NOTHING PERMANENT

NOTHING PERMANENT
Modern Architecture in California

TODD CRONAN

University of Minnesota Press
Minneapolis / London

The University of Minnesota Press gratefully acknowledges the financial assistance provided for the publication of this book by Emory University.

Portions of chapter 1 were previously published in "The Secrets of the Material: Contingency and Normativity in Adolf Loos," *Umění/Art* (2021); "Getting Over the Bauhaus," *The Philosophical Salon* (January 11, 2021); and "Bauhaus contra socialisme," *Lava Revue* 14 (September 29, 2020). Portions of chapter 3 were previously published in "Between Culture and Biology: Schindler and Neutra at the Limits of Architecture," in *Émigré Cultures in Design and Architecture,* ed. Alison Clarke and Elana Shapira (Bloomsbury, 2017), 203–20. Portions of chapter 4 were previously published in "'Danger in the Smallest Dose': Richard Neutra's Design Theory," *Design and Culture Journal* 3, no. 2 (Summer 2011): 165–92. Portions of chapter 6 were previously published in "Architects in the Hands of an Angry God," review of *An Eames Anthology,* ed. Daniel Ostroff, *Los Angeles Review of Books* (May 25, 2016).

Every effort was made to obtain permission to reproduce material in this book. If any proper acknowledgment has not been included here, we encourage copyright holders to notify the publisher.

Published by the University of Minnesota Press
111 Third Avenue South, Suite 290
Minneapolis, MN 55401-2520
http://www.upress.umn.edu

ISBN 978-1-5179-1519-3 (hc)
ISBN 978-1-5179-1520-9 (pb)

Library of Congress record available at https://lccn.loc.gov/2023001551.

Printed in the United States of America on acid-free paper

The University of Minnesota is an equal-opportunity educator and employer.

30 29 28 27 26 25 24 23   10 9 8 7 6 5 4 3 2 1

Such architectural flowers . . . were not made to endure. They charmed as nothing permanent could.

—Harwell Harris on R. M. Schindler, 1979

The permanent value of society was helped enormously by the impermanence of its architecture. Those values then take on other than a physical or monumental aspect.

—Charles Eames, 1956

One of my main objectives was to *prove that man is stable.* . . . It *was* possible to make an *enduring* design.

—Richard Neutra, 1962

Contents

Abbreviations

These abbreviations are used for significant sources throughout the text and notes.

AD   Reyner Banham, *Scenes in America Deserta* (Layton, Utah: Gibbs M. Smith, 1982)

DC   Reyner Banham, *Design by Choice,* ed. Penny Sparke (New York: Rizzoli, 1981)

EA   Charles and Ray Eames, *An Eames Anthology: Articles, Film Scripts, Interviews, Letters, Notes, Speeches,* ed. Daniel Ostroff (New Haven, Conn.: Yale University Press, 2015)

ED   John Neuhart, Marilyn Neuhart, and Ray Eames, *Eames Design: The Work of the Office of Charles and Ray Eames* (New York: Harry N. Abrams, 1989)

EMR   Esther McCoy, *Piecing Together Los Angeles: An Esther McCoy Reader,* ed. Susan Morgan (Valencia, Calif.: East of Borneo, 2012)

LA   Reyner Banham, *Los Angeles: The Architecture of Four Ecologies* (New York: Harper & Row, 1971)

LS   Richard Neutra, *Life and Shape* (1962; reprint, Los Angeles: Atara Press, 2009)

MA   Vincent Scully, *Modern Architecture, and Other Essays,* ed. Neil Levine (Princeton, N.J.: Princeton University Press, 2005)

MCH   Esther McCoy, *Modern California Houses: Case Study Houses, 1945–1962* (New York: Reinhold, 1962)

NN   Richard Neutra, *Nature Near: Late Essays of Richard Neutra,* ed. William Marlin (Santa Barbara, Calif.: Capra Press, 1989)

OA   Adolf Loos, *On Architecture,* ed. Adolf Opel and Daniel Opel, trans. Michael Mitchell (Riverside, Calif.: Ariadne Press, 2002)

OC   Adolf Loos, *Ornament and Crime: Selected Essays,* ed. Adolf Opel, trans. Michael Mitchell (Riverside, Calif.: Ariadne Press, 1998)

PD   George Nelson, *Problems of Design* (New York: Whitney Library of Design, 1957)

SD   Richard Neutra, *Survival through Design* (New York: Oxford University Press, 1954)

SF   Raphael Soriano, *Substance and Function in Architecture,* interview by Marlene Laskey (Los Angeles: Oral History Program, University of California, 1988)

TD   Reyner Banham, *Theory and Design in the First Machine Age,* 2nd ed. (Cambridge: MIT Press, 1980)

WA   Wassily Kandinsky, *Complete Writings on Art,* ed. Kenneth C. Lindsay and Peter Vergo (Boston: G. K. Hall, 1982)

YM   Sigfried Giedion, *Architecture, You and Me: The Diary of a Development* (Cambridge, Mass.: Harvard University Press, 1958)

Introduction
Connections in California Modern Architecture

It's the universal problem. No building exists for very long without some heavy-footed person walking around in it and changing everything around. . . . I wish I'd been a poet, it's so much easier because you don't have clients.

—Kevin Roche, interview in *Kevin Roche: The Quiet Architect,* 2017

The literature on California Modern is abundant: scholarly monographs, guidebooks, collections of photographs by Julius Shulman, and style guides to living "midcentury modern." Commercials, magazines, and websites are awash in light-filled California living spaces defined by midcentury post-and-beam architecture, glass walls, period furniture, and futuristic accessories. Far less abundant are studies that attempt to understand the meaning of California Modern, an approach that brackets the entire question of style. Although it is style that gives us the terms *California Modern* and *midcentury modern* in the first place, it is also style that erases the differences between intentions, creating unities that were never there and obscuring meaningful connections that were. By looking closely at the debates that drove the innovations of modern architects in California, I aim to excavate those intentions and offer a new interpretation of an extraordinary and influential moment in architectural history. And while I do not address all or even most of the players involved in California Modern architecture between 1920 and 1970, focusing instead on four core figures—R. M. Schindler, Richard Neutra, and Charles and Ray Eames—I suggest that the problems that defined the practices of these four were shared by many in their milieu.

The major themes that emerge in my account center on the survival and control of architectural intent in the face of inhabitants' uses and abuses, modeling and performance, impermanence and permanence, and the shifting boundaries of intentionality. I explore a range of responses to the "universal problem" of use and misuse by a structure's inhabitants, from Neutra's attempt to control every aspect of the user's experience to the Eameses' reluctant acceptance of the inevitable loss of meaning when a work left their hands.

No doubt my most controversial claim concerns the status of architectural media and materiality. As I argue, the fault lines of California Modern fall along the divide between those architects who embrace media and materiality as a form of *agency* and those who construe their medium and materials as part of the process of communication (at once resistance and support, disabling and enabling), but never as displacing their intentions. Ultimately, the question is an urgent one—it is *political*—with implications far beyond the history of modern architecture: Do materials make meaning of their own accord, or do the intentions of those who shape materials (however relational that process may be) make the meaning?

For the former, I trace the history that flows from August Endell in the 1890s through the Bauhaus, through Neutra and his colleagues, sketching the ways in which contemporary architecture is committed to an idea of media that grants agency to things at the expense of human agents. Thus, my account of media and materiality from Endell to Neutra is a genealogy of the present. As a counter to this media-based approach, I follow an alternative genealogy, from Loos in the 1900s to Schindler to the Eameses and their circle in the 1960s and 1970s. These architects and designers saw media and materiality as creative and resistant tools for communicating ideas to users, ideas that were as prey to miscommunication and opacity as understanding and connection.

Intention

Intention is a formative concept for this book as a whole, and one that often gives rise to a series of misunderstandings.[1] As I use the notion here, it has nothing to do with artists' writings, letters, biographies, documents, mental contents, or ideas that are then deposited, materialized, or executed in matter and received as "messages" by viewers or inhabitants. While these materials may be useful in helping one to understand what an architect meant, they do not supply some key to unlocking the meaning of a work of art. Artists are often unaware of what they mean, at least in discursive terms. To suggest that intention functions along the lines of an inside/outside (mind/matter) binary is the precise mistake I aim to address. The mistake was writ large in 1957 when Marcel Duchamp fatefully observed the "difference between the intention and its realization."[2] Duchamp erroneously defined an intent as a private interior space that is separable from materials. For Duchamp and others, the latter is given primacy over the former, always with the belief that they are separable. According to this view, during the process by which a work is made the intention is either annihilated or rendered irrelevant.

Robert Rauschenberg, following Duchamp, provided perhaps a succinct version of the mistake when he stated, "I don't want a painting to be just an expression of my personality." Rauschenberg identified this kind of inner world *with intention itself* and separated it from the process of making. He insisted that he was "opposed to the whole idea of conception-execution—of getting an idea for a picture and then carrying it out." Against this inner (idea), outer (material) account, one that is dependent on "conscious manipulation and control" of the material, he proposed as his alternative "*collaboration* with materials," a process he construed as *anti-intentional*.[3] When, fifty years later, Maria Gough critiqued Buckminster Fuller for his putative commitment to "prior ideation" over and against the "artist's discovery through making"—his "assumption that the materialization of a structure or an object was essentially secondary to its ideation"—she was simply reiterating the Duchamp/Rauschenberg "critique" of intention.[4]

At the same moment Duchamp and Rauschenberg were introducing their fateful picture of intention as inner, Stanley Cavell was describing how this was a "bad picture" of intent, bad in the sense that it imagined some "internal, prior mental event causally connected with outward effects."[5] The "good" picture—the one put forward by Elizabeth Anscombe in *Intention* of 1957 (while I do not address *Intention* here, I am indebted to it at every turn)—conceives of intent as *an action*, one that *inseparably combines* inner and outer, idea and execution, artist and medium.[6] Throughout this book I suggest that a range of modern architects grasped the necessary entwinement or endless circuitry of inner and outer, thought and materialization; alternately, I address a number of architects, most of them in the grip of fantasies of material agency, who were anti-intentionalist and also adhered to a bad picture of intent.

The Duchampian picture swiftly entered the architectural discourse and there too it became orthodoxy. Paul Rudolph, in 1973, makes the same point as Duchamp when he insists that "*intentions* in architecture and the results are two entirely different things."[7] Rem Koolhaas, in 2012, makes the same point, but now in terms of the afterlife of a structure, saying that "a building has at least two lives—the one imagined by its maker and the life it lives afterward—and they are never the same."[8] It is hard to imagine what use the latter (truistic) claim might have, except insofar as one aims to *deny* the loss of control, which is precisely what Koolhaas does in his pursuit of "evolving" architecture. Vast stretches of architectural literature are devoted to the same pseudoproblem raised by Koolhaas and others. Consider the opening gambit of Stewart Brand's *How Buildings Learn*. Brand observes that "between the world and our idea of the world is a fascinating kink. Architecture, we imagine, is permanent. And so our buildings thwart us."[9] Between what we intend and what happens there is a permanent gap. Brand's point is that we should aim to create buildings that cannot be thwarted, by letting them grow. And as Koolhaas and so many others—Neutra, for instance—would agree, the idea is not to *accept the inevitability of the gap,* to draw a line between work and world, architect and inhabitant, but to fantasize the kinds of building that will displace the difference.

The Conflicted Field of California Modern

The contention of this book is that California Modern—an approach established by a group of architects and designers working in California between 1920, when Schindler arrived in Los Angeles to work for Frank Lloyd Wright, and 1970, when Schindler's Viennese colleague and rival Neutra died—was not a single, coherent movement but one that was divided and conflicted through and through.[10] Schindler and Neutra, the most influential California Modern architects, were formative in shaping modern architecture in the United States in the interwar period and after, and it was from their contrasting approaches that the dominant currents of architectural practice in California emerged. Schindler was devoted to the ideals of his mentor Loos and inspired architects Gregory Ain and Harwell Harris but also, more surprisingly (and far more indirectly), Craig Ellwood and the Eameses. Neutra, by contrast, embraced the aims and principles of the expressionist and Bauhaus architects in Germany. Neutra, among the most influential and productive architects working in the United States during his lifetime, in turn influenced architects such as Raphael Soriano and Pierre Koenig, as well as critics like Sigfried Giedion, Peter Blake, Arthur Drexler, and Reyner Banham. At the center of the debate between these two factions was the question of architectural intention: What is inside a work and what is outside? Where does a structure end and the world begin? What are the limits, if any, of architectural agency? What role do materials play in architectural meaning? How do architects address the inhabitants of their works (the fact of inhabitants being the defining feature of architecture in relation to other media)? It is the intensity with which these questions were engaged that makes this period and this place so fascinating, not least because these are the questions that define architecture at large.

What follows below is a brief survey of the four dominant approaches explored in this book—those of the Eameses, Neutra, Ellwood (and other steel-based expressions of the Case Study House Program), and Schindler—in terms of their reactions to the problems of change and survival, response and form, all of which hinge on the surprising status of architectural connections. It is my contention that it is through those connections, or lack of them, rather than through larger stylistic issues, that one gains clearest access to the basic aims of the architects whose works are examined here.

Eames, Connections, Control

One of the most well-known maxims to emerge from the Eames Office, a kind of summary of the firm's design aims, is "The details are not details. They make the product, just like details make the architecture. The connections, the connections, the connec-

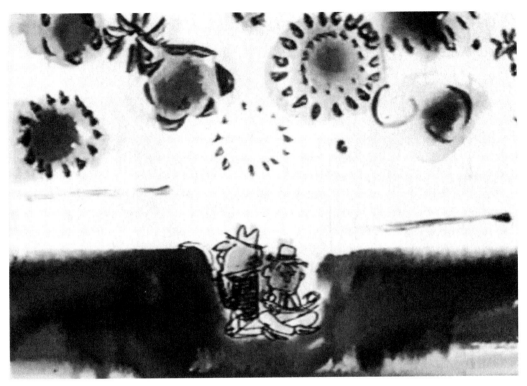

FIGURE I.1. Charles and Ray Eames, still from *ECS*, 1961.

tions."[11] As Ralph Caplan observes in his essay for the 1976 exhibition *Connections: The Work of Charles and Ray Eames,* "Nothing [Charles] or anyone else has ever said or written comes closer than that to the heart of the work, and thinking, and convictions."[12] The phrase first appeared in the 1961 Eames film *ECS,* which focuses on Eames Contract Storage, a system of sleep, study, and storage furniture units (Plate 1). Part animation, part live action, the film opens with a description of the best method for tackling complex design problems. Charles Eames, the narrator, suggests that one should "study an extreme case" (the words are also framed on the wall of the designer's office). Here the extreme case is the college dormitory. Drawings depict two figures in a trench (the designers) with bombs bursting and gunfire flying overhead (the college students attacking their furniture) (Figure I.1). The narrator states, "If the designer, the manufacturer, and the system can survive this extreme, we will be confident that the normal, unusually rugged use should prove no problem" (*EA,* 224). A 1961 spread in *Interiors* magazine reinforced the idea of ECS as furniture for a war zone. Under the heading "Maintenance, Durability, Security," the article exhorted ECS for its resistance to damage—including the *irremovability* of components, however small. Drawers cannot be taken out. Neither can the bolts that hold the parts together: none of the standard screwdrivers will fit the heads. . . . Built-in security advantages include the fact that all protruding handles and bars are strong enough to take tremendous punishment. The bed bar can be chinned on, the wire drawers climbed on.[13]

At the root of the problems explored in this book is the extremist ideal of survival as it relates to architects' desire for control within settings beyond their control—those defined by inhabitants' use (or abuse).[14]

For the Eameses, survival was about the capacity of the idea to endure its inevitable alteration and distortion in the course of production and consumption, the changes that occur between an idea and its execution. The Eameses put it this way: "When the concept is formed it represents about 5 percent of the design effort—the remaining 95 percent of the effort being used to keep the concept from falling apart" (*EA,* 247). Once again, design is a war zone: with a "beautiful idea," "if only you can survive, if you can just survive and keep your head up" and avoid doing "something that you will be completely ashamed of, it is about that time that you start looking for the lifeboat" (*EA,* 253). The Eameses pinned their hopes on the capacity of the idea to survive conditions of production and consumption, so that even if the rest, the product itself, went under, the idea would survive.

The Eameses were part of a larger pattern of architectural thinking at the time, one that spread far beyond the borders of California. Hugh Stubbins, for instance, in his "Thoughts on Architecture," offers a striking commentary on the Eamesian approach to design, remarking on the conflict between idea integrity and physical and ideational dispersal. Stubbins describes his own peculiar way of *denying* the reality of dispersal. Thinking (rather literally) of a building as his baby, he reflects on how strange it is that an architect "who has nursed his concept so carefully and possessively while it is still only a concept, tends to cut the umbilical cord completely once the building becomes part of the public experience." Stubbins refuses to let go, noting how there is the potential that the work could go on forever, endlessly gathering data from use and plugging information back into the system. He wonders, does the architect "ever really find out how people respond to and use his buildings"? There is no reason the architect must "abandon[ ] his offspring once it is out in the world." Stubbins imagines a situation where the child never has to leave home, as there is "much to be learned in watching a building grow and change over a period of years in response to the needs and activities of its users—much that could be fed back into the design experience to become part of the objective language of architecture."[15] Under this perspective, everything is potentially architecture all the time, which is precisely the view expressed by Charles Moore: everything is part of the work, it is "all architecture," because there is no way of "cutting off anywhere and saying that it's somebody else's province, or irrelevant to mine" (this is Moore's version of Derrida's "There is nothing outside of the text").[16] As attractive as this vision of unending design might be, a vision close to the one elaborated by Neutra, the Eameses came to terms with the inevitable decay of their concepts, although they devoted every shred of their energies to delaying the inevitable.

The Eameses took an extreme position in response to the threat of distortion of their ideas; in a way, their approach was to drown ideas in advance by aiming to *not* produce anything that might be consumed without their full authorial weight behind it. In practice what this meant was an embrace of *modeling*—a very capacious category for the Eameses—and a turn away from built architecture and even furniture. A model was a way to try something out without actually making the thing it modeled, and it could take the form of architecture, exhibition design, slide show, or even furniture. But above all, the turn to modeling was a turn to *film*: film as a form of modeling problems or films of models that model problems. The Eameses described their films—one hundred of which they made between 1950 and 1979—as "models before the fact, or models after the fact," the fact being some event, product, or plan (*EA, 347*). What was compelling about film, for the Eameses, was control. As Charles Eames explained, you can

> make statements on film that you just can't make any other way. Certainly not in designing a product, and not even in writing a book. You have certain elements of control—over the image, the content, the timing—that you can't have in other media.[17]

Another attraction of film was its survival capacity, the way it could keep an idea intact; ideas expressed through other media, by contrast, were inevitably distorted by users. Caplan glosses this specialness of film for the Eameses, noting how "viewers . . . are unable to break the designed sequence of presentation. They cannot skip ahead, speed by, see the exhibit in reverse order, or turn to something else."[18] Or as Charles told Paul Schrader, speaking of the film the Eameses created to rally support for a national aquarium, "I've discovered that not even a senator dares to stand up and interrupt a film." Elaborating on the central attraction of film, he observed that it offers the illusion of a "perfectly controlled medium; that after the mess of production, when it is all in the can, nothing can erode it—the image, the color, the timing, the sound, everything is under control."[19] As Charles frequently explained, the Eameses' initial turn from architecture to chairs (around 1950) was motivated by the same fated effort at control. Speaking to Studs Terkel in 1965, he noted how with a building, "an architect almost loses control, for at a vital moment when it goes out and it becomes so many hands, the scale is so great that he can't really control it. And I suspect that in doing a chair, for that instant, he is almost able to control a piece of architecture." He then added immediately that even here the architect "finds out that he really can't quite do it, but . . . it's an approach to it."[20] As I will later argue, the linguistic hedging that saturates Charles's speech is entirely to the point, as he staves off final expression through mounting qualifications. Charles found his true approach in the turn to film; it was there that the contingencies of "so many hands" were reduced to a minimum. He asserted (against all the facts) that of the more than one hundred films the Eameses had made, he "shot almost all of it."[21] This too was a fiction of control, but one that Charles seemed best able to live with.

This inflated but also fragile vision of control—the ability to communicate an idea that is immune to distortion by a user—seemed to entail a denial of the point of making a film: that it is for an audience. When the film is in the can, the work is sealed shut; the film has achieved a kind perfection, the idea is intact, no erosion is possible. But the film that is in the can is not fully a film unless it is seen by an audience (in fact, most of the Eameses' films were never shown for audiences). As Charles fully recognized, the film in the can is "just an illusion," and "thoughtless reproduction, projection, and presentation turn it into a mess again."[22] The world intervenes, the seal is broken, the unspooled film becomes a mess on the ground. The Eameses tended to avoid the seemingly inevitable, and sensible, process of communication whereby one aims to get across the main drift of what one means and accepts the inevitable losses (and gains) that come with expressing oneself to another. Such an approach seemed to entail too much loss for the Eameses.

Charles was explicit in formulating the problem of communication as the problem of *audience*. Audiences introduce the threat of miscommunication, the failure of an idea to be (fully) understood. And this is what Charles meant when he exclaimed—in perhaps his most unguarded moment—that "audiences scare the hell out of me" (*EA*, 269). Audiences mean unpredictable responses, unpredictable uses. Of course, without an audience, art sacrifices the notion of communication itself; the work loses its point. Moreover, how can one conceive architecture without an audience? Models, for the Eameses, were a basic but also paradoxical solution to the problem of audience; they were, so the Eameses imagined, permanently suspended between idea and application. Models could survive the "mess" of the world, but at the expense of being fully in the world. To be clear, this is not to suggest that the Eameses literally refused to engage the problem of audience. They did not deny the reality of audience (even if they did flirt with this fantasy) but attempted to work through the basic artistic (but also human) problem of getting one's intent across to another with minimal loss of sense. Again, they believed this issue to be particularly pressing for architects, as audience uses and misuses are structural to architecture in a way they are not, or at least not as immediately so, for other media.

Neutra, Photography, Survival

The idea of film as survival—the notion that the least material of media is, by that very fact (less to lose), the most durable in sustaining an idea—captured the passing imagination of Richard Neutra, the antagonist of this book, whose work represents the most influential architectural expression of California Modern. As Neutra noted a few months before his death, the architectural photography of Julius Shulman "will survive me. Films are stronger, and good glossy prints are easier shipped than brute concrete and stainless steel—or even ideas." Neutra reflected on how all of architectural history has depended on "stones," citing the Roman proverb "Saxa loquuntur." It was stones that were "supposed to talk for themselves and forever." But even stones decay, disappear, remain mute. "*Film* is of the stuff to talk!" (the Eameses could not have agreed more).[23] Shulman's vast archive of photographs of Neutra's work (going back to 1936; Figure 3.47), Neutra came to believe, would outlive not just concrete and steel, but the audiences, the inhabitants who shaped and misshaped his dwellings to their needs. By all accounts, Neutra maintained strict control over the photographs of his work, shooting his own rolls of film and plotting out the shots in advance of Shulman's arrival. As Shulman later described these initial shots, they were intended to strip the work of its first layer of reception: poor construction. Neutra was "devious," Shulman said: "He would attempt to cover up, change, improve, hide certain elements that were not done according to his design intent."[24] Moreover, Shulman's remarks about Neutra's photographs reveal a lot about how Neutra construed the relation between intent and reception: "Neutra told me that one of his great pleasures was to take my 8 × 10 pictures to bed and mark the prints, studying them. He said he didn't get pleasure in the process of construction because of the constant fighting, but he enjoyed the great pleasure he obtained studying the 8 × 10 prints."[25] Architectural anxiety over construction, as the all-purpose sign for loss of control, is a motif that recurs throughout this book. And this late admission by Neutra, that his intentions were more accessible in the photographs (although even here he edited them), clarifies the kind of (impossible) control he sought to achieve. For Neutra, as for so many, architectural photography seemingly kept the idea intact and immaculate, before the inevitable decay that came with the reception of the work.[26]

Neutra was likely inspired here by the example of Frank Lloyd Wright.[27] In his 1932 autobiography, Wright describes photography as keeping the "thought-form" of architecture alive long after the work has disappeared:

> I never grieve long now that some work of mine has met its end; *has had short life,* . . . consoled by the thought that any design has far-reaching effect, today, because our machine so easily gives it, as a *design,* to the mind's eye of all. . . . Prevalence of the idea in some graphic thought-form—certainly one of the best things the machine has done for us in this age. Even in this "matter of record," those architects failing to establish so-called "permanence" may get free from any desire to do so.[28]

If Neutra showed begrudging assent to the necessity of photography for sustaining the idea when the work was gone, then Wright's final thought about freeing oneself of the desire for permanence—the "thought-form" survives in its graphic representation—could not be more foreign to Neutra's approach.

In an early article, a review of the 1937 *Mural Conceptualism* exhibition at the San Francisco Museum of Art, Neutra channeled all his doubts about audience into the minds of contemporary painters. Architects were there to rescue the painter from permanent exile in the sales gallery and provide contemporary art with the only home it would ever know. Never once did Neutra imagine (at least in writing) that the uncertainty of the painter was his own. Neutra's practice was a lifelong effort to deny the "horrible uncertainty" of the situation he attributed to other media.

> In periods of the past, when the architectural environment had harmonious unity, it presented a defined frame of reference. Van Eyck, painting an altar piece, knew beforehand the space characteristics of a cathedral, its properties of illumination day and night, the focal distance from which his work would be viewed, the accompanying color scheme to surround it, the emotional and intellectual frame of mind of his audience facing the unfolded triptych on a holiday.
>
> When a few hundred years later a man like Vermeer painted easel pictures not designed for a given spot in a particular building, he nevertheless was fully familiar with the genre character of a Dutch living room in the middle of the seventeenth century. His work would fit, whether Mr. van der Soandso or Mr. van der Suchandsuch purchased the picture for his home.
>
> Contrast this favorable situation with the horrible uncertainty of a contemporary artist . . . who composes a piece of art without any possible anticipation as to whether it will be placed in a mission type, an English cottage or a Georgian living room, with adobe imitation, jazz plaster, patterned wallpaper or gypsum astragals

as competitive details all around it; for a room with light or dimmed down with velour drapes to mid-Victorian dignity.

He cannot anticipate anything. He thinks of the . . . sales gallery as the happiest background for his picture. And there in the sales gallery the picture hangs, never bought, not tempting a purchaser who has no place to put it.[29]

Neutra's fantasy of a shared "frame of reference" for earlier artists is matched only by his fantasy of total lack of reference for contemporary art. But if the painter could not anticipate anything, the architect, by contrast, could anticipate *everything*, or so Neutra imagined. In one of his more telling admissions, he noted that the architect should aim to achieve the impossible, to "foresee and gauge every last wrinkle of individuality in all of the people who might someday occupy his design" (*NN*, 151). Neutra clung to this all-or-nothing conception because anything other than anticipating everything or anticipating nothing meant being exposed to the kinds of risks of uncertainty that he sought to eliminate.

Neutra was haunted to his bones by the problem of survival. And while he could be more generous than many architects about the capacity for photography to sustain meaning, he, like so many others, ultimately construed photography as a pale copy of multisensory experience. Two years prior to his tribute to Shulman, Neutra took a far more typical approach to architectural photography, focusing on the titanic set of "limitations" of the genre. He was emphatic that "all-around architecture [is] ALIVE, not merely consumed through a photo lens." Every second, every moment of the day and night, changes the nature of the work, he asserted, pointing to the impossibility of capturing "all these things and their relation, which to behold changes in seconds our inner-most chemistry!" Neutra's photographic solution to the infinitely changing nature of architectural experience was to sublime photography out of existence. Only a "colossally complete series of still photographs" might manage to capture even the most fleeting dimension of an architectural "experience."[30] (It is difficult to conceive what this colossal set might look like.) Or again, as he explained in his introduction to Shulman's *Photographing Architecture and Interiors* (1962), architecture sets one's "sensitivities . . . in flux, they do not remain static as on a fabricated film. Everything in our reactive life-body changes every second, but everything is rigid on that 8 × 10 print."[31] Neutra's solution to the problem of survival took a more extreme form than the deathly freeze of photography (a standard trope of the literature) that Shulman and the Eameses embraced. As he argues in his extraordinary book *Survival through Design* (1954), survival is a matter of absolute architectural control, an infinite nuancing of structure to survive any contingency. Neutra sought to achieve a mode of practice that could "endure the ordeals of use" in perpetuity (*NN*, 62). Survival, for Neutra, meant never

letting go. For the Eameses, by contrast, however materially attenuated their work became, there was "always" a moment when you "call[ed] it off" (*EA*, 170).

The Limits of Control

As should be clear, Neutra and the Eameses were equally extreme in their commitment to a vision of architectural control, but they differed in their views of how far that
control extended and in their solutions to the problem of loss of control. The Eameses
pursued furniture, film, and modeling because these afforded the designer, as they saw
it, control not only over the communication of meaning but also, to an extent, over the
conditions under which this communication took place, where and how ideas were conveyed. The Eameses understood the challenge in particular terms. First, they broadly
accepted that what they had to convey were meanings that were perpetually capable of
being misunderstood—this also helps to explain their desire to saturate their work
with their intentions. One must "face the job of really transmitting meaning . . . ; every
tear is sort of pertinent to the meaning" (*EA*, 253). Second, even though the Eameses
"were not at all sure when" the work was "finished," an extensive number of pieces were
finished and went into the world, where they were received by millions of users (and
abusers).[32] The Eameses recognized that sending their work into the world limited their
control, that the world was a war zone. They responded by making things—furniture,
films, and models—that were ideally protected from the worst forms of misuse, but the
loss of control was inevitable and they tentatively accepted it as such.

The contrast with Neutra here is stark. For Neutra, control extended to every facet of
the work and its reception. More significantly, control for Neutra meant creating works
for which misunderstanding was irrelevant. Neutra intended his works to be surefire
in their capacity to generate effects in the inhabitants. In this way, then, Neutra's intentions became irrelevant (and with them, misunderstanding); only the effects he
engineered mattered. For Neutra (following the Bauhaus here), it was the materials
that shaped the inhabitant; his role was to marshal the "meaning" inherent in those
materials, but the materials were never conceived as giving expression to his intentions. Neutra subscribed to his own version of "vibrant matter," observing, "Materiality
is alive with stimuli." The new science, he insisted, was "disclosing that matter is dynamically infused with all manner of significance," a fact that inspired his search for
the "meaning of architectural matter" (*NN*, 63). Meaning, in other words, was not *his*
meaning, but something that was there "in" things. The consequences of this displace-
ment of human meaning in his work—it is the matter that means—were that the inhabitant was not able to understand what the architect meant, the architect was not able

to make his intentions known, and the critic was not able to interpret the meaning of the architect's structures.

In a certain sense, the aims of Neutra and the Eameses are susceptible to every aspect of Jacques Derrida's deconstruction of the problems of communication. Derrida's "Signature Event Context"—written in 1971 for a conference titled "Communication"—opens with a critique of the entire endeavor to make communication "rigorously controllable, and transmittable." It takes direct aim at those who conceive their work as bearing a "unity and wholeness of meaning" that will remain unaffected "in its essence" through every "alteration" of context.[33] Any writer—and the point holds for any mode of expression—who sees communication as a "continuous and homogeneous reparation" of the idea through states of distortion is in denial about the "essential drift [dérive] bearing on writing as an iterative structure, cut off from all absolute responsibility, from consciousness as the ultimate authority, orphaned and separated at birth from its assistance of its father."[34] No doubt these are the kinds of concerns that haunted the architects discussed in this book (Esther McCoy, for instance, observes how Schindler sought to "maintain complete control over every detail of his buildings").[35] Notice too that Derrida seeks out his own reparative gesture in the claim that the "mark" is prior to and outside the space of communication.[36] This is a large topic, but suffice it to say that for Derrida, the mark defines an "essential" materiality that persists over and against any meaning "imposed" on it in a text. Moreover, Derrida's fixation on the failure to achieve "absolute" or "ultimate" transparency of meaning—a failure that he uses to authorize his account of the mark—reflects a desire to displace the kinds of complex communicative problems Neutra, the Eameses, and others sought to work through. The Eameses were tempted by a picture of "rigorously controllable" meaning, but they discovered in practice, over and over again as it were, the impossibility of attaining that goal, and this discovery led them to embrace inventive, but also bewildering, makeshifts, such as modeling, that could at once satisfy their need for expressive clarity and bypass some of the complications of communication. If Derrida made an abstract claim about the impossibility of conveying intentions with a mark, then Neutra concretized that abstraction by turning his work into machines for the production of material effects.

Communicative Fantasies

The problem of survival is basic to art making. It is about artists' capacity to sustain their intentions in the face of audiences or receivers who might ignore, dispute, or, more often, be unaware of or unresponsive to those intentions; it is this possibility that gives rise to the opposite fantasy of total control. Can one make works that defeat the unresponsiveness of receivers? Can one make works that are unable to be misunderstood?[37] Can one invent a mode of communication that is, on some level, transparent and eludes the worst contingencies of context? This is what Buckminster Fuller was after when, in his innumerable expressive fantasies, he spoke of the "communication of ideas by [an] author to other minds in a referential form more permanent than if they were to be just orally expressed," a "method of broadcast beyond the power of human speech."[38] Speakers standing before an audience witness them "'talk back' so instantaneously to them that they know just what their audiences are thinking and they can converse with their audiences, even though the speaker seems to be the only one making audible words. The feedback by eye," Fuller noted, "is so swift as to give him instantaneous, spontaneous reaction and appropriate thought formulation." Eyes and brains are "telepathic transceivers": "Several hundred thousand different wide-band radio sets can at any time be tuned in anywhere around our biosphere," and such arrays "operate even within our brains."[39] Fuller's dream, more extreme and more literal than the Eameses' or Neutra's, was for communication not beyond human speech but beyond the human. Mathematics "made possible continuity of expression of truth beyond the 'great wall' of the body and of personal death."[40] New technologies promised "infinity-of-survival-and-growth" up to and including "continuity of living" beyond death.[41] As tempting as Fuller's communicative utopia was for both the Eameses and Neutra, it was not a live option.[42]

Fuller's utopia, however, has proved tenacious, recurring in the most unlikely places, as Beatriz Colomina's highly influential 2001 account of the Eameses indicates (Marshall McLuhan's account of the medium is where Colomina and Fuller meet). Colomina blithely dismisses what she calls the "individual factoids [the Eames films] offer, or even the story they tell" (not that she gives us any sense of what that is).[43] Denying the very idea of architectural intention, Colomina is committed to laying bare our contemporary "mode of perception."[44] What the Eameses showed us is what the "MTV and the Internet generation" already knows; the Eameses proleptically "spelled out" the "logic of the Internet."[45] The only difference between a multiscreen film like the Eameses' *Glimpses of the USA* (1959) and the Internet is that the Eameses "intensified"—that is to say, *visualized* (the optical register is important)—an "existing mode of perception," a mode that was reflected in "television, space programs, and military operations" (all differences collapse in the space of the screen).[46] Because, Colomina maintains, the "eye cannot escape the screens" in a constructed space like *Glimpses* or *Think* (1964), the multiscreen "enclosure" shows us the "kind of space we now occupy continuously without thinking."[47]

Reinhold Martin reiterates Colomina's claims when he describes Fuller's vision of

Spaceship Earth—including the World Game and geodesic domes—as providing a "replica of the postmodernist 'new machine.'" But this is a "mirror world" in the way that Eamesian image enclosures critically mirror postmodernity. Writing of the "Fly's Eye Dome" of 1965, Martin describes it as a dome "made up of dozens of other, smaller dome-shaped units that refracted the image of the globe at finer scales" (again, the optical register is a given).[48] Here Fuller's seamless global utopia is "reversed," as the "unitary spaceship piloted by a unitary astro-cosmonaut" is "suddenly and jarringly" turned into an "external totality," as the world "is fed back into the machine itself," producing nothing but a crossfire of mirrored reflections. Martin's question is Colomina's question: "how to escape the self-reflexive, self-contained regime of risk management, the hall of mirrors in which the entire game is played."[49] Colomina's paranoid image enclosures are Martin's hall of mirrors; both require a moment when the enclosures become *visible,* thus offering a "way out." Insofar as the problem is *images*—perhaps *the* problem for the art historical professional managerial class—the solution is critical mimesis. Image saturation and its "critical" mirror reversal are designed to leave political economy untouched.

I will not dwell any further on this spectatorial mode of argumentation. I only flag here the seemingly durable fantasy of asserting the existence of both a mode of perception we "all" now occupy (immersively and uncritically) and one that we need specially privileged critics and artists to show us—we the unthinking automatons of the "MTV and the Internet generation"—from a detached point of observation.[50] Fuller's communicative fantasy similarly depends on the existence of the privileged "intermediary" who can lift the "average human mind" to see the import of great evolutionary events.[51] Fuller consistently warned "geniuses" not to share their ideas prematurely with average minds, those "non-teleologists" who would only "pauperize" their ideas, turning them "into mere means of dogmatic formularizing, inevitably short-circuiting rationalization growth."[52] Architects and critics of this period voiced an increasing dissatisfaction with human agency, a dissatisfaction tragically compensated for by an assertion of the "agency" of materials—screens, here—to do the work humans fail to do.

Connections I: Eames Details

The survival of intent is among the most acutely gripping problems for architecture, in ways that it is not for other media. Architecture, by definition, requires an active user, not just a viewer or beholder. In this it differs from the other arts, which are often satisfied to be housed in galleries or museums, awaiting audiences that may or may not respond. Further still, museum works are not (one hopes) confronted with the kinds of alterations that haunt architecture. Inhabitants hang pictures on the walls of houses, altering the spaces in manifold ways, a fact that creates problems for some architects (Neutra was surely one of them).[53] A book that remains unread retains meaning all the same, and even if you tear out its pages, the meaning persists; a musical score that remains unplayed is still music. To respond to architecture, by contrast, is to materially change it, to live in it. The architects discussed in this book regarded the fact of literal and metaphorical "erosion" or "entropy" (as the Eameses called it) as a vital threat to the communication of their intentions, even as they begrudgingly accepted that to communicate at all was to live with that erosion. Their responses to that threat, however, not only differed but also conflicted.

In the film we began with, *ECS*, the Eameses offer a clear solution to the potential of audience misuse. Their object again is the extreme case, a college dorm, which functions as a kind of allegory for the "noise" of the world. The focus of the film is on the *system*, the underlying structure, which will ideally survive its abusive users. (This is what Hugh Kenner means when he says, "Things break. The system abides." It is, he maintains, "invulnerable."[54] The Eameses were not so certain.) Charles describes how the system is secured by two structural sections, wall brackets, in the shape of a C with inwardly turned ends (Figure I.2). The sections are attached to the wall at levels of 1 foot and 7 feet, and divider panels with horizontal shelves provide lateral bracing.[55] Finally, hollow-core doors are hung on the divider panels. The narrator extols the virtues of the system (half tongue-in-cheek) for housekeepers, the department of sanitation, and comptrollers, as it delivers the most design value "per foot, per person" (*EA*, 224). It is at this point, after the system's ability to survive extreme conditions has been demonstrated, that Charles famously mentions "the connections, the connections, the connections," which include "the gauge of the wire, the selection of the wood, the finish of the castings" (*EA*, 224). The viewer is then presented with a barrage of photographic details through twenty-one shots in under as many seconds (Figure I.3). This quick-cut method came to define the Eamesian aesthetic, an approach described by Schrader as "information overload."[56] Charles always resisted this description, preferring instead to call the surplus of imagery an attempt to assert "credibility," to maintain unity of message in the face of a skeptical or distracted audience (that he always conceived of the audience as skeptical warrants further attention).[57]

Charles was relentless in his focus on the details of furniture. Narrating the development of the chair design process for a television show, he formulated the issues around the connections between seat, back, and legs. The biggest hurdle in the development of the famous molded plywood chair was finding a shock mount "connection that would take half a million flexes" (Figure I.4). Next came the "frame, more connections. This time, metal to metal. Braces, welds, working." Here too "the connection is the same" (*EA*, 117). Looking back on the chair, Charles declared his satisfaction that

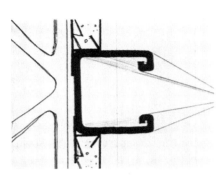

FIGURE I.2. Charles and Ray Eames, still from *ECS*, 1961.

FIGURE I.3. Charles and Ray Eames, still from *ECS*, 1961.

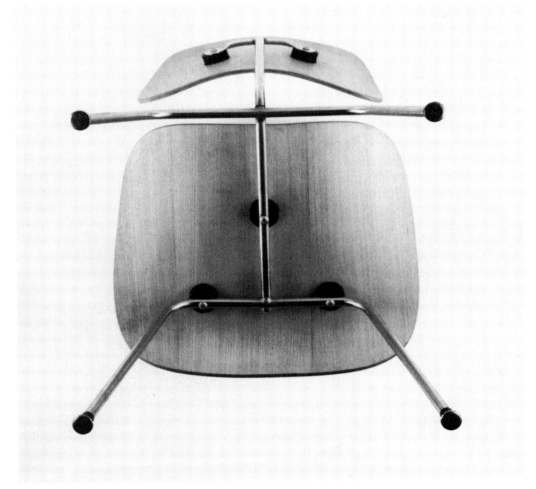

FIGURE I.4. Charles and Ray Eames, Eames Dining Chair Metal (DCM), 1946.

it provided a "clear statement of the handling of the connection between two different materials" (*EA*, 167).

Charles's eye seemed to fixate on connections, as though the bulk material of the object was a kind of intrusion on, or extraction from, the fine details.[58] Connections pointed to the structural principle of a work, the element he thought could survive any degree of abuse. As Caplan rightly notes, the connections were not only "between such disparate materials as wood and steel" but also, and more importantly, "between such seemingly alien disciplines as physics and painting, between clowns and mathematical concepts, between architects and mathematicians and poets and philosophers and corporate executives."[59] Caplan's point is that the disparate can be meaningfully related, a fact that a visually refined connection can express. Early on in the Eameses' practice, it was about the connections between materials in furniture and in architecture (wood, rubber, steel, glass), but after their 1953 film *A Communications Primer*—with their turn to film and exhibition design—the emphasis fell on connections between disparate *ideas*. As Charles later noted, looking back on their career, what they sought to show again and again was how "eventually everything connects—people, ideas, objects, etc. . . . The quality of the connections is the key to quality per se."[60] When Charles said this, the Eames Office had just completed *Powers of Ten* (1977), a film that aimed to show the connections among "everything," from the vast reaches of space to the smallest particles of matter. In the early film *House: After Five Years of Living* (1955), the Eameses made connections the thematic meaning of the work. The film is composed of hundreds of still photographs, and the sixteenth and seventeenth shots draw a seemingly improbable connection between the diagonal cross bracing on the titular house's façade—an element that connects disparate aspects of the structure—and the diagonal orientation of a leaf against the wood planks of the entranceway (Figure I.5). The point is to suggest there is some deep connection between natural and human elements, that steel, leaf, and wood organically fit together, despite, or rather because of, the disparities among them.

In a more extreme register, the Eameses' fascination with connections resulted in a film that offers an extravagant reading of Charles Babbage's Difference Engine. Conceived in the 1820s as the first digital computer, the Difference Engine is the subject of the Eameses' 1968 film *Babbage's Calculating Machine or Difference Engine*, the opening frames of which display a profusion of images featuring the number 901—the famous street address of the Eames Office in Venice, California. One can hardly fail to see the relation, but it is much harder to construe the meaning, which turns out, according to the Eameses' own account, to be that their office was in fact an unconscious exemplification of the principles of Babbage's device created more than a hundred years earlier (Plate 2).[61]

FIGURE I.5. Charles and Ray Eames, stills from *House: After Five Years of Living*, 1955.

Whatever connections the Eameses drew between disparate, even random, elements, they were intended to be *seen as drawn* for the viewer. The Eameses were pointing to relations internal to a work that were—so they hoped—made meaningful by
them. This understanding of connection should be contrasted with the strictly metaphysical notion of it that saturated the work of their friend and colleague Buckminster
Fuller. Fuller's idea of "nature's geometry," which built on the transcendental insight
he called the "coordinate system of nature," was very different from that of the Eameses.
"Nature," Fuller stated, "has a superb, rational coordinate system," the first principle
of which is that "all structure in the universe is made up of tetrahedronal parts." The
tetrahedron is "the minimum prime divisor of omni-directional universe," a discovery
that Fuller insisted he would be "most remembered for."[62] Fuller did not draw connections between disparate things—an icosahedral virus, tetrahedral carbon molecules,
and a geodesic dome, for instance—but instead asserted an existing *identity* underlying
difference. He did not see the relation in a meaningful way; rather, he emphasized an
identity that existed beyond any intention. The Eameses made connections that expressed their intent; Fuller pointed to identities presumed to persist in the world.[63]

For the Eameses, the highest value was the quality of "continuity," the creation of a
connection between seemingly disparate elements within a limited set.[64] They believed
that past, tradition-based, cultures had a deeper sense of the connections among the
various aspects of life, from the largest to the smallest and vice versa. Modernity, by
contrast, was defined by the division of labor, specialization, the separation of the faculties, a split between mind and body—a disjunct the Eameses summed up with the term
"discontinuity." Their project was to rectify the discontinuity rather than to reestablish
continuity ("We are doomed to be aware," Charles asserted).[65] The only kind of wholeness available within modernity, in their view, was "nondiscontinuity" (*EA,* 356).[66]

In the PBS documentary film *An Eames Celebration* (1975), Charles, leaning on the work of Jacob Bronowski, lays out his basic philosophical view of the nature of connections, focusing on the fraught relation between art and science:

> There seems to a general assumption that science and art form a kind of a discontinuity, and I don't think anything could be farther from the truth—when a poet, for example, views two entirely different things that seemingly have no relationship but builds a beautiful simile out of it. It's exactly the same as when a scientist, Newton, for example, when he saw the moon and he saw the apple fall, two seemingly unrelated things of which he built one of the most exquisite theories, principles, of all time.[67]

Despite Charles's insistence, these are not the same. Poet and scientist relate on one level and part ways on another. Just as the poet must "build" a connection between disparate things because it does not appear independent of the poet's making, Newton, in building a new relation between the moon and an apple, makes something appear that was not there before. But in another sense, art and science are dissimilar. The simile constructed by the poet is not a literal connection but a figurative one (even if it might change how we see things). For Newton, what matters is the underlying order, which exists beyond the apple or the moon. Newton, in this sense, is seeing a relation that is already there, while the poet is making a connection that would not exist without the poem. As I argue, there is a formative tension in the Eameses' oeuvre of construing artistic practice as analogous to scientific discovery, *as though* a poem (or any work of art) could be a natural object.[68]

Connections II: Craig Ellwood and the Case Study House Program

In 1962 Charles Eames laid out a series of possible subjects for films about architecture. He called one *The Connections* and described it as "the story of architecture—'moment of truth'—when one material is made to meet another" (*EA*, 230). The Eameses would have been familiar with a version of this story as it unfolded in the pages of the magazine *Arts and Architecture,* edited by their friend and colleague John Entenza, a crucial figure in the world of modern architecture in California. It was Entenza who, in 1945, launched the seminal Case Study House (CSH) Program, which fundamentally reshaped the landscape of modern architecture in California.[69] Charles and Eero Saarinen designed Entenza's house, CSH 9 (1950), on a property neighboring that of the Eameses' house, CSH 8 (1949). Both CSH 8 and 9 were constructed of factory-made parts, assembled, as Colomina puts it, like an "infinitely rearrangeable storage system."[70] Like the Eameses' house, Craig Ellwood's CSH 18 (1958) featured connections

FIGURE I.6. Craig Ellwood Associates, Case Study House No. 18 (Los Angeles, California), 1956–58. College of Environmental Design Archives, Special Collections, Cal Poly Pomona.

and a system that bound its disparate elements of steel, glass, and stucco panels together into a "nondiscontinuous" whole (Figure I.6). And like the Eameses, Ellwood sought a means to keep his form alive through all the uses and abuses that its reception entailed. As Ellwood observed in a frequently repeated phrase, the "substance of architecture is *form,* and this alone has survival value."[71] Form for Ellwood was made of the same stuff as it was for the Eameses: the structural system. When all else failed, it was the system that ideally survived every form of use and abuse.

Ellwood and the Eameses came to hold similar views of form and audience for roughly the same reasons. The Eameses moved from architecture to furniture and from furniture to film because those media allowed them to assert more control. Charles described the noise of architectural practice and how to counter it:

> Practicing architecture is a super-frustrating business. You work on the idea, but then standing between you and the event itself are many, many traps to dilute it.

> The finance committee, the contractor, the subcontractor, the engineer, the facili-
> ties guys, the political situation—all of them can really degenerate the concept.
> Going into furniture or film is a deviation of a sort, but at least we have a more
> direct relationship with the end product—better chance to keep the concept from
> degenerating. (*EA*, 315)

It is likely that Charles followed Ellwood here in his account of the specific nature of
architectural dissatisfaction. In a 1959 feature on CSH 18 in *Progressive Architecture*,
Ellwood described the rewards and frustrations of architecture.

> The most rewarding aspect is the self-satisfaction of somehow—through the frus-
> trating maze of the antiquated processes of the building industry, and in spite of
> archaic building codes, needless deed restrictions, reactionary architectural com-
> mittees, sloppy subcontractors, and nervous, anxious periods when it is part of the
> job to act as arbitrator-analyst-mediator-diplomat—being able to produce a building
> without serious flaws, buildings that conspicuously display perfections, regardless
> of what has seemed to be every effort by all concerned to effect the exact opposite.[72]

Ellwood was far more willing than the Eameses to compromise with the world. He
was forthright about the "impossibility of building it perfectly," but he was satisfied
if what came across was the ability to "display perfections." In other words, Ellwood
concurred with the Eameses that architecture is defined by a high loss of meaning, but
he accepted these losses, and that allowed him to continue in architecture (at least for a
time), while the Eameses, unable to accept the losses, abandoned architecture in favor
of other, more durable, modes of expression (such as modeling).

Ellwood dominated the pages of *Arts and Architecture* in the 1950s, and his work
explicitly borrowed themes introduced by the Eames and Entenza Case Study Houses.[73]
CSH 9, the house Eames and Saarinen designed for Entenza (Figure I.7), established a
pattern that Ellwood would exploit many times over. Ellwood replicated such features
as the separation of the outer envelope from interior partitions and the folding down
of the roof plane of the garden façade to create a *brise-soleil*. In many ways, however,
CSH 9 was more conventional in its approach than CSH 8 (also known as the Eames
House), and it was the latter that had the deeper impact on Ellwood's thinking. As
Eduardo Contini, engineer on CSH 9, observed, "The intention of the Entenza house
is to eliminate structure—to be anti-structural" (quoted in *MCH*, 57). By removing
columns and beams from view (with the exception of one visible interior steel column),
Eames and Saarinen stressed the sweeping nature of the spatial envelope, what McCoy
calls "elastic space," as well as provided an expansive view of the natural world stretch-
ing out to the Pacific (*MCH*, 54) (Figure I.8). The Eames House, by contrast, was far

FIGURE I.7. Charles Eames and Eero Saarinen, Case Study House No. 9 (Los Angeles, California), 1950. Photograph: Julius Shulman, 1950. Copyright J. Paul Getty Trust. Getty Research Institute, Los Angeles (2004.R.10).

more structurally assertive, with the stress given (in Charles's words) to the "materials themselves—the texture of the ceiling, the metal joists, the repetition of the standard sash, the change of the glazing from transparent to translucent." The Eameses accorded the greatest importance to the expression of the "structural web," the system connecting the parts; it was the web that held "in a unit the stucco panels of white, blue, red, black and earth" (*MCH,* 57) (Plate 3). For Ellwood Associates, the impact of the Eames House was in the way it managed to join an array of disparate materials—steel, glass, and stucco panels—and the house became a crucial model for Ellwood's most highly publicized house, CSH 18.[74]

Designed in 1955, CSH 18, by Ellwood Associates, with Jerrold Lomax as chief designer, was built over several months in 1957 and 1958.[75] The first plans for CSH 18 appeared in 1955, and Ellwood Associates had received heavy exposure for its two earlier

FIGURE I.8. Charles Eames and Eero Saarinen, Case Study House No. 9 (Los Angeles, California), 1950. Photograph: Julius Shulman, 1950. Copyright J. Paul Getty Trust. Getty Research Institute, Los Angeles (2004.R.10).

CSHs (16 and 17) through the early 1950s in *Arts and Architecture* and other magazines. The work of Ellwood Associates was published in *Arts and Architecture* more than twenty-five times from 1952 through 1958, more than that of any other architects of the 1950s, and CSH 18 was the magazine's most publicized house, with nearly month-by-month reports from 1956 through 1958. Neil Jackson rightly calls the house a "manifesto" and "didactic" in its aims, and one might see it as a summation of the claims of the Case Study House Program as well as the ambitions of *Arts and Architecture* in the 1950s.[76]

Structurally the house was organized on an 8-foot module with 2-by-2-inch-square steel tube columns and 2-by-5½-inch rectangular steel I beams.[77] The 8-foot module was fitted into sixteen prefabricated steel bents (units of beams and columns) to create a 32-by-72-foot rectangle.[78] CSH 18, Ellwood declared, was the first Case Study House to have "truly reflected in the design the system utilized," a point he made repeatedly. As he described the system: "One connection applies to all exterior wall conditions:

panels, glass, sash and sliding glass door units connect to structural tubes in the same manner." It is the "versatility of the system [that] allows its adaptation" to a "multiplicity of combinations."[79]

Like the Eameses, Ellwood stressed the importance of systemic connections to the meaning of the structure.[80] It was the system of connections—what Ellwood simply called the "form"—that would survive when nothing else would. The March 1958 issue of *Arts and Architecture* features the unique wall plan sections of CSH 18 (Figure I.9), details meant to exemplify how "one connection method applies to all 'in-line' exterior wall conditions," a claim illustrated with six photographs detailing the mode of connection between all the various in-fill materials.[81] The first illustration shows the mode of connection between two prefab wall panels; the second, the connection between prefab panel and fixed glass. The third photograph shows the connection between fixed glass and sliding glass wall, and the fourth shows the connection between fixed glass and jalousie or louvre windows. The fifth shows a corner section connecting jalousie sash and prefab panel. According to the accompanying caption, "All other corners conditions, any combination of panels, sash, fixed glass and 'Steelbilt' [sliding glass] units, attach in a similar manner." The sixth and final photograph details the basic framing materials, the rectangular steel beam and the square steel column. Displayed on the page of *Arts and Architecture,* these six connections constitute a featured expression of the house, the formal means that could survive any degree of use and abuse.

It is a commonplace of the literature on the Case Study Houses to point to the difference between the second-generation steel architects (the Eameses, Ellwood, Soriano, and Koenig) and the first-generation wood-and-plaster architects (J. R. Davidson, William Wurster, Whitney Smith, and Rodney Walker), a difference I will touch on here. Davidson's career, for instance, clarifies the changing nature of modern architecture in California. Like Schindler and Neutra, and unlike architects in the generation that followed, Davidson had no interest in structural expression. It was in the treatment of the plan that he expressed his mastery of the medium. Davidson's plan for the first CSH of 1946 was reused at least four times; McCoy calls it "the neatest plan ever devised for a small house."[82] As Davidson explained, what he valued above all in houses were the qualities of "serenity and cheerfulness," which were generated by the plan. The plan derived its force through the primacy of *line*. In his most programmatic statement, Davidson reflected how "serenity is achieved through order. The continuous line is the restful one. . . . I make it a design habit that nothing hangs free of the continuous line except for the accent."[83] It was the emphasis on linearity and on the image of continuity that put him at odds with the problems of connection that are at the heart of the issues explored in this book. As McCoy explains, Davidson's Old World values ultimately conflicted with the changing nature of architectural expression at midcentury (McCoy fixes on 1949 as a turning point).[84] With the Dann House of 1950 (Figure I.10), McCoy

CASE STUDY HOUSE NO. 18

DESIGNED BY CRAIG ELLWOOD ASSOCIATES

These photographs show the ease of installation of the pre-fabricated wall panels in Case Study House #18. The panels are 9/32" thick "Harborite" plywood, glued and nailed to both faces of 2" (net) Douglas fir framing. "Harborite" is a marine grade Douglas fir plywood, plastic-faced with resin-impregnated overlays to prevent common plywood failures such as grain-raise, checking and delamination. The plastic face also allows a smooth application of paint, free from grain transfer.

All interior and exterior wall panels in the house were erected after pre-fabrication as shown here. Panels to receive wiring and plumbing were built with one open face to allow access. All panels are thermal acoustic insulated with "Celotex" insulating blankets, a highly efficient, fireproof mineral wool.

Also shown here are typical wall plan sections of actual components. One connection method applies to all "in-line" exterior wall conditions. Pre-fab wall panels, "Steelbilt" sliding glass wall units, "Cal-State" louvre sash and fixed glass attach directly to the 2" square structural steel tube or are held in place with a 2" wide, 3/16" thick, continuous steel batt attached to

(Continued on Page 32)

1. ACTUAL 1" LONG EXTERIOR WALL SECTION. THIS SECTION SHOWS PRE-FAB INTERIOR WALL PANEL CONDITION AT EXTERIOR WALL. THE 1"x1"x1/8" CONTINUOUS STEEL ANGLES AT INTERIOR PANEL EDGE ALLOW THE PANELS TO BE UNDERSIZED FOR TOLERANCE AND "TRIM" THE JOINTS.

2. EXTERIOR WALL SECTION. CONDITION AT PRE-FAB PANEL AND FIXED GLASS. GLASS AND PANEL ARE HELD IN PLACE WITH THE CONTINUOUS 2" WIDE, 3/16" THICK STEEL BAR.

3. EXTERIOR WALL SECTION. CONDITION AT FIXED GLASS AND "STEELBILT" SLIDING GLASS WALL JAMB. HERE AGAIN THE CONTINUOUS 2" STEEL BAR "FIXES" GLASS AND THE "STEELBILT" UNIT. THE CONTINUOUS WHITE MASTIC BEAD IS WEATHERPROOFING.

4. EXTERIOR WALL SECTION. CONDITION AT "STEELBILT" JAMB AND JALOUSIE SASH. THE JALOUSIE FRAME ATTACHES TO A CONTINUOUS LIGHTWEIGHT FORMED STEEL CHANNEL WHICH IS ATTACHED TO THE 2" SQUARE TUBE. THE JALOUSIE SCREEN FRAME ATTACHES TO THE OUTER FACE OF THIS LIGHTWEIGHT CHANNEL.

5. EXTERIOR WALL SECTION. CONDITION AT CORNER. THIS IS TYPICAL CORNER OF JALOUSIE SASH AND PRE-FAB PANEL. ALL OTHER CORNER CONDITIONS. ANY COMBINATION OF PANELS. SASH, FIXED GLASS AND "STEELBILT" UNITS. ATTACH IN A SIMILAR MANNER.

6. ACTUAL SECTIONS OF 2"x5-1/2" RECTANGULAR STEEL BEAM AND 2" SQUARE STEEL COLUMN. BOTH SECTIONS HAVE 1/4" THICK WALLS. THE BEAM WEIGHS 11.9# A LINEAR FOOT. THE COLUMN 5.6# A LINEAR FOOT.

PHOTOGRAPHS BY MARVIN RAND

P. E. PHILBRICK COMPANY, GENERAL CONTRACTORS

DETAILS AND DESIGN COPYRIGHT 1955 BY CRAIG ELLWOOD

FIGURE I.9. Craig Ellwood Associates, Case Study House No. 18 (Los Angeles, California), 1956–58. *Arts and Architecture,* March 1958.

FIGURE I.10. J. R. Davidson, Gustav Dann House (Los Angeles, California), 1950. Photograph: Julius Shulman, 1952. Copyright J. Paul Getty Trust. Getty Research Institute, Los Angeles (2004.R.10).

writes, Davidson fully entered the "spirit of the day," as the house was a "collage of rectangles and squares on different planes, of different materials and transparency."[85] It was precisely Davidson's embrace of material and spatial complexity, of connecting disparate elements into a compact whole, that clashed with his primary commitment to linear continuity. For the first time in his career, it was connections, "not the floor plan," that shaped the expressive whole.[86] Davidson's 1950s post-and-beam work replaced his truss-and-mullion approach, a difference that resulted in the kinds of spacing that resisted his genius for tracing closely knit lines across intimately defined spaces.[87] He was forced to multiply, expand, and enlarge built-ins, fireplaces became dominant features, and the two-axis living room—perhaps the core feature of his domestic program— while retained, felt stranded within increasingly undefined spaces.

Unframed Space

If Ellwood stressed the connecting joint at CSH 18, then critic and architect Peter Blake picked up on an earlier idea and focused on the difference between frame and walls. For Blake, the point was to see how the wall expressly neutralized its structural function:

> Using his light steel cage as a space-module, Ellwood . . . preceded [sic] to fill in the voids [with] sheets of clear or frosted glass . . . or he would insert panels of wood, stucco, concrete, brick—anything that seemed to suggest a flat, non-structural plane in opposition to the delicately detailed structural frame.[88]

Blake's coordinates—frame/wall, structure/plane—were those of the International Style and informed the debates about it. Writing in 1952 about Ellwood's first steel, glass, and stucco structure, the Hale House (1951), Entenza similarly noted, "Space is not bound by the perimeter of the rooms; the uninterrupted motion of the ceiling pattern and the interpenetration of house and garden through the transparency of glass result in a visual freedom that suggests unlimited expanses beyond."[89] Entenza picked up on Neutra's terms. It was Neutra who insisted that the modern house is "not closed in all directions" but rather an open-ended spatial container, unbounded by walls.[90]

Ellwood's CSH 16 of 1951–53 was interpreted along these same lines. An extensive 1953 *Arts and Architecture* editorial on the house stressed the "impression of unrestricted space," a quality the architect created by lifting the roof slab over the wall planes and lifting the walls from the floor slab.[91] By 1960, Blake's Miesian reading of Ellwood had become a kind of critical consensus. In that year the *Architectural Review* published a piece describing CSH 16, as depicted in the famous Marvin Rand photograph of the house, as a giant "erector set," one that went beyond the example set by the Eames House to an "extreme point," one where "the whole structure becomes a neutral space-grid of horizontal and vertical members, with no apparent scale of their own, and the house is made by skinning over the top range" (Plate 4).[92] Part of the fascination with Rand's photograph was its unusual point of view, which privileges the unfinished lower half of the structure where it meets the ground, suggesting a kind of endless grid, as though the house were extruded from empty space. And yet other aspects of the photograph point to the *limits* of the frame, as the left side of the structural frame lines up with the literal frame of the photograph. Consider too how the floor of the house nearly bisects the left edge of the literal frame. It is as though the internal framing system reiterates at every point the square shape of the photographic frame. Rand's point seems less about the photographic nature of Ellwood's space than about the internal division of the work, how the deep perspective suggested by the glass walls and angled members is in tension with the hard stoppages of the structural frame. Moreover, Rand captures the precise quality of impermanence that Ellwood Associates' works project, a quality aptly described by David Gebhard as "Miesian, cardboardy, and fragile."[93] Except, of course, the word "Miesian" alongside "cardboardy" exposes all the difference in the world between California Modern and other approaches.

Well before seeing Ellwood's work, Blake had developed a vision of modern architecture as unrestricted space. In his plans for an ideal museum—a structure inspired by Mies's Small Museum Project (1941–43)—Blake filled the space with Jackson Pollock paintings, which doubly functioned as walls. According to Blake, "Jackson and Mies seemed to have a very similar attitude toward the nature of space." It was a "'Dream of Space'—a dream of endless, infinite space in motion."[94] In a daring conceit, Blake put Pollock's art into "motion" by setting a large mirror perpendicular to each side of Pollock's *The Key* (1946), the effect of which was to project Pollock's paintings into space. Blake's museum was the subject of an influential 1950 article in *Interiors* magazine by Arthur Drexler evocatively titled "Unframed Space" (Figure I.11).

> The paintings [in the ideal museum] seem as though they might very well be extended indefinitely, and it is precisely this quality that has been emphasized in the central unit of the plan. Here a painting 17' long constitutes an entire wall. It is terminated on both ends not by a frame or a solid partition, but by mirrors. The painting is thus extended into miles of reflected space. . . . Its sole purpose is to heighten our experience of space.[95]

Blake's and Drexler's picture of "unrestricted space"—a variant on Miesian "universal space"—did not capture either the Eameses' or Ellwood's aims at CSH 18 (nor Mies's own practice).[96] As Ellwood continually emphasized, his aim was to discover a system of connections to allow for a kind of infinite flexibility of enclosing materials. The point of separating the structure from the walls was not to create open-ended space but to

Without its roof the project's spaciousness is more apparent. Close-up, below, shows a mirrored wall with a painting reflected in it. Other Pollack pictures hang in the background on walls of Betty Parsons' gallery.

Unframed space; a museum for Jackson Pollack's paintings

Peter Blake has given the open-plan treatment to the paintings of Jackson Pollack, but in this case not merely to effect a circulation of visitors so rapid that no one stops to look at the exhibits. The pictures are heavily pigmented designs whose continuous rhythms often appear to end because there was no canvas left for more, and Mr. Blake feels that their distinguishing characteristics are best revealed by open space and by the absence of frames. The paintings seem as though they might very well be extended indefinitely, and it is precisely this quality that has been emphasized in the central unit of the plan. Here a painting 17' long constitutes an entire wall. It is terminated on both ends not by a frame or a solid partition, but by mirrors. The painting is thus extended into miles of reflected space, and leaves no doubt in the observer's mind as to this particular aspect of Pollack's work.

The model also includes three small polychrome sculptures made by the artist for Mr. Blake's use, and one of them stands before a curved screen of perforated brass. This is the only wall in the ensemble which serves exclusively as a background. The largest of the sculptures rests on a square base, while the other two stand on the floor.

In its treatment of paintings as walls the design recalls an entirely different kind of pictorial art; that of the Renaissance fresco. The project suggests a re-integration of painting and architecture wherein painting *is* the architecture, but this time without message or content. Its sole purpose is to heighten our experience of space.—*a.d.*

Peter Blake *New York City*

Arthur Drexler

90

FIGURE I.11. Arthur Drexler, "Unframed Space: A Museum for Jackson Pollock's Paintings," *Interiors,* January 1950.

afford "design flexibility not otherwise possible" and to allow a multitude of choices with respect to the wall panel material.[97]

In a brief essay titled "On the Future of Architecture," published in 1959 but written circa 1955–57, Ellwood discussed the structural system at CSH 18 and related structures, again focusing on the future of prefabrication:

> Of the many pre-fab structures thus far produced, few have truly reflected in their design the system utilized, and this will be the proper means to variety. To avoid stereotype architecture, the need will be for a great assortment of component parts which will allow a multiplicity of combination. And there will have to be a diversity of structural and plastic concepts, among these, possibly, a new machine sculpture.[98]

The system made possible a combination of parts, and the system could be thematically featured in the structure. The abundant visual record supports Ellwood's claim about the privileged role played by connections at the house. The house was completed and opened to the public in May 1958, and it was featured in the June 1958 issue of *Arts and Architecture,* in a twelve-page spread that included no fewer than thirty-one Rand photographs (Figure I.12), the plan of the house, and an essay by Ellwood titled "The Machine and Architecture."[99] The novelty of the house was not in the steel frame itself (the first steel-frame house went back to Neutra's Lovell House of 1927–29) or in its spatial conception, but in the advertised structural system.

The idea behind the "one jointing detail" at CSH 18 and the language used to describe it were modeled on the example set by Konrad Wachsmann and Walter Gropius's General Panel Corporation. Wachsmann, a longtime friend of the Eameses, introduced Ellwood to modern architecture in 1947 when they collaborated on a duplex.[100] The November 1947 issue of *Arts and Architecture* featured an article by Wachsmann and Gropius titled "'House' in Industry."[101] This article came to shape how Ellwood, the Eameses, and others thought about connection and also how designers more generally thought about prefabrication. McCoy aptly describes Wachsmann's aim: to "create a market for building elements from which any kind of building could be assembled, in any variation or combination, for any purpose" (*EMR*, 135).

Wachsmann stressed the novelty of a new universal system of connection:

> The building elements are joined together by a unique method of connection. Every part, of whatever nature, is put together with the same device called the "wedge connector."
>
> This method of connection . . . is three dimensional because it is exactly the same, whether horizontal or vertical members are joined together. With the General Panel joint it is not necessary to know beforehand which panel goes into

18

Jerrold E. Lomax, Associate
Albyn and Charles Mackintosh,
Consulting Structural Engineers
Craig Ellwood Associates, Interiors
Carroll Sagar & Associates, Furniture
Warren Waltz, Landscape Architect

P. E. Philbrick Company, General Contractor

All furniture, except garden furniture,
dining table and beds, by Herman
Miller Furniture Company, Zeeland,
Michigan

This house, the last of a series of three that Craig Ellwood has designed for our continuing Case Study House Program, is certain to provoke new thinking and new construction techniques in the residential field.

For some time is has been Ellwood's contention that the increasing cost of labor and the decline of the craftsman will within not too many years force a complete mechanization of residential construction methods. All houses, except those with very high budgets, will someday be constructed of factory-built components designed for fast and easy site assembly.

Unlike the typical pre-fab, where the designer and the manufacturer believe it a requisite to copy past and current styles and where a supreme effort is made to make the product appear to be job built, no attempt to disguise has been made here. The architecture of this house is based upon the system utilized and the visual organization properly reflects this system. The elements of the system are strongly defined with color: ceiling and panels are off-white and the steel framework is blue. Since room partitions occur on module or mid-module, there is unity between structure and plan and structure and form. The color-defined frame thus provides a visual rhythm which emphasizes this unity.

The plan is oriented to the site for best advantage of southern exposure and the view of city lights, the coastline and distant hills. For ample off-street parking, a large paved motor court was provided. Landscaping was designed to supplement and complement the existing natives already growing on the site. The complete landscaping was described in February 1958 ARTS & ARCHITECTURE.

Past and present pre-fab panel houses actually produced integrate structure with panel, i. e., the panel itself is designed and constructed to carry vertical loads and resist the lateral forces of earthquake and wind. Since panels are structural, they are heavy and difficult to handle, and panel connections, designed to transfer structural forces, are by necessity complicated and costly.

This house differs in the fact that the structure and panel are separated. Each, however, is pre-fabricated. In the development of an ideal pre-fab system it seemed logical, considering the earthquake factor here in California, to use a modular structural frame

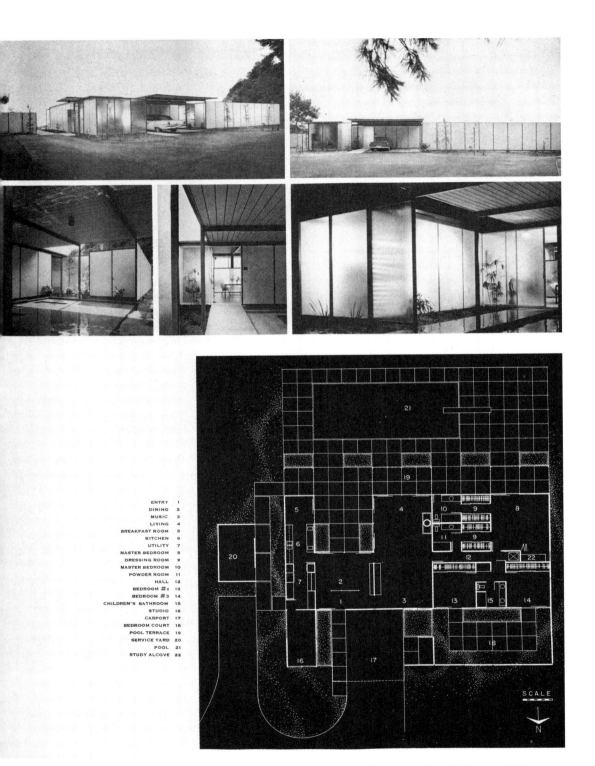

FIGURE I.12. Craig Ellwood Associates, Case Study House No. 18 (Los Angeles, California), 1958. *Arts and Architecture*, June 1958.

which part of the building. That the uniformity of the edge and the connection have great usefulness for the manufacturer need not be emphasized. . . . Any house can be constructed merely by joining these elements together like an Erector set. . . . Theoretically the design variation is unlimited.[102]

Ellwood was surely fascinated by Wachsmann's view that with the universal wedge connector it was finally "possible to effect any desired combination, whereby all the elements are interchangeable," although what Wachsmann meant by "all the elements" was a puzzle, as the wedge had to be fitted inside the framing element, which limited its application to wood panels.[103] A full-page illustration of the connector showed how the wedge was put together as well as its application (Figure I.13).[104] It consisted of four steel parts that were paired with four die-cast wedges inserted into the frame; crucially it was invisible, buried within the support—there was no effort to grant it visual expression.

At the same moment Wachsmann was broadcasting his vision of the universal connector, Eero Saarinen was exploring a similar concept for his massive commission for the General Motors Technical Center in Warren, Michigan. Among the many innovations he achieved at this vast complex, Saarinen remarkably, and poignantly, insisted that his "greatest gift" to the building industry was "the development of the neoprene gasket weather seal, which holds fixed glass and porcelain enamel metal panels to their aluminum frames." At stake with the gasket were precisely the kinds of effects and potentials of universal material connectivity imagined by others in his generation (Figure I.14). As Saarinen described it, his gasket was "truly windproof and . . . capable of allowing the glass or panels to be 'zipped out' whenever a building's use changes"; for these reasons, it became "a common part of the language of modern architecture."[105]

Another essential step in the development of the universal connector emerged from Raphael Soriano's work on the unnumbered CSH of 1950 (Figure I.15). Soriano, a devoted admirer of Neutra, took his cue from unfulfilled aspects of Neutra's early commitment to industrial technologies, especially steel. Soriano also picked up on what McCoy describes as Neutra's long-standing pursuit of the "weightless space" pavilion.[106] Soriano's CSH was featured no fewer than eleven times in *Arts and Architecture* from December 1949 through December 1950, including in two major Shulman photographic essays in November and December 1950. Once again, it was the section detail that was of specific interest to Ellwood, even if Soriano's approach was starkly different from his in the end. As Soriano explained: "I make a thorough study of a section of a beam and column and try it out two or three ways. One is always the best—it performs in all ways. After I have found the best solution for a detail I won't vary it" (*MCH*, 74). (Soriano accepted Fuller's formula that "material affairs can be handled in but one best

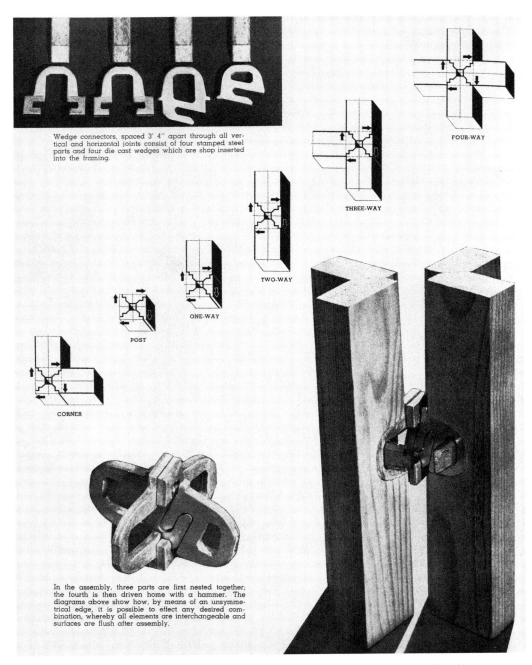

Wedge connectors, spaced 3' 4" apart through all vertical and horizontal joints consist of four stamped steel parts and four die cast wedges which are shop inserted into the framing.

FOUR-WAY

THREE-WAY

TWO-WAY

ONE-WAY

POST

CORNER

In the assembly, three parts are first nested together; the fourth is then driven home with a hammer. The diagrams above show how, by means of an unsymmetrical edge, it is possible to effect any desired combination, whereby all elements are interchangeable and surfaces are flush after assembly.

FIGURE I.13. Konrad Wachsmann and Walter Gropius, "'House' in Industry," *Arts and Architecture,* November 1947.

FIGURE I.14. Eero Saarinen, General Motors Technical Center, installation of gaskets (Warren, Michigan), 1949–55. Photograph: Lionel Freedman, circa 1948. Eero Saarinen Collection (MS 593), Manuscripts and Archives, Yale University Library.

mechanical way.")[107] McCoy glosses Soriano's approach by saying that "steel to him is a problem of connections" (*MCH,* 74), which he had solved; having solved (and disposed of) the problem of the connector, he saw no need to give it any expression.

What is striking about the extensive visual record of the house is that Soriano

FIGURE I.15. Raphael Soriano, Case Study House 1950 (Los Angeles, California), 1950. Photograph: Julius Shulman, 1951. Copyright J. Paul Getty Trust. Getty Research Institute, Los Angeles (2004.R.10).

clearly had little interest in presenting the section detail. In fact, the first appearance of his "solution" to the connector was in McCoy's 1962 *Modern California Houses*. That is, Soriano (or was it McCoy?) highlighted the section detail only after Ellwood had featured it in publications focused on CSH 18. Indeed, Soriano's section detail (Figure I.16), like Wachsmann's, was anything but elegant, and he purposefully concealed it within the structure. It was never meant to be seen, and the system was never intended to be part of the expression. Rather than the connections, Soriano's emphasis was on Miesian "universal space."[108] McCoy notes that to create an open-ended space, Soriano pointedly "de-emphasized the wall," while Ellwood, by contrast, "had a particular affinity for it." In Ellwood's CSH 18, just as at the Eames House, "there is an immediate awareness of the textures of the materials used as infilling in the steel frame" (*MCH*, 81). This was no simple aesthetic distinction. The contrast between Soriano's emphasis on open-ended space and Ellwood's on the nature of connections between disparate

The wide flange beams cut through the fascia channel to span an opening in the partially-roofed dining court.

FIGURE I.16. Esther McCoy, detail of flange beams at Raphael Soriano, Case Study House, 1950. *Modern California Houses,* 1962. Courtesy of Hennessey and Ingalls.

materials marks a basic divergence in approach that defines one of the central conflicts of California Modern.[109] At stake were conflicting accounts of the work of art. The open-ended work displaced artistic intention (even as it surreptitiously finessed every detail, those details were not meant to be read or felt as significant), while the closed structure made intention perspicuous, every detail hinging on the shaping sense of the architect and every structure reducible, at least conceptually, to its details.

It is important to note—albeit in passing—that Pierre Koenig, who was responsible for some of the best-known expressions of the CSH Program, including CSH 21 and 22, and of California Modern more generally, worked briefly in Soriano's office and adhered closely to Soriano's approach to connections and to space. As McCoy remarks about Koenig in her discussion of CSH 21, "Like Soriano . . . he is impatient with panel aesthetics." While Koenig rejected 4- and 8-foot modules primarily for reasons of cost, he shared Soriano's view—again in opposition to Eames and Ellwood—of the role of connections, noting, "His joints are simple and correct" (*MCH,* 117). Like Wachsmann, Soriano, and Neutra, Koenig believed the point was to find a solution to the joint, not to make the connection an expressive feature of the work. Koenig poked fun at the obsession with detailing, observing of CSH 21 that it had "two details—one north/south and one east/west."[110] And like Soriano and Neutra, Koenig drew attention away from the joints and the panels and instead highlighted extensive, open-ended space.[111] Neil Jackson aptly describes CSH 22, which survives as the most famous expression of California Modern, as a "bold demonstration of expansive space. At its most minimal, it is little more than a steel frame beneath an oversailing roof, the glass walls dematerializing any sense of barrier or containment."[112]

Two details suffice to capture something of Koenig's approach to unrestricted space. The first is one of Shulman's famous nighttime views from the living room of CSH 22 (Figure I.17). Shulman situated himself at the steel jamb of the massive 10-foot sliding glass door—half the length of the vast 20-foot-square grid—that separated the swimming pool from the kitchen and living room, looking across the living room outward, with a 270-degree view over Los Angeles. What is most striking about the photograph is the correlation Shulman draws between the vast perspective generated by the rhythmic pattern on the galvanized-steel T-decking of the roof plane and the perspective of the lit-up city streets below. The effect is to suggest a kind of infinite space, that the architecture is an extension or mirror of the world around it. Another view, this time internal to the structure, creates a similar effect of unending perspective (Figure I.18). Looking through the clerestory of the master bedroom to the children's bedroom, Shulman creates a hypnotic effect with the seemingly endless repetition of the T-decking, suggesting a space that extends well beyond the walls of the house, as though the house itself

FIGURE I.17. Pierre Koenig, Case Study House No. 22 (Los Angeles, California), 1960. Photograph: Julius Shulman, 1960. Copyright J. Paul Getty Trust. Getty Research Institute, Los Angeles (2004.R.10).

were some cut in a vast, open continuum, the rooms being temporary fixtures within an unending matrix of space.

Koenig's steel formulas were perhaps more in flux than his completed works suggest. In 1962, Koenig designed the Bethlehem Steel Exhibit Pavilion, a traveling exhibition space advertising the wonders of the steel-frame house. Among the various items on display were four photographs of wood–steel connections highly evocative of Ellwood's details for CSH 18. That Koenig construed the problem of how disparate materials connect as worthy of careful and ongoing exploration, even if these elements were rarely an expressive feature of his work, shows the unresolved nature of his thinking at this moment.[113]

For Ellwood and the Eameses, in contrast to Neutra, Soriano, Koenig, Drexler, and Blake, the system ended with the work. Even if the system evoked a larger mathemati-

FIGURE I.18. Pierre Koenig, Case Study House No. 22 (Los Angeles, California), 1960. Photograph: Julius Shulman, 1960. Copyright J. Paul Getty Trust. Getty Research Institute, Los Angeles (2004.R.10).

cal order, it was nonetheless a closed one. As Charles Eames observed, if "you develop a system . . . it has to come to an end. There is always the problem, once having developed the system, of when do you call it off?" (*EA*, 170).[114] No doubt discovering the moment when a connection started to obtrude, began to suggest disconnection, was an ongoing problem, but it was one they courted: films were finished, models were completed, exhibitions concluded and packed away. For Neutra, Soriano, Koenig, Drexler, and Blake, by contrast, there was no end: the work was a cut in universal space that stretched to infinity, and their aim was to produce structures that, as Neutra emphasized, "endured" beyond the limits of human agency.

But what, finally, of Ellwood's efforts at CSH 18 to create a universal system to handle all connections? Looking back on that moment in his career, Ellwood came to a disenchanted conclusion. Even though he and his associates had "tried to standardize our detailing," in the end, he realized, "you can't standardize." The reasoning was simple and devastating: "Each building is a different problem and we found we couldn't standardize anything to do with the exterior wall details because we ended up with a hundred and some odd details, none of which could we use again or reapply."[115] The move from six basic exterior details at CSH 18 to a hundred was the kind of leap the Eameses were increasingly reluctant to make. And the sense of reality departing from the system paradoxically reinforced their commitment to a mode of production—modeling—that would retain the idea even if it meant letting go of more and more material qualities of execution. Near the end of his life Charles looked back and noted that the "end-product" of the Eames Office was "more often than not in the nature of a model." Over time they had "gotten away with not taking the very last step of the process." The last step, of course, was to make something based on the model. If the idea remained intact, it was because they had found a way to make something that might not be used.[116]

Connections III: R. M. Schindler at Midcentury

Schindler was undoubtedly the most significant figure, alongside Neutra, in introducing avant-garde architectural expression to Los Angeles, but it would be wrong to think his concerns were rooted in an earlier world.[117] It was Schindler who first devised the flexible connection system put into effect by Wachsmann, Soriano, Ellwood, and the Eameses. In 1943, Schindler called his system, which he had first outlined in 1935, "'panel-post' construction." This "system for prefabrication," he explained in 1949, used "a skeleton of structural posts connected by exchangeable wall panels of various materials including glass," adding that the system achieved "utmost permanent flexibility" and permitted "changes in the ceiling heights of the various rooms, allowing better architectural articulation outside and inside."[118] Like the Eameses and Ellwood, Schindler thought of the work in terms of manipulable units. He described the architect's task as the "creation of individual form and character through varied combinations," combinations of what he called the "montage unit."[119] Schindler conceived of flexibility in different terms from Ellwood and the Eameses, in that he believed the unified spatial conception would resist the changes wrought by use. In line with Ellwood and Eames, McCoy observes how the changes made to Schindler's Lovell Beach House of 1926—structural elements as well as the enclosure were painted white—inevitably led to a loss of meaning. With the paint's erasure of the separation between the concrete structural frames and the wood-and-glass cube, "a certain meaning is lost," but the change also throws into relief the formal unity of the whole: "The space development is built-in, it can't be changed."[120] McCoy's suggestion that "built-in" refers to more than furniture and includes the whole spatial conception signals her belief that there are qualities resistant to ongoing user defacement.

Along these lines McCoy stresses, in her first essay on Schindler, the difference between architects and "all other artists." The architect, she writes, must come to terms with the fact that "so much of his work is canceled" along the way from concept to execution. The work is subject to "changes to satisfy the client, to satisfy the building department, the long period during which working drawings are made," and finally come the estimates, where often works at the "point of being born die." There is "nothing analogous to this in the other arts," McCoy declares (*EMR*, 110). The architect must continually find the line between artistic demands and the demands of the client. Schindler's response was to find a way to *delay* the inevitable disintegration of his ideas. His survival strategy was to give his "clients a variety of choices, but never on matters central to the success of the design. All his wiles and ingenuity went into the protection of the kernel of the plan."[121] Options, options, options, except for what mattered.

Schindler died in 1953, and in May 1954 *Arts and Architecture* presented an extensive photographic memorial, arranged by McCoy, featuring thirty of his works (Figure I.19) accompanied by testimonials from McCoy (who worked in his office), Neutra, Gregory Ain, William Wurster, Harwell Harris, Philip Johnson, and several others. Harris, who worked briefly in the Schindler studio, helped close the generational and intellectual gap between Schindler and later architects. In his testimonial, he noted that "for me [Schindler] was the first to point out in the connection of a frame, or a method of flashing, a theme sufficient to regulate an entire composition," demonstrating that it was Schindler's deep engagement with connections that impressed the next generation of architects.[122] Harris's formula was remarkably in sync with that of the Eameses, who remarked in 1953 that in "the design of any structure, it is often the connection that provides the key to the solution" (*EA*, 115).[123]

Connections meant something very specific in Schindler's hands. He frequently discovered his basic architectural motifs in sets of difficult constraints (a central theme for the Eameses): program, materials, finances, local ordinances, views, and site (Schindler had a penchant for difficult hillside settings). McCoy succinctly defines Schindler's approach as an "impatience to set up new problems for himself" (*MCH*, 39).

Four brief examples serve to exemplify Harris's point about how connecting elements became a theme in Schindler's work.[124] At the How House in Silver Lake (1925), Schindler used a "slab-cast" mode of construction, a system he devised that utilized movable wood plank formwork. The lines etched by the formwork created horizontal courses at 16 inches, an effect that Schindler made a structural theme for the house as a whole, crossing concrete and wood and turning the arbitrary into the expressive

R. M. SCHINDLER

1890   1953

1916: *Buena Shore Club, Chicago, work of Schindler in his middle twenties, designed two years after his arrival in the United States. Building pays tribute to his beloved teacher Otto Wagner as well as Louis Sullivan. In 1918 Schindler was invited to Taliesin, where the Imperial Hotel was on the board. He spent four years in Wright's drafting room.*

1922: *Kings Road house, Hollywood. After supervising construction on Wright's Barnsdall house, Schindler remained in Los Angeles to open his own office. The S-shaped house is built on concrete slab with walls of tapered concrete panels cast on ground and tilted into place, panels joined by ribbons of glass through which light and space filter. Sliding canvas doors open rooms to gardens.*

1926: *Design for one of the group of League of Nations buildings is work of Schindler and Richard J. Neutra, who shared an office for two years in the Kings Road house. League of Nations design was one of the award winners. (Buildings never executed.)*

1927: *Sachs Apartments, Silverlake district, Los Angeles, was first of a number of apartment houses in which Schindler eliminated the long central hall, using instead covered outdoor passages, and opened all apartments to private garden spaces or terraces. This plan did much to overcome bad lot subdivision.*

Gregory Ain:

I first met Schindler when I was a college sophomore, majoring in physics. He was the first architect I had ever known, and his house was the first stimulus toward my interest in architecture. That house revisited recently arouses the same wonder and delight that it did almost thirty years ago. Powerful, yet delicate, vibrant yet serene, it is distinguished in detail by innumerable innovations which have since become the common language of modern domestic architecture, but which have rarely since, I believe, been used with such sensitive meaning or to so rich a cumulative effect. The house and the garden are literally one, and the garden is as private as the house. How different from the current cliché of "indoor-outdoor integration" in which the house is as public as the garden! Schindler's garden was planted with near weeds—castor bean, tobacco plant, and bamboo; but it had the rare charm and depth and excitement that marked all of his work, and which revealed a genius of composition which is still too little recognized because the artist was so unconcerned with publicity.

Schindler was an architect who had not merely mastered engineering. He felt and thought in terms of structure, which was an inherent element in his design. He invented, successfully employed, and then discarded dozens of structural systems and mechanical devices which, if patented and commercially exploited, could have earned him a fortune. Three decades ago he poured concrete wall slabs on the ground and tilted them up vertically; he developed an inexpensive vertically sliding form for high concrete walls poured in place; he shot pneumatic concrete against one-sided forms to obtain thin ribbed bearing shells; he employed stucco not merely as a skin but as a load bearing structure by plastering it over light cages of metal lath; he made flush ceiling lights, pin-point spotlights and concealed garden lights long before these appeared on the market; he built flush front cabinets, remote window operators, pullman type lavatories (out of kitchen sinks), sliding sheet metal framed doors and windows, and a multitude of gadgets for two-way fireplaces, folding chairs, and drainboard stoves. And these ingenious inventions were regarded by him merely as incidental elements in the execution of small and inexpensive buildings. Many of these ideas developed on the building site, where much of his actual designing took place. He rarely built from finished working drawings. His plans were usually the roughest sketches of a building, just as his buildings were sometimes just rough sketches of a subtle and wonderful idea. (Continued on Page 35)

1928: *Entrance detail of Wolfe house, Catalina Island, shows the strongly articulated forms which were becoming characteristic of Schindler's work. Three-story house appears to hover over steep slope of its sea-edge setting, rather than adding to the hill mass.*

1937: *House for Henwar Rodakiewicz, Beverly Hills, set in a citrus grove, follows the slope. Outdoor living area extends out from main or second floor level. By 1937 Schindler had abandoned the balloon frame and was developing his own system, which allowed for a free use of clerestories and varying ceiling heights. By placing his plate line at door height the horizontal continuity of the design became a structural reality.*

1944: *Bethlehem Baptist Church, Los Angeles, breaks with clichés to utilize a limited area sensibly. Street side where traffic is heavy presents solid wall. Church has two wings to seat worshippers, together with roof terraces, affords space for outdoor gatherings.*

FIGURE I.19. R. M. Schindler memorial, edited by Esther McCoy, *Arts and Architecture*, May 1954.

(Figures 3.23 and 3.24). For the Elliot House (1930), also in Silver Lake, Schindler noted how the proximity to the neighbors led him to create a trellis scheme for privacy. The trellis in turn became the "leitmotif of the building"; the entire image of the design was driven by the lines of the oversize trellis shape.[125] At the DeKeyser House (1935) in Hollywood, Schindler took the extraordinary step of turning the inexpensive green asphalt roll roofing into a horizontal motif for the house as a whole (Figure I.20).[126] What was a financial necessity became an inventive device that covered the roof and then reappeared, folded over the horizontal plane and lining the eastern elevation, creating a unified surface of roof and siding. The drama continued on the north side, where the roofing extended all the way down the upper level, wrapping it like a present.[127] Harris's observation about how flashing became a theme was likely inspired by the Van Dekker House in the San Fernando Valley (1940). Its elaborate green copper roof was an inspired response to the site, a synthetic equivalent of fallen leaves. The roof generated problems that became an unlikely source for the design. "Since the runoff from copper roofs stains, a system of gutters was introduced to protect the stucco," Schindler explained. "They became part of the architectural scheme."[128] The gutter line motif was not only elaborated along the roof but also reappeared in the interior, in the form of hidden light sources that created light troughs, the light analogizing water running through a gutter.

Unlike the works of the Eameses and Ellwood, which flaunted their visible orders, Schindler's structures seemed personal follies without a system. And for decades this is how Schindler was received. Attitudes toward him changed dramatically, however, in the early 1990s, when Lionel March used Pythagorean calculations to understand his work.[129] March's perspective, coming up against the canonized "complexity and contradiction" account of Schindler by David Gebhard, could not have been more out of step with the mainstream view of Schindler's work at the time.[130] March's approach was vindicated in large part with the discovery in 1999 of Schindler's 1916 Church School lecture notes, which presented a clear mathematical framework for his architecture. "Mathematics: Everything under its laws. Architecture to be conscious of it, usually employed to find proportions. . . . Play with numbers," Schindler declared.[131] What had seemed to many the exemplification of architectural improvisation—casual, bohemian, romantic, expressionist—turned out to be highly organized statements of an underlying mathematical order. It is this "new" Schindler, the author of seemingly temporary, ephemeral productions that were also rigorously composed according to an underlying system, who is closely related to the Eameses.[132]

Connections appealed to architects like Schindler, the Eameses, and Ellwood because it was in the smallest details of the structure that a system was evoked that could

FIGURE I.20. R. M. Schindler, DeKeyser House (Los Angeles, California), 1935. Photograph: Grant Mudford. Courtesy of Grant Mudford.

survive all the inevitable transformations that come with built and lived-in structures. In practice, what this meant was that architecture could be reduced to the merest of elements; it could potentially dispose of the greater mass of the structure and still retain its underlying order. Schindler, Ellwood, and the Eameses flaunted the temporary and seemingly revocable nature of the work as a means of emphasizing, rather than refusing, the survival of an idea of which it was an expression.

The Tent and the Cave: Schindler's Impermanent Ideal

Schindler construed the history of architecture as comprising two "archetypes": the tent and the cave. If history was dominated by the "static" and "permanent" qualities of the cave that "protects . . . all of life's actions," then the new architecture of the tent was defined by the opposite: transience, mobility, and impermanence.[133] Schindler famously described his own house and studio as a camper's shelter, "a protected back, an open front, a fireplace and a roof."[134] It would not be an exaggeration to say his houses frequently suggested the character of a tent or other temporary dwelling.[135] A patio view of the 1946 Kallis House captures the tentlike character of Schindler's approach (Figure I.21). The first archetype

> originates with the idea of the tent, the igloo, etc. Its essence is mobility and its scheme based on the idea of a sheltered bed rather than a house. . . . The need for mobility was first during the period of nomadic life. . . . [In Japan] the constant earthquake danger enforced a specification for house building which is akin to the one of the nomad—lightness, flexibility, ease of rebuilding. The Japanese house shows us the tent in its mature development.[136]

Schindler was intimately familiar with the threat of earthquakes both from his work in Los Angeles and in connection with Frank Lloyd Wright's Imperial Hotel in Tokyo, which famously survived the 1923 earthquake in part because of its flexible foundations.[137] If Wright famously derided Neutra's work as "cheap and thin," for Schindler, such a remark could only be taken as a compliment.[138] Harris provocatively described Schindler's houses as "architectural flowers"; they were not, he observed, "made to endure," but "they charmed as nothing permanent could."[139] Harris identified Schindler's works with Wright's Ocotillo desert camp in Chandler, Arizona (1929), a set of temporary structures built of wood and canvas. Like Wright's camp, Schindler's works were "ephemera."[140] As it turns out, Wright likely took his inspiration for the Ocotillo camp from Schindler's work. Here is Wright in the second edition of his *Autobiography* (1943), his language now borrowed from Schindler's account of the cave dweller:

FIGURE I.21. R. M. Schindler, Maurice Kallis House (Los Angeles, California), 1946. Photograph: Robert C. Cleveland, circa 1951. R. M. Schindler Collection, Architecture and Design Collection, Art, Design & Architecture Museum, University of California, Santa Barbara.

I believe we pay too slight attention to making slight buildings beautiful, or beautiful buildings slight. Lightness and strength may now be synonymous.

Usually we spend so much too much to make buildings "last," as we say. Unqualified to build, we are still busy making caves for cave-dweller survivals.

So, "Ocotillo"—our little desert camp—you are "ephemera."[141]

Harris's image of the "architectural flower" synced up remarkably with Schindler's own vision; in an unpublished 1952 manuscript, Schindler noted that "the color cry of a flower is as short-lived as it is intense, as fleeting as the breathtaking moment of the rainbow or the sunset."[142] What Schindler could not have known was that his vision of architecture as a fleeting shelter that nevertheless reflected a formal order would have broad ramifications for the meaning of California Modern.

Overview

This book comprises six chapters and a Conclusion. Chapters 1 and 2 establish the background conditions for my account of California Modern. Chapter 1 presents the two conflicting architectural approaches explored in the book: on one side, Adolf Loos, mentor to both Neutra and Schindler; on the other, the tradition that runs from August Endell in the 1890s through Wassily Kandinsky and the Bauhaus in the 1930s and on. Looking back today, what is striking about Loos's practice is the depth of his resistance to a vision of materials as bearing meaning intrinsic to their nature. That is, Loos resisted an increasingly popular and eventually dominant aesthetic-political fantasy about the ability of architecture to shape subjectivity, the view I describe at length as a vision of "human sculpting," or *Menschenbildnerei* (a term first used by Adolf Behne to describe Bruno Taut's Glass Pavilion of 1914). Against the widespread claims that construed architecture as a mode of affective formalism, Loos affirmed the limitations of human capacities to plumb the depths of matter and media. For Loos, meaning was historical, situated, and contextual. The architect's job was to understand the complex relations of site, program, cost, and materials and how those functional elements related to the history of forms. Bringing all of these elements together, the architect could create a "mood," one that was open to the contingencies of time and use.

The second and longer part of the chapter engages one of the dominant modes of architectural thinking in the twentieth century, one that still bears results today. Looking at a range of works by Kandinsky, Paul Scheerbart and Taut, Gropius, and László Moholy-Nagy, I address the complex intersection of medium-based thinking and its political implications. Tracing a history of architecture as a mode of human sculpting, I consider how artists in the Bauhaus circle invented a new form of architectural politics, one that was driven by a dissatisfaction with human modes of artistic and political agency and that they replaced with nonhuman "agencies"—a kind of object-oriented ontology *avant la lettre*—that would compensate for all the perceived failures of the human. My contention in the chapters on Neutra that follow is that his basic mode of architectural thinking evolved from his sympathies with expressionist and Bauhaus ideals in ways that qualified his loyalty to Loos.

A brief note on the relationship between Neutra and the Bauhaus, a subject that has not received adequate attention. Although it is little discussed in the literature, the time that Walter Gropius spent in Los Angeles in May 1928 during his six-week trip to the United States had major consequences for the history of architecture in the region. Gropius was in Los Angeles to visit Neutra and to view his latest works, including the just-completed Jardinette Apartments, and to see the designs for the Lovell House

FIGURE I.22. Richard Neutra, Demonstration Health-House (Lovell House), 1927–29. Photograph: Willard D. Morgan, 1930. Copyright Barbara and Willard Morgan Photographs and Papers, Library Special Collections, Charles E. Young Research Library, UCLA.

(Figures I.22, 3.20, and 5.11).[143] He had traveled to the United States to investigate the prospects for industrial house production—an idea he later partially realized in his collaboration with Wachsmann—and Neutra's Lovell House, although a high-priced luxury item, hinted at the possibility of factory-made assembly. At the heart of Gropius's concerns in 1928 was the status of what he called the minimum existence dwelling *(Existenzminimum)*: the minimum standard based on "biological facts" stripped free of any "traditionally imagined historical needs."[144] What both Gropius and Neutra envisioned was a combination of the collective housing represented by the Jardinette Apartments and the factory-based production of the Lovell House.

Not long after Gropius left Los Angeles, Neutra went to lecture at the Bauhaus, taking up residence in the fall of 1930 at Mies's invitation. For his course, Neutra asked students to produce competition designs for the Ukrainian state theater in Kharkov, a competition for which Gropius also submitted a design. Mies saw that Neutra and the Bauhaus had common interests and published a statement expressing a desire to inaugurate a new Bauhaus in the United States under Neutra's direction. "Richard J. Neutra, the progressive American architect who has taught Architecture both in the European Bauhaus as in the U.S. was delegated to develop preliminary plans how to promote in America the idea of such cooperation," Mies stated.[145] Neutra, near the end of his life, affirmed his commitment to Mies's ideas, writing of his desire to "widen their influence in this country—creating an American counterpart to the Bauhaus" (*NN*, 177).[146] The conflicting examples of Loos and the Bauhaus circle considered in chapter 1 provide orientation for the chapters that follow on Schindler, Neutra, the Eameses, and Banham.

Chapter 2 engages the first and second waves of criticism of modern architecture in California, focusing on the writings of East Coast critics Henry-Russell Hitchcock, Talbot Hamlin, Elizabeth Mock, Sigfried Giedion, and Vincent Scully. The subject here is the shift in attitudes toward California Modern, from Hitchcock's and Mock's mixed reactions to West Coast work in the 1940s to Giedion's global vision of the 1950s to Scully's dismissal of domestic and suburban forms in the 1960s. As I argue, modern architecture in California has largely been understood under a set of misguided terms, especially with respect to domestic or private scale versus public monumentality. The second half of the chapter looks at the work of George Nelson, who frequently collaborated with the Eameses, and at Nelson's influential but also wavering efforts to capture the basic sentiments of a new vision of impermanent architecture emerging from the West Coast.

Chapter 3 confronts the infamously fraught relationship between Schindler and Neutra, the competing pillars of California Modern. Neutra, from the first, sought to provide a biotechnical foundation for modern forms, one that would allow him to shape the lives of those who inhabited his structures down to their chromosomes or (after 1954) DNA. Schindler, by contrast, who carried on aspects of the work of Loos, sought to ground his practice in changing local problems of site, building codes, clients, and cost. At stake here is the question of limits: Neutra sought to deny the limits of the work by conceiving modes of control that would persist long after he and his clients died, while Schindler worked within a set of tight constraints, construing the work as expressive within the clear limits of the architectural frame. The last part of the chapter is a close examination of a series of late houses by Schindler (his midcentury moment). What I describe there is a wholly new conception of architectural space and time, an impermanent ideal motivated by what I call "rotational spaces," meaning houses designed to generate a sense of circular or rotational movement around a still center.

Chapter 4 offers a reading of the most powerful document of architectural thinking at midcentury, Neutra's *Survival through Design*. At the root of Neutra's concerns was the capacity of design elements to both advance and destroy human sensory life.

The chapter explores the shift in his thinking from the early 1930s, when he embraced notions of open planning, user interactivity, and design plasticity, to the postwar period, when he turned to a psychoanalytically informed architecture. In his postwar structures Neutra aimed to re-create the protective sensation of the womb as well as the traumatic experience of birth. Despite a clear shift in aesthetic and rhetoric from interaction to therapy, he remained consistent in his basic approach. Underlying both phases was an emphatic interest in shaping the lives of those who inhabited his structures through materials that produced effects independent of human intentionality.

Chapter 5 explores the previously unrecognized conflict between the aims of Neutra and those of the Eameses. Beginning with the work of Neutra's disciple Raphael Soriano, I explore Soriano's and Neutra's most extravagant discursive and architectural commitments to contemporary forms of "scientific" analysis. What is revealed by Neutra's later fascination with "biochemical individuality"—a highly controversial concept originated by biochemist Roger Williams—is a picture of architecture that seeks to break down the defenses of its inhabitants, to the extent that the architect can begin to alter and shape the DNA of his clients and their offspring. The second half of the chapter introduces the work of the Eameses as a contrast to Neutra's example. The Eameses lived for eight years in a Neutra-designed apartment, and their house—CSH 8—was adjacent to Neutra's highly publicized CSH 20. I rely on a close look at the two houses as well as a consideration of the trip that Neutra and the Eameses (alongside George Nelson and Robert Motherwell) took together through Germany in 1954 to characterize the central conflict between the Eameses and Neutra. Far more explicitly than has been recognized, by 1960, Neutra was taking direct aim at the Eameses, as though they represented a standing threat to architecture itself.

Chapter 6 offers an attempt to think through the Eameses' vast oeuvre. Looking first at their early film *A Communications Primer,* I establish the basic pattern of their concern with noise as the distorting mechanism that haunts every communicative act. Seemingly obsessed with interferences that block communication, the Eameses sought ways to bypass or neutralize the barriers to the transference of ideas from architect to receiver. Taking a rather grim view of the "decadence" and "degeneracy" that haunts communication, the Eameses pursued two approaches to architectural expression designed to circumvent noise. The first, modeling, aimed to create something that might remain perpetually suspended between idea and execution, concept and application. The second was a form of production, but also a nascent politics—the only one they could fully embrace—that *equated production with consumption.* Festivals, celebrations, and rituals defined an ideal mode of making that left *no remainder;* the product was fully dissolved (literally consumed or self-consuming) in the action, with nothing left over.

The Eameses' vision of the temporary arts, one that goes back to Schindler's impermanent architectural ideals, leads to a comparison with the most influential account of Los Angeles in the twentieth century, Reyner Banham's *Los Angeles: The Architecture of Four Ecologies* (1971). Banham took his cue from both Schindler and the Eameses, but he ultimately came to a conclusion that diverged from theirs regarding the goals of modern architecture. Banham reduced science to technology and architecture to performance, a perspective at odds with Schindler's fascination with mind and the Eameses' commitment to modeling. Looking back at Banham's infamous essay "A Throw-Away Aesthetic" (written in 1955 and published in 1960) and related writings, I show the continuity of his thinking over time and how he was primed to see Los Angeles in a way that, I argue, falsifies the significance of the phenomenon he was trying to describe.

What has gone unexamined in the literature is the depth of Banham's political commitments, which should be characterized as libertarian. In a sense, Banham *invented* a picture of Los Angeles that shaped the way the city came to understand itself. Inheriting the terms and arguments (but not the aesthetic) of the Bauhaus generation, Banham powerfully brought them to bear on California Modern. My aim is to displace this now canonical, and politically conservative, model by looking closely at the aims and intentions of the architects who produced a widely influential but misunderstood body of work. At stake are competing notions of obsolescence and impermanence, one devoted to the "biologically" driven consumer, the other to the permanence of ideas and the impermanence of architecture. Is it tragedy or irony that it took a British libertarian to package an image of California and sell it back to the world? Californians today, despite their progressive self-image, too often follow in Banham's ideological footsteps. Politically conservative in their fixation on individual responsibility—as though the problems of environmental collapse are a matter of more electric cars and recycling—and antistatist and antitaxation (at least since the passage of Proposition 13 in 1978) in their desire to hold on to their money above all else.

In the end my argument is about the persistence and consistency of a set of failed ideas concerning the capacity of artworks to alter their audiences—to shape them, create them, produce them—as a substitute for the complexities of a normative notion of political life. For many architects and theorists the attraction of architecture, as opposed to other arts (except for film), lies in its immersive quality, the ways in which the inhabitant is all but subsumed by the work over time. This quality is attractive because it seemingly allows the work to function at a level beyond or below the threshold of awareness, thereby taking hold of the inhabitant unawares. This attitude is political in a dual sense: it is pessimistically committed to the idea that normative notions of human agency are unreliable, untrustworthy, flawed, and it is optimistically committed to the idea that this flaw or weakness in human agency can be addressed at the level of form, that structures alter being, and that specific kinds of formal arrangements can create desirable kinds of human actions, precisely the ones Mies fantasized when he spoke of "very specific spiritual-political goals" at the Bauhaus.[147]

This is one half of the story told here. The other half concerns the creation of architectural spaces that express, reflect, and attract forms of life rather than generate them. For Schindler, Ellwood, and the Eameses, for instance, architecture served as a model for progressive living, embracing complex modes of experience that included material, formal, intellectual, psychological, and social dimensions. For these architects, what was at stake was nothing less than fully embodied experience, reflecting the full range of what it is to be an embodied creature. What they shared was a sense that to express the full range of human experience, their work had to express its impermanence, to exemplify the ways in which the work was not reducible to a set of material qualities but subsisted both within and beyond them.

1

The Medium Has No Message
Media Politics from Adolf Loos to the Bauhaus

> But the members of the *Werkbund* are confusing cause and effect. We do
> not sit in a particular way because a cabinetmaker has constructed a chair
> in this or that way, the cabinetmaker makes the chair in a particular way
> because that is the way we want to sit.
>
> —Adolf Loos, "Cultural Degeneration," 1908

Two ideas drove the divergent tendencies of California Modern. One was Adolf Loos's emphasis—picked up by Schindler—on putting people before environment, along with his resistance to a contemporary tendency in design to "confuse" the causality of the two; the other was an insistence on the part of Loos's adversaries—like August Endell and Hermann Obrist—as well as Wassily Kandinsky, Paul Scheerbart, Bruno Taut, and the Bauhaus, that human agency is unreliable and therefore "material" agencies, "cultures" of paint, glass (and the camera lens), and steel, must do the political work that humans are no longer capable of. The replacement of intentionality with the agency of media has by now become a dominant way to talk about art at large (not just architecture), and my aim here is to provide a genealogy for that mistaken approach, and to show how it was resisted from its inception.

Adolf Loos

In his 1898 essay "Old and New Style in Architecture," Loos observes that the architect's main task is to use "materials to arouse feelings [erzeugen gefühlen] in us," adding that whatever feelings are aroused in the spectator, they are "not inherent [nicht inne-wohnen] in those materials themselves."[1] The feelings stimulated by architecture are "acquired, not inborn [anerzogen, nicht angeboren]," and so the architect needs to study the history of forms in order to understand how past forms generate their effects. An architectural education consisted of finding out what buildings "aroused those feelings in the past" and then taking those "acquired feelings into account" in the design of new structures. Loos was not making an appeal to tradition in order to suggest that the past holds the key to a set of eternal qualities; rather, he saw tradition as offering a reliable set of answers to problems faced by both past and current architects.

Loos never deviated from this basic idea. He raises these points again in "Architecture" (1910): "Architecture arouses moods [erweckt stimmungen] in people, so the task of the architect is to give these moods specific expression" (*OA*, 84). To achieve this mode of expressiveness the architect must turn to the "buildings of the past which aroused those moods in people." Here he offers an example of what it means to have an acquired rather than innate sense of expression: "For the Chinese, white is the color of mourning, for us black. Therefore our architects would find it impossible to create cheerful moods with black paint" (*OA*, 84). It is a simple but also surprisingly controversial idea: expressive meaning is culturally, historically, and socially specific and susceptible to change. As I argue, Loos's account of historically changing effects was at odds with the increasingly dominant approach of naturalizing architectural effects adopted by architects from August Endell in the 1890s to Neutra in 1930s and beyond. According to Neutra, an informal student of Loos, science had "proved that certain sensory responses which we regard as acquired are really primary and innate."[2] Neutra attempted to formulate his practice in light of these fixed and enduring properties. For Loos, the rate of change of architectural meaning could be quite slow. The emotional tenor of certain structures could remain stable for years or whole eras, but however long-standing, the response to a building is not innate and always open to revision. This seemingly radical notion of history was merged with another, potentially more troubling idea. As Loos never tired of saying, the "best form is always there already and no one should be afraid of using it." Or as he even more emphatically put it, "Let us keep on repeating ourselves. Let one building be like another" (*OA*, 117). However fixated Loos was in his attachment to the past, he nonetheless left open what "being like" another building might mean.

While Loos advocated reusing past forms, he was nevertheless averse to *copying* them, a distinction that goes back at least to Johann Joachim Winckelmann's account of the difference between *Imitation* or *abbilden* (a kind of rote repetition) and *Nachahmung* (imitating an underlying principle). Although "everything created in earlier times *can* be copied," Loos stressed, no one *should* copy earlier works. Or rather, no one should ever "*consciously echo* a past style."[3] But how do we make sense of the demand to repeat past forms and yet avoid consciously copying them? Can one repeat the past without copying it? What Loos was asking architects to repeat was not the look of the past, but what he called the "reason for the form." It was Loos's complex, if not impossible, proposition that the ideal architect was one who would repeat the principle of past forms without consciously appealing to those forms.[4]

Potentially complicating his affirmation of the historical nature of expressive form, Loos had a distinct preference for classical Greek art and the "superiority of classical antiquity" (*OA*, 33). If meaning changed with time and place, then how could it be that classicism created a "common Western culture," a "common ground" that spoke beyond "differences of languages and frontiers" (*OC*, 187)? It may seem that this partiality compromises the distinction between "acquired" and "inborn" meaning, but Loos was not being disingenuous when he spoke of the expressive differences between Chinese and European forms.[5] He could consistently maintain both that certain colors do not intrinsically express particular emotional states and that these contrasting cultural patterns were anything but equal in his eyes. His affirmation of the *superiority* of the Greek ideal (Figure 1.1) over that of the Chinese (or any other culture) was grounded in a judgment of taste, one that was permanently open to revision.[6]

For Loos, claims of superiority or inferiority were qualitative and had "nothing to do with racism" (in the sense that neither is inherited or biological). He could argue that the distinction between how an "Englishman or a Greek" would design an object and how a "non-Greek, the German," would (*OC*, 135) "come[s] from the times and not from the blood" (*OC*, 139). In Loos's view, a "German" designer could *become* an "English" or "a Greek" one if he took care to ensure that his goods had practical applications. That is why he could speak of German culture "being returned" to the Germans "by the English" (*OC*, 82–83).

At this point, I want to return to Loos's claim that the primary task of the architect is to arouse feelings or moods in the spectator (his most common term for the audience was *Beschauer*). Implicit in this claim is the notion that the architect *stands apart* from his materials and organizes them in such a way as to generate feelings in the spectator.[7] This aesthetic is not, in other words, a *process* aesthetic, one in which meaning is derived in the making; rather, Loos privileged the architect's capacity (shared with composers) to create "inner" designs that are then handed over to the builder to be executed. This begins to suggest a clear inside/outside logic, an idealist conception of inner idea and outer execution. Loos seems to be making just such a distinction in "The Principle of Cladding" of 1898, where he observes that the true "*architect* must first feel the effect that he intends to produce and then see with his inner [geistigen] eye the space that he wants to create" (*OA*, 42). The inner idea comes first, the material execution second; the inner or spiritual term is privileged over the outer or material expression.

But for all of Loos's admiration for classical antiquity, it would be a mistake to see him as reiterating a Platonic conception of artistic production. Just before he suggests that the architect must use materials to arouse feelings in the spectator, he insists that

THE CHICAGO TRIBVNE COLVMN

FIGURE 1.1. Adolf Loos, project of the Chicago Tribune Column, 1922. Adolf Loos Archiv, Albertina Museum, Vienna, ALA378. Copyright 2022 Artists Rights Society (ARS), New York / Bildrecht, Vienna.

the architect should do "more of his work at the building site." Asserting that drawing details in the studio is superfluous, Loos argues that the architect should have "models" present "at the construction site" (Figure 1.2) so that he can make a "close study of the lighting and the distance" of details as they appear on the ground (*OA,* 32). Loos further recommends that the architect put "corrections in with his own hand" in view of specific and changing material conditions on the site, conditions inaccessible to any drafting table design, and architects who built on paper were often the targets of his criticism. It is important to see, nonetheless, that Loos retained a distinction between

FIGURE 1.2. Adolf Loos, model for Villa Alexander Moissi in Venice, 1923. Adolf Loos Archiv, Albertina Museum, Vienna, ALA2439. Copyright 2022 Artists Rights Society (ARS), New York / Bildrecht, Vienna.

idea and execution in his stress on keeping a *model* on the site. He was hands-on *with the model,* but he saw this form as still separate from the act of building, suggesting he could not quite traverse the elemental barrier between inner and outer.

Loos's retention of a distinction between the idea and its realization even as he questioned the distinction between the studio and the site is also evident in his attitude toward photography. In *On Thrift* from 1924, Loos once again states his aversion to drawing: "I do not need to draw my designs." But if he rejected drawing, he also maintained that an architectural "concept" can be "written down" (*OA,* 178). He negatively associated drawing with photography and stated outright his opposition to photographing interiors. "Drawing-board" designs are spaces that might "look beautiful in photographs," but they are, he insisted, dead as lived environments. The "light and shade" of the photograph is "mechanical" and distorts the lived experience of changing

FIGURE 1.3. Adolf Loos, Hans und Anny Moller House, interior of study (Vienna), 1927–28. Adolf Loos Archiv, Albertina Museum, Vienna, ALA2451. Copyright 2022 Artists Rights Society (ARS), New York / Bildrecht, Vienna.

light and shade in a built structure. Loos's opposition to photography was driven by his sense that it *"dematerializes* reality"; he aimed to do the opposite, to create rooms where the occupants would "feel the material around them." "I want it to have its effect on them," he stated (*OA*, 178). So while Loos was emphatic about his commitment to a kind of experiential materialism—he wanted people "to feel the material, the wood, to see it, touch it, to perceive it sensually, to sit comfortably and feel the contact between the chair and . . . their peripheral area of touch" (Figure 1.3)—he was just as emphatic about his belief that the architectural "concept" is notionally separate from its material embodiment (*OA*, 178–79).

There is one more turn in Loos's thinking that requires attention. Readers might have been struck by Loos's consistent emphasis on the difference between acquired feelings and innate ones, and in this distinction they may have detected an echo of Jean-Baptiste Lamarck's discredited theory of inheritance of acquired characteristics. Loos's picture of evolution—most notoriously laid out at the beginning of "Ornament and Crime"—comes strikingly close to Lamarck's theory. Loos's Lamarckianism is clearest perhaps in his brief 1912 essay "The Mystery of Acoustics," in which he suggests that the mystery of the great concert hall is not to be found on the "drawing board," in "diagrams," or in "acoustical theory." He ponders what would happen if a new hall were made using the exact measurements and the same materials as an old theater. The result, he insists, would be "terrible." By way of contrast, he considers the history of the opera house in Vienna. When it first opened in 1869 it had poor acoustics, but over time it became a "model theater for acoustics" (*OA*, 109). What happened? Here Loos treads deeply speculative terrain. He contends that the "material the hall is made from has changed" over time. The walls have literally "soaked up [eingesogen] good music" for forty years; they have been "impregnated with the sound [stimmen] of the Philharmonic and the voices of our singers," which has resulted in a change in the "molecular structure" of the room. With this charged language, Loos suggests that the walls of the concert hall have been inseminated over time by the sensual sounds of singers and the orchestra, and thus have given birth to a new form that is superior to the original. Materials take on the qualities of their users—good or bad, beautiful or ugly—over time, what Loos calls in the brief and ironic "Beethoven's Sick Ears" the "spirit build[ing] the body" (*OC*, 178). Half-jokingly, Loos asserts that, over time, Beethoven's middle-class critics have been slowly shaped by being subjected to his music: all of their "anatomical details, all their ossicles, labyrinths, drums, and trumpets, have taken on the . . . forms of Beethoven's ears" (*OC*, 178). Loos remarks that the changing wood of violins that have been played for many years or many generations displays the same phenomenon of acquired characteristics.

While Loos's speculative vision may strain credibility, the idea that materials change over time (an assertion very different from claims to biological inheritance) also informs his more well-known and uncontroversial view that architecture is never actually finished. "Our home was never finished," he states. "It developed with us, and we with it" (*OC*, 58). Moreover, he maintains that a home "must never be completed" (*OA*, 182). He takes the same view with respect to human beings, asking rhetorically whether we are "ever finished, complete in our physical and psychological development" (*OA*, 182). While from a Darwinian perspective, the answer is yes, we have inherited certain traits that are fixed at birth, even if not yet given full expression, from a (discredited) Lamarckian perspective, meaning changes with use, and the environment shapes the outcome to an uncertain end. Armed with this belief, Loos hoped that classical beauty, given its superior qualities (as he saw them), would over time shape the world in its image. And while this desire was grounded in a profoundly elitist notion, it was not exactly racist, as Loos rejected out of hand the idea that there could be a form of life resistant to change. We may and likely do reject Loos's judgments, but the solution to our disagreement with his judgments would be to replace his evaluations with those we find more persuasive, because to deny that we have the capacity to make judgments is, to his mind, to deny the capacity for people to change.

Loos's commitment to normative ideals contrasted sharply with a growing consensus in the architectural discourse of his period and after. Although Loos's view that there are no laws of emotion that automatically generate emotional states in an observer may seem uncontroversial, he and his circle waged a many-sided battle in defense of this view with a range of ahistorical, essentialist architects, artists, writers, and philosophers. As Éric Michaud has argued, the problem predates Loos's work. In his groundbreaking essay "La Fin de l'iconographie (une nouvelle rhétorique du sensible)," Michaud shows how in the aftermath of the French Revolution some artist-educators sought a means by which to inculcate morality in their subjects directly. Allegory was too slow, too complicated, and required an educated audience to understand its often complex language. Architecture was the first to find a way around allegory toward a universal and immediate production of moral attitudes. Michaud cites the architectural treatises of Louis-Pierre Baltard, C.-N. Ledoux, and Étienne-Louis Boullée in their pursuit of a "universal language" that could directly educate the senses of the viewer. Baltard sought through decoration a means to have "direct influence on our senses and on public morality." Ledoux insisted on pure geometrical signs, because there "should not be a stone in the architect's works which did not speak to the eyes of passersby." Boullée similarly argued that architecture should restrict itself to simple geometrical figures because "by their properties," by "the analogy they have with our bodies," they have a direct "power over our senses."[8]

August Endell, writing in 1898, described the new attitude toward "pure form" when he suggested the possibility of "formal creations that are nothing and that signify nothing, but that have a direct effect on us without any intellectual mediation, like the tones of music."[9] In his "Beauty of Form and Decorative Art" of 1897–98, Endell similarly noted the "power of form upon the mind, a direct, immediate influence without any intermediary stage, . . . one of direct empathy." He went on to explain in detail how "feelings [are] aroused by form," outlining the "emotive effect of the elements of form and their constituent parts" as well as the "psychological explanation" for various kinds of arousal through forms.[10] Endell provided readers with a famous chart of formal effects that could be marshaled to produce any emotional state one might wish (Figure 1.4). In 1900, Hermann Obrist similarly described art as the "transmission of a natural sensation." For the artist, art is "giving amplified sensations . . . and for the consuming layman . . . it is empathizing with the amplified sensations so presented."[11] Henry van de Velde, in "The New Ornament" of 1901, observed how "a composition of lines could have the same logical and constant relationships as numbers and musical

FORMENSCHÖNHEIT UND DEKORATIVE KUNST

boshaft	höhnisch	hochmütig	pathetisch	kalt	unerbittlich	grausam		fürchterlich
frivol	übermütig	herausfordernd	stolz	streng	gewaltsam	wild		grässlich
kokett	chic	prächtig	kühn	rücksichtslos	wuchtig	kolossal		scheusslich
geziert	graziös	elegant	energisch	kraftvoll	derb	ungeschlacht		roh
süsslich	zierlich	geschmeidig	feurig	stark	gedrungen	gewaltig		entsetzlich
fade	zart	hingebend	gross	vornehm	machtvoll	ungeheuer		furchtbar
nüchtern	einfach	innig	warm	ernst	tief	erhaben		grausig
stumpf	kraftlos	müde	bekümmert	traurig	schwermütig	düster		finster

FIGURE 1.4. August Endell, "Formenschönheit und dekorative Kunst, Part II," *Dekorative Kunst*, 1898.

tones."[12] This was the basis for what he called (in 1902) the coming "scientific theory of lines and forms."[13] Even Frank Lloyd Wright was far from immune to the new "science" of form. In his early "Philosophy of Fine Art" of 1900 he observed that the "laws of the Beautiful are immutable as the laws of elementary physics," adding that certain combinations of "forms, lines, and color have . . . natural significance and inevitably express something."[14] The "scientific theory" of line and form stood at the basis of Bauhaus teaching. Walter Gropius, in "The Theory and Organization of the Bauhaus" of 1923, closely followed Endell, van de Velde, and (especially) Wassily Kandinsky when he observed that architectural materials are a "means of expressing different emotions and movements." In terms directly counter to Loos on color, Gropius described how red "evokes in us other emotions than does blue or yellow," while "round forms speak differently to us than do pointed or jagged forms."[15] Gropius never wavered from his early "science" of form. As late as 1968, he argued that "color and texture of surfaces have an effective existence of their own, sending out physical and psychological energies which can be measured as such."[16] And as I will argue, there is little ultimate gap separating Endell in the 1890s from Gropius in the 1920s, Neutra in the 1950s, and affective theorists today. "The importance of . . . an artistic work lies in its charge in affects, its force of contagion. Rather than what it means, the essential is in what it does and causes to be done," Robert Hurley writes, summing up Jean-François Lyotard and Gilles Deleuze.[17]

Thomas Mann, in his 1903 story "Tristan," which he called a "burlesque," parodies the fashionable affective formalism of his day, an attitude he identifies with Wagnerian histrionics. "There are certain notes I cannot so much as hear without feeling the extraordinary sting of tears in my eyes," Gabriele Kloterjahn (Isolde) tells Detlev Spinell (Tristan), another hypochondriacal patient, a failed writer, at the sanatorium where she is staying. "Nothing else affects me this way. You wouldn't believe it." Spinell leaps to his feet, "I believe it! Oh, to think I wouldn't believe it!"[18] He has built his world on a vision of how the details of one's environment trigger affective responses—that is the point of Mann's satire (I imagine Loos laughing along with Mann): "There are times when I simply cannot do without Empire, when I absolutely must have it, if I'm to feel even moderately well. Clearly one feels one way amidst furniture that is sinfully soft and comfortable, altogether different amidst the austere lines of these tables, chairs and draperies. . . . This brightness and severity . . . they impart composure, madam, and dignity. The result is an inner cleansing and convalescence, a moral elevation. Of that I'm absolutely sure."[19] The point of the story is to show just how flimsy, how *unsure,* this pathos-driven ideal ultimately is.

Loos judged all of these claims about the nature of form and affect (he witnessed many variants of it) as backward in their logic, "confusing cause and effect" (*OC,* 163). As he argued tirelessly, the "consumer is the primary factor, the producer the secondary," and this too was a variant on Lamarckian principles (*OC,* 186). He defined cultural degenerates as artists who feel they are "held in subjection" to the changing needs of their clients as well as to a wide range of material constraints and so take revenge on the consumer by "impos[ing] their forms on mankind" (*OC,* 189). The consumer rightly rejects the imposition; he "wants to shape [his] life [himself], and does not want it imposed on [him] by some league of producers or other" (*OC,* 189). According to Loos, affective formalists—those who believe they can master and marshal the emotional energies "inborn" in materials—are driven by the desire to master those who are subject to their forms. But this artistic domination is itself a denial of the capacity to *be* a subject, as the one harnessing the "inborn" energies of materials is playing with forces that "express themselves" rather than any idea generated by the architect in his changing and contingent engagement with materials, program, client, and site.

The great failure of affective formalism, according to Loos, is its denial of the "possibility of error" (*OA,* 38). Loos offers his most probing meditation on the errors and contingency of the artistic act in his brilliant 1904 essay on pottery.[20] He evokes the image of a master potter waiting before the kiln, unsure how the work he has been making will turn out. "Will it give tangible shape to my dreams, or will it eat them up?" the potter wonders. "The spirit of the material has not yet been overcome," the potter declares, and Loos retorts that it "may it never be!"

> May the secrets of the material always remain mysteries to us. Otherwise my potter would not be sitting in happy agony at his kiln, waiting, hoping, dreaming of new colors and clays, which God in his wisdom forgot to create, in order to allow mankind to participate in the glorious joy of creation. (*OC,* 149–50)

Loos's vision of the artisan sitting in "qualvollem glück" as he awaits the results of his efforts is one that makes chance and contingency paramount in the process of making, that draws attention to the vicissitudes of working with a medium—fire—that is forever beyond our control. Once again Loos opposes a scene of empty mastery, the drawing board, with the site where human agency reconciles itself with contingency, the furnace. A whole "world separates" the two. Loos starkly opposes the "exactitude of the compass" with the "uncertainty of chance, of fires, of human dreams and the mystery of becoming" (unbestimmtheit des Zufalles, des Feuers, der Menschenträume und das Mysterium des Werdens) (*OC*, 150).

Rejecting any putative laws of form, Loos took his cue from three sources: materials, place, and form.[21] While he believed one might look to the past to see how different spaces evoked different emotional states, he rejected the idea that a secret essence or law could be extrapolated from a form and be used to automatically generate emotional states in viewers. According to Loos, if, by appealing to the "laws" of form, the architect can never fail to generate an emotional effect, then he can never succeed either, as the effect is independent of his intention—the contingency of expressive meaning is essential. The ability to maintain expressive control, but also the capacity to fail to express, depends on the architect's separating himself, at least nominally, from materials and site and creating the work "in his mind's eye." It is in the *practical*, rather than theoretical, gap between idea and execution that a space is opened up for failure and for success. Loos explained this idea by way of reference to human beings' capacity to "participate" in God's unfinished work. For Loos, it was never a matter of finding order *in* the world, never an act of artistic divination, but rather a matter of making an order to fit changing needs. And it was this distinction between human and divine orders that put him at odds with dominant trends in architectural thinking of his moment.[22] For those who deny the difference between art and life also deny the "possibility of error." The denial of error—the fascination and fixation with the "laws" of form and affect—is a denial of the human (but also the divine) for Loos. To be human is to accept and even solicit the "uncertainty of chance," as it is only through chance, and the risk of error, that something like a human order might be created. "The works of man should not compete with the works of God," Loos declared, an idea that shaped Wittgenstein's early writings. The works of human beings are an expression of their fallibility and their capacity for order in the face of it (*OA*, 123). Although Loos's ideas and practice were largely formed well before the rise of the Bauhaus, his views stand as perhaps the most prescient rejoinder to those of the Bauhaus, whose architects, just like their earlier Viennese counterparts, sought to crack the mystery of materials (glass, steel, concrete, and the camera lens) and marshal those hidden forces to shape a new and better form of human that would fulfill the demands of the Bauhaus for the right kind of political future, one in which the failings of human agency did not figure.

The Bauhaus

In March 1922, three months after his return to Germany from Russia, Wassily Kandinsky was offered the position of head of the mural workshop at the Bauhaus. At this same moment, he addressed the status of realism in modern art in the pages of *Das Kunstblatt*.[23] According to Kandinsky, the rise of realism was in part a reaction to the freefall of financial markets, but it was also a progressive tendency, one that, he noted, he had outlined in "Über die Formfrage" of 1912, his central contribution to the *Blaue Reiter Almanach*. Looking back on that essay, he said his aim was to show that the "coming realism" was identical to the "coming abstraction." Realism and abstraction share in the "great age of the Spiritual," whose collective task is to "liberate and develop all the senses, so that they are able to perceive the living element in 'dead' matter" (*WA*, 481). Contrary to what might be assumed, Kandinsky and his colleagues at the Bauhaus made no significant distinction between realism and abstraction; the only distinction that mattered was that between dead form and live matter.

In the 1935 "Line and Fish," Kandinsky argues that from a spiritual point of view there is "no essential difference between a line . . . and a fish." An "isolated line and the isolated fish alike are living beings with forces peculiar to them," he observes.[24] Kandinsky illustrates his point with the painting *Each for Himself* of 1934 (Figure 1.5). Although they share certain qualities, the nine biomorphic forms depicted in the painting inhabit separate universes; the thick, glowing membranes that encase them are doubled by the incomplete geometrical grid that brackets them off from each other. Whatever similarities obtain between these entities, the aim is to exemplify their particularization—"each for himself"—rather than their integration into the larger whole.[25] Moreover, there are "forces of expression for these beings," Kandinsky asserts, describing an ontology he never wavers from, and these forces struggle to get heard; they require the hand of the artist to be heard by human ears. "It is the *environment* of the line and the fish that brings about a miracle: the latent forces awaken," and the environment is the "*organized* sum of the *interior* functions (expressions) of every part of the work," which are *not* the artist's expressions but the objects themselves that the artist helps us to hear.[26] Neutra made the same point when he observed, following Jakob von Uexküll on animal consciousness, how "each life plays in its own world."[27] We are not far here from Graham Harman's speculative realism, where experience "is applicable to the . . . psyches of rocks and electrons as well as to humans."[28] What Harman's phrase "as well as to humans" betrays is an overarching desire to deflate the human, even if at the same time Harman grants a kind of mystical agency to humans, who recognize their equivalence to rocks.

Kandinsky addresses the question of realism most directly in his 1912 essay "Über

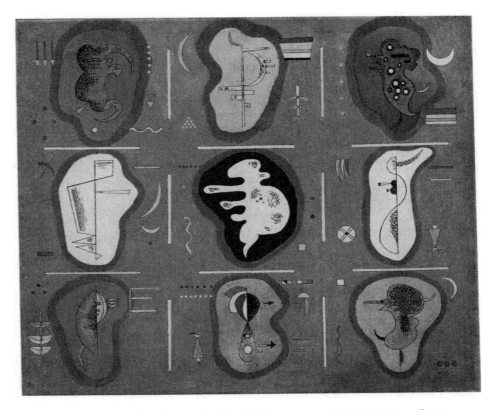

FIGURE 1.5. Wassily Kandinsky, *Each for Himself (Chacun pour soi)*, 1934. Private collection. Copyright 2022 Artists Rights Society (ARS), New York.

die Formfrage" ("On the Question of Form"), an accompaniment to *Über die Geistige in der Kunst* (1912) that was intended to provide practical analogies for the claims made in the book. He summarily dismisses the question he raises in his title: "*The question of form does not exist.*" Why? Because it is "not form (material) that is of . . . importance, but content (spirit)" (*WA*, 238). Form is nothing but the "external expression of inner content," and for every artist, the inner content is different. For every artist, "their own form is the best, since it best incorporates what they are obliged to communicate" (*WA*, 238). Because all forms are equally valid expressions of diverse inner contents, stylistic debates about realism and abstraction are meaningless. It is of "*absolutely no significance whether the artist uses a real or an abstract form. For both forms are internally the same*" (*WA*, 248). Beyond every formal difference lies a single expressive content: "*to hear the whole world just as it is*" (*WA*, 243). For Kandinsky, hearing the world "as it is" means, above all, *not* hearing the artist's voice. The term *expressionism* is particularly useless when it comes to Kandinsky. When Arnold Schönberg, in a 1911 letter, told Kandinsky, "Art belongs to the *unconscious!* One must express *oneself!* Express oneself *directly!*" Kandinsky showed little interest in this kind of expressionism.[29] When he was asked whether he painted his inner life, he retorted that the "desires of the artist . . . are irrelevant. . . . I have no desire to paint my own psychic states, since I am firmly convinced that they cannot be of any interest or concern to others. . . . It is preferable that people I do not know should plaster my [artistic] stall with all kinds of misleading labels" (*WA,* 345). Studying the nature of the "misleading labels"—affective response—was the theoretical task of Kandinsky and the Bauhaus.

The foundational argument in "Über die Formfrage" is formulated around two examples: one using alphabetic letters, the other using grammatical marks. Kandinsky asks his reader to consider the letters that constitute the words in the essay not as signs with meaning but rather as *things.* "If the reader of these lines looks at one of the letters with unaccustomed eyes, that is, not as a *sign [Zeichen]* for a part of a word, but as a *thing [Ding],* then he will see in this letter, apart from the practical purpose created by man . . . another bodily form, which independently produces a specific external and internal impression" (*WA,* 245). Kandinsky is drawing a fundamental distinction between signs that bear meaning and those that make an impression or impact: lines and colors—as well as *everything else in the world*—both signify and make physical and psychological impressions on the beholder; signification is the cultural expression of materialism, while psychological experience is the expression of *Geist.*

Two autonomous expressive elements, Kandinsky argues, characterize every letter. First is the letter's "overall appearance," which can be variously described as "cheerful," "mournful," "striving," "defiant," "ostentatious," and so on. Then there are the letter's individual lines, which are "bent this way or that." Like the overall appearance, these individual lines produce a specific "internal impression" (*WA,* 245).

Kandinsky interrupts his account of letters to issue a crucial proviso. He advises the reader not to worry about the fact that "this letter will affect one person in one way, another person in another," as this is "incidental and can be understood": "Every being [Wesen]," he writes, "will produce a different effect upon different people" (*WA,* 246). So while I might see the letter *K* as defiant with a hint of remorse, you might see it as cheerful but insincere. And this applies to works of art as well. Every picture, when construed as a *thing* and not as a signifying entity, inevitably produces "a different effect upon different people" because just as pictures are lines and colors "with their own life," a life beyond what the artist intended them to mean, so too every viewing body constitutes a life independent of every other. What makes my body mine is a whole set of contextual factors that results in the fact that it responds differently from yours when looking at the same set of lines and colors. My body has a particular size, shape, viewpoint, history, and memory that constitutively differ from those of every other body, and owing to this variety of qualities that constitute my body, I experience *K*s (or pictures) differently from any other viewer.

After issuing this proviso, Kandinsky drops the thought, but he picks it up again in his second contribution to the *Blaue Reiter Almanach*, "Über Bühnenkomposition" ("On Stage Composition"), where he explains that artists instinctively know they have achieved the right form for their inner content when they feel a vibration they are compelled to relay to the beholder. He reiterates one of his famous musical metaphors from *Über die Geistige*: "Color is the keyboard. The eye is the hammer. The soul is the piano with its many strings. . . . The artist is the hand which, by playing on this or that key [i.e., form], affects the human soul in this or that way" (*WA*, 160). The vibration that occurs in the artist, once it finds its proper material form, causes "a virtually identical vibration in the receiving soul" (*WA*, 258). But as Kandinsky himself acknowledges, there is a problem, because the viewer's soul has *many* strings, and when the hammer falls it can set off unintended vibrations. This imprecise response he calls the "excitation of 'Fantasy' in the receiver, who continues to exert his creative activity upon the work" (*WA*, 258). The danger of this kind of "collaboration," or *Mitwirkung*, between artist and viewer is that viewers' reactions may "drown the original sound" to such a degree that they "cry when they hear 'cheerful' music, and vice versa" (*WA*, 258). Kandinsky's solution to this problem is to argue that even if the "individual effects of a work of art [change with every] receiving subject," that does not mean that the "original sound is destroyed"; on the contrary, the original sound survives and continues to "work . . . imperceptibly [unmerklich]" on the beholder, and over time, Kandinsky insists, "every work is correctly 'understood'" and in "every man without exception a vibration [is produced] that is . . . identical to that of the artist" (*WA*, 258). The "imperceptible" nature of the effect is essential to the account of material agency that defines the history I am tracing from the expressionist painters and architects through Neutra.

The imprecision of the artistic hammer's contact with the soul was not the only problem Kandinsky found himself having to address. The subject's affect system, he recognized, responds to *everything* in the environment. The "world," he observes, "resounds by tone, color, and line" (*WA*, 102). We are flooded with a world of resounding objects; we need the artist to orchestrate their sounds into a symphony: "Every object, regardless if it is natural or manmade is a *being*" that bears "its own effect. . . . 'Nature' . . . continually sets the strings of the piano (the soul) in vibration, by means of the keys (objects)" (*WA*, 168). Artworks, *like any natural object*, generate unlimited responses. For Kandinsky, these effects were essential to the expressive life of art, but he feared that treating a work of art like a natural thing would make its expressiveness so unlimited as to make it empty. Works of art are natural things, but the effects generated by an artwork, unlike those generated by the natural world, are channeled and intensified by the artist's hand.[30]

Kandinsky's solution to the problem of limitless affectivity was to show how individuated responses to things are "incidental," while shared responses to things are essential. He offers an example in his account of letters. While the individual lines that make up a letter might be "cheerful," the letter as a whole can nonetheless register as "mournful." Which is to say, the first element, the overall appearance of the letter, subsumes the second element, the individually bent or straight lines. It is the individual lines that stimulate individuated responses, but those responses are inevitably subsumed under the experience of the letter as a whole. Thus, while Kandinsky wants to erase individuated affects generated by particular viewing bodies, he emphatically wants to *preserve* affects that are shared by bodies in general.[31] While it might seem like Kandinsky's commitment to beholder response negates his flat realist ontology of lines and fishes, it is closer to the opposite. The subjectivity inscribed in Kandinsky's response-driven accounts is the condition for his vision of the "agency" of objects. Kandinsky's abstraction—in contrast, for instance, to that of Kasimir Malevich and Piet Mondrian—is defined by its near overload of visual incident, a kind of filling up of a vacuum with narrative or subnarrative action. Babies, children, lovers, elderly beggars, knights, kings, queens, merchants, musicians, priests and religious figures, a cemetery, a church, a castle, and a forest populate Kandinsky's diminutive universe of *Das Bunte Leben* of 1907 (Figure 1.6). The painterly handling reinforces the effect of animation with its array of unmodulated dots of color in the foreground, creating a tapestry effect without ever compromising the singularity of the specific events. Indeed, Kandinsky's work from *Das Bunte Leben* to *Kleine Welten* to *Each for Himself* attempts to figure worlds full to the brim with animate but inscrutable objects, conveying the impression that every particle is vibrating with life.

At the conclusion of his account of letters, Kandinsky summarizes his concept of the dual effectiveness of objects by saying that a letter produces both "an effect as a sign having a particular purpose" and an effect *not as a form* but as an "inner sound," which is "completely independent" of the form (*WA*, 246). He underscores the latter point by stating unequivocally that signification and "inner sound" are *unrelated*. Every work of art and every object in the world is characterized by two competing and ontologically separate phenomena. Kandinsky asks his reader to "look at any object you please on your table, even if it is only a cigar butt [in an ashtray]" (*WA*, 250). Within the cigar butt "the reader will notice at once the same two effects of body and soul, form and content." "*The world sounds*," and with the right *attitude* the cigar butt will tell us that we live in "*a cosmos of spiritually affective beings. Thus 'dead' matter is living spirit*" (*WA*, 250). Kandinsky reiterates this point in an anecdote he relates in his *Reminiscences*:

FIGURE 1.6. Wassily Kandinsky, *Das Bunte Leben (The Colorful Life)*, 1907. Städtische Galerie im Lenbachhaus und Kunstbau München, Leihgabe der BayernLB. Copyright 2022 Artists Rights Society (ARS), New York.

Everything "dead" vibrated[;] . . . a cigar butt lying in the ashtray, a patient white trouser-button looking up at you from a puddle on the street, a submissive piece of bark carried through the long grass in the ant's strong jaws to some uncertain and vital end, the page of a calendar, torn forcibly by one's consciously outstretched hand from the warm companionship of the block of remaining pages. Likewise, every still and every moving point . . . became for me just as alive, and revealed to me its soul. (*WA,* 361; see also 778, 804)

Although there is little discussion of this in the literature, Kandinsky's attitudinal aesthetics were codified and made influential all over again in the United States by John Cage, who explicitly took his cue from Kandinsky's work. Cage spoke frequently of his mentor, animator and filmmaker Oskar Fischinger, who was close with Kandinsky and László Moholy-Nagy. Cage met Fischinger through Galka Scheyer, an art dealer and collector who founded the Blue Four artists' group, which comprised Kandinsky, Paul Klee, Lyonel Feininger, and Alexej von Jawlensky. Scheyer lived in a house designed by Neutra, and Cage frequented her home.[32] It was through Scheyer that Cage brought the works of the Blue Four to Seattle. Fischinger seemed to supply Cage with some of the core claims of Bauhaus thinking on art. Fischinger, Cage wrote in 1948, "spoke to me about what he called the spirit inherent in materials and he claimed that a sound made from wood had a different spirit than one made from glass."[33] "The spirit," Fischinger told Cage, "is inside each of the objects of this world"; "all we need to do to liberate that spirit is to brush past the object, and draw forth its sound." Cage took these words to heart: "Wherever I went, I always listened to objects"; "I began hitting, rubbing everything, listening, and then writing percussion music, and playing it with friends."[34] Cage drew his example of a musical object directly from Kandinsky:

> Look, for instance, at this ashtray. It's in a state of vibration. We're sure of that, and the physicist can prove it to us. But we can't hear those vibrations. . . . Well, now, instead of listening to myself, I want to listen to this ashtray. . . . I'm going to listen to its inner life thanks to a suitable technology.[35]

That Cage's Kandinsky moment lasted a lifetime is evident from his 1980 mesostic on Fischinger's name (Figure 1.7). Again in 1984, Cage reflected that Fischinger "made a remark which was very important to me. He said that everything in the world has a spirit which is released by its sound, and that set me on fire, so to speak."[36]

I call this the Bauhaus ashtray ontology. In all these instances what is at stake is a change in one's *attitude* toward things, a shift from hearing oneself to listening to the thing. Is this object ontology or correlationism?[37] Does this rid the world of the self or project it everywhere? In a certain sense my argument about Kandinsky echoes Douglas Kahn's about John Cage, which is that every aspect of the world is subject to the composer's unrelenting will to turn noise into music, nature into sound.[38] But what Kahn fails to acknowledge—because he embraces it—is the rejection of intentionality as the precondition for object agency. The moment one declares one is no longer "listening to oneself" but only to objects is the moment ashtrays become subjects and human subjects become ashtrays. And it is at this moment, when decentering self-denial sets in, that it makes no difference whether one calls oneself an idealist or a realist. Changing one's attitude toward the world in such a way that we can recognize spirit requires that we replace the attempt to understand, express, or communicate with one another with an effort to plumb the imponderable life of things. If we can assume the right attitude toward people and things, an attitude properly responsive to their "inner life," we can solve the problem of communication by bypassing it entirely.

when yOu
Said
eaCh
inAnimate object
has a SpiRit

that can take the Form of sound
by beIng
Set into vibration
i beCame a musician
it was as tHough
you had set me on fIre
i raN
without thinkinG
and thrEw myself
into the wateR

FIGURE 1.7. John Cage, "Mesostic for Elfriede Fischinger, 8 May 1980." John Cage Trust.

Following his discussion of the letter, Kandinsky offers a related account of the abstract components of picture making, this time based on what he sees as an onto-logical difference between a grammatical mark that helps to articulate meaning and a material one that does not. A dash, he writes, "used in the right place—as here—is a line that has a practical and purposive significance" (*WA,* 246). He then wonders what would happen if one lengthened the line a little. If it appeared in the *same place,* both the "sense of line" and "its significance" would be retained. And yet, he adds, the surplus of lineness would imbue it with an "indefinable coloration" and cause the reader to ask why it is longer and to question its grammatical purpose (*WA,* 247). What happens then, he asks, if a dash is put in the wrong place "(as in this—instance)"? At this point, the mark loses its practical purpose—it no longer functions as a grammatical character—but it is also not *purely* expressive, because it is still framed by a discursive context. "As long as this or that line remains *in a book,*" he explains, "the practical or intentional element cannot be definitely excluded" (*WA,* 247). Once the dash has been released from a setting in which it is presumed to have meaning, or rather to allow meaning to emerge, then its expressive purpose comes to the fore. Kandinsky provides an example of how a signifying dash becomes a nonsignifying mark: "Let us put a line in a setting that is able to avoid completely the practical-purposive" and place it on a canvas (*WA,* 247). It is at this point, when the dash becomes a *mark,* that "the spectator, no longer the reader," is forced to take a different attitude toward the line from the one he did when he encountered it in a discursive setting.[39]

Kandinsky describes the crucial difference in attitude between materialism and spirituality as the difference between reading and seeing. When the *reader* becomes a *spectator,* his "soul is ready to experience the pure, inner sound of line," which "functions as a *thing . . .* that leads its own material life" (*WA,* 245). Kandinsky assumes that we are always and at the same time readers *and* spectators of the world, but these two experiences unfold along separate ontological axes. A line, he says, is "just as much a chair, a fountain, a knife, a fork, etc.," but it is also, when it is put out of *use,* a sensory thing with an inner life (*WA,* 247). Cage's *Variations VI* of 1967 follows Kandinsky's dualist ontology. During that performance, "everything was wired with contact mikes— forks, knives, plates, glasses."[40] So Kandinsky's world of things—line, fish, chair, fountain, knife, fork, ashtray, button, bark—carry their own messages, and it is the audience's job, a job the audience is tasked with by the artist, to assume the right attitude to hear the spiritual messages delivered up by things. Hearing those messages requires that one abandon the idea that one's attitude toward something is irrelevant to what that thing means.

In 1920, just before his tenure at the Bauhaus, Kandinsky published a condensed and revised version of "Über die Formfrage" for a Russian audience. The Russian version was accompanied by a questionnaire that I think best characterizes the nature of Kandinsky's ambitions at the Bauhaus and beyond. Here, Kandinsky expanded on the discussion of letters and lines, including an account of shape:

Do you notice in yourself (whether clearly or just vaguely) any kind of experiences when you contemplate or observe specifically elementary or complex drawn forms (for example, a point, a straight, bent or angular line, a triangle, square, circle, trapeze, ellipse, and so on, or a free drawn form not subject to geometric definition)? . . . How do you see a triangle? Would you say that it moves and, if so, in which direction? Would you say that it is smarter than a square? Is not the sensation elicited by a triangle more similar to that elicited by a lemon? What is the singing of a canary more like, a triangle or a square? Which geometric form is like the bourgeoisie, talent, fine weather, and so on?[41]

He asked a similar set of questions about color:

Which color is more like the singing of a canary, the mooing of a cow, the whistling of the wind, of a whip or of a human being, talent, a storm, disgust, and so on[?][42]

It is hard not to see this as pure suggestion, as leading his students to the conclusions that he wanted them to draw (any of the associations he lists seem entirely products of Kandinsky's imagination, even as he passes them off as universal). It is not a question of whether or not "red is warm" and "blue is cool" are notions that might generate widespread consensus, because even at the lowest levels of common sense there is no way to disentangle biology and convention. Science might demonstrate some loose correlations between color, line, medium, and affect, but no matter how natural these correlations may appear, there is no way to separate them from a wider context of meaning. More to the point, there is nothing loose or low level about Kandinsky's vision of the relation between form and affect, and there is nothing loose about the work of those scientists today using fMRIs to understand what happens to us when we look at a Van Gogh or listen to Ariana Grande.[43] Kandinsky, like neuroaestheticians today, wants to insist that there is a correlation between the colors we paint our walls and the effects they produce, on the one hand, and the colors that appear in paintings and their effects on beholders, on the other. But paintings are not walls. (We do not typically interpret the paint colors of classrooms or lecture halls, but we do interpret the colors in Kandinsky's paintings, or at least we should, even if he did not intend that we should.)

Kandinsky codified the core of the Bauhaus project in his 1920 essay "Program for the Institute of Artistic Culture," in which he asserted that "to investigate any art in theoretical terms, we must use the analysis of the media of this art as a point of departure. . . . We know, for example, the powerful and invariable effect of different colors (proven by experiment): red (in a color bath) increases the activity of the heart, which is expressed, in turn, by the acceleration of the pulse; blue, however, can lead to partial paralysis. Facts such as these have great importance for art" (*WA*, 458). Marshaling these "facts" in order to produce reliable results was at the core of the Bauhaus mission. Manfredo Tafuri rightly describes the impact of Kandinsky's 1920 program on Bauhaus teaching, noting that with it "new themes began to circulate within the Bauhaus environment—from the analysis of the specific means of artistic communication, to the influence of forms on the public, to the relationships between formal structures and behavior."[44] Walter Gropius, László Moholy-Nagy, and Walter Benjamin all shared a view about the connection between media and subject formation, a view that had little to do with art and everything to do with politics. It is to the political side of the equation—the consequences of Kandinsky's realism—that I turn now.

Environmental Determinism in Scheerbart, Taut, and Behne

Published in *Der Sturm* in 1914, Bruno Taut's expressionist manifesto "Eine Notwendigkeit" ("A Necessity"), the title of which refers to Kandinsky's "inner necessity," called for a new form of building, one that would be "not only architecture, but in which everything—painting and sculpture—all together will form great architecture and wherein architecture once again merges with the other arts." The new artist, Taut wrote, "has to incorporate all possible structural forms into his work just as we find them expressed in . . . the compositions of Kandinsky." Drawing the arts together, creating a new collective art by breaking down traditional boundaries—which was of course one of the primary aims of the Bauhaus—could be accomplished, Taut explained, only if "every thought of social intentions" was removed from the work.[45] But Taut did not just want to eliminate social intentions; he wanted to eliminate *all* intentions beyond those generated by media. At this task media were more effective than artists, whose efforts to express what they meant were dogged by failure and misunderstanding.

Paul Scheerbart, in his highly influential treatise *Glass Architecture,* a kind of biblical text for the Bauhaus generation published in 1914 and dedicated to Taut, made the equation between material properties and political results clear. In the famous opening section of the book, titled "Environment and Its Influence on the Development of Culture," Scheerbart announced the principle guiding his medial politics:

> In order to raise our culture to a higher level, we are forced, whether we like it or not, to change our architecture. And this will be possible only if we free the rooms in which we live of their enclosed character. This, however, we can only do by introducing a glass architecture, which admits the light of the sun, of the moon, and of the stars into the rooms . . . through as many walls as feasible, these to consist entirely of glass—of colored glass. The new environment, which we thus create, must bring us a new culture.[46]

Scheerbart's assertion that glass architecture could introduce a new culture rested on the prior assumption that "social intentions," or even what an artist attempts to express with or through glass, are insufficient to generate cultural change. "Reform the environment, don't try to reform man," was Buckminster Fuller's laconic way of making Scheerbart's point.[47] Esther McCoy, writing in 1974, ironized Scheerbart's glass utopia, one whose reality had shaped Los Angeles:

> Scheerbart foresaw floating glass architecture on rivers, lakes, and seas, glass leviathans in the air, glass express trains, the mountains above Lake Lugano illuminated at night from inns with glass walls. "A paradise on earth," he wrote, leading inevitably to "a composed and settled nation." The shot starting WWI, so close in time, must not have flashed on Scheerbart's crystal ball. (*EMR*, 285–86)

What McCoy ironized Benjamin endorsed. Benjamin followed Scheerbart in his description of the "glass-culture" of modernity.[48] What has "now been achieved by Scheerbart, with his glass, and by the Bauhaus, with its steel" is an architecture that can transform humanity itself, Benjamin wrote. Benjamin quoted Scheerbart—fatefully, and without irony—saying, "It follows from the foregoing that we can surely talk about a 'culture of glass.' The new glass-milieu will transform humanity utterly."[49] It was Scheerbart's view that "a person who daily sets his eyes on the splendors of glass *cannot* do wicked deeds."[50] The idea was literalized with Taut's use of Scheerbart's phrase "Colored glass destroys hatred," which was inscribed along the entablature of the Glass Pavilion at the 1914 Cologne Werkbund Exhibition (Figure 1.8). Taut also made the point in reverse: "Stone houses make stone hearts."[51] Scheerbart did too, in words that likewise appeared at the Glass Pavilion: "Brick culture can only do us harm." It is the culture of materials that produces the human culture that inhabits it. This is a standard claim of media studies, and versions of it have been made in connection with film, television, video, Internet, Twitter, and other screen cultures.

Adolf Behne made the point in prescient terms in the first major article on Taut. Writing of Taut's early functional work at the Gartenstadt Falkenberg in Berlin, he observed: "Every fulfilled function has become for Taut a lever to obtain a new man. The inhabitants have everything at hand and the architect has the inhabitants in his hand through functionality. All art is ultimately human sculpting [Menschenbildnerei]. Architecture is simply the strongest and most visible."[52] By arranging his materials in specific ways and relying on the agencies stored within the media, the architect is able to "sculpt" the unaware inhabitant. For Taut, Behne argued, "art is always human sculpting, not picture painting and statue modeling, not exhibiting, selling and storing away."[53] Behne's metaphor was sculptural, but his model was architecture. "It is the

FIGURE 1.8. Bruno Taut, Glass Pavilion, Werkbundaustellung, Cologne, 1914. Copyright Bildarchiv Foto Marburg / Art Resource, New York.

deepest truth that all other arts are inessential next to *building*! Building as an *elementary* activity can transform mankind." It was not art and not even building that Behne had in mind, but a specific medium. "Glass building," he insisted, would be the "surest method to make a human being out of the European."[54] Detlef Mertins sums up this view: "Glass architecture created a new environment . . . for a new subjectivity," what he rightly calls (without a hint of skepticism) "environmental determinism."[55]

Scheerbart literalized the human sculpting potential of media through his aversion to what he thought to be the contagious qualities of brick. "Brick becomes rotten. . . . It produces moldiness. . . . In the vaults of brick houses the air is impregnated with these bacilli: the architecture of glass has no need of vaults."[56] The brick phobia shared by Scheerbart and Taut was immortalized in the saying, penned by Heinrich Zille and quoted by Moholy-Nagy, Behne, and Neutra, "You can kill a man with a dwelling just as surely as with an axe" (Figure 1.9). Or, as Erich Baron put it in his contribution to Taut's

FIGURE 1.9. Adolf Behne, *Neues Wohnen–Neues Bauen,* frontispiece quoting Heinrich Zille, Leipzig, 1927.

FIGURE 1.10. Ludwig Mies van der Rohe, Glass Skyscraper project (view of lost model), 1922. Airbrushed gouache on gelatin silver print, 7⅜ × 5⅜ inches (18.8 × 13.7 cm). Digital image copyright The Museum of Modern Art. Licensed by SCALA / Art Resource, New York. Copyright 2022 Artists Rights Society (ARS), New York / VG Bild-Kunst, Bonn.

The City Crown, "The gloomy wrinkle creates anger, the clear view creates serenity and harmony."[57] It is an idea literalized in Mies's 1922 Glass Skyscraper, the design for which, first published in Taut's journal *Frühlicht,* positioned the deadening brick structures huddled around the pristine glass structure, as though gasping for breath from the life-generative light reflected off the towering glass cathedral (Figure 1.10). Mies too, at least at this moment in his career, regarded the morally advantageous effects of glass and the destructive effects of brick as products of agencies lodged within the materials that could be released onto their victims or beneficiaries by the architect.[58]

Taut's *Alpine Architecture*

Material shortages during World War I made even Taut's counterfactual utopia at the Cologne exhibition seem a distant fantasy. Taut channeled his energies instead into writing a series of extraordinary treatises, the second of which, *Alpine Architecture*, was conceived as an homage to Scheerbart, who died in the fall of 1915. Divided into five parts, *Alpine Architecture* comprises a sequence of drawings of utopian structures built among mountain landscapes. With the decline in architectural production Taut shifted his emphasis away from master architects and toward a gothicized *Volk* who were able to generate an architecture from an irrepressible need to build. With this shift from architect to *Volk* also came a rhetorical shift in Taut's object-based materialism to include a corresponding *materialism of labor*. Building the alpine cathedrals would require the united efforts of humanity; it would "most certainly involve unheard of difficulties and sacrifices," but it would "not be impossible."[59] However, these architectural forms, unlike the sacrifices for the war, were not to be undertaken in the name of "power, murder and wretchedness."[60] Works made without regard for profit produce, through exigent labor, a society that has no need for profit. Alternately, making architecture for profit or any practical purpose leads to a violent society. "To concentrate upon practical matters is boring," Taut reflected. "Children who are bored, fight—and nations make war, i.e., they murder, lie, steal—therefore, architectural projects are of supreme importance!"[61]

Gropius, chairman of the Arbeitsrat für Kunst, affirmed the "cleansing effect of the war," which was "necessary" for the new "type of life" he conceived.[62] Summing up Scheerbart's vision, Baron likewise affirmed that "no life arises without death."[63] Gropius's defense of Rosa Luxemburg and Karl Liebknecht makes sense in this context. Luxemburg and Liebknecht were driven by "pure idealism," according to Gropius, and their only mistake, the "same as their rightist counterparts," was their use of "force."[64]

Apolitical Socialism

Taut's most explicit statement of his aims appears in the caption to plate 16 of part 3 of *Alpine Architecture*. Here he calls on the PEOPLE OF EUROPE! and admonishes them to FASHION FOR YOURSELVES A HOLY ARTEFACT—BUILD! This is Taut as Zarathustra offering a full-tilt "last man" speech:

> Yes! Impracticable and without profit! But has the useful ever made us happy?— Profit and even more profit: Comfort, Convenience—Good Living, Education— knife and fork, railways and water-closets: and then—guns, bombs, instruments for killing! . . . Boredom brings quarrelling, strife and war: lies, robbery, murder and wretchedness, blood flowing from a million wounds. . . . Preach the socialist idea: ". . . Get organized! and you can all live well, all be well educated and at peace!"—As long as there are no tasks to be done your preaching will echo emptily. . . . Harness the masses—for a gigantic task. . . . A task whose completion can be felt to have meaning for all. . . .—Boredom disappears and with it strife, politics

and the evil specter of War. . . . There will be no more need to speak of Peace when there is no more War.[65]

Scheerbart, Taut, and Behne all drew on Friedrich Nietzsche's vision of the *Übermensch* in *Zarathustra*.[66] As Iain Boyd Whyte notes, "Bruno Taut and his associates nurtured a profoundly Nietzschean view of their role and their responsibilities as artists, as uniquely gifted individuals standing isolated above the masses."[67] As early as 1904, Taut wrote to his brother, "I've read Nietzsche's *Zarathustra* over the last three months—a book of enormous and serious vitality. I've learned a lot from it."[68] And although "only a few hear it," Behne wrote in *The City Crown*, Scheerbart's poetry and Taut's architecture proposed a "reevaluation of all values."[69] For Nietzsche, creators are responsible for shaping the lives and values of a whole people, not, as one might assume, the state.[70] Therefore, if one desires a "change of values," then that means a "change of creators."[71] This is Nietzsche's version of *Menschenbildnerei*. Baron made the Nietzschean point clear in his contribution to *The City Crown*:

> Prophetic heralds, passionate politicians, visionary poets, all transformed the people with their own fire and lifted them above themselves. Whether they are poets or apostles, musicians or painters, sculptors or architects, Fyodor Dostoyevsky and Leo Tolstoy, Walt Whitman, Cervantes and Strindberg, Hamsun and Gerhart Hauptmann are, like all great artists, the true creators of the people, who sanctified the people from within their own souls.[72]

In addition to offering a hymn to the Zarathustrian creator, Baron extolled the power of media, praising how in the "luminosity of the glass, architecture is redeemed from its heaviness."[73]

Taut, like others in his generation—and many today—gave voice to a special and categorical blend of pessimism and optimism. He was pessimistic about human beings' capacity to alter their situation by virtue of their actions but optimistic about the combined power of media and all-consuming labor to effect changes that human agents fail to bring about. Architectural design, or the traditional problem of *form*, had nothing to do with Taut's materialism. Even if Taut came to believe that "the first and foremost point at issue in any building should be how to attain the uttermost utility"— the *exact opposite position* from his wartime view about function—his view of labor and materiality did not change in the least. Rather than tempering his argument regarding the subject-producing nature of media, however, in *Modern Architecture* of 1929 Taut reiterated it, now within a strictly functionalist context:

> If everything is founded on sound efficiency, this . . . utility will form its own aesthetic law. . . . The architect who achieves [functionality] becomes the *creator* of an

ethical and social character; the people who use the building for any purpose, will, through the structure of the house, be brought to a better behavior in their mutual dealings and relationship with each other. Thus architecture becomes the creator of new social observances.[74]

Taut's vision of the political stemmed from what he saw as the problem with contemporary society, namely, that it was obsessed with *Gemütlichkeit* (coziness). We "should not call it architecture," he argued, "to provide a thousand useful things, homes, offices, railroad stations, market halls, schools, water towers, gas tanks, fire stations, factories, and the like."[75] Behne, in a review of Scheerbart's *Glass Architecture,* described the devastating effects of glass on the European desire for comfort:

> The European is right when he fears that glass architecture might become uncomfortable. Certainly, it will be so. And that is not its least advantage. For first of all the European must be wrenched out of his *Gemütlichkeit*. Not without good reason the adjective *"gemütlich"* intensified becomes *"saugemütlich"* [swinishly comfortable]. Away with comfort! Only where comfort ends, does humanity begin. Comfort is of no value. . . . Glass architecture breaks with the perpetual state of spiritless painful coziness, in which all values become dull and worn, and substitutes for it a state of bright consciousness, a bold activity, and the creation of ever more new, ever more beautiful values.[76]

For Behne and Taut the battle waged against comfort was a battle waged against *bürgerlich* values, against the spiritless society, the *geistlos Gesellschaft,* that was in danger of slowly degenerating community, *Gemeinschaft*.[77] It was a battle directed against rich and poor alike, as both desired empty comforts and the meaningless satisfactions of material progress.

The stakes of Taut's psychological or attitudinal socialism were made explicit in *The City Crown,* a text completed in 1917 but published in 1919, which inspired many of the basic claims of Gropius's Bauhaus program of a few months later:

> Both the poor and rich follow a word that resonates everywhere and promises a new form of Christianity: Socialism. It is the urge to somehow enhance the well-being of mankind, to achieve salvation for self and thus for others and to feel as one, solidly united with all mankind. This feeling lives, or at least slumbers, in all mankind. Socialism, in its non-political sense, means freedom from every form of authority as a simple, ordinary connection between people and it bridges any gap between fighting classes and nations to unite humanity. If one philosophy can crown the city of today, it is an expression of these thoughts.[78]

Taut's real utopia lay not in building glass cathedrals on mountaintops but in imagining the problem of capitalism as the problem of *hierarchy* and *authority*, of how we *see* each other, to see capitalism as a matter of domination rather than exploitation. For Taut, to bridge the "gap between fighting classes" one need only make an appeal to people's innate resistance to power and authority. It was Scheerbart's ideal, cited by Taut, to see "kings walk with beggar-men, . . . artisans with the men of learning." Baron, writing in *The City Crown*, similarly claimed that the "'people' is an active and suffering embodiment of the inhabited earth, including emperor, king, gentleman, peasant, burgher, and beggar."[79]

Taut believed, as Lisbeth Stern put it in a review of *The City Crown*, in "a better future, in which man will stand with mankind . . . without the barriers of the classes."[80] The political aim was *not to eliminate the classes* but to dissolve the barriers between them, to, in effect, *naturalize class relations*. Taut's utopia was a world in which the spiritual barriers between classes are broken down—in which the beggar walks arm in arm with the king. It was also Gropius's: "Let us then create a new guild of craftsmen without the class distinctions that raise an arrogant barrier between craftsman and artist!"[81] Which is to say, neither Kandinsky nor Scheerbart nor Taut nor Gropius had much interest in ridding the world of either kings or beggars. The problem was not that there were rich and poor but rather how the rich and poor *treated* one another; the problem was their *attitudes* toward one another, the "arrogant"—not economic— barriers between them. For Scheerbart and Taut the problem was class*ism*, and the solution to that problem was class *respect*. "The level of cultural progress cannot be measured by how it climbs into higher classes," Baron smugly asserted in his contribution to *The City Crown*.[82] Class conflict on this score is a *bürgerlich* ideal.

From Environmental Determinism to Biological Determinism

Although it has never been construed in this light, Moholy-Nagy's *Von Material zu Architektur* (published in English as *The New Vision*) of 1928 sums up the art-political conclusions of his generation:

> Not only the working class finds itself in a position today; *all* those caught within the mechanism of the present economic system are, basically, as badly off. . . . At best the differences [between rich and poor] are material ones. . . . The revolutionist should always remain conscious that the class struggle is, in the last analysis, not about capital, nor the means of production, but actually about the right of the individual to have a satisfying occupation, a life-work that meets inner needs, a balanced way of life, and a real release of human energies.[83]

Moholy-Nagy never tires of clarifying that the "standard for architects" is not "economic class," nor is it form. Rather, it is the "biologically evolved manner of living which man requires."[84] This is neither Marxism nor socialism (a critical feature of both of which is subjects who collectively organize for political change) but rather represents a view of what art can do when humans fail—and they always fail—to change their lot in life. Media (glass, steel, paint, or the whole built environment) *create subjects* with or (better still) without their consent.

It would be understatement to say, as Frederic Schwartz does, that the goal of the Bauhaus was "to reform the look of the products offered consumers and not so much the system itself (the consumer sector of a highly developed capitalist economy)."[85] And yet Schwartz still contends that even though there was nothing "*inherently* progressive . . . in a political sense" about the Bauhaus, the "identification of objects and buildings with a political stance had a certain logic."[86] This logic, however, is far more than just compatible with a capitalist economy, as evidenced in Sigfried Giedion's suggestion in *Mechanization Takes Command* (1948) that mechanization "transcend[s] the purely economic" and should not be seen as "tied to any one system." Labor is a "basic human problem," and the "class struggle," according to Giedion, falls outside that.[87] In other words, Giedion is simply restating the Bauhaus line on economics, labor, and automation: architects need to ignore their historical setting and conceive of them as abstract "human" problems that affect the rich and poor alike.

Moholy-Nagy's views were consistent with Gropius's own principles prior to the war. In Gropius's 1913 essay "The Development of Modern Industrial Architecture," his primary concern was satisfying the worker (architecturally, that is), which also inevitably helped the bottom line:

> A factory which has come into being through the combined energies of employer and architect will possess advantages which the organization as a whole is bound to share. . . . It should not be forgotten that from the purely social point of view it is of the utmost importance whether or not a factory-hand carries out his work in airy well-proportioned rooms or squalid forbidding quarters resembling a barracks. A worker will find that a room well thought-out by an artist, which responds to the innate sense of beauty we all possess, relieves the monotony of the daily task and he will be more willing to join in collective undertakings. If the worker is happy, he will take more pleasure in his duties and the productivity of the firm will increase.
>
> One or two enterprising owners who have recently been calling in architects with training in the fine arts as well are plainly deriving incalculable reward from their farsightedness.[88]

As Gropius insisted, it "pays in the long run" to involve artists in mass production, because "not only have leading firms earned themselves a reputation for promoting culture but, which is equally important in business, have considerably increased their financial gain."[89]

If the politically reactionary nature of the Bauhaus has been frequently glossed as revolutionary media theory, then the more astonishing lapse in the critical literature is the lack of attention given to the Bauhaus vision of the *biological*. Virtually every major document generated by the Bauhaus was invested in a vision of what Moholy-Nagy called the "biological ABCs." Moholy-Nagy defined the Bauhaus educational program as "striving toward the timeless biological elements of expression which are meaningful to all people and useful to all people."[90] If you satisfy those elementary biological needs—and that can be done with architecture—then the political problems dissolve.

In the later 1920s the Bauhaus architects sought to incorporate these biological essentials into industrial production with their "minimum existence dwellings."[91] Part of what Gropius was aiming to research during his visit to the United States in 1928 was a new approach to industrial housing and a new form of life in the industrial house. It was on this topic that Gropius and Neutra found common ground. In fact, Neutra was far more successful in enacting on a large scale Gropius's vision of the minimum existence dwelling. Gropius defined the minimum dwelling, combining mass production and health benefits, as the "elementary minimum of space, air, light and heat required by man in order that he [may] fully develop his life functions without experiencing restrictions due to his dwelling."[92] As it turned out, humans do not need much to live. Gropius cited the work of contemporary hygienists who observed that with "good conditions of ventilation and sunlight, man's requirements of living space from the biological viewpoint are very small." Gropius deduced a formula for the new house: "Enlarge the windows, reduce the size of rooms, economize on food rather than heat." If in the past people overestimated the "value of food calories in comparison to vitamins," then the minimum dwelling was the vitamin exchange for the excess calories of "larger apartments."[93] Under this broader social-diet austerity regime—smaller dwellings, bigger windows; fewer possessions, more air and light; less food, more vitamins—Gropius affirmed, the "individual and his independent rights" would replace the "economic plight of urban populations."[94] Less socialism, more individual rights. As Paul Overy rightly observes, the ideals of the *"neue Wohnung"* were "an undisguised attack on traditional working-class and lower middle-class domestic relations." From the architect's perspective, workers were all too *"petite bourgeois,* i.e. aspiring to unprogressive lower middle-class values: a kind of social *un*hygiene." In contrast, "by carefully controlling the plan of the *neue Wohnung* it would be possible to produce the *neue Mensch* and the *neue Frau.*"[95] But the fundamental problem was not the classism of the architects (real as that was), but the naturalization of class relations embodied in their commitment to the affectively oriented plan.

Racial Biology at the Bauhaus

Among the "timeless biological elements" noted by Moholy-Nagy was *race*. Johannes Itten—the defining character of the first phase of the Bauhaus—was explicitly racist. In 1921 he designed the House of the White Man (Figure 1.11), and he and his colleagues published essays celebrating "the white race [as] represent[ing] the highest level of civilization."[96] Virtually every narrative of the Bauhaus stresses the difference between its early expressionist phase—the period dominated by Itten—and its second, industrial-technological phase, marked by the arrivals of Oskar Schlemmer and Moholy-Nagy in 1922 and 1923. And yet what is the difference between the House of the White Man and the celebrated Haus am Horn by Georg Muche built in 1923? Is Itten's instinctive racism any different from Gropius's and Moholy-Nagy's "scientifically" inflected account of race? After all, at the same moment Itten was ousted from the Bauhaus, Gropius and his colleagues were busy courting racist industrialists for jobs by appealing to their racism. In a collective letter to Henry Ford and William Randolph Hearst in 1923, the Bauhaus wrote: "We make our appeal to yourself, who have the privilege of living in the Land whose population today is in the act of taking the reins of Leadership of the White Race into its grasp."[97]

Gropius was in fact a virulent anti-Semite, and the class character of his racism was evident from the start. Here he is during World War I:

> We can fight battles as much as we want to but the weaklings and the pigs at home will destroy everything we achieved. The Jews, this poison which I begin to hate more and more, are destroying us. Social democracy, materialism, capitalism, profiteering—everything is their work and *we* are guilty that we have let them so dominate our world. They are the devil, the negative element.[98]

As the equivalence drawn here between "social democracy" and "the Jews" indicates, Gropius's political program was identical to his views on biology, and biology was at the center of the Bauhaus project at large.

There is plenty to show that Kandinsky and Schlemmer held similarly malignant anti-Semitic views. Arnold Schönberg, once a close friend of Kandinsky, wondered about the rumors of anti-Semitism at the Bauhaus and addressed them in a 1923 letter to Kandinsky: "I heard that even a Kandinsky sees only evil in the actions of Jews and

FIGURE 1.11. Johannes Itten, *House of the White Man (Haus des weißen Mannes),* from the portfolio *New European Graphics,* first portfolio: Masters of the State Bauhaus, Weimar, 1921 (Neue europäische Graphik, 1. Mappe: Meister des Staatlichen Bauhauses in Weimar, 1921). Dallas Museum of Art. Copyright 2022 Artists Rights Society (ARS), New York / ProLitteris, Zurich.

in their evil actions only the Jewishness." Schönberg ended the friendship, saying, "We are two kinds of people. Definitively!"[99] As late as the 1960s, Ise Gropius, now living in Lincoln, Massachusetts, had this to say about her Jewish servants: "We never allowed them to come upstairs of course, because you know Jews, they always stink."[100] Here Gropius's class politics synced up with his racism: presumably, the Jewish servants did not need to go upstairs, as the family had other maids for that.

The Bauhaus's collective and sustained aversion to political socialism was inseparable from its vision of the "materialist" Jew, and its commitment to a primitivist view of racial difference went beyond its embrace of the existence of a Jewish-socialist cabal. Although his comments have gone unremarked, Moholy-Nagy noted in *The New Vision* how, in the Bauhaus foundation course, it was "interesting to observe . . . the differences in sensory training in different races. A Japanese, for instance, has doubtless a more active relationship to tactile values than a European. This difference was also evident in the touch exercises with blindfolded eyes. In contrast to his fellow-students, who usually attempted to ascertain what the material was by stroking it, Mitzutani danced his fingers on it."[101] What Moholy-Nagy thought he saw here was evidence that form is both generated by biology and responsive to different biological determinants. Germans, Japanese, and Jews respond to the world differently; it is part of their "biological essentials."

I will not dwell on the well-researched subject of the ties between Ludwig Mies van der Rohe, last director of the Bauhaus, and the Nazi Party.[102] When confronted by the Nazis, Mies held the Bauhaus party line: "The Bauhaus has a certain idea," he maintained, "but this idea has nothing to do with politics."[103] He meant, of course, socialist or communist politics. He was trying to deflate the image of the Bauhaus as a Bolshevik-socialist breeding ground. And there is no doubt the Bauhaus was *perceived* by authorities (as it is by current-day academics) as having progressive political commitments. The problem is that scholars have been far too generous in accepting that perception; they seem to assume that just because the Nazis closed the Bauhaus, the Bauhaus was in fact progressive. But Mies was correct: the Nazis had nothing to fear from Bauhaus politics.

Behne, in one of his many celebrations of the Bauhaus, was clear about what it meant to have no politics in Germany in 1930:

> No one can doubt that the new building methods as such question absolutely nothing about men or about human goals. Sing Sing [prison] will be built in as modern a way as a new market hall, a department store as fashionably as a new housing colony, and when a somewhat larger new prison becomes important for a new military—or maybe even a giant new factory for gas bombs, so they too will be truly modern.[104]

Apologists want to call this opportunism, but one is hard-pressed to see it that way. It is better to see it as the determined affirmation of technocratic capitalism. R. M. Schindler saw it this way when he tersely noted in the same year, "Glass houses may be prisons."[105] This is the politics that defined the Bauhaus proclamation of 1923, "Art and Technology—A New Unity."

The Bauhaus was under the leadership of a socialist for two years in the late 1920s. Hannes Meyer was sincerely dedicated to leftist politics, and those politics inevitably put him at odds with the views of Gropius and Mies, his successor as director of the Bauhaus.[106] But it would be wrong to think that Meyer's architectural vision was in any way at odds with the dominant commitment to biological determinism at the Bauhaus. Meyer repeatedly described the house as a "biological apparatus," one based on the "careful study of every biological factor." Meyer's reputed functionalism was not grounded in the materially situated demands of client, materials, program, or site but rather in "a strict biological methodology." At every turn, Meyer stressed that the new architecture "deliberately employed the results of biological research" to achieve verifiable results that bypassed the contingencies of changing social realities.[107]

As I have been arguing, the "very specific spiritual-political goals" (as Mies put it) of the generation of architects and theorists working in Germany between the *Blaue Reiter* and the Bauhaus—a set of spiritual-political goals emphatically expressed by Neutra—can be defined by the battle against a loss of spirituality, a battle entirely compatible with and even necessary for the success of capitalism.[108] In a sense, my case stands at a distant remove from John Willett's view that "nothing emerges more clearly from a study of [art under the Weimar Republic] than that it was founded on a broadly socialist, and in many cases communist ideology."[109] And if some commentators have backed off on the assertion that the Bauhaus was intrinsically progressive, they have doubled down on the "indeterminacy" of the Bauhaus project. Barry Bergdoll, writing in the *New York Times,* sustains the fantasy that the Bauhaus was "universally misunderstood." According to Bergdoll, what we all fail to get about it is "the huge diversity of forms, ideologies, opinion and experiments." With the overuse of the word *Bauhaus* to describe anything modern—like the word *Eames* on Craigslist or eBay—we fail to "understand how little ideological coherence the Bauhaus maintained." According to Bergdoll, it was fractured during its lifetime and continued to fracture in its afterlife: "In the end the Bauhaus was a school, never a static style or a single-minded movement."[110] But style is one thing, single-mindedness another, and the Bauhaus was indeed single-minded. Those not happy with the idea that the Bauhaus cannot be pinned down may choose to go the theoretical route, as Juliet Koss does, and claim that Bauhaus works are "insistently refusing to postulate a firm stance of any kind."[111] Except every stance seemed to find its way back to the biological ABCs. Not at the level of style, which might change (Itten's work often looks different from Moholy-Nagy's), but at the level of *idea.*[112] The Bauhaus was unwavering from beginning to end in its refusal of socialism and its commitment to biodeterminism, the latter serving as the justification for the former.[113]

Bauhaus Today

It is important to mention, if only in passing, the strong influence of Scheerbart's and Taut's writings and practice on the works of several present-day artists. A range of recent projects—Josiah McElheny's being the most high profile—have been explicitly situated in dialogue with Scheerbart's and Taut's glass architectural ideals, including Ian Kiaer's *Scheerbart-Bed* (2005), Heather Rowe's *plans that have fallen through* (2006),

Lee Bul's *(Untitled) After Bruno Taut* (2008), and McElheny's *Projects 84* at the Museum of Modern Art (2007) and *Bruno Taut's Monument to Socialist Spirituality (after Mies van der Rohe)* (2009). For the latter, McElheny produced a model of Mies's 1922 Berlin skyscraper project but replaced the clear glass of the original designs with colored glass windows modeled on Scheerbart's and Taut's glass ideals (Figure 1.12). McElheny intended to suggest a missed opportunity, to offer a counterfactual history in which Mies's corporate glass image—the architectural language of corporate capitalism—is replaced with the colored glass image of Scheerbart's and Taut's spiritual socialism. As the wall label at the Portland Art Museum suggests of the piece, "McElheny's sculpture imagines a different history for twentieth-century architecture, one that embraced lively, transcendent spaces rather than the monochromatic monoliths of capitalism that evolved from Mies's radical thinking." How different, though, is McElheny's history? If color is socialist and monochrome is capitalist, the solution is where McElheny thinks he has found it, namely, not in architecture but rather in a shift in the medium. But is it true that a significant difference between Mies's and Taut's visions boils down to clear versus colored glass? Is there a difference between Taut's nonpolitical socialism and the corporate capitalism putatively projected by Mies? Or is this vision of glass architecture—whether Scheerbart's, Taut's, Mies's, or McElheny's—precisely the cultural socialism capitalism needs? Artist Gary Indiana sums up the core attraction of Scheerbart's project for contemporary art politics: as a "utopian artist, Scheerbart was most fiercely concerned with making the case that social reality and its outcomes are primarily determined by the constructed environment."[114] This is of course a very attractive vision for the artist. At a moment when art is at its weakest, when it seems irrelevant to our social-political reality, something like the fantasy of its absolute centrality comes into view—maybe this was the point all along.

What was clear to the Bauhaus generation was that the new media politics was the compensation for failed human politics. Behne described the new art-political regime in his review of Scheerbart's *Glass Architecture*: "It is not the crazy caprice of a poet that glass architecture will bring a new culture. *It is a fact!* New social welfare organizations, hospitals, inventions, or technical innovations and improvements—these will not bring new culture—*but glass architecture will.*"[115] Although Behne neglected to include education among the chief social ills of modernity, he did not fail to indict "welfare organizations" and "hospitals" as generators of botched subjects. In his role as managing director of the Arbeitsrat, Behne made clear that its members "did not aim to put through small *reforms,* calculated for the day, by compromising with officials."[116] Socialism, he wrote, is not a matter of "laws, paragraphs, force, and regulations."[117] And while a socialist government can be "manufactured with paragraphs," it would be utterly

FIGURE 1.12. Josiah McElheny, *Bruno Taut's Monument to Socialist Spirituality (after Mies van der Rohe)*, 2009. Hand-blown and molded glass modules, wood, and hardware, 105¾ × 75 × 55 inches. Copyright Josiah McElheny 2022. Courtesy of the artist and James Cohan, Corbett vs. Dempsey, White Cube.

devoid of the (apolitical) essence of socialism. Behne was preaching to the choir when he wrote to Gropius in 1920 that the Arbeitsrat stands "far from party politics, on Socialist grounds, of course, but independent of any party connection."[118] As Gropius himself put it in his essay for the Arbeitsrat exhibition of unknown architects, "Ideas die as soon as they become compromises."[119] Gropius insisted on a "clear watershed between dream and reality, between longing for the stars and everyday labor."[120] And by September 1919 he wistfully concluded that "cultural values are the only goods our enemies cannot take away from us."[121]

Looking back on this moment we might see that the real watershed was not between dream and reality, between cultural values and material ones, but between two kinds of politics: dreaming *as* politics and "social intentions." "*Build in imagination,*" Gropius declared, and rather than "permit any compromises," it is preferable to "accomplish practically *nothing*."[122] My argument has been that the Bauhaus artists and architects were never satisfied to accomplish *nothing* but were committed from beginning to end to "very specific spiritual-political goals."[123] And my aim has been to suggest *not* that uncompromising and imaginative architecture was misguided, but rather that the members of the Bauhaus generation never really conceived of their forms in imaginary or autonomous terms. Imaginative or dream architecture was for Kandinsky, Scheerbart, Taut, Behne, Gropius, Moholy-Nagy, and Benjamin an explicit mode of *politics*; it changed culture without any set of beliefs or agents having to do it themselves. Humans, after all, are fallible in ways that media never are.

Taut made his politics clear when he observed that "one might . . . see a connection between the synchronous erection of the Crystal Palace and the Communistic manifestoes of Marx and Engels."[124] This was also the connection Benjamin saw when he declared that "to live in a glass house is a revolutionary virtue par excellence." The searing light flowing through the glass house would "liquidate the sclerotic liberal-moral-humanistic ideal of freedom."[125] Like Taut, Benjamin defined the latter in terms of its empty commitment to "pragmatic calculation." One should not misunderstand the claim here. Glass walls did not *figure* something like the transparency of a democratic society; rather, they were thought to *materially generate* a politically transparent world.[126]

Benjamin concluded his study of surrealism with a rhetorical question: "How are we to imagine an existence oriented solely toward Boulevard Bonne-Nouvelle, in rooms by Le Corbusier and Oud?"[127] If for Benjamin this connection between consumerism and glass architecture was unimaginable, it takes no imagination at all to see that connection today. In fact, it was exactly what was on Le Corbusier's mind when he was designing the Pavillon de l'Esprit Nouveau, the inspiration for which he took from

Nous donnons une photographie des échafaudages des magasins du « Bon Marché »
qui nous fournissent l'échelle des immeubles-villas dessinés en prolongement

FIGURE 1.13. Le Corbusier, *immeubles-villas* as extensions of the Bon Marché, from *Œuvre complète*, vol. 1, edited by Willy Boesiger and Oscar Stonorov, 1929. Copyright 2022 F.L.C. / ADAGP, Paris / Artists Rights Society (ARS), New York.

scaffolding affixed to Paris's Bon Marché department store (Figure 1.13).[128] Maybe it is better to forget that relation altogether and say there is no material correlation between the shape of a room and patterns of consumption within it, between glass walls, the glass of the camera lens, and the subjects who engage media. Media do not make a subject unless the subject no longer aspires to be one.

2

Not Learning from Los Angeles

The city does not suffer from the horrible permanence that afflicts most cities. . . . Wood frame and stucco offer less resistance to movement, to change. The appalling blight of the modern urban environment is a thick and heavy crust upon the land. The crust is thinner in Los Angeles. It can be more readily penetrated and scraped away.
                    —Arthur Gallion, "Architecture of the Los Angeles Region," 1956

Monumentality at MoMA

Among the more dispiriting accounts of California Modern is Henry-Russell Hitchcock's 1940 contribution to *California Arts and Architecture,* "An Eastern Critic Looks at Western Architecture." Hitchcock notes at the outset that most of the best architecture on the West Coast had come out of Oregon (he singles out the work of Pietro Belluschi), but he lauds the anonymous drive-ins of Los Angeles, noting that they "represent a very model of what exposition or resort architecture ought to be, light, gay, open, well executed and designed to be as effective by night as by day." Every word of this is a backhanded compliment, however, because he goes on to say, "Nothing in the East compares with the best things of this sort in Los Angeles."[1] He is offering high praise for works of low value ("this sort" of thing).

Hitchcock seems to see a glimmer of hope in the work of Neutra, but here too the praise is half-hearted. Neutra has "mastered a method of building suited to Southern California which assures economy in various types of structure, ordered if frequently somewhat monotonous design, and able, if at times idiosyncratic planning."[2] Hitchcock's terms—"inexpensive," "monotonous," "idiosyncratic," and above all "regional"—haunt the literature. In the 1932 *Modern Architecture: International Exhibition* catalog, Hitchcock notes that Neutra's Jardinette Apartments are an "adaptation of modern European ideas," even if "not a distinguished" one. The Lovell House is an "advance" on European forms but an "inconsistent" one, introducing "more complexities than are required by the plan so that the general effect is lacking in clarity."[3] Hitchcock solicited the help of a distinguished educator, Helen Parkhurst, for comment on Neutra's Ring Plan School (1926), and he reports that she found the plan to be "unduly decentralized"; she also challenged a host of features, including the overhead lighting, exposed swimming pool, placement of the kitchen, relation of the track to the classrooms, lack of locker space, and inadequate reception rooms near the entrance.[4] Neutra's "City of the Future," Hitchcock concludes, would require wholesale revision in light of "actuality."[5]

When Hitchcock considers other prominent modernists working in Los Angeles—Gregory Ain, Raphael Soriano, and J. R. Davidson—he notes that "aesthetically as well as technically there remains an abstractionist rigidity continued from the European twenties in the work of the Neutra group." Neither Ain nor Davidson would have assented to the association with Neutra. The Wrightian execution of Harwell Harris—here at the height of his fame—Hitchcock finds "inferior to the general Los Angeles standard" (a standard low to begin with).[6] Most famously, Hitchcock was averse to Schindler's work. It is hard to overestimate the impact of Hitchcock's withering terms on the immediate reception of the architect:

> The case of Schindler I do not profess to understand. There is certainly immense vitality perhaps somewhat lacking among many of the best modern architects of the Pacific Coast. But this vitality seems in general to lead to arbitrary and brutal effects. Even his work of the last few years reminds one inevitably of the extreme Expressionist and Neo-Plasticist work of the mid-twenties. Schindler's manner does not seem to mature. His continued reflection of the somewhat hectic psychological air of the region, from which all the others have attempted to protect themselves, still produces something of the look of sets for a Wellsian "film of the future."[7]

Hitchcock manages to denigrate Schindler and West Coast architecture in one breath. If the architects around Neutra were monotonous and rigid, Schindler was animate and chaotic; they represented two sides of the same phenomenon. Vital, immature, and futurist, Schindler was a psychologically unstable expressionist throwback. And for Hitchcock, this too was a regional expression, Hollywood science fiction.

McCoy, in an early assessment of Schindler (1945) that she wrote while she was still working in his office, explains how she read a letter sent to him from "an importer of the International Style from Europe to the East Coast" (*EMR*, 74). The letter was Hitchcockian in tone and sentiment, if not in fact from him. Schindler's "attitude toward architecture," it stated, "is undoubtedly colored by life in California. It is of great advantage for architects to travel to different parts of the country and so vary their surroundings and broaden their views." McCoy offers a properly caustic retort: "How could *not* the life of an architect be colored by his surroundings?" The greatness of Schindler, for McCoy, lay in his capacity to "let the land dictate the house," the contour map of the site being his essential guide with every project (*EMR,* 71). Schindler "had dug into the place where he had settled" (*EMR,* 74). McCoy recalls Thoreau: "I have traveled much in Concord." It was a bold turn to draw together Concord and Los Angeles, northeastern Puritanism and the putative laxity of Southern California.

When Hitchcock takes up Schindler's work a second time, in the preface to David Gebhard's 1971 monograph on the architect, he seemingly wants to atone for his sins. And yet all he can summon up is how Schindler's futuristic expressionism was "premonitory" of things to come (yet another backhanded compliment).[8] He congratulates Gebhard for providing a historical framework for Schindler's work, noting how it might make possible "a significant, if not a full, appreciation" for a body of work that "found so little acceptance from critics of the Eastern Seaboard such as myself."[9] Gebhard's groundbreaking study went a long way toward reconciling Schindler with the terms established by the critics on the East Coast, deploying Robert Venturi's notions of complexity and contradiction to understand Schindler's little-known body of work. Gebhard's style-based criticism, while decisively raising the reputation of Schindler's work, fundamentally dissociated the architecture not only from its settings but also from its logical core; it was style that determined form, not the "dictates of the land" or the logic of the method.

In 1942, Talbot Hamlin, writing in *Harper's Magazine,* launched a broad attack on the claims of East Coast critics. Citing the "pathetic misapprehensions of architecture" produced along the West Coast, Hamlin singled out the Southern California work of Wright, Neutra, and Harris in observing that West Coast designers were producing "a kind of house architecture that is perhaps the most advanced domestic architecture in the world today." This architecture of "long, low, rambling houses with their broad sheets of glass, their free and open spaces" was "new in the world because it represents the reaction of sensitive artists to a new ideal of what human living may be."[10] Hamlin's assessment had an immediate impact on the status of California Modern. In 1942, the Museum of Modern Art published *What Is Modern Architecture?,* a text that in effect reversed the terms of the *Modern Architecture: International Exhibition* of ten years earlier. Following Hamlin, the 1942 catalog went so far as to claim that "more good architecture is found in California than anywhere else in the United States."[11] Gebhard seemed to confirm that early consensus many years later, writing in *Artforum* in 1964:

> Certainly from 1935 to 1942 California—both in the Los Angeles area and in the Bay region to the North—was the architectural center of the United States. The East Coast had its Gropius, its Breuer—all imported vintages—but it could not boast of a Neutra, a Schindler, an Ain, or a Harris. Perhaps as Gregory Ain once commented, it was alive because it was evangelistic. To commit oneself to the ideals

FIGURE 2.1. Installation view of the exhibition *Five California Houses*, March 17–April 18, 1943. Photographic Archive. Photograph by Soichi Sunami. Digital image copyright The Museum of Modern Art. Licensed by SCALA / Art Resource, New York. The Museum of Modern Art Archives, New York.

of progressivism in architecture meant that one was aligning oneself against the establishment.[12]

Gebhard struck a moralizing tone: evangelistic, progressive, antiestablishment. He was not willing to name the politics outright: Ain was a communist, and Schindler was a fellow traveler (and their clients were frequently political radicals).[13]

Hamlin's remarks ushered in a reevaluation of California Modern. In its publicity for the *Five California Houses* exhibition of 1943, MoMA reprinted most of Hamlin's essay (Figure 2.1).[14] *Five California Houses* was the beginning of MoMA's direct and lasting engagement with West Coast architecture and featured the work of Harris and Neutra. Neutra exhibited what he called the "Last of an Era House," otherwise known as the Nesbitt House of 1942 (Figure 2.2), made of "non-critical materials."[15] The Nesbitt House was in fact the first-of-an-era house, a seminal work reflecting Neutra's changing attitude toward wood, a turn that definitively shaped his postwar approach to materials.[16] But it was Elizabeth Mock's 1944 and 1946 MoMA exhibitions and catalogs

FIGURE 2.2. Richard Neutra, John B. Nesbitt House (Los Angeles, California), 1942. Photograph: Julius Shulman, 1941. Copyright J. Paul Getty Trust. Getty Research Institute, Los Angeles (2004.R.10).

Built in USA: 1932–1944 and *If You Want to Build a House* that established the basic terms of the narrative on California Modern.[17] Both exhibitions and catalogs heavily featured works by California architects, and both were determined to spotlight the limitations of domestic architecture, limitations whose origins were thought to be deeply inscribed in the California Modern approach.

In *Built in USA* Mock surveys the development of modern American architecture since the International Style exhibition of 1932. John Funk's 1939 Heckendorf House in Modesto, California, appears on the catalog's cover and is featured in its opening pages (the house would appear again in *If You Want to Build a House*). After a brief review of the International Style exhibition, Mock informs readers that when American architects began revisiting homegrown forms in the 1930s, "it was suddenly discovered that California had been enjoying a continuous but curiously unpublicized tradition of building."[18] Mock begins her survey with two works by Wright (Mock studied at

Taliesin)—Fallingwater and the Winkler-Goetsch House of 1939—which she follows with an account of Funk's Heckendorf House, Gardner Dailey's Owens House in Sausalito, and Harris's 1935 Fellowship Park House in Los Angeles (his Lowe House of 1934 is featured in the catalog's opening essay). Significantly, Mock discusses Gropius's and Breuer's houses after surveying West Coast works.

Work by California architects (including Ain; Reginald Johnson and the architectural firm of Johnson, Wilson, Merrill and Alexander; Harry Thomsen and William Wurster; Vernon DeMars; Neutra; Franklin and Kump and Associates; Dailey; Raphael Soriano; and John Stokes) receive the most coverage in the catalog. But as it turns out, Mock does not really endorse the California work she features. In the two closing sections of her catalog essay—on urbanity and monumentality, respectively—she casts the works in a more skeptical light. "Must we resign ourselves to the social vacuum of the 'residential suburb'?" Mock asks, looking back on developments since the International Style. Can an "institutional effect" be avoided in housing schemes? Most problematic, from Mock's perspective, is that recent American works lack public scale and significance (a criticism also made by Hitchcock). A "democracy needs monuments, even though its requirements are not those of a dictatorship," Mock asserts.[19] Whatever California could deliver in "good architecture," it could not deliver what was most needed: monumentality. Domestic scale seemed to be written into its regional DNA.

Ever since the International Style exhibition, modern architecture had been moving toward small-scale, residential, informal, flexible, open-plan, site-specific works, and above all in the direction of suburban building, as Mock outlines in a section of *Built in USA* titled "A Human Basis for Design." But as she observes in her conclusion, the days of suburban modernism were over. "There must be occasional buildings which raise the every-day casualness of living to a higher and more ceremonial plane, buildings which give dignified and coherent form to that interdependence of the individual and the social group which is of the very nature of our democracy."[20] Readers may be stopped short by this description. What Mock has been presenting as exemplifying a new architectural order is now construed as "every-day casualness," a modality that fails to deliver on the need for public ceremony. One would be hard-pressed to find instances in the exhibition that could fulfill this new demand for monumentality. Eschewing monumentality might have been the point of the show, but even if it was not, that was the result. In her conclusion Mock reflects that the "need [for monumentality] is apparent, but the answer is still nebulous." The answer she proposes—"the complete collaboration of architect, city planner, landscape architect, painter and sculptor"—is prophetic. Although it has "scarcely yet been considered in modern terms," Mock foresees the "monumental possibilities of the city square."[21] Undeniably, the show was at once the apotheosis of California Modern and the seal on its historical fate. At the same moment as *Built in USA,* Sigfried Giedion was very publicly criticizing what he called "pseudo-monumentality" in "The Need for a New Monumentality," his contribution to Paul Zucker's symposium "New Architecture and City Planning" (1944). Every word of Giedion's essay could have been directed against the works featured in *Built in USA* and *If You Want to Build a House.*

Giedion directly addresses the city square problem in "The Heart of the City," his commentary on the theme chosen for the eighth CIAM conference, held in Hoddesdon, England, in 1951. In this essay Giedion both traces the development of modern architecture that he sees as ending with California and voices concern over what will come after the demise of the suburban phase:

> If we examine, from a human point of view, the road which architecture has been obliged to follow during this century in order to come to terms with its own period, we shall find this divided into two distinct stages.
>
> The development started as a fight against an "infected atmosphere and as a moral revolt against the falsification of forms" (Henry van de Velde) . . . in the nineteenth century with William Morris' purification of the immediate human environment. . . . From here it passed on to architecture, nowhere more markedly than in the single-family houses built around 1900 by Frank Lloyd Wright and others in the suburbs of Chicago. The American spark reached Europe. The work of the Stijl Group in Holland, Mies van der Rohe's projects for country houses, Le Corbusier's first Paris house in reinforced concrete, were all produced early in the century and all were single-family houses. A study of the single-family house—man's most intimate environment—enables one to understand better than anything else whether a man really knows how to build. The climax of this development came later in California.[22]

By "California," Giedion means Greene & Greene, Irving Gill, Wurster, DeMars, Harris, Soriano, and Ain, all of whom he cites in passing.[23] He is also likely referring to the first phase of the Case Study House Program initiated in 1945 by *Arts and Architecture* magazine. (Giedion's *Mechanization Takes Command* was reviewed by Neutra in *Arts and Architecture,* and the book was advertised in the magazine's pages.)

Without a doubt, it was Neutra who figured as the prime representative of the modern house in California. Giedion situates Neutra's 1923 Diatom prefabricated house (Figure 2.3) alongside the "architectonic vision" of Theo van Doesburg and Cornelis van Eeesteren's 1923 Maison Particulière, Mies's brick country house projects, and Le Corbusier's Dom-Ino project. This architectonic phase, the dominance of the "dwelling unit"—a development that ran from William Morris in the 1850s to California in the 1950s—was, in Giedion's view, "no longer sufficient" (*YM,* 202). After the mastery of the "single cell" must come the "reconquest of monumental expression" (*YM,* 27).

FIGURE 2.3. Richard Neutra, Diatom prefabricated homes, presentation drawing, 1923.

California and the new monumentality ran at cross-purposes. Hitchcock, speaking at the 1948 MoMA symposium "What Is Happening to Modern Architecture?," reaffirmed Giedion's message. If West Coast architecture—what he and Alfred H. Barr Jr. referred to as "cottage style"—sought to give "a looser and an easier expression" to domestic architecture, then these were "activities centered on what is frankly not one of the important problems of the architecture of the present day." Of "serious importance," according to Hitchcock, were mass housing, the industrial production of "housing components," and the "field of monumentality."[24]

It was not exactly a compliment, then, when Giedion wrote in the 1950 introduction to Neutra's collected works that Neutra "preserved in practice the artistic integrity, which emanated from the schemes of the early twenties."[25] By claiming that Neutra "never diverted" from the architectonics of the 1920s—the "consistent basis of his entire later work"—Giedion was in effect condemning him to the past. Giedion's essay is full of begrudging respect, offering a kind of nostalgic glance at what used to be modern. And yet glimmers of promise appear in two of Neutra's projects: the Channel Heights "settlement" of 1942 and the Warren Tremaine House of 1948. Giedion singles out two monumental aspects of the Tremaine House for comment: the relation between the massive concrete pillars and the slender beams and roof slabs and the relation between the master bedroom and the natural world seen through the plate-glass walls (Figure 2.4). Both express the "transcendence of mere function" into "psychic value," the

FIGURE 2.4. Richard Neutra, Tremaine House (Montecito, California), 1947–48. Photograph: Julius Shulman, 1948. Copyright J. Paul Getty Trust. Getty Research Institute, Los Angeles (2004.R.10).

feeling of mass and grandeur.[26] Giedion situates the Tremaine House within a sweeping historical development, crediting Neutra with transcending the "architectonic vision" and developing what he calls a "natural form of life." The contemporary "form of life" has become "more and more similar to that of primitive nomads," Giedion explains.[27] In a surprising turn, he regards the view from the Tremaine bedroom as the appropriate setting for the new nomad. "The waking man . . . prefers to see things close at hand and only gently illuminated," as though he is a caveman rising from a primal slumber. As one looks out from the bed, one's "eye wanders along gentle slopes, losing itself in the intimate nearness of green plants and rough stones, and the structure of the furrowed, evergreen oaktrunks." Architecture falls away, and what remains is a direct confrontation between self and world. The new habitat for the new barbarian is one where the architect does "almost nothing."[28]

FIGURE 2.5. Richard Neutra, Channel Heights housing project (Los Angeles, California), 1942. Photograph: Julius Shulman, 1950. Copyright J. Paul Getty Trust. Getty Research Institute, Los Angeles (2004.R.10).

The wandering nomad expresses a "new stage of civilization," one in which the "human being as such—the bare and naked man—will find a direct means of expression" (*YM*, 127). Actively revolting against the earlier phase of development that resulted in the domestic-scale setting of California Modern, Giedion suggests that nomads have no need for single-family dwellings but rather require collective spaces for "spontaneous social intercourse" (*YM*, 126). What is "demanded today," he insists, "is an almost completely neutral contact between person and person—not intimate relationship." The nomadic subject exists "apart from the family circle," participating in ever-changing "neutral relationships outside the dwelling" (*YM*, 202).

For Giedion, Neutra's Channel Heights housing project for dockworkers of 1942 (Figure 2.5) exemplifies his most actively nomadic space, an environment where one finds "the [black man], who suns himself Sundays on the lawn at his house."[29] It was this project that would graft "urbanistic ideas" onto chaotic suburban sprawl, creating an "unspoiled, undulating terrain." Los Angeles, for Giedion (as for most critics), was a "catastrophe of city planning. No beginning, no end."[30] At the edge of the Pacific and split off from the city, Channel Heights was the nomadic counterimage to the unplanned urbanism of Los Angeles.

Beginning in 1937, Giedion emphasized the need to transcend domestic modernism and shift toward monumental urban environments that could act as a "symbol or mirror of [human beings'] inner desires" (*YM*, 3). Without this external image of their inner life, he believed, modern subjects would be lost, aimless. Only the artist, in Giedion's view, could create a condensed public symbol for the seething and aimless inner life of modern man. If human beings were ever to find a way to "cope with the new reality" of industrialization, they would need monumental symbols for their "fate or destiny" (*YM*, 28). The problem, according to Giedion, was that those who "govern and administer public taste"—sounding the essential antistatist note—lack the "emotional understanding" required to provide satisfying symbolic spaces. Giedion called for artists, those professionally charged with providing "shape [for] our emotional life," to be given free rein over the environment, to "work upon the living body of our period" (*YM*, 33). It is here, in his "demand for shaping the emotional life of the masses" rather than his call for monumentality, that Giedion crosses paths with the tradition that runs from Endell through the Bauhaus and Neutra (*YM*, 34). It is this quality of shaping the masses, of *Menschenbildnerei,* that is the underlying ideal (even if it seems to produce "almost nothing")—the new nomads are stripped of the inheritances of premodern thought and thus ideally susceptible to the new mode of thinking that integrates mind and body.[31]

In "On the Force of Aesthetic Values" of 1947, for example, Giedion notes that the "humiliated human instincts," otherwise suppressed, are given expression at the micro level of the environment:

> Aesthetic values are inherent in things. They emanate from them, somewhat as odors do from food or from flowers. Like intangible perfumes they determine our sensitive or emotional reaction.
>
> Aesthetic impacts influence us at all moments. Consciously, or in most cases subconsciously, they provoke friendly or hostile reactions. Evading our rational strongholds they directly attack our emotions and are therefore out of our control.
>
> This means aesthetic values are no simple trimmings but, indeed, have their roots in the depth of the soul. Their impact on man's decisions reach even to the most practical problems, into the shaping of things of daily use . . . and, above all, of our human environment. (*YM*, 67)

Every word here is in sync with the literalism of the affective formalism I consider in chapter 1. No doubt such extravagantly literalist claims about the architect as "builder of contemporary life"—humans as a pliable material to be shaped by the architectural medium—are not foregrounded in Giedion's highly influential *Space, Time and Architecture,* but they underlie his argument at every turn. Near the end of that book he clarifies his position:

> When we go to the bottom . . . we see that contemporary architecture takes its start in a *moral* problem. Architecture has emerged from the realm of narrow specialization. And by taking off his specialists' blinders, the architect has greatly extended his influence. . . . Following an impulse which was half ethical, half artistic, [modern architects] have sought to provide our life with its corresponding shell or framework. And where contemporary architecture has been allowed to provide a new setting for contemporary life, this new setting has acted in its turn upon the life from which it springs. The new atmosphere has led to change and development in the conceptions of the people who live in it.[32]

In a sense, Giedion's claims are modest. The problem is specialization, and the solution is greater integration, to render the architect a whole person (a classically Bauhaus position). And yet it is anything but modest to suggest that the "conceptions of the people" are altered by the new "atmosphere" created by architects. Giedion embraces the literalist logic that construes the environment of a dwelling as shaping the conceptions of the inhabitants. Agency runs from material to architects to inhabitants. And architects are intentionally submerged in the diffuse "aesthetic values" of the settings they produce, their responsibility at once unlimited and dispersed.

As early as 1937, with Giedion's turn to monumentality, California Modern was construed as a polite Scandinavian reduction of the revolutionary claims of the earlier generation. Barr's famous insult that California Modern was the "*neue Gemütlichkeit* with which to supersede the *neue Sachlichkeit* of the 1920's" had not just shaped the reception of California work but had come to be applied to all modern architecture imported into the United States.[33] Commentators have casually asserted that when modern architecture arrived in America, "it lost its political character and became a metaphor for a better life."[34] And they have just as casually asserted that the *neue Sachlichkeit* bore political significance (recall Willett's [patently false] claim that "nothing emerges more clearly from a study of [art under the Weimar Republic] than that it was founded on a broadly socialist, and in many cases communist ideology").[35] It is tempting to say that the truth lies somewhere in the middle, but the record will not substantiate that view. Ain, for instance, was described in his vast FBI file as the "most dangerous architect in America" by J. Edgar Hoover. Many architects working in Los

Angeles, including Neutra, were under either frequent or intermittent surveillance by the FBI, suspected of communist activities.[36] What the record suggests is that the modern intervention at the domestic level could generate significant political panic of a sort that the monumental simply did not. These matters are beyond the scope of this discussion, but they should suggest the stakes attached to casual assertions of political consequence based on the claims of architects, critics, and historians. As I argue in the Conclusion, the turn to monumentality was vigorously and almost immediately challenged by Banham and the Brutalists. But at the same time, their love of California— "the most potent current version of the great bourgeois vision of the good life in a tamed countryside"—was the reductive equal and opposite of the embrace of monumentalism at MoMA.[37]

Vincent Scully's Monumentality

It would be no exaggeration to say that Vincent Scully developed an architectural vision that was almost the direct inverse of the one elaborated by Giedion in *Space, Time and Architecture*. If Giedion thought that the modern *Weltanschauung* was defined by continuous space-time, then Scully saw it in the closed and sculptural forms of late Le Corbusier, Louis Kahn, and Robert Venturi. But, like Giedion, Scully pursued an antisuburban modernism, one defined by a turn to urbanism and monumentality. Quoting a 1947 lecture by Alvar Aalto at Yale, Scully recalled the shock of him saying, "In Finland in the reconstruction we shall build no temporary buildings, because not by temporary building comes Parthenon on Acropolis."[38] Scully's quoting of Aalto was deliberate. To invoke him—and not, for instance, Le Corbusier—on the importance of monumentality was to use him in a targeted way against his West Coast admirers.

Beginning in 1954 Scully inaugurated a wide-scale attack against what he saw as the suburbanization of modernism. In "Archetype and Order in Recent American Architecture" Scully retracted his support of Wright's vision of "richly interwoven, structurally complex, spatially fluid buildings."[39] The new churches by Philip Johnson and Paul Schweikher defined a vision of ceremonial spaces where "nothing flows together" (*MA*, 66). The new sacred architecture

> breaks sharply with some aspects of Wright's philosophy. . . . The forms created by this generation are urban forms, contained, generalized, civil in their relationship to other forms. As such they indicate a turning away from romantic isolation, from the modern suburb. . . . They seek instead the qualities of the city. . . . One can observe that the majority of the illustrated projects have had religious programs. (*MA*, 73)

Just like Giedion, Scully dated the antisuburban revolt to 1937, when Mies arrived in the United States. Mies in Chicago inaugurated the effort to "reject . . . compulsive continuity and its concomitant asymmetry and to create instead a more fixed and symmetrical kind of design." Closed blocks were no longer forced to "define a continuous and fluid space" (*MA*, 82). Scully took aim at Giedion's "continuous" space conception, rejecting "thinness and weightlessness" on the grounds that "space is still the 'reality' over matter, and the solids are either simply a frame or a thinly stretched membrane which encloses a volume" (*MA*, 83). Matter, rather than space or volume, Scully averred, was finally and decisively reaffirmed in Le Corbusier's late work: "The human being returns to the landscape; he no longer dissolves into it as he may do in the lonely dream of Wright" (*MA*, 85). Here too Giedion could only agree. By the late 1940s Giedion had turned against the continuous phase of the modern spatial conception, a phase that came to a definitive end for Scully and Giedion with Le Corbusier's vast urban scale at Chandigarh.

It is well beyond my aims here to delve into the controversies surrounding Chandigarh at midcentury.[40] But a brief glance at Arthur Gallion and Simon Eisner's *The Urban Pattern* (1950), a book written while both were teaching at USC, which remains among the most influential textbooks on urbanism (the sixth edition of 1993 is still in print), offers an overlooked response to the terms set out by Giedion and Scully around Le Corbusier's urbanism. Is Brasília, this "monumental expression of concrete and glass," "really for people?," Gallion and Eisner ask.[41] And comparing Chandigarh with the city of Fatehpur-sikri from the Mogul period, they argue that in Fatehpur-sikri the "relation between buildings and space, the light and shade of arcades and sheltered areas, convey a vivid impression that the place was meant for *people*," a quality that they conclude is "not present at Chandigarh."[42] While Gallion and Eisner maintain that a commitment to space is at the core of modern urbanism, they reject the idea that the skyscraper is its best expression. "Horizontal space," they observe, "contact with the earth . . . on foot," answers the most basic human need. It is here, on the grounds of "horizontal space," a progressive image of urban sprawl, where "interior and exterior living space merge into unity," that Gallion and Eisner draw a connection between the new urbanism and California Modern.[43] That their vision rests on what they call the "human desire for a house on its land" could not have put them at deeper odds with the dominant thrust of the postwar period.

Scully delivered his infamous broadside against Gallion and Eisner's modernism in "Doldrums in the Suburbs" of 1965, published simultaneously in the *Journal of the Society of Architectural Historians* and *Perspecta*. It is worth pausing to consider this article at length, as it reveals an almost paradigmatic (or pathological) aversion to the expressions of California Modern that I consider in this book. Scully reserves his deepest scorn for the works of the "American Bauhaus," the sweeping polemical banner under which he classifies all suburban modernism.

The article opens with paired photographs that are captioned as Gropius and Breuer's 1938 Gropius House and Harris's 1949 Johnson House, but as the article appeared in the *Journal of the Society of Architectural Historians,* the second illustration in fact depicted Harris's 1941 Birtcher House. The photograph Scully chose to illustrate the Birtcher House (a photograph that was widely disseminated at the time) was taken by Man Ray.[44] Scully summarizes his claims up front, arguing that "during the 1930s in America architectural theory suburbanized itself up to the point where it became almost nonexistent; and where, indeed, architecture itself, or architecture as a topic of general urbanistic meaning, almost ceased" (*MA,* 128). He recalls coming to this conclusion in light of the 1948 MoMA symposium "What Is Happening to Modern Architecture?," during which Alfred Barr Jr. and Lewis Mumford squared off on opposing accounts of contemporary architecture. Mumford, in his opening statement, outlined the claims of "organic" architecture associated with the Bay Region School. Scully illustrates Mumford's point with the example of a house "not from the Bay Region but more or less of that type, a house in Los Angeles, the Johnson house" (*MA,* 129). Scully casually conflates Bauhaus, Mumford, Harris, Los Angeles, and Bay Region architecture to make the point that the old polemic of inorganic versus organic is dead. "We were," he states, "more or less being told that Gropius' art was classic or classicizing and that the art of the Bay Region School was romantic," but, he counters, "there was basically no difference between these architectures at all: no important difference between Gropius' house at Lincoln and Harris' house at Los Angeles" (*MA,* 130). This is meant polemically, but for many readers it could already have registered as a cliché. Mock had observed in *Built in USA* (twenty years earlier) that the "heated controversy of Wright vs. Le Corbusier no longer seems important." Nor was the "schism itself any longer so absolute," as the two architects had drawn closer to one another.[45]

Scully aims to define modern American architecture monolithically, referring to it all as "American Bauhaus" and thereby dispensing with the distinctions between East and West and inorganic and organic in one blow. It could only be beside the point for Scully (if he was even aware of it) that Harris was engaged in a long-term struggle against Gropius's aims; that in 1943, while teaching at Columbia University, Harris was involved in the CIAM Chapter for Relief and Postwar Planning and found himself in direct opposition to Gropius and Giedion; that Harris was present at the 1948 symposium alongside Scully, Barr, and Mumford and that he clashed there with Breuer; and that Harris had famously addressed the problem of regionalism in his 1954 "Regionalism and Nationalism in Architecture" and a range of other writings.[46]

Scully assumes what can only be described as a Wölfflinian distance from architectural controversies of the moment. From his bird's-eye view he observes the following of Gropius's and Harris's houses:

> Both are small, single-family suburban houses. Both of them are built of wood; both of them are light in weight; neither of them has anything whatever to do with the problem of urbanism. In fact, both of them, in the suburbs, embody an attempted escape from the larger questions of monumental architecture and city building as a whole. . . . They are small in scale and anti-monumental, and they have nothing to do with the larger architectural problem of urbanism with which, in its own way, the International Style as a whole also had a rather curious record. (*MA*, 130)

Scully adds that the houses are both "fundamentally pictorial," by which he means everything about them evokes "transparency, flux, flow, no weight, no symmetry." Whether it is Los Angeles, the Bay Area, or anywhere else, "you will see," he claims, "that the passage of planes, the maximum thinness, the lightness, the asymmetry, and so on is that of Moholy-Nagy. Ergo: Bauhaus and Bay Region all in one" (*MA*, 133).

Scully punishingly singles out Breuer as the most public "victim" of the Bauhaus attitude. For all of Breuer's late efforts toward monumentality, everything he built expressed "basically the same pictorial, small-scale, designer's sensitivity" (*MA*, 135). Breuer's "insectile tension" bears all the "characteristics of small-scale, anti-monumentality, asymmetry, tension of line, and so on, which had been characteristic of his pictorial education" (*MA*, 135). It was Breuer's "small-scale graphic sensibility," Scully contends, that "made it impossible for him to build a monumental building." Scully disingenuously claims that this is "not an attack upon Breuer"—his insectile designs meandering through suburban doldrums apparently are an achievement—but Scully's final comparison of Breuer's work with the late work of Le Corbusier is intended to be crushing. Like Giedion, Scully regards Le Corbusier's Chandigarh as the model for the new monumentality:

> One would say, looking at the work by Le Corbusier, that the force that Chandigarh has derives from the fact that it elevates to heroic scale the standing figures of men; whereas in the Breuer there is *no* possibility to associate oneself empathetically with the form lifted. The relationships are insectile, small-scale, and related to furniture design. (*MA*, 137)

Scully's verdict is sweeping and misogynistic: modern architecture from Wright on is ultimately scaled-up furniture design—graphic, planar, insectile, small, "rather feminine."[47] Against this tendency, Scully cites Mies's work in Chicago and the late works of Aalto and Le Corbusier, all of which express "muscular force," "monumental mass and structural weight," a return to the cherished empathetic values Scully sees in Louis Sullivan's skyscrapers (*MA*, 137).

Although Scully uses the East Coast Breuer as his scapegoat, he makes it clear the Bay Region "wing" of the Bauhaus was no more capable than its eastern counterpart of producing "monumental urban architecture"; its commitment to "the single-family house," its "special preoccupation with wood and also with a conscious desire to make architecture as shack-like as possible" relegated it to the past, or to the dustbin (*MA*, 137). Like Hitchcock and Giedion, Scully makes no distinctions among Oregon, the Bay Area, and Los Angeles, or among any of the architects practicing there: "The California group or the West-Coast group" are equally guilty, equally incapable of transcending decor. What Scully entirely fails to grasp is the nature of the conflict outlined in this book between affect-driven accounts and ones driven by expressive intent, a conflict that does not follow consistent stylistic or morphological lines. In my account the sweeping stylistic use of the term *Bauhaus* is, like the use of *midcentury modern* later, devoid of content.

Like Giedion, Scully concludes his attack on the "anti-monumental suburbanization of architecture" with a story of rebirth. It was Mies at the Illinois Institute of Technology in 1939 who ushered in the new era of monumentality. Or almost, as "late Mies was not begun to be understood until about 1949" (*MA*, 139). The 1949 publication of Rudolf Wittkower's *Architectural Principles in the Age of Humanism* ultimately ratified the new monumentality and the resurgence of interest in cross-axial planning, symmetry, mass urban scale, everything Renaissance, and everything that was forbidden by the gothicizing graphism of the American Bauhaus. The official rebirth occurred with Louis Kahn's Yale Art Gallery of 1951, the entrance to which serves as Scully's closing illustration. As Scully declares in his parting line: "We have an architecture again" (*MA*, 141).

"Nothing Is Left": Nelson on Obsolescence

For Scully as for Giedion, ambitious civic and ceremonial structures were the means of breaking the hold of residential modernism in the postwar period. In "The Need for a New Monumentality," Giedion laments how modern architects, when entrusted with "monumental tasks involving more than functional problems," fail miserably (*YM*, 32). George Nelson, who presented a paper after Giedion at the "New Architecture and City Planning" symposium, offers a similar set of dismal reflections:

> The contemporary architect, cut off from symbols, ornament and meaning-
> ful elaborations of structural forms, all of which earlier periods possessed in

abundance, has desperately chased every functional requirement, every change in site or orientation, every technical improvement, to provide some basis for starting his work. Where the limitations were most rigorous, as for example in a factory, or in a skyscraper where every inch had to yield its profit, there the designers were happiest and the results were most satisfying. But let a religious belief or a social ideal replace cubic foot costs or radiation losses, and nothing happened. . . . Faced with the problem of monumental building—the building in which function and structure become secondary problems—the modern architect seems to lose his creative faculties and he becomes a critic. (*PD*, 116)

Nelson points to a series of "contradictions": between the social drive toward "immortality" and the architectural drive toward the "ephemeral" and between the "demand for monumentality" and a "lack of faith in the institutions normally glorified in monumental architecture and sculpture" (*PD*, 117). Embracing Giedion's terminology, Nelson proposes a solution in a "new concept of the community." The "structures devoted to production" would no longer carry the burden of architectural meaning. The "Roman roads are not an expression of a traffic system, but of what was then a new world outlook, which stemmed from a system of social unification" (*PD*, 118). Nelson is tellingly vague about the nature of the new outlook, but he insists that the age of austerity—minimum-existence idealism—has come to an end. Architecture, he declares, has been "preoccupied with closets and minimum shelter and undersized bedrooms and all the minimal paraphernalia of a penny architecture long enough" (*PD*, 118).

Although in 1944 Nelson was under the sway of MoMA monumentality, by 1945 his outlook had changed because he began seriously engaging, for the first time, with the work of Fuller and the Eameses. Nelson had known Fuller from their tenure at Time, Inc. (1938–40), but Fuller did not begin to shape Nelson's thinking until Nelson visited Beech Aircraft, the manufacturing site of Fuller's Dymaxion house, for a cover story for *Fortune* magazine (the story appeared in April 1946) (Figure 2.6).[48] In December 1945, during a preview exhibition of Eames furniture at the Barclay Hotel, Nelson looked closely at the Eameses' designs for the first time. What both events signaled, as McCoy reflects, was "the spirit of an age that questioned marble monumentality and permanency" (*EMR*, 185). It was also in 1945 that Nelson and Wright published their best-selling guidebook *Tomorrow's House*. The heavily illustrated volume features no fewer than seventy-two photographs of modern architecture in California (the only other state given equal attention is Nelson's home state of New York). Showcasing well-known work by Harris, Wurster, and Neutra, as well as lesser-known work by J. R. Davidson and Raphael Soriano, Nelson and Wright single out "reduction in bulk" and "flexibility of control" as defining features of the new house.[49]

FIGURE 2.6. *Fortune* magazine, April 1946.

Nelson first publicly lauded the Eameses' work in a long article titled "The Furniture Industry," which appeared in *Fortune* in 1947. At the conclusion of the article Nelson discusses the March 1946 Museum of Modern Art exhibition *New Furniture Designed by Charles Eames*, at which Eames introduced the Dining Chair Metal, or DCM (Figure I.4), a plywood side chair shock-mounted to a steel frame. Nelson's encounter with "molded plywood, plastic impregnated papers, metal and rubber" that was "light in weight, extremely durable and comfortable" at least in part moved him to abandon his interest in monumentality (he now observed the "steadily diminishing size of dwellings" without a hint of regret).[50] Nelson stopped referring to the urgent need for monumentality, and he replaced notions of permanence and immortality altogether with what he came to call the arts of "obsolescence." After seeing the Eames furniture display, Nelson told the president of the Herman Miller furniture company, D. J. De Pree, that he "must get Charles."[51] Following the show, the Eameses joined Herman Miller as design consultants, positions they held until the end of their lives.[52]

Nelson also contributed to the 1948 MoMA symposium "What Is Happening to Modern Architecture?" Responding to bitter remarks by Mumford, Barr, Hitchcock, and Gropius, Nelson—like Scully—suggested that there was "no contradiction" between "'machine look' and 'living,'" claiming the argument was "disposed of twenty years ago," presumably referring to the invention of the Dymaxion house.[53] He went on to review his argument from his 1944 essay, but although he still maintained that "no architect alive has produced a church or government building that evokes a deep emotional response from the beholder," he did not, as he did in 1944, reject the factory aesthetic; on the contrary, he now insisted that "architectural validity today" existed solely in the "factories, commercial structures and projects like TVA." If factory thinking was the problem in 1944, it was the solution four years later. All housing, modern and traditional, looked equally conventional in comparison to commercial technology. Nelson, with Scully-like sweep, asserted that the "difference between the Tugendhat house and a dwelling in the 'Bay Region Style' is almost invisible" when one compares the two together against industrial buildings. It was the difference "between the Tugendhat house and Buckminster Fuller's Dymaxion house," he contended, that was truly at stake. Nelson concluded, in a moment of utopian excess, that Fuller's "catastrophic" inventions introduced a gap between *all* building of the past and the new world of structural possibility, a change ushering in a "No Man's Land of future professional battles."[54]

In "After the Modern House," published in *Interiors* magazine in 1952, Nelson extravagantly claims that the "modern house is already obsolete" (*PD*, 135).[55] Going further than in his MoMA address, Nelson insists that the International Style / Bay Region style dispute and the dispute between modern architecture and traditional housing

FIGURE 2.7. Ludwig Mies van der Rohe, Concert Hall project (interior perspective), 1942. Digital image copyright The Museum of Modern Art. Licensed by SCALA / Art Resource, New York. Copyright 2022 Artists Rights Society (ARS), New York / VG Bild-Kunst, Bonn.

are equally irrelevant. The future is with "the factory or office building, . . . not the house." Nelson cites Mies's Concert Hall project of 1942 (Figure 2.7) and his Minerals and Metals Research Laboratory at IIT of 1943 as well as Albert Kahn's Chrysler Dodge Half-Ton Truck Plant of 1938 and Toledo Scale Plant of 1939, referring to them as *"the master type of space enclosure of our time"* (*PD*, 139).[56] The "space container" or "controlled shelter," he states, will come to replace the house. His examples of the new shelter environment are more predictable: the Eames House, Soriano's Curtis House, Mies's Farnsworth House, Johnson's Glass House, and Bruce Goff's Bavinger House. Nelson asserts that with the triumph of the "conditioned shell," architecture will disappear altogether and be replaced by interior and industrial design (what he would describe in 1979 as the end of architecture).[57] Picking up on Charles Eames's account of the opacity of architectural meaning, Nelson reflects on the inordinate barriers to expressive transparency. An architect, he observes,

> has a relatively limited time to solve a very complex set of problems, and when he has done so his design is picked up by a motley crew of masons, plumbers, carpenters and others who then proceed to execute it in a thoroughly unpredictable fashion. Furthermore, his design is a one-of-kind-thing, and on the next house he has to start again from scratch. (*PD*, 147)[58]

Like the Eameses, Nelson worried about the "unpredictable" aspects of execution and how designers might maintain the integrity or survival of a design once it left their hands. One solution to unpredictability that he proposes, charting an opposite course from his 1944 talk, is a new mode of tentlike shelter. The "post" modern house will remove "all heavy interior construction," the space being divided by "glorified pup tents" (*PD*, 148). These ideas express the aims of Fuller, and by this point Nelson was a member of the so-called Fuller Research Foundation.

Nelson's most sustained vision of this new type of architecture is found in his seminal essay "Obsolescence" of 1956, republished in 1957, 1965, and 1967.[59] By the mid-1950s Nelson had been describing what he called "Kleenex Culture" for several years—"more and more consumer products shift from a semi-permanent to a disposable basis," he observed (*PD*, 12)—but it was with "Obsolescence" that he elaborated a broad theoretical account of this new attitude. In this essay, Nelson asserts that the prospects for a design with "perfectly planned disintegration" are over. Swamped in an "infinity of variables," the contemporary designer has no chance of balancing all the elements to achieve a long-term equilibrium (this is exactly what led the Eameses to quit architecture). Nonetheless, there is a new type of obsolescence, one that seemingly requires high levels of "waste" to generate a product, much as fish have to lay many eggs and oak trees have to drop many acorns in order to ensure that at least "a minute percentage" of their progeny survive (*PD*, 44). Nelson's point is that from the right perspective what looks like waste (to Europeans looking at Americans) is not waste at all. From fish and oaks, he turns directly to cars. Quoting at length from economist Peter Drucker, he suggests (optimistically) that there is a perfected industrial equilibrium of new and used cars. One of Nelson's favorite images is Fuller's (fantastic) idea of the equilibrium attained on a highway, where constant feedback between motorists creates a harmonically balanced traffic system (*PD*, 76).

The only way of achieving this kind of widespread systemic balance—what would later be christened an ecology—is through competitive industry. Consumers put pressure on industry for new products. Nelson considers those pressures to be largely irrational, but, however misdirected, they are a progressive force, what the Eameses famously describe as a growing "universal sense of expectation" (*EA*, 351). As Fuller argues, with the rise of automation, workers are being replaced in the "industrial equation" by consumers. "People are going to be utterly essential as consumers—what I call *regenerative consumers*," Fuller writes.[60] These new "critical consumers" consult their "individual human chromosomal ticker-tapes" to determine what is valuable and what is not.[61] For Fuller, as for Nelson, a direct line can be drawn between the immediacy of one's inner desires and the choices that result from those desires, leading to purchases in the marketplace. The "critical consumer" is perfected direct democracy, as there is (putatively) a perfect accord between absolute need and industrial production, insofar as industry listens to the demands of consumers and is flexible enough to meet and fulfill those particular needs. Consumers expect more and more for less and less. While they demand generalized newness, industry attempts to gauge the seriousness of consumer demands. Industry has a reliable set of instruments for judging products: "performance pressure." Nelson notes that "if performance were always measurable and demonstrable, obsolescence rates would be higher than they are now" (*PD*, 46). His example is a bomb. Bombs are measured by megatons, and more of them is better: a "ceiling of 60,000 feet is better than 50,000" (*PD*, 46).[62] As Nelson sees it, "When a performance can be evaluated so directly, product design becomes very pure and the appearance of the product, highly satisfying esthetically" (*PD*, 46). Nelson elaborates at length on the beauty of weapons in his short film "How to Kill People," which aired as an episode of CBS's arts and literature program *Camera Three* in 1960. He ironically wonders if "the Greeks or Romans ever produce[d] anything as beautiful" as the bomb dropped on Hiroshima while lamenting that designers "have designed the excitement out of killing" (now that it is done at the push of a button).[63] It is an irony-soaked statement that Nelson made at a deeply pessimistic moment in his career, but it also sits uncomfortably with his only slightly earlier gushing over the beauty of bombs (which lacks the ironic gloss) and his later utopian fantasy of capitalist ephemeralization.

At the same moment Nelson was outlining his performance principle, Charles Eames was describing the making of a kite in these terms. What is "marvelous" about the "kite problem," he points out, is that "one can definitely judge its success or failure, that it will *fly* or it will *not* fly. I wish more problems could be so beautifully defined" (*EA*, 148). I consider this point at length in chapter 6, but for now let me say that it was not at all the case that the Eameses wished for problems to be reducible to evaluative performance—rather, it was more like the opposite in that they sought to delay performance or avoid it altogether. Nelson, by contrast, sees the bomb/kite problem as providing a rule: "*The more accurately performance can be measured, the higher the rate of obsolescence*" (*PD*, 46). And he points to *how* we might measure performance: "We tend to accept without question *anything that will do more with less*" (*PD*, 47). Nelson is sounding an orthodox Fullerian note. There is an unconscious and unstoppable universal demand for ephemeralization. He gives a thumbnail version of Fuller's history of invention: from truss bridge to suspension bridge, from vacuum tube to transistor, from piston to turbine, everything tends toward "reduced weight, bulk, or both" (*PD*, 47).

Nelson devotes the rest of his essay to explaining how it is that the universal demand for change emerged. There is, he asserts, a "master area" in every culture: "Every society lives out its span in the grip of certain ideas which are so powerful and so widely held that people are scarcely aware of them" (*PD*, 49). In the thirteenth century it was the church; in twentieth-century America, it is business. As Nelson explains it, the drive for newness, which is "completely valid" in business, is so powerful that it has spread to the culture at large. The attraction to change has permeated society, spreading to aspects of life where "basic pressures are not operative" (*PD*, 48). In other words, optimization slips from the hands of business and from the hands of the designer into the culture at large.

The designer's role, in Nelson's account, is to advance us along the path of progress toward ephemeralization. There must be the "active element," "someone restates the problem at hand . . . and comes up with a better answer" (*PD*, 48). Nelson's example, a charged one, is the prefabricated house. The designer, using industrial techniques (and so making the handmade house obsolete), needs "to step up the performance of the product" (*PD*, 49). Designers, Nelson maintains, are performance obsessed; it is in their blood. Everything they see is construed as obsolete the moment it is made: "To a designer, anything that is, is obsolete" (*PD*, 49).

In the final turn in his essay, Nelson directly crosses paths with the Eameses. The designer needs to marshal every available tool of the information age to achieve the highest levels of optimization. The designer needs "increasing quantities of information, not only technical, but scientific, metaphysical, economic, social, psychological" (*PD*, 50). If the designer really wants to "plan our various kinds of obsolescence," then that "means a lot of work for somebody" (*PD*, 50). Nelson repeats the Fuller-Eames mantra: obsolescence "provides a way of getting a maximum of good to a maximum of people" (*PD*, 50). He concludes with his famous assertion that what "we need is more obsolescence, not less." But what Nelson meant by obsolescence was not at all what the Eameses had in mind. As the Eameses saw it, getting "the best to the most . . . people for the least" meant *refusing the performance principle,* an idea that was in tension with Nelson's (as with Fuller's) whole approach (*EA*, 73).

Nelson typically could not see past the performance principle, but on occasion he did glimpse an alternative. Notably, his essay "The Designer in the Modern World" of 1957 goes in a different direction from the rest of his writings collected in *Problems of Design.* He begins the essay conventionally enough, arguing that designers are producers who take the modern world as their "target." But he quickly turns his attention to the status of the modern artist. If in the past there was little use for artists—who were denigrated for being dreamers—then today the vindicated artist reappears on the scene as a mirror of the designer. "The existence of the industrial designer marks one phase in the reassimilation of the artist into society" (*PD*, 76). The main difference between artist and designer is that the designer works in an organization; we all need organization, Nelson insists, to cope with "increasing quantities of information." In the past there was "common ground" that enabled us to process all information, but today there is nothing to help us deal with the chaos of information. The period of shared educational curriculum is over; the current aim is to seek a "new common ground," one that "will be found in *methods* of organizing and transmitting information" (*PD*, 76). Designer, artist, scientist, and businessman meet on the ground of *abstraction*:

> One common element with interesting possibilities is the widespread use of abstractions. A man trained for management learns to deal with abstractions consisting of some two dozen alphabetical symbols, a handful of Arabic numerals and special kinds of pictures called charts or graphs. He does not as a rule think of these as abstraction, just as Moliere's *bourgeois gentilhomme* did not realize that he had been speaking prose all his life. Yet it is true that the powerful images used by management have no visible resemblance to the physical world and might correctly be described as abstractions. (*PD*, 76)

Nelson's businessmen are *unconscious* of their use of modeling. While they think in terms of application, they are in fact practicing *theory*. It is as though the product made by the tools of abstraction is reducible to the tool, as though every businessman is always and already an artist.

And if the artist vindicates the designer, so does the designer vindicate the artist. Because artists deal with symbols, they are really the same as the designer: both "deal with constellations of abstract symbols" (*PD*, 77). Communication occurs through shared methods of abstraction. Further, Nelson conceives of a mode of *practice* that matches this account of abstraction (rather than vice versa), one that offers an alternative vision of obsolescence compared with the one he describes in his 1956 essay. He imagines a kind of educational process whereby the aim for creators is to "destroy their work at the end of most sessions," leaving behind the method, absent its application (*PD*, 83). He elaborates on the idea in the context of what he refers to as the "Office Revolution," "the main problem" of which is to "rediscover productive inefficiency again."[64] More profoundly—and here he crosses paths with the Eameses' early film *Bread* (1953), part of the collaborative Georgia Experiment—Nelson superbly glosses the "traditional lunch of the Finnish peasant":

> He goes to his work carrying a hard-crusted, round loaf of black bread. His wife has already cut a wedge from the top, inserted a large dollop of butter, and replaced the wedge. Once at his work the peasant puts it under a hedge, where its thick, shiny crust is immune to the attacks of the hungriest insects. When the lunch time comes, he takes it, breaks it open, spreads the butter and eats it. Nothing is left, for the package is the meal. If he drops a few crumbs, the birds dispose of them. The ideal, I suspect, is unattainable. But I cannot imagine a better symbol for the goals of the new generation of package designers.[65]

A work in which nothing is left after consumption would be one in which production equals use. Nelson's admission that the ideal is likely out of reach is honest and also speaks to his larger and more central commitment to "control over nature," which defines his practice from beginning to end (PD, 57). Even if Nelson glimpses the "nothing is left" ideal explored by Schindler and the Eameses, he almost uniformly circumscribes it within the space of optimized performance. He ends the essay with a Fullerite ephemeralization fantasy, reflecting that *the greater the internal stability of a modern regime, the lighter its buildings,"* as though there are causal connections among method, medium, and politics (PD, 77). This ephemeralization fantasy stands in contrast to his brilliant refusal of media politics in "Good Design: What Is It For?" There he remarks that design "cannot transform a dark brown little life into a large, brightly colored one—only the person living the life can do that." Directly criticizing the affective formalist tradition I describe in chapter 1, Nelson stresses that design "is not a vitamin pill or a sulfa tablet" (which is precisely how Gropius described it). Design reaches its potential when "it is experienced by a person fully equipped to understand . . . what it has to communicate" (PD, 13). Nelson, on this account, refuses to imagine design as a mode of "human sculpting," leaving it to already cultivated consumers to come *to* modern design. Nonetheless, Nelson's ideal house does not exactly communicate much; it is Fuller's empty background for life. The Dymaxion house was "a home wherein the real individualism of man and his family may be developed, as a minimum of time is given to what he *has* to do, willy-nilly, eat, sleep and be clean."[66] As Hugh Kenner glosses this point, the Dymaxion house "doesn't perform the most important office of a house in most people's lives: it doesn't tell you what to do with yourself, doesn't give you so much as a hint. That's up to you." The user of the new house needs "no directives from the brickwork."[67] On the one hand, Nelson emphatically rejects the idea that design creates subjects. On the other hand, he does not imagine spaces that put any kind of pressure or limits on action—they are more like blank pages for "real individualism," whatever that means.

Nelson first broaches the topic of abstraction in his contribution to the famous collaboration Art X—The Georgia Experiment (1952), with Charles Eames and Alexander Girard. The group's lecture, called "A Sample Lesson: Subject 'Communication,'" is broken down into eight parts, six of them film and two of them multiscreen slide shows.[68] Part 4, by Nelson, is called "Abstraction," and it runs for eight minutes. The point of it is to show that "the use of abstraction is necessary in communications, since it is rarely possible to send a *total* message" (PD, 22).[69] Nelson's examples are Picasso's *Still Life with Watermelon* (1946)—the work is inverted in reproduction in the publication of the talk—maps of London, and cathedrals in England and France. The variety of maps—street patterns, subway routes, garage locations—is meant to show that there are different ways of collecting and presenting data via abstraction. The cathedral is described as an abstraction because it is the "result of a filtering process which has gone on for centuries" (the Eameses make this same claim about tools) (*PD,* 17). Nelson's point is that abstraction provides a new set of "attitudes, methods and techniques designed for the widest possible applicability," offering "general flexibility in relation to almost any situation" (*PD,* 31). With abstraction Nelson touches on something that the Eameses go on about at length: that the flexibility of application suggests an end point beyond application itself, opening up a space for modeling. But it is not a place that Nelson thinks to linger; his eye is on the latest technology, the perfected Fullerite tool of the future—furniture, appliance, house—able to do "more with less."[70] Capitalism freed of its shackles brings utopia. Nelson illustrates his late essay "Miniaturization, Ephemeralization, Dematerialization" (1978) with an IBM microchip and remarks how it inevitably evokes the "mysticism" of the "True Cross."

> Accepting the hypothesis that the brighter we get, the more we can do with less, it presently follows that if this is a good thing, then doing *much* more with *much* less must be an even better thing. Then, if we cautiously extend the evolutionary line in the direction of infinity we come to the interesting realization that the ultimate goal of technology has to be *doing everything with nothing.*
>
> This, of course, is precisely what God did. . . . One wonders if the conjunction of mineral reserves being depleted to an eventual vanishing point, and the real goal of technology doing everything with nothing, is serendipity or something more.[71]

No doubt the early designers in Silicon Valley believed the same Fullerite gospel (no doubt they also ironized it as protection against heresy). And no doubt this is the lesson that most of the critics and admirers of California Modern learned from it. But, as it turns out, it was the wrong lesson.

3

Between Culture and Biology
*R. M. Schindler and Richard Neutra
at the Limits of Architecture*

> His plans were usually the roughest sketches of a building, just as his
> buildings were sometimes just rough sketches of a subtle and wonderful idea.
> —Gregory Ain, "R. M. Schindler," 1954

Biology was at the center of Richard Neutra's aesthetic, philosophical, social, and architectural concerns. Neutra assumed and acted on the belief that, as he writes in his autobiography, *Life and Shape* (1962), there is an *"organic common denominator of the species."*[1] "Everywhere, it appeared to me, human beings, in mixture and in clash, held nevertheless a common denominator beneath their biological individuality—in spite of ethnic variety" (*LS*, 230). But in the exact same breath he affirms the fundamental unassimilability of the *"biological individual"* (*LS*, 192), noting that we possess a "constitutional trait" that necessitates "emphasizing our peculiarities, dwelling on ethnic distinctions, our subtly diversified creeds and geographical distances" (*LS*, 303). Beyond ethnicity and nationality, what truly "interrupts human homogeneity," Neutra observes, is "biological individuality, even within our single family, with stomachs of very different volume, shape, and position, and windpipes of remarkably different diameter, and so many oddities of variation" (*LS*, 304).[2] It is only in light of a shared biological basis that an account of the profound "oddities of variation" can emerge. Uniformity is the condition for difference in Neutra's work. Neutra was uninterested in ethnic differences because those differences are superficial and above all *contingent*, and because they obscure the more fundamental expressions of biological variation. Knowing that his clients had specific kinds of stomachs and windpipes—even or especially if they were themselves unaware of these differences—he could (he thought) accurately calculate the effects his structures would have on his subjects over the long term. What America, or rather California—the "cradle of anthropology" to which Neutra immigrated in 1925 and where he remained for the rest of his career—meant to Neutra was freedom for himself and for others to live "closer to biological requirement" (*LS*, 215, 216). In California one could live "as man had originally," according to "his original physiology."

Neutra's attitude toward immigration was shaped by Loos's optimistic account of life in the United States. For Loos, America was the "classical country of immigration"; it was the "great melting pot" where all immigrants were "absorbed into its civilization," and he often emphasized the "converting influence of the American entry port on the incoming polyglot flood of immigrants" (*LS*, 170). Crucially, Neutra notes that Loos never spoke of "machine civilization" or architecture; he never explained "what the city's . . . impacts were, nor what it was that made for this influence" (*LS*, 177). Neutra recalls his first conversation with his host upon his arrival in Chicago in 1923. "You will like it here," his host told him. "It is a very interesting enterprise to change immigrants over into Americans" (*LS*, 181). But what both his host and Loos had shown him were merely a *"passing show into progress"* (*LS*, 177), as the impacts and influences of northern cities were temporary and superficial. Real progress, real shaping force, required a different environment. Again and again Neutra mentions "man the Southerner" (*LS*, 309).[3] It was the desert outside Los Angeles where superficial differences were erased and true biodiversity flourished.

R. M. Schindler took a far different view of his adopted home of Los Angeles. It was the mountains rather than the desert that he admired, but he stayed in the city owing to its mild climate and its bohemian clientele. California, for Schindler, represented the complete "pacification of the world."[4] Nature there had been fully conquered by civilization, the precondition for the birth of "culture," the defining quality of his architectural enterprise. Unlike Neutra, Schindler showed virtually no interest in a biological justification for his forms; form was a human construct and a human achievement. And space—the defining feature of culture—was an expression of and a model for the "limitless powers of the human mind."[5] In other words, for Schindler, California was an ideal place to live because there one could be free of the demands of nature *and* civilization, there one could be free to be fully human for the first time in history.

For five turbulent years the Schindler and Neutra families lived together at Schindler's Kings Road House (also known as the Schindler House) in Los Angeles (Figure 3.1). Schindler and Neutra met at Loos's *Bauschule* in Vienna, and both remained devoted to Loos's ideals for the rest of their lives. Nonetheless, they disagreed vehemently over the nature of Loosian principles. The disagreement centered on a basic distinction between the spatial and temporal aspects of Loos's project.

In 1914 Schindler took Loos's advice and sought out architectural work in Chicago, where he ultimately found a position in Frank Lloyd Wright's firm. By late 1920 Schindler had moved to Los Angeles to supervise the construction of Wright's Hollyhock House for Aline Barnsdall. Neutra had intended to follow Schindler in 1914, but he did not end up moving to Los Angeles until February 1925. Between 1925 and the summer of

FIGURE 3.1. R. M. Schindler *(right)* with Richard, Dione, and son Dion Neutra at the Kings Road House, 1928. R. M. Schindler Collection, Architecture and Design Collection, Art, Design & Architecture Museum, University of California, Santa Barbara.

1930, Schindler and Neutra lived together and formed a collective architectural identity, which they ambitiously called the Architectural Group for Industry and Commerce, or AGIC. The only lasting achievement of the short-lived AGIC was its 1926 design entry for the League of Nations competition (although Neutra designed the Jardinette Apartments under the AGIC name, the structure is solely Neutra's design) (Figure 3.2). The design failed to receive a prize but was selected to be part of a traveling exhibition hosted by the German Werkbund.[6] This minor triumph for the AGIC was also the source of a growing rift between Schindler and Neutra. The collaborative plans were exhibited throughout Europe under Neutra's name, and, despite Neutra's efforts to correct the error, Schindler took this "breach of professional ethics" as a matter of personal betrayal. No public break between the architects occurred until several years later when Neutra was included in MoMA's 1932 International Style show but Schindler was not. After that, the simmering tensions between the two flared into the open, and their connection was severed for the next twenty years.[7]

FIGURE 3.2. R. M. Schindler and Richard Neutra, League of Nations competition entry, perspective of assembly hall facing lake, 1926. R. M. Schindler Collection, Architecture and Design Collection, Art, Design & Architecture Museum, University of California, Santa Barbara.

Schindler and the Meaning of Space

The first public exposure of the feud between Schindler and Neutra unfolded in the pages of the Texas-based *Southwest Review* in the spring of 1932 (Figure 3.3). The terms of the debate involved the question of functionalism. Neutra took the "pro" position and Schindler the "contra."[8] In his response, Schindler rehearsed, nearly word for word, his 1912 manifesto, where he declared that the "architect has [finally] discovered the [true] medium of his art: space."[9] Schindler situated this spatial discovery within a vast evolutionary history of humankind's civilizing of natural forces through which humans achieve, for the first time on earth, a culture worthy of their free spiritual being. This evolutionary shift from civilization to culture marked the formative distinction for Schindler's architectural thinking as a whole. In lecture after lecture

Schindler described this difference as like the one between the newspaper editorial and literature, or what Loos's friend Karl Kraus described as the difference between a chamber pot and an urn.[10] Loos notoriously construed most forms of architecture, as a strictly practical medium, as falling along the chamber pot side of the divide. Against Loos, Schindler defended architecture as an art form. "Arch[itecture] can be Art," he declared. "Usefulness [is] no hindrance as long as purpose influences only 'content' and not conception of form," Schindler wrote in another variation on his distinction between civilization (content) and culture (form).[11] According to Schindler, all architecture prior to his own was prehistoric in the sense that it was *defensive* by nature. "The behavior of our ancestors was overshadowed by constant defense reactions against real and imaginary enemies," he reflected.[12] "Fear dictated originally the form and spirit of the house," and it was fear, he argued, that continued to dictate the form and spirit of functionalism. Functionalism "emanated from the sickbed of a frightened European culture" that was alarmed by the "new culture," by the modern achievement of physical and mental freedom.[13] By fixating on the process of civilization, functionalists were hiding in prehistoric caves whose defensive character was veiled by technological packaging. The expressive language of past architecture derived from its function as bulwark, and its history was the result of a dialogue between this language and evolving structural possibilities. Schindler described artist-architects like Le Corbusier as driven by a "defense reaction" to overcome their training in the visual arts. Their emphatic "use of structural forms seems to be in direct proportion to the limitations of their constructive ability. The architect who is temperamentally unmechanical will be so preoccupied with his handicap that he is likely to accept the solution of the structural problem as the sole aim of his architectural effort."[14] It was specifically the volumetric and sculptural qualities of Le Corbusier's *pictorial* work that were paradoxically reflected by his overemphasis on structural clarity in his architecture.

Schindler concluded that "all architecture of the past . . . was nothing but the work of a sculptor dealing with abstract forms," and that "the aim of all architectural effort was the conquest of structural bulk by man's will for expressive form."[15] He fundamentally believed that the time had come to end this defensive phase of architecture's history. With the "mathematical victory over structural stresses" structure had lost its expressive character. Once architecture had achieved "complete control of Space, Climate, Light, Mood," there was no need to dwell on the process of civilization; the age of fear was over.[16] Space, climate, light, and mood—rather than mass, materials, and structure—were the new coordinates of expressive form making. The architecture that would truly represent the contemporary cultural situation, Schindler argued, would be

POINTS OF VIEW

FUNCTIONALISM AGAIN

PRO

By Richard J. Neutra

EUROPEANS suppose Americans to be a hard-boiled, money-ridden people who are inclined to figure all values in terms of dollars and cents. Therefore they call Americans materialistic. But this is a narrow view, for although dollar-and-cent values are determined by the mechanics of a conventional market, they are frequently influenced by an emotionalism which sales geniuses direct. And thus nature steps in again at the back door.

For example, a Los Angeles realtor may invent a Hollywood Spanish house; then the prospective consumer, immigrating not from Spain but from Iowa, is made to fall into a fervor of purchasing and honestly believes that he is following an old tradition. Falling into a fervor and believing are activities of an emotional nature; and dollar-and-cent computations based on them are by no means so materialistic as Europeans assume.

When the sales talk comes to Spanish, French, or "half-timber" bungalows, it is silently agreed that the price has really not so much to do with these esthetic values as with whether the house has six or seven rooms, one or two baths, a one- or a two-car garage, and two or three coats of paint. Within an individual style class the price is actually governed by floor footage, although Mediterranean roof-tile in pressed cement might cost more than artificially weathered French shingles.

Now beyond any doubt a computation of cost for a real Balearic peasant house would be significantly different from that for a Scandinavian lumber cottage. Fundamentally different techniques and methods are used in these structures, in relation to different materials and different climatic demands. A true computation proportioning correctly the cost of preparatory labor

CONTRA

By R. M. Schindler

I HAVE read with pleasure "Toward a New Architecture" in the Winter issue of the *Southwest Review*. Although I have experimented in architecture for some twenty years, I am not inclined to share the optimistic belief of Messrs. Broad and Ford that we are already well on our way. New needs and new methods of construction do not create architecture. It is impossible to explain the architectural styles on the basis of functional variations. The Egyptian and the Greek temples served very similar needs and were constructed on the basis of very closely related techniques, but with architectural results which are worlds apart.

The source of architectural form is the spirit, and its meaning is a cultural one. This is completely forgotten by the modern "functionalist", who is not an architect at all, but an engineer who has taken to building houses. By being master of our technique and our modes of production he weaves his product into the fabric of contemporary civilization, but can never pretend to be an agent of culture at a time when such a culture does not exist. We are so excited about the marvels of the new mechanical toys which have been presented to us by our inventors that we entirely forget such things as architectural problems.

The line of development of a contemporary architecture lies outside the turmoil of publicizing an international style. I feel that the present status of architecture is one of experimentation with a new medium. Only with the rise of a new culture will the medium be able to convey a meaning.

The program for our architectural work which I suggested back in 1912 is still unfulfilled, and may serve for quite a few years to come:

The cave was the original dwelling. A shallow adobe pile was the first permanent house. To build meant: to gather and

FIGURE 3.3. Richard Neutra, "Points of View: Pro," *Southwest Review,* Spring 1932, and R. M. Schindler, "Points of View: Contra," *Southwest Review,* Spring 1932.

one that "give[s] us [complete] control of our environment, without interfering with our mental and physical nakedness."[17]

In a certain sense Schindler was an unmitigated functionalist. He imagined that the current stage of technological achievement allowed human beings to "manufacture" their "own climate" and to fully harness and domesticate nature by servicing it through "pipes, ducts, and wires."[18] Here Schindler followed Frank Lloyd Wright, who claimed in the Wasmuth portfolio that the machine meant "mastery over an uncivilized land—comfort and resources." The machine, Wright declared, "can only murder the traditional forms of other peoples and earlier times."[19] Schindler echoed Wright's sentiment here when he claimed that the "problems" of civilization "have been solved" and all past "styles are dead."[20] The aspect of functionalism that Schindler rejected was the ideologically charged insistence that *humankind had yet to fully evolve* and that for architecture there were ongoing problems of defense, control, and containment of nature.

Nothing, for instance, could have been more anathema to Schindler's vision of the new culture than Neutra's 1935 designs for the Von Sternberg House (Figure 3.4), which included a "moat," a "medieval scheme of protection" that Neutra insisted "would have to be supplemented by electronic devices to do away with intruders who entered" it; "flipping a switch . . . over the night stand in the bedroom would suddenly electrically charge the water," and Neutra half-jokingly noted that the unexpected budget overrun on the house was due to the "electric incinerator" that would be required "to dispose of the bodies fished out of the moat in the morning" (*LS*, 289). The explicit identification of function with defense at the Von Sternberg House exemplifies the basic aesthetic conflict between Neutra and Schindler.

Everything Schindler rejected he construed as the misplaced expression of "plastic structural mass." The new architecture, by contrast, was not "concerned with objects" but with "shapes and relations," "spaceform, texture and color."[21] "The modern architect conceives the room and forms it with ceiling and wall plates."[22] As Lionel March has argued, Schindler worked with Loos on the *Raumplan* just before he left Vienna, particularly as it bore on Loos's plans for the log house at the Schwarzwald School, an idea that Schindler took up with his 1918 Log House project (Figure 3.5). Unlike Loos's structures, Schindler's projects tend to revolve around a central aesthetic paradox. As March notes of the Log House, it is oriented around the "dominant mass" of the hearth. The hearth, March continues, "rises . . . from the ground as a sculptural, masonry mass some 13' by 6' in plan and 16' high, the chimney itself being a massive 6' × 4' in plan." The hearth, which "occupies one-sixth of the habitable floor space" is "monumental in the ordinary sense of the term."[23] In other words, if space architecture is defined by "surfaces" made up of "thin wall screens," then there is little evidence of it here.

FIGURE 3.4. Richard Neutra, Josef von Sternberg House (Los Angeles, California), 1935. Photograph: Julius Shulman, 1947. Copyright J. Paul Getty Trust. Getty Research Institute, Los Angeles (2004.R.10).

More significantly, virtually every instance of Schindler's space architecture contains a monumental element, and it is this feature that requires explanation. Given Schindler's unmitigated rejection of "sculpture" and massing as a source of architectural meaning, what is the status and role of these clearly defined sculptural elements in Schindler's practice?

Consider, for instance, the street view of the almost finished Kings Road House (Figure 3.6), whose massive concrete outer walls are laid directly on a no less massive concrete slab. Elizabeth Smith rightly notes that their shape derives from Schindler's "idea of a cavelike enclosure" and that the overall appearance of the street façade is not unlike a fortress.[24] That is, its basic form derives from everything that Schindler rejected in both contemporary and past architecture. "The mainspring of primitive life was fear," Schindler observes. "'My house is my castle' shows how that emotion [of fear] adhered to man throughout his development up to the immediate present." In

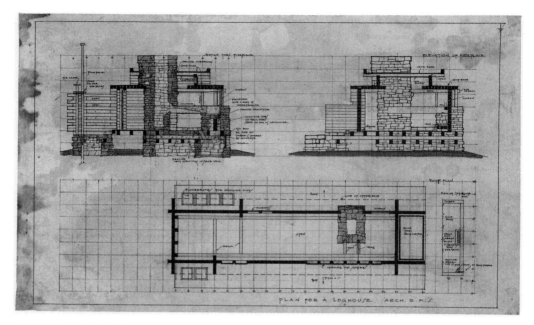

FIGURE 3.5. R. M. Schindler, Log House (project), section through fireplace, elevation of fireplace, and roof plan, 1918. R. M. Schindler Collection, Architecture and Design Collection, Art, Design & Architecture Museum, University of California, Santa Barbara.

the past, houses "tried to appear comfortable by emphasizing their safety through their heavy walls, small windows . . . and dim light."[25]

Such castle-like features as mark the Kings Road House are frequent in Schindler's practice. The best commentators on his work have struggled to account for these sculptural features within his larger project. David Gebhard, Reyner Banham, Esther McCoy, Lionel March, August Sarnitz, and Judith Sheine have all proposed variety, complexity, ambiguity, contradiction, and play as basic aesthetic categories for understanding his work.[26] My account of these monumental features, eruptions of prehistoric form into Schindler's spatial designs, is different and is grounded in Schindler's view of the architect's basic function as "an agent of culture at a time when such a culture does not exist" and in the idea that the medium of space would "be able to convey a meaning" only once a new culture had arisen.[27]

Schindler envisioned his structures as being capable of educating the inhabitants to accept and embrace the new culture, the new freedoms of body and mind that modernity were about to achieve. Schindler's works thus *thematize* this world historical shift from mass to light, from fear to freedom, from civilization to culture, from "shelter"

FIGURE 3.6. R. M. Schindler, Kings Road House (West Hollywood, California), view of concrete walls, circa 1922. R. M. Schindler Collection, Architecture and Design Collection, Art, Design & Architecture Museum, University of California, Santa Barbara.

to "playground," as he put it in a 1926 article for the *Los Angeles Times*. Inhabiting his spaces, one could measure the difference *between* civilization and culture, one could bear continual witness to the conquest of the fear-dominated mass by the floating translucent screen. His structures, that is, bear an evolutionary history inscribed into their forms; they are agents of history, not expressions of a posthistorical world.

If the Log House plan reflects the monumental dimension of Schindler's practice, then his well-known works of the 1930s express his fundamental sense of spatial dialectics. The one-bedroom apartment along the right side of Schindler's Buck House (1934), for example, appears to be one solid sculptural mass, a bulky form that is crucially lifted above and recessed behind the thinly walled surfaces of the house at left (Figure 3.7). The roof at the left seems to almost hover above the wall planes below,

FIGURE 3.7. R. M. Schindler, Buck House (Los Angeles, California), 1934. Photograph: Julius Shulman, 1979. Copyright J. Paul Getty Trust. Getty Research Institute, Los Angeles (2004.R.10).

suggesting the shifting limits of a pure space container within. The opposition between the sculptural volume and the floating planes rehearses the opposition between old and new ages of architecture. As I argue at length in the final section of this chapter, Schindler conceived of the fundamentally conflictual character of his spaces, exemplified by the Buck House and related structures, largely in terms of stasis versus movement, of the 90-degree angle played off against the 45-degree angle.

Schindler's Oliver House (1933–34) (Figure 3.8) displays a similar dialectic between the raised sculptural mass along the right and the thin transparent planes at left, this time reversing the convex-concave orientation of the Buck House, with the convex pressure of the bulking distant plane opposed to the recessed and open street-side container. Schindler's Lovell Beach House of 1926 (Figure 3.9) offers a model for the thematic opposition between mass/plane, sculpture/transparency, structure/space, echoing the play between massing and transparency at the Kings Road House. Although the whole structure is painted one uniform color, the elements are nonetheless meant to be read as functioning in different ways. The northern façade emphatically displays its con-

FIGURE 3.8. R. M. Schindler, Oliver House (Los Angeles, California), 1933. Photograph: Julius Shulman, no date. Copyright J. Paul Getty Trust. Getty Research Institute, Los Angeles (2004.R.10).

crete structural members, which lift the narrow mass of the sleeping porches off the ground, while the recessed and translucent western façade rests on a raised concrete tray. Schindler decoratively treats the large window plane with thin horizontal features as though seeking to model the light that floods into the interior from the unobstructed view toward the ocean. Schindler's treatment of glass walls stands in sharp distinction to Neutra's unobstructed views; for Schindler, every *given* dimension of the world must be remade or shaped by human values in the sense that the architect's hand must be visible (a quality that informs every square inch of the house's design). The hallmark of Schindler's works is this formalized disjunction between the demands of civilization and the freedoms of culture. From Schindler's perspective, Neutra's project failed because Neutra aimed to *willfully harmonize* civilization and culture and by doing so to *deny the autonomy of human culture, to deny its difference from the naturally given.*

FIGURE 3.9. R. M. Schindler, Lovell Beach House (Newport Beach, California), façade facing the beach, 1922–26. R. M. Schindler Collection, Architecture and Design Collection, Art, Design & Architecture Museum, University of California, Santa Barbara.

Neutra's Temporal Architecture

Like Schindler, Neutra was fixated on the idea that architects have the capacity to create culture. And like Schindler and so many modernists, Neutra believed humankind was on the brink of a world historical transformation of its basic material condition. Despite their early conflict over the question of functionalism, the far more basic disagreement between Schindler and Neutra centered on a philosophical, and ultimately political, difference as to the relative importance of *spatial* versus *temporal* design. Neutra prioritized the temporal, noting in his account of functionalism that with the "entrance of the time element into architecture . . . modern civilization distinguishes itself sharply from what has gone before." In one sense, what Neutra was referring to in mentioning the new "time element" was the role of "modern financing" in architectural possibilities. "Paying of interest on loans, specific paper-planning, advance computation of exact cost," he said, all "place a wide gulf between every style of the past and our own."[28] What was new about modern, financed, architecture was that the architect had to foresee possibilities years, even decades, down the road, which meant the amortization period had artistic significance, an idea that Neutra credited to Loos. But by "time element" Neutra was also referring to the fact that the experience of a built environment unfolds over time and changes with the changing lives of its inhabitants.

The preponderance of Neutra's extensive body of writing is devoted to the question of audience response. From the opening page of *Survival through Design* he stresses that designers must "foresee the [widest] range of individual responses" and "program" those responses into their designs from beginning (*SD*, v). It was entirely characteristic of Neutra to suggest that even if it is impossible for an architect to "foresee and gauge every last wrinkle of individuality in all of the people who might someday occupy his design"—a remarkable understatement—it is still the architect's job to grasp as many of these possibilities as conceivable (*NN*, 151). Neutra's commitment to physiology and, specifically, neurology derived from his interest in managing audience response. He argued that "brain physiology" must and in time will be able to "interpret all . . . sociological effects and phenomena" (*SD*, 66). Neutra became increasingly convinced over his long career that all human experience is reducible to neurological terms, and this commitment—one he shared with the designers associated with the Bauhaus both in Germany and the United States—now seems incredibly prescient as well as deeply suspect.

These are the kinds of question Neutra often pondered: "What are these nerves a designer's life effort is concerned with? What can he learn about [nerves] and about their anticipated reactions? What is their response to a stimulus? What occurs in them when impulses travel down the length of their path and hurdle synapses with measureable speed? . . . How does a synapse operate, how is it activated?" (*SD*, 198). With neurology Neutra thought he had discovered the royal road by which he could control all of the "anticipated reactions" to his structures, not just on a day-by-day, moment-by-moment basis but potentially *in perpetuity*. The consequences of an architect's neuronal assault on the inhabitant *unfold over time*: "The 24-hour-a-day, 365-day-a-year stimulus impact of designed environment . . . [will] 'physiologically teach,' by molding the nervous make-up . . . of an adult and the alteration may take place through continuously stimulated neuron extension" (*SD*, 205). A "practical designer," Neutra contended, can "manipulate . . . directly the entire and manifold sense equipment with which his client, the consumer, the human species is endowed. Schools that train the student will be *obliged* to familiarize [the architect] with this physiological keyboard on which he must try to play with understanding and harmony" (*SD*, 201).

Neutra's "physiological keyboard" is an updated version of Kandinsky's comparison of the artist to a pianist, who by "playing on this or that key . . . [can] affect the human soul in this or that way" (*WA*, 160). Neutra's affective keyboard includes heavy artillery against a whole city of pliable human souls. If architects "could grasp more fully all that is involved [in brain physiology], the missiles they devise would reach their aims more effectively and their ballistics would be less accidental. They could conquer many a now toughly resistant rampart. They could almost manipulate at will cortical spreads of excitation and inhibition, as well as inductive effects" (*SD*, 217). Neutra's language, saturated with images of unconscious manipulation and response control—concerns that further displace both the architect's intentionality (he is manipulating "objective" facts) and that of those who engage his structures (they are not agents but pliable nervous systems)—again speaks to issues of defense and survival, placing Neutra in direct opposition to Schindler, whose vision entailed a cultural sublation of nature.

Neutra offered one of his most explicit and public responses to Schindler's spatial aesthetic in a talk he delivered at the School of Architecture at the University of Southern California in 1956. Taking aim at Schindler (who had died three years earlier), Neutra contended that

> architecture is not a space art, but it is a space-time art. You see a morning in the desert. The reflectiveness of the pool is rather symbolic for the intent of the composition. The architecture reflects the mood and the unstable characteristics of a landscape as it changes dynamically during a day or during the seasons of the year.
>
> This is a blue sky with white clouds, you see, coming over the water. The pool looks quite different now, and the wide banks of window draperies are being opened. Modern architecture is capable of dynamically participating more than ever before in the changing moods of the natural setting. . . .
>
> . . . Looking into the cavity of the interior . . . now . . . everything closed, overcast sky, and the whole building seems to be modified, together with the landscape, turned into a new emotive modality or scale.
>
> When the afternoon comes and the sun is low, the building is again different. This has nothing to do with structure. It has nothing to do so much with static forms or colors. Evidently the color play is going on *in nature, surrounding it, merely echoed* by the sensitive man-made . . . assembly, placed within this great nature, which extends from the stars into our innermost being. For all the stimuli of this wide range we have our millions of [sensory] receptors.[29]

The famous pool at the Edgar Kaufmann House in Palm Springs—a nearly ubiquitous image in Neutra's writings and one that has rightly come to signify his practice at large—exemplifies Neutra's basic architectural intentions. The pool is an infinitely changing reflective surface that mirrors the natural surroundings within the static frame of the design. As Neutra describes it, architecture can participate in this dynamically changing environment by echoing the surrounding world. When Neutra speaks of architecture "reflect[ing] the mood and the unstable characteristics of a landscape," he does not mean that the architecture dissolves into the natural setting or even that it is defined by the changing landscape. Rather, he is suggesting that the architect is sensitive enough to respond to the changing environment and *code those changes into the terms of the architectural composition from the beginning*. The pool, then, is an allegory for the architect's total command of the shaped environment. The architect, on this account, is able to include the highest degree of instability within the changing but nonetheless controlled experience of the architectural setting. Julius Shulman's sequentially unfolding photographs of the Kaufmann pool—there were two major early photographic campaigns in 1947 and 1949, both merged into a single view in publications—aim to make Neutra's point at length (Figures 3.10–16).[30]

The sequence of images of the east pool begins with a view looking north across grass and rocks, out toward the house (Figure 3.10), and into the open living room on the left, while drawn curtains close off the bedroom to the right. The next image situates the viewer precipitously, as though hovering over the pool (Figure 3.11), and focuses across the water now on the master bedroom, the interior of which is not visible owing to the drawn curtains. The third image is similar to the second, except now the curtains have been poignantly drawn aside, and, for the first time, we are given a view into the bedroom, as well as a fleeting glimpse of a female inhabitant who appears just to the left of the foreground steel column (Figure 3.12). In the next photograph, the stark objectivity of the previous images is interrupted by the appearance of a young girl seated on a lounge chair (although notably not one of the high-end Van Keppel-Green lounge chairs visible throughout the sequence) looking out at the pool (Figure 3.13) and dwarfed by a massive boulder along her left side, her body partly obscured by the rock. The next view moves away from the pool and house, situating both within a vastly larger terrain, an expansive mountainous landscape, the whole suggestive of an almost cosmic unity (Figure 3.14). This is followed by the most famous photograph of Neutra's career, the evening view with Mrs. Kaufmann reclining on a cushion beside the pool (Figure 3.15), taking in the transition from day to night (on a single sheet of film Shulman took three exposures over forty-five minutes). The dusk-to-twilight image was carefully calculated to achieve at least two things: to draw out formal relationships between disparate elements—notice how Shulman has opened a door in the bedroom that lines up with the vertical line of the chimney, which is analogized to the numinous mountain peaks beyond—and, more centrally, to create an atmosphere that draws together *temporal* and *changing* elements into an overall unity (in this sense the photograph decidedly reiterates the point of the sequence as a whole). The final image is the little-seen nighttime view, laid out with a strict geometry so that the perspective line of

FIGURE 3.10. Richard Neutra, Edgar J. Kaufmann House (Palm Springs, California), 1946. Photograph: Julius Shulman, 1947. Copyright J. Paul Getty Trust. Getty Research Institute, Los Angeles (2004.R.10).

FIGURE 3.11. Richard Neutra, Edgar J. Kaufmann House (Palm Springs, California), 1946. Photograph: Julius Shulman, 1947. Copyright J. Paul Getty Trust. Getty Research Institute, Los Angeles (2004.R.10).

FIGURE 3.12. Richard Neutra, Edgar J. Kaufmann House (Palm Springs, California), 1946. Photograph: Julius Shulman, 1947. Copyright J. Paul Getty Trust. Getty Research Institute, Los Angeles (2004.R.10).

FIGURE 3.13. Richard Neutra, Edgar J. Kaufmann House (Palm Springs, California), 1946. Photograph: Julius Shulman, 1947. Copyright J. Paul Getty Trust. Getty Research Institute, Los Angeles (2004.R.10).

FIGURE 3.14. Richard Neutra, Edgar J. Kaufmann House (Palm Springs, California), 1946. Photograph: Julius Shulman, 1947. Copyright J. Paul Getty Trust. Getty Research Institute, Los Angeles (2004.R.10).

FIGURE 3.15. Richard Neutra, Edgar J. Kaufmann House (Palm Springs, California), 1946. Photograph: Julius Shulman, 1947. Copyright J. Paul Getty Trust. Getty Research Institute, Los Angeles (2004.R.10).

FIGURE 3.16. Richard Neutra, Edgar J. Kaufmann House (Palm Springs, California), 1946. Photograph: Julius Shulman, 1947. Copyright J. Paul Getty Trust. Getty Research Institute, Los Angeles (2004.R.10).

the pool intersects with the horizontal planes of the house at the other end, creating an opaque shimmering substance framed by a grid of lines (Figure 3.16). This sequence was intended to suggest how the architect conceived of his spaces unfolding in time, to indicate how he had fully taken into account the changing visual, emotional, and psychological qualities of the setting from the beginning, programming all aspects of the "24-hour-a-day, 365-day-a-year stimulus impact"—one that imaginatively reaches back to prehistory and forward to the most up-to-date technology—into the design. Neutra contended that these organized experiences of change had profound and lasting effects on the inhabitants of his structures even or especially if the inhabitants were unaware of the degree of formalization.

Neutra saw his time-based architecture as standing in stark contrast to Schindler's spatial abstractions. Schindler's works were, in his view, dead containers of geometrical space projecting the final remnants of a static vision of the universe. Whereas Neutra's time, he believed, was lived, durationally unfolding, Schindler's temporality was spatially *represented*; that is, time was pictured for Schindler's inhabitants.

In chapters 12 through 19 of *Survival through Design,* Neutra offers a critique of Schindler and focuses on the subject of upper-level brain associations, the historical remainders of myth and symbol that are slowly being erased by science. The last great myth, according to Neutra, is the static vision of Euclidean and Newtonian space. To conceive of architecture "in relation to space alone is in itself a defective approach" (*SD,* 185). A "*time-foreign* design appears to by-pass life or cripple it in its most important dimension" (*SD,* 173). Neutra here imagines static spaces as literally incapacitating their inhabitants. "A windowless, dust-proof, air-conditioned hospital ward . . . with measured ultra-violet irradiation to substitute for the health factor of sunshine"—a "statically set interior, from a neural point of view"—compares "unfavorably," he states, without missing a beat, "with the dungeon of old," which "had at least one little grilled window opening, and so provided one important comfort: an ever-changing play of light and color on the walls, the floor, and the heap of straw on which the prisoner rested. The wretched man could at least watch rosy or golden reflections and wandering shadows as the hours and months slipped by" (*SD,* 184–85). Improbable as it is, the prisoner locked in the dungeon and the figure who sits beside the pool in the Shulman photograph share an experience of the space-time continuum, one that Neutra thinks is denied to the inhabitants of Schindler's static structures.

And if Neutra could affirm the Palm Springs–like reflections on the dungeon wall, then he could also envision how architecture was *responsible* for the person who ended up in the dungeon, or at least in the mental hospital. He was fascinated with what he described as the "gravely damaging effect" of neon signs on innocent bystanders. In a 1967 interview, he observed that although neon signs were "only fifteen years old," it

> may be possible to make an adjustment of your organic equipment . . . whereby you can stand glowing red before a black background, but this will take something, I estimate, like 200,000 years! But now you are required to do it immediately. So instead you go to pieces. That is why we have 18,000,000 . . . Americans [annually] cooling their . . . heels in psychiatric waiting rooms. . . . You just wonder how they all found a place to park their cars to get to this psychiatric waiting room, but they *didn't* find a place to park their cars and that is why their nervous system is so disturbed![31]

Neon signs and parking spaces, the finish on a countertop, the sound a floor makes— all create the blind, deaf, and unconscious subjects who encounter them. Neutra's most basic thought revolves around the idea that form produces function, that the shapes that make our environment make the self at its most molecular level, which is why for Neutra what is at stake in the least visible trace of the built environment is our very sanity and survival.

If the neon signs on the highway and the fluorescent lights of the hospital are the negative figures for the fatally spatialized design sense, then the reclining figure beside the pool embodies Neutra's temporally extensive subjective ideal. Neutra imagines us in our capacity as lived subjects as beings who can indulge in a vision of nature as a sequence of "endless complexities," as beings who have security enough to "abandon the effort to understand the world" and to "resign ourselves to the amorphousness around us, as though we were listening to a conversation in a foreign tongue that we have given up trying to understand." As we look out across the reflective surface of the pool, "purposes are forgotten"; "all has turned into a . . . gurgling and tinkling polyphony" (SD, 125–26). As listeners "in leisure," we enjoy "the voices of nature as something . . . lacking any intention, without that order or form which dominates human routine"; we perceive "no rhythmic laws or differentiated notes, but merely sound . . . diffused" (SD, 126). Neutra's ideal listener or viewer looks out on the "endless complexities" of nature, seeing them—quite literally—reflected in, and *programmed into,* the architectural setting but never straining to understand what they mean. Neutra conceives of an exacting proportion between the degree of architectural agency he exerts (although the elements themselves are "objective") and the utter lack of agency exerted by his inhabitants. The more fully he has thought through the least details of the architectural setting, the more fully its inhabitants can give up the effort to understand the world they occupy.

One of Neutra's most compulsively repeated images is that of an astronaut floating in his space capsule. "It will not be just spacemen who will in the end be encapsulated in interesting transparency," he writes in his last published volume. "Ordinary earth dwellers can also daily be regenerated explorers as they look through large clear thermopane glass at windswept tree-tops under morning clouds."[32] Large plates of clear glass, like the one at the Tremaine House in Montecito (Figure 3.17), thus function in the same way as the reflecting pool; they are the upright and vertical equivalents of the horizontal mirror that offers a view onto changing nature. In a dramatic Shulman photograph taken from the living room of the Wise House in San Pedro (1956) looking out at the Pacific Ocean below (Figure 3.18), the Wise children sit hypnotized by the view from the window wall, as does Neutra, characteristically slouched behind them in a Hardoy butterfly chair, all of them passive or anesthetized consumers of a natural spectacle (the two empty chairs in the photograph, in this context, feel more active than the figures, as though the general telos is toward the ground and the endless sea beyond). The architect produces complex settings that generate experiences equal to

FIGURE 3.17. Richard Neutra, Tremaine House (Montecito, California), 1947–48. Photograph: Julius Shulman, 1948. Copyright J. Paul Getty Trust. Getty Research Institute, Los Angeles (2004.R.10).

the "endless complexities" of the natural world, enabling the ideal dweller to linger passively over the changing "panorama of the world."

Neutra and the Meaning of Educational Environments

If the reflective pool and the view through the thermopane window are Neutra's imaginative figures for the kinds of architectural control that are available to the neurodesigner, then school design, or design for children more generally, marks an even more primary figure for Neutra's aesthetic (Figures 3.19 and 5.2). It was obvious to Neutra that the transformative capacities of a house in the desert commissioned by a millionaire offered the experimental (and financial) grounds on which his larger architectural practice could thrive. The endless plasticity of the pool and the changing en-

FIGURE 3.18. Richard Neutra, George E. Wise House (Los Angeles, California), 1956. Photograph: Julius Shulman, 1958. Copyright J. Paul Getty Trust. Getty Research Institute, Los Angeles (2004.R.10).

vironment seen through the window wall were analogs for the plasticity of the human subject in its earliest stages. The healing powers his structures could pass on to their inhabitants were in a sense unnecessary at the primary stages of human development. If he could produce environments for children, then the problem would shift from the healing and survival of the distorted adult to the shaping and nurturing of the unformed child. Healthy inculcation from the beginning would avert the need to address the problem of survival in the future.

It was Neutra's fundamental commitment to the production of subjectivity—healing the adult, creating the child—that made every one of his designs appear as a variant on the famous school projects he produced throughout his life. From the Ring Plan School of 1926 to schools in Puerto Rico from 1943 through 1945 to his final work in 1969 on dormitories at the University of Pennsylvania, Neutra designed and built more

FIGURE 3.19. Richard Neutra, Corona Avenue School (Bell, California), 1935. Photograph: Julius Shulman, 1953. Copyright J. Paul Getty Trust. Getty Research Institute, Los Angeles (2004.R.10).

than 150 structures for educational settings.[33] Even the Lovell House, Neutra insisted, should be understood as an educational environment; its extensive outdoor spaces were designed to make it possible for the client's children to receive an open-air education (Figure 3.20).

Remarkably, for Neutra, the school was too far down the chain of influence; the architect was necessarily involved in the education of children *before they were born*. If the maternal womb presented the perfect architectural design, then birth trauma was being thrust into the architect's arms. "In the moment it is born, the human baby is . . . delivered right into the hands of the hospital architect, *who will remain as powerful as he is* . . . in his ominously influential practice" (*LS*, 273). The architect's "influence . . . confronts us from morning to evening, works on us 'from cradle to the grave,' from the

FIGURE 3.20. Richard Neutra, gymnastic equipment on the southeast side of the Lovell House (Los Angeles, California), 1927–29. Photograph: Willard D. Morgan, circa 1928–29. Copyright Barbara and Willard Morgan Photographs and Papers, Library Special Collections, Charles E. Young Research Library, UCLA.

maternity ward and infant nursery to the funeral parlor; no escape" (*LS,* 271). When Neutra says there is "no escape" from architecture he means that architecture, quite literally, reaches into our chromosomes and alters it:

> [Even w]hat seems hereditary . . . is often influenced by [the architect]. Whether [a mother] spends the months of pregnancy in a cave . . . or in a residence with controlled climate and insulation . . . [these] encompass the designer's influential

FIGURE 3.21. Richard Neutra, Tremaine House (Montecito, California), 1947–48. Photograph: Julius Shulman, 1948. Copyright J. Paul Getty Trust. Getty Research Institute, Los Angeles (2004.R.10).

contributions to what may be early death of the infant or later appear as its inherited constitution. The limits of these contributions and so the formidable powers of design often seem almost beyond scrutiny. (*SD,* 230–31)

Here we are at the limit case of Neutra's vision of temporal design and the furthest limits of intentionality. By imagining, as he seems to here, that design can alter an un-born child's hereditary structure, he gives voice to a conception of absolute architectural agency and an *equally absolute lack of agency* for his audience. Of course, even Neutra's desire for control has little to do with his expressive intent, as the forces he is marshaling are "facts" that are not his, nor do they bear meaning.

In one of his illustrative commentaries on the Tremaine House, Neutra describes the "living space" of the living room as something that "sweeps on through [doors of glass] and reaches out for miles until finally it is closed off by the mountain" (Figure 3.21). The natural world functions as the architectural frame. Is this an instance of nature producing art? Is it an instance of architect formalizing nature? What, or *where*, is the line between art and life? "The mountain," Neutra reflects, "is the 'back wall' of this stupendous living room."[34] Once again, this is not a metaphorical suggestion. Natural and human-made walls produce a kind of symbiotic whole; the building is the lung that nature fills with breath. It is never a matter of *fusion*, of a *merger* between art and life, but rather a matter of mutual exchange. Neutra refuses (Wrightian) fantasies of the house that "sprout[s] from the ground." "The simply sprouting, the *naturally automatic*, has been restrained and replaced by man. If he wants to survive amidst the mass of his new inventions, he must consider deeply and responsibly what is natural in his design and also what cannot be assimilated. The natural must not be defeated. . . . Every human creation is an 'insert,' an addition to that infinite natural landscape."[35] Access to nature is not exactly automatic for Neutra; rather, it is only through the "full-height thin-framed sliding doors of glass" that nature emerges as a vital reality.[36] Within Neutra's structures, nature is continuous with the work by virtue of the stamp of the architect's all-but-invisible and always receding hand. Testing the limits of minimal architectural presence to produce a maximalization of sublime natural effects is the basis of the architect's aesthetic. This does not mean of course that the architecture disappears; rather, a concrete roof slab physiologically registers as protective without obtruding into consciousness as mass.

Schindler and the Site

Compare this set of procedures with Schindler's approach to landscape. David Gebhard notes how in the late 1920s Schindler "divorce[d] the building from its site," observing that the Wolfe House carries the "dissociation between site and man-made object to a dramatic level."[37] Gebhard further points out how the garden at the Rodakiewicz House of 1937 "exemplifies Schindler's view that the surrounding landscape should be left alone, thereby contrasting with the building." Here the eastern and southern patios are treated as "direct, controlled extensions of interior spaces," while the setting that stretches out past these two "precisely bound areas" is akin to a "romantic English garden" with "a dense jungle" beyond.[38] McCoy similarly argues that Schindler's "interest in the garden stopped with the terrace."[39]

How, then, do Schindler's works relate to the world? Consider, for instance, the plan for Schindler's Packard House of 1924 (Figure 3.22), whose eccentric Y-shaped design extends out into three wings, the geometrically organized garden spaces clearly articulated against the terrain around them. Gebhard is mistaken to think that Schindler sharply divorced the work from the site—as Sheine observes, he sought profound connections between work and site, and his elaborate planting schemes aimed to make the

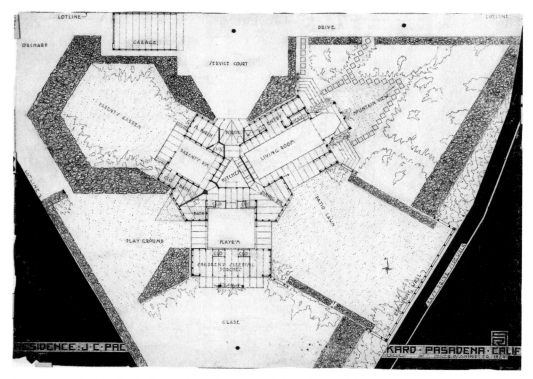

FIGURE 3.22. R. M. Schindler, Packard House (South Pasadena, California), plan, 1924. R. M. Schindler Collection, Architecture and Design Collection, Art, Design & Architecture Museum, University of California, Santa Barbara.

connections deeper over time—but it is essential to see how Schindler distinguished the inside of the work from the outside, that the work/site unity was calibrated to separate itself from the world at large. The dissociation between architecture and world is an instance of Schindler's more fundamental dissociation between civilization and culture. For Schindler, the unaltered landscape and the machine were both marked by *repetition*. Life, like the machine, is endless. "Although rhythmic, [the machine] has no inherent quality of development, no fate," Schindler observes in an unpublished essay on construction. The machine, like nature, has no meaning. Following Loos, Schindler argues that the house must continually "reply to our experiences," it must embody the "unrepeatable" quality of our everyday lives. The house, unlike nature or the machine, is a changing "mirror" of human fate; it is "produced by . . . our cultural, social and etymological surrounding."[40] Like Neutra, Schindler favored the use of the "large sheet of plate glass," but less as a means of extending the frame into nature and more as a "means of living out-of-doors at will."[41] It was the very mobility, the *responsiveness,* of sliding glass doors that he valued; one could leave the interior with only the slightest effort. Schindler valued new materials for their capacity to "respond quickly to our intentions" and to provide "ease and freedom of action."[42] For Schindler, it was imperative that architectural elements respond "fluidly" to human actions; for Neutra, what mattered was that human beings respond to the healing over time that the architect effected by building with nature.[43] The speed and ease with which Schindler hoped his structures would respond to human action matched the projected responsiveness of the works to the processes that would inevitably alter them. Neutra, in contrast, hoped to *anticipate from the start,* to *plan for,* every conceivable mode of responsiveness to his structures. Change—even of the most complex and fantastic degree—was an intended part of each structure from the work's inception.

Neutra's Nature, Schindler's Culture

From a certain angle, the difference between Neutra and Schindler is a version of the difference between Josef Hoffmann and Adolf Loos. Like Hoffmann, Neutra envisioned a mode of architectural design that would encompass every aspect of the built environment. But for Neutra, it was less a matter of explicit control of shaped matter, of the artist's hand manipulating every aspect of the lived space, than of a *maximum surplus of environmental imponderables,* aspects of design that receded from the inhabitant's eye but were all the more effective by virtue of their lack of visibility.

Neutra's emphatic commitment to an ideal and imagery of change, variety, and duration defined itself against Schindler's vision of architecture as "space-forms . . . visualized and created in [the architect's] mind."[44] If Neutra's design spaces are oriented around the changing forms of water and the changing views through thermopane windows, then Schindler's spaces are organized around a humanly scaled system of modular units (Neutra's modules, by contrast, were intentionally dissolved into the total experience). The architect, Schindler insisted, "must establish a unit system which he can easily carry in his mind."[45] This extratemporal "mental image" held in the architect's mind could be manipulated to produce highly complex spatial arrangements organized around a simple modular unit.[46] The idea went back to Schindler's 1916 Church School lectures; in the notes for them, he warned that students should "not start to draw before everything is shaped by your mind—conception not to surpass reach of imagination."[47] The opposition between Neutra and Schindler is an opposition between the management of experience, on the one hand, and the spatial realization of the architect's idea, on the other. Ultimately, this is a difference about what architecture is and what kind of agency an architect exercises. For Neutra, the "sheer endless experience" of shape existed prior to, and gave rise to, every codified form of human experience (*LS,* 239).

Those shapes that make our environment could either destroy or save humanity, and that is why we need architects to protect us from pernicious shapes and surround us with healthy ones. Schindler, by contrast, maintained that architectural agency should not be confused with *and could never replace* human agency. For Schindler, the survival of humanity depended not on design but on its limits, on designers' knowing and thematizing the difference between art and life, between culture and civilization.

Impermanent Civilization, Permanent Culture

For Schindler, permanence connoted a cultural value, and to confuse it with civilization was to mistake fear for freedom. Civilization is fear based, and its expression is a massing against an unknown threat. Culture, by contrast, expresses freedom, and its architectural expression is the house as "playground": it is close to the ground and is a "simple weave" of inexpensive materials; the walls are "few, thin, and removable"; all of the rooms are part of an "organic unit"; the garden is part of the house; the difference between indoors and out is fluid.[48]

When Neutra came to address the nature of permanence and impermanence, he distinguished between commodities and housing, a hard distinction that Schindler and, later, the Eameses refused to make. While "ladies' apparel may be designed to last only for a season," Neutra writes, it would be a "sorry mistake to be similarly carefree or arbitrary in designing a house" (*SD*, 122). Impermanence is "indigenous" to the world of "hectically changing fashions," but in building, "such fashionable changes first bewilder the consumer and then repel him" (*SD*, 62). Chapter 36 of *Survival through Design* takes up the subject of disposable commodities; for Neutra their interest lies exclusively in their distinction from architecture. In terms of "movable belongings, one cannot but notice that they have . . . increased in number but decreased in permanency" (*SD*, 258). In the past, the "feeling of having, of owning, things was very conscious and permanent, while use . . . was rarer and more intermittent" (*SD*, 258). That trend has reversed: now use is the proper index to quality (*SD*, 260). Nowadays "possession has become less enduring, more fluctuating, and in more and more cases it tends to be superseded, even obliterated, by the idea of use" (*SD*, 259). Neutra measures the distance traveled from "treasured family china to cardboard picnic dishes and Lily cups, from grandmother's linens to paper napkins, paper handkerchiefs, and perhaps paper underwear discarded after a single use" (*SD*, 259). Whatever "ingrained aversion" there might be against the "tendency to impermanence," it is "unavoidable in a civilization of inexpensive, mass-produced commodities." The trade-off for the "abandonment of permanence" is classically modernist in formulation: "less subsequent toil to restore, to repair, to clean" (*SD*, 259).

But impermanent commodities are the equal and opposite of permanent housing. Neutra's psychological point is that all aesthetic "appeals should be graded with respect to their duration" (*SD,* 121). The "basic rule" for creative practice, he explains, is the "anticipated duration of exposure and appeal." As I have argued, Neutra nursed profound fantasies concerning his capacity to anticipate future uses. The exposure and appeal of commodities is short-lived; that of architecture long. Not surprisingly, Neutra construes this "neuromental criterion" as having sublime consequences: "Neglect or disregard of the relevance of the time factor in design is a frequent and yet a fatal sin" (*SD,* 122).

Neutra's view of women's fashion stands in sharp contrast to that of his mentor, Loos. Loos saw fashion in terms of the progressive evolution of "self-determination" *(Selbstbestimmung)* (*OC,* 109). Free employment for men and women lent itself to forms of clothing that allowed physically free movement. That both men and women could wear trousers reflected as well as facilitated their free employment and increasingly liberated their mental worlds (*OC,* 110). Moving into a "newer, greater age," women no longer needed to "appeal to sensuality" or use the whole ornamental apparatus of "silk and satins, ribbons and bows, frills and furbelows" to achieve equal status with men. Through growing "economic and intellectual independence," the "new woman" would "become equal with men," and both would shed their ornamental clothing (*OC,* 111).

Schindler closely follows Loos in his commitment to contemporary forms of "self-realization." Cultural problems are "problems of growth and development of the human being himself. Its products are the result of self-realization."[49] Like Loos, Schindler construes self-realization as a sweeping evolutionary process that encompasses both the "house and the dress of the future," each defined in terms of the extent to which it controls "our environment, without interfering with our mental and physical nakedness."[50] Mental and physical culture are on the same trajectory, leading to a future in which matter will be impermanent and mind permanent. Schindler concludes his "Furniture and the Modern House" with a celebration of "light," the last artistic medium. Humankind's "power will be complete," he writes, "when the present primitive glass wall develops into the translucent light screen."[51] For Schindler, the glass wall is "primitive" because it still reads as a wall, albeit a transparent one. What is valuable about the new materials is not their innate qualities but their responsiveness to the will. The role of clothing, like that of architecture, is to reflect and assist in the expression of the full range of human intentionality.

Schindler downplays the significance of the materials in order to prioritize human agency, in direct opposition to the Bauhaus approach. His structures express a general impatience with materials. "Structural materials, walls, ceilings, floors, are only means to an end," he explains. "They lose their individual importance and are simplified to the utmost—a simple weave of a few materials articulates space into rooms."[52] McCoy describes Schindler's "particular vision" as one predicated on the view that "materials, even the structural systems he developed, were always incidental." Schindler discovered how to "organize forms irrespective of structure."[53] Schindler pursued his ideal vision of cultural progress toward the pure medium of space with his translucent house project for Aline Barnsdall in 1927, and first realized his vision fully in three late translucent houses—the Janson (1948–49; Figures 3.29–3.30), Tischler (1949–50; Figures 3.32–3.33), and Skolnik (1950–52; Figures 3.51–3.53) Houses. Everything that he found problematic about the sculpted matter of past architecture was capable of being redeemed through the sculpted character of immaterial light. "The character and color of the light issuing from [the translucent screen] will permeate space, give it body and make it as palpably plastic as is the clay of the sculptor."[54] It would be no exaggeration to say that Schindler's deepest motivation was to achieve the translucent house, an architecture that would represent the full expression of human self-realization. As he declares in the final line of "Furniture and the Modern House": "Only after the space architect has mastered the translucent house will his work achieve its ripe form."[55] A colored screen transforms the glass wall into colored radiance, altering the character of everything in the house. Colored light is the final "medium to serve as the vehicle for human expression."[56] Schindler declares in his manifesto that it is the "mind" that "destroyed the power of the tyrant." It is the mind that is "asking for its monument."[57] The translucent house is the ideal expression of the possibilities of culture, and the impermanence of light is the best figure for the permanence of mind. It was in Schindler's last works, in the period from 1945 until his death in 1953, that he gave his fullest expression of translucent architecture as well as explored an entirely novel conception of the nature of the plan. In the last works, the house itself became a figure for the impermanence of the material world and the enduring character of mind. At the end Schindler conceived of every aspect of built space as potentially transfigured by colored light and turning under one's feet as though in the slow rotation of a cosmic dance.

Late Schindler: Rotational Spaces

In the Introduction, I considered Schindler's special relation to the core problematics of connection, a problem he shared with a younger generation of architects who, at least in part, looked to him as a model. Here, I want to consider Schindler as part of that younger generation, Schindler at midcentury (1945–53), when his concerns were in many ways in advance of his younger colleagues in terms of his commitment to a vision of impermanence predicated on a novel way of conceiving architectural space as

FIGURE 3.23. R. M. Schindler, James E. How House, exterior, frontal view (Los Angeles, California), 1925. R. M. Schindler Collection, Architecture and Design Collection, Art, Design & Architecture Museum, University of California, Santa Barbara.

fully dynamic—specifically, as *rotational*. Before I consider that moment in Schindler's career, the final seven years of his practice, I need to establish the basic premises of his work prior to 1945.

Following his own Kings Road House of 1921 (Figure 3.6), his next major achievement was the concrete and redwood How House of 1925 in Silver Lake (Figure 3.23). At street level, the house appears to be a single, compact story sheathed in wood, its basic character evoking a cube or boxlike shape. From the back it emerges as a two-story structure hugging the side of a hill, the lower section comprising massive slab-cast concrete walls that join the redwood boards at the upper register. Creating a prominent visual feature across the whole exterior are the 16-inch-wide horizontal lines incised into the concrete, which are mirrored (and reversed) in the protruding drip strips on the redwood above. The lines, which establish a sense of seemingly endless continuity across the variety of surfaces, derive from the wood formwork used to create the concrete walls as well as from the moldings inserted between the wood boards. As I noted in the Introduction, it is basic to Schindler's approach to turn practical features of a structure into a thematic motif for the whole. Making meaning out of the functional, as Schindler sees it, marks the difference between civilization and culture.

While the plan is emphatically square, with a series of projecting porches and terraces, the main experiential axis slices through the square at a 45-degree angle (Figure 3.24). Everything in the space is oriented around the dramatic diagonal axis of symmetry that cuts through the living room and is further expressed in the ceiling forms as well as the mitered corner windows leading to the terrace. By introducing a dramatic double cantilever above the two fireplaces, Schindler hollows out the core of the square, emptying it of its mass, further opening up the core to provide vertical and horizontal transparency from the corner window (at the entrance) through to the terrace and the view beyond.

It was with the Bergen Free Library project of 1920 that Schindler first introduced an emphatic 90-degree/45-degree orientation, a structural arrangement that defined his body of work from 1920 through 1944 (Figure 3.25). Here, roughly a dozen square and rectangular spaces are ordered into a broad L, and the seemingly emphatic quality of stasis projected by the 90-degree orthogonal is assertively undercut by the 45-degree angle of the entranceway, which reaches right into the center of the building and terminates at the perpendicular of the central book counter. Schindler continued to play with more and more complex variations on the static and the dynamic, setting up seemingly stable forms that were then subtly but also continuously undermined by the presence of 45-degree angles. McCoy rightly stresses the active character of Schindler's spaces, insisting that his houses are "in movement; it is in becoming. Form emerges from form" (*EMR*, 73). The sense of movement is set in play by the counterpoint of an immobile square, an inert form that is forced—in McCoy's romantic turn of phrase—to take flight "like a bird that has just touched earth, its wings still spread but at once part of the earth" (*EMR*, 73). Schindler described his aim as dislodging the static character of "formal harmonies."[58] The closed formal harmony of the box suggested to him a wide range of premodern feelings associated with defense, security, and fear of the outside world.

In his early work Schindler embraced concrete as the most modern material, one that was visibly free of the constraints of structural expression. Concrete was especially expensive during the Great Depression, so he shifted his practice to plaster-skin design (1930–44), essentially wood frame covered in stucco, the whole structure seemingly extruded from a single pliable material covering inside and out. As Schindler explained it, in plaster-skin design, "all surfaces of the structural skeleton are covered by a plaster coating which then speaks with its own form vocabulary."[59] The Buck House of 1934

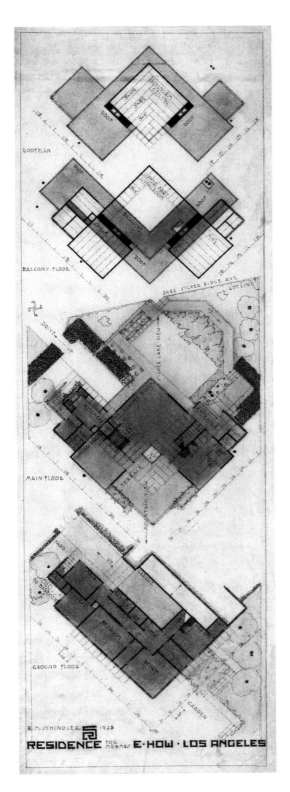

FIGURE 3.24. R. M. Schindler, James E. How House, presentation drawing (Los Angeles, California), 1925. R. M. Schindler Collection, Architecture and Design Collection, Art, Design & Architecture Museum, University of California, Santa Barbara.

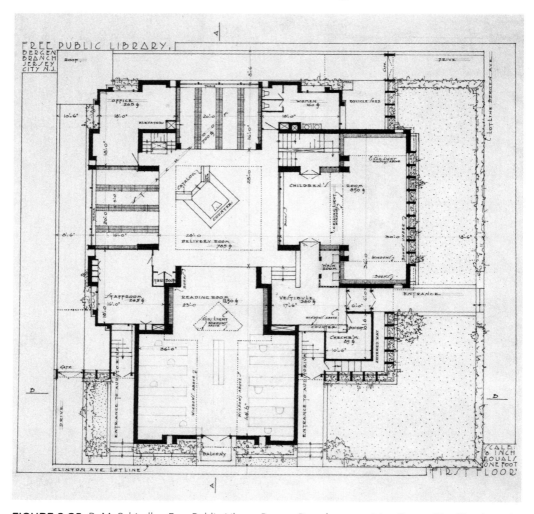

FIGURE 3.25. R. M. Schindler, Free Public Library Bergen Branch competition (Jersey City, New Jersey), 1920. R. M. Schindler Collection, Architecture and Design Collection, Art, Design & Architecture Museum, University of California, Santa Barbara.

is a particularly lucid expression of the plaster-skin approach (Figure 3.7). The plan of the Buck House is a double L, with one L formed by a three-bedroom house wrapping around a large patio and the second L defining a private patio for a one-bedroom apartment over the garage (Figure 3.26). As is almost always the case with Schindler, one enters the house at the knuckle of the primary L, where one is exposed to a long diagonal view into and across the patio. As at the How House, the inhabitant experiences mixed signals from the pervasive use of right-angle shapes against the strong 45-degree angle

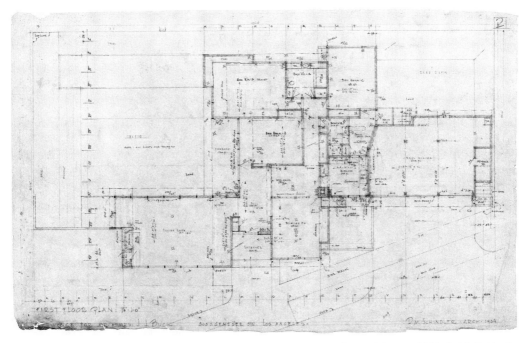

FIGURE 3.26. R. M. Schindler, John J. Buck House, plan (Los Angeles, California), 1934. R. M. Schindler Collection, Architecture and Design Collection, Art, Design & Architecture Museum, University of California, Santa Barbara.

that slices through the right angles, destabilizing the static shape and putting into motion the inert character of the "formal harmony" of the square. A similar expression of movement occurs throughout the seemingly infinite play of concave and convex boxes that define the exterior and interior spaces. While the "boxes" themselves are set at 90-degree angles, as they project away from or cut into the wall, the 45-degree angles of the corners, producing shadows, become active presences that set the square into motion.

Throughout the 1930s and 1940s, Schindler wrung innumerable changes from the 90-degree/45-degree push and pull of "cubes" at the levels of both the plan and the façade, as well as innumerable interior details, including ceiling heights and built-in furniture. In an essay first published in 1967, McCoy offers a useful interpretation of the broadly "cubist" approach to the plan in Schindler's pre-1945 work, what she describes as the "ever-changing relationship between solid and void":

My special feeling for the buildings of the '30s comes from the way in which the cube is formed and reformed; and yet the cube is implicit in the subtle movement in and through the geometric form. [Schindler] carved so delicately at the geometry of the spaces that certain forms almost but not quite detached themselves from the overall form to create their own hierarchy of spaces. Then they rejoin the whole. (*EMR*, 105)[60]

In an unpublished essay McCoy similarly observes how Schindler's "forms were concentrated but, as the observer moved around them, they dissolved and reappeared in new contexts."[61] As McCoy tells it, Schindler's 1930s structures relied on his constant and seemingly infinite capacity to break down, dislodge, and reform the cube. The continually shifting sense of movement between solid and void, concave and convex, derived from the constant pressure of the 90-degree angles of the cube playing against the implicit 45-degree angles of the corners, as well as the dominant axis of the structure.

It was not until 1944, with the Bethlehem Baptist Church in south-central Los Angeles, his one and only religious structure, that Schindler appears to have wrung his last effective change from the 90-degree/45-degree contrast and reached the limits of "cubist" space (Figure 3.27). As several commentators have observed, Bethlehem Baptist bears a striking resemblance to the How House of twenty years earlier (Figure 3.23). The two buildings are similar in terms of materials—the stucco exterior bands at Bethlehem mirror the redwood siding at the How House—and, more significantly, in terms of their plans. The interior sweep of Bethlehem Baptist reiterates the diagonal thrust of the How House, although the contrast, essentially a scaling up of secular effects for a religious space, has slackened. It is here at Bethlehem Baptist, I would suggest, that the diagonal impulse no longer provides the kind of expressive effect of unsettling the inactive character of the square; it has become a kind of theatrical tool, one that has settled into a new kind of formal order (Figure 3.28). The comparison with the How House suggests, as Gebhard first observed, that it was with Bethlehem Baptist that Schindler began to exhibit an "increased tendency . . . to look back to his own past, in a sense to plagiarize a number of his earlier concepts."[62] Gebhard's charged assertion of plagiarism is surely overdrawn. Rather than plagiarism, what Schindler engaged in after Bethlehem Baptist Church might more accurately be described as a wholesale process of retrospection and revision.

In the wake of Bethlehem Baptist, Schindler began to make the seemingly inevitable comparisons between his later and earlier works an explicit and active, rather than simply passive, part of his expressive program. In this period, he turned to the past for raw material for a new mode of expressing movement, one that elaborated on and revised the earlier 90-degree/45-degree approach.

The Ellen Janson House of 1948–49, perhaps the ne plus ultra of Schindler's impermanent architecture, was made for his girlfriend, the poet Ellen Janson, and Schindler spent the last days of his life there (he died of cancer at sixty-five, four years after the

FIGURE 3.27. R. M. Schindler, Bethlehem Baptist Church (Los Angeles, California), 1944. Photograph: Julius Shulman, 1949. Copyright J. Paul Getty Trust. Getty Research Institute, Los Angeles (2004.R.10).

FIGURE 3.28. R. M. Schindler, Bethlehem Baptist Church (Los Angeles, California), 1944. Photograph: Julius Shulman, 1949. Copyright J. Paul Getty Trust. Getty Research Institute, Los Angeles (2004.R.10).

FIGURE 3.29. R. M. Schindler, Ellen Janson House (Los Angeles, California), 1948–49. R. M. Schindler Collection, Architecture and Design Collection, Art, Design & Architecture Museum, University of California, Santa Barbara.

house was built) (Figure 3.29). One of the most striking features of the house is the highly uncharacteristic exposure, or dramatic overelaboration, of the building's structural, weight-bearing materials. The crisscrossing latticework of the base projects a strong sense of unfinish, as though architectural scaffolding has been left in place at the construction site. McCoy evocatively describes the house as a "jack-in-the-beanstalk structure; it grew like a light vine from the bottom of canyon up to the road, clinging to the narrow ledge of the level land at the top by structural tendrils."[63] Janson, in her 1952 book of poems dedicated to Schindler, describes a "Bamboo House" whose "intricate clamor of leaves . . . Marshall the light."[64] Gebhard, glossing the effects of impermanence at the house, reflects how the "general feel" of the structure is that of "incompleteness, as if the builder had through neglect left his temporary scaffolding behind, or as if upon being built it was found that the layered boxes would fall down the hillside unless some quickly erected supports were desperately put into place."[65] Beanstalk, bamboo, or scaffold, the emphasis has shifted to the tensile framework for the structure, as the boxlike living space is delicately poised atop a sea of sticks, threatening to topple with a strong breeze.

The plan is a shallow cruciform defined by a series of balconies, terraces, and trellises angling out from the base (Figure 3.30). The walls at the corners are "translucent," made of colored fiberglass panels so that the interior space changes colors as sunlight passes from east to west. At night the lighted corners would "release color into the air" as Schindler sought to project the colors outward into the space around the house, further dematerializing the square.[66] Sheine rightly observes that the Janson House is a "direct commentary" on one of Schindler's early designs, the Monolith House of 1919, sketched while he was working for Wright (Figure 3.31).[67] In terms of the plan, the Janson and Monolith Houses are nearly identical and rather severely boxlike. And yet at the Janson House, Schindler has reversed the polarity, so to speak, of the solid and void of the earlier design, turning the "monolith" into a treehouse. What was massive, weighted, and compact about the 1919 house is made thin and fragile, turned literally and figuratively into light.

Similar concerns underlie the aims of the Tischler House of 1949–50 near the University of California, Los Angeles (Figure 3.32). This is Schindler's most extreme expression of his dream of a "translucent house," as the gabled roof is composed of blue corrugated fiberglass, so that a powerful blue hue is projected over the whole of the interior (Figure 3.33). Like the Janson House, the Tischler House takes up an earlier work and reverses the polarities between mass and light, opacity and transparency. The living room of the Tischler House reverses the terms of the 1924 Packard House (Figure 3.34) and once again inverts the basic character of the two spaces. At the Janson House, Schindler engages the monolithic box, and at the Tischler House he takes up

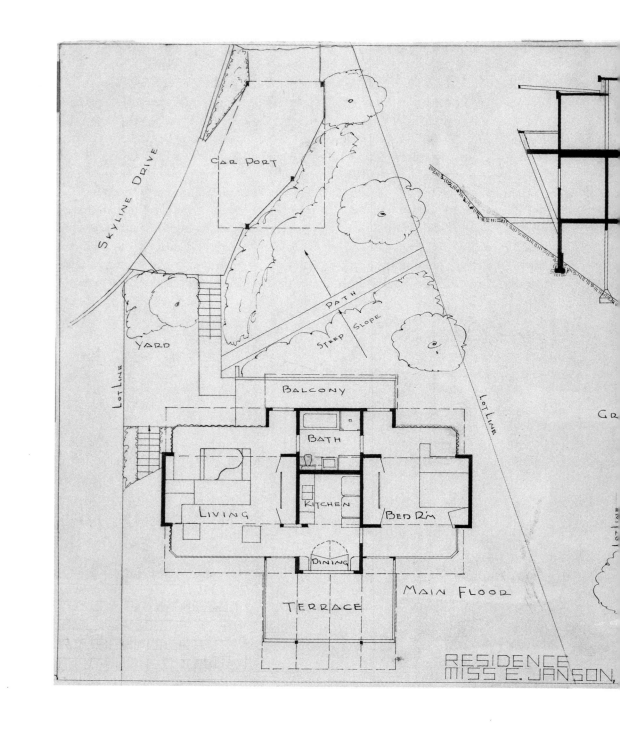

SKYLINE DRIVE

CAR PORT

PATH

STEEP SLOPE

YARD

LOT LINE

LOT LINE

BALCONY

BATH

LIVING

KITCHEN

BED RM

DINING

MAIN FLOOR

TERRACE

GR

RESIDENCE
MISS E. JANSON

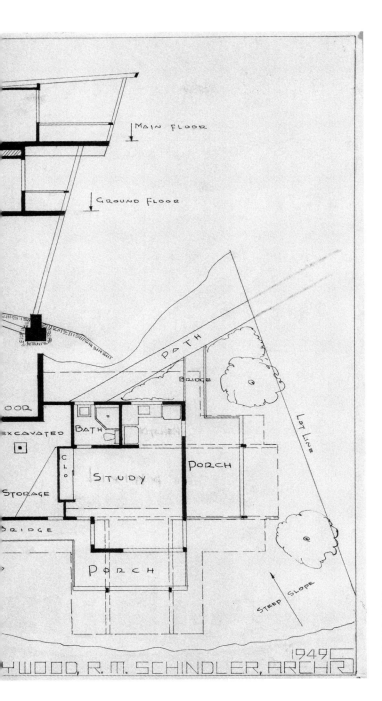

MAIN FLOOR

GROUND FLOOR

PATH

BRIDGE

LOT LINE

OOR

EXCAVATED BATH

CLO STUDY PORCH

STORAGE

BRIDGE

PORCH

STEEP SLOPE

1949

YWOOD, R. M. SCHINDLER, ARCH

FIGURE 3.30. R. M. Schindler, Ellen Janson House, plan (Los Angeles, California), 1948–49. R. M. Schindler Collection, Architecture and Design Collection, Art, Design & Architecture Museum, University of California, Santa Barbara.

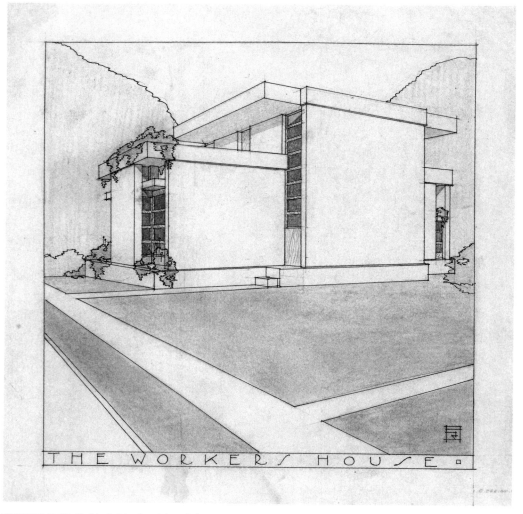

FIGURE 3.31. R. M. Schindler, Monolith House, perspective sketch of exterior, 1919. R. M. Schindler Collection, Architecture and Design Collection, Art, Design & Architecture Museum, University of California, Santa Barbara.

the gabled roof associated with religious spaces. What is solid, weighted, and dark at the Packard House becomes void, colored transparency, or glass at the Tischler House.

For Schindler, the return to and revision of these earlier designs, turning the permanent impermanent, emerged alongside a related and ultimately deeper investigation of the nature of the plan. If the pre-1945 work expresses a many-sided conflict between solid and void, orthogonal and diagonal, symmetry and asymmetry, down to the

FIGURE 3.32. R. M. Schindler, Adolph Tischler House, view from the street (Los Angeles, California), 1949–50. Photograph: Marvin Rand. R. M. Schindler Collection, Architecture and Design Collection, Art, Design & Architecture Museum, University of California, Santa Barbara.

FIGURE 3.33. R. M. Schindler, Adolph Tischler House, view from living room to terrace (Los Angeles, California), 1949–50. Photograph: Lotte Nossaman, circa 1950. R. M. Schindler Collection, Architecture and Design Collection, Art, Design & Architecture Museum, University of California, Santa Barbara.

smallest elements of design, then beginning in 1945 Schindler's approach expresses a new commitment to qualities of *rotation* or *turning,* suggesting something like the lived experience of the rotation of a wheel, a fan, a watch, a compass, or a cog, or, most suggestively and explicitly, the turning and rolling of a body bathing in the light of the sun. The strong sense of rotation is evident in the entrance path along the right side of the Tischler House, in the circular shape of the workshop on the mezzanine level, and, above all, at the entrance to the house on the upper floor, where one is ushered in and around the central fireplace, with its metal hood's sweeping and reflective curves. The whole structure seems to be set in motion, turning around the freestanding fireplace (Schindler includes an "arrow" shape on the plan at the mezzanine level as though to notate the direction of the circular movement).

FIGURE 3.34. R. M. Schindler, Packard House, living room (South Pasadena, California), 1924. R. M. Schindler Collection, Architecture and Design Collection, Art, Design & Architecture Museum, University of California, Santa Barbara.

While referring specifically to the interior of the Skolnik House, McCoy effectively sums up the character of Schindler's late houses in general: "essentially a carousel, an open space with a merry-go-round in the middle."[68] In his late work Schindler conceived of the house not as the struggle to mobilize the static shape of the square but rather as something that is never static to begin with, as though it were always in perpetual rotational motion around a still center. This turning effect was the product of

Schindler's new interest in eccentric angles, especially his elaborated use of 15-degree angles throughout his later work.

Schindler signaled the change of his late period with an important essay titled "The Schindler Frame," illustrated with Shulman photographs and published in *Architectural Record* in 1947. Here Schindler notes that the new framing system allows him to cut all wall studs at 6 feet, 8 inches, or door height, above which he inserts a clerestory course capped with a roof or, more often, a series of roof planes. The Tischler House provides a clear expression of the new frame as the light from the clerestory illuminates the interior from all directions. These multiple light sources have the effect, in Schindler's words, of "forcing all objects in [the space] to become active parts" of the composition.[69] Again, the point for Schindler is about "forcing" any potentially *inactive* given or static elements of the space to become activated, meaningful, a quality he achieves in part through the interplay of roof planes and clerestory lighting as they modify all the elements in the space below.

"The Schindler Frame" opens with a Shulman photograph of the living room of the Gold House, an image that elaborates on the ways in which light pours in at different heights around the room. Directly to the right of where Shulman stood to take this photograph, Schindler introduces a highly expressive statement of his late approach to the plan. At the entrance to the house, Schindler offers a kind of programmatic expression of two overlapping coordinate systems (Figure 3.35). It is programmatic in that the two angles are placed side by side, as though offering an illustration of how the house as a whole is organized. A column floats in space, with the lower half articulating a 45-degree turn of the partition wall for the dining room (to the left), while the upper part, situated a few inches back, follows the beam and outlines the 90-degree angle of the living room. It is as though the 90-degree angle is *balanced on* the 45-degree angle beneath it, giving priority to the tilted center of gravity over and against the stable orthogonal shape of the living room.

The ways in which Schindler overlaps the two coordinate systems is still a bit hesitant at the Gold House, as he is still ordering spaces in terms of 90- and 45-degree angles, even if those angles begin to generate increasingly eccentric shapes. The dining room, breakfast nook, and both bedrooms expose and elaborate the two overlapping coordinates rather than attempt to mitigate or reconcile the angles into a larger whole. The breakfast nook, in particular (it was destroyed long ago), in the shape of hexagon, picks up the curved shape of the patio and the lawn, exemplifying the sense of rotation that suffuses one's sense of the space as a whole.

Beginning with the Kallis House of 1946 in Studio City, Schindler opened a new direction in his work (Figure I.21). Once again, the door height datum at 6 feet, 8 inches creates a continuous line that runs throughout the whole of the house (Figure 3.36).

FIGURE 3.35. R. M. Schindler, J. Gold House, living room (Los Angeles, California), 1940–41. Photograph: Todd Cronan, 2021.

FIGURE 3.36. R. M. Schindler, Maurice Kallis House and Studio, living room (Los Angeles, California), 1946. Photograph: Grant Mudford. Courtesy of Grant Mudford.

Above the door height, Schindler inserts a clerestory course over which floats a thin roof plane, creating the effect that the roof hovers free in space. A characteristic detail emerges along the upper region of the wall shared by the living room and bedroom as Schindler pulls back the wall to create a cutaway. Here, as elsewhere, Schindler pierces the walls below the horizontal datum so that one can literally see and, more important, *feel* the continuity between rooms, as though the walls form temporary enclosures within one larger space. In order to reinforce the sense of total continuity, Schindler goes a step further than clerestories and cutaways, canting the walls of the house outward (below) and inward (above) at 15-degree angles. As Sheine describes it, the "angled plywood . . . helps to turn [the overall shape] into a volume rather than just a wall."[70] In a sense, the difference between a 105-degree or 75-degree angle and a 90-degree angle is subtle, but it is also all the difference in the world. It is the moment when a "formal harmony" becomes a vital force—it is the instant one begins to *notice* the shape of the space, as though for the first time.

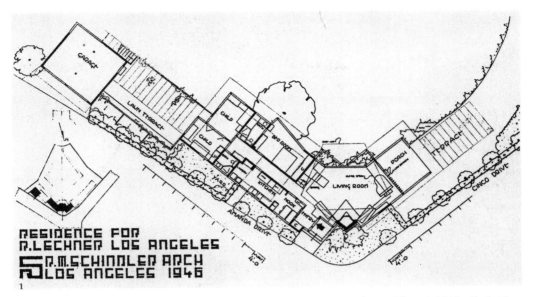

RESIDENCE FOR R.LECHNER LOS ANGELES
R.M.SCHINDLER ARCH LOS ANGELES 1946

FIGURE 3.37. R. M. Schindler, Richard Lechner House, plan (Los Angeles, California), 1946–48. R. M. Schindler Collection, Architecture and Design Collection, Art, Design & Architecture Museum, University of California, Santa Barbara.

It is tempting to read Schindler's introduction of the 15-degree angle, a design feature that is ubiquitous in the late work, as driven by the nature of the site or some explicitly practical purpose. Writing of the A. van Dekker project of 1947, Jin-Ho Park and Joung-Lan Park observe that it is "regulated by angles of 30°, 60°, 90°, and 120°." They suggest that the "method of employing the various angles" may be "a result of the drafting equipment [Schindler] used, such as the T-square and 30°–60° and 45° triangles."[71] Most readings assume that the eccentric angles are driven by the siting of the structure. But, as I am arguing, a strictly functionalist reading would be a mistake. Schindler writes of accepting the "odd angle[s] of the lot lines" and then using them as a motif to "introduce[ ] similar angles into the shape of the rooms."[72] As Gebhard rightly notes, writing of the 1946 Toole House, which is situated on flat land, it is "not the irregularity of the terrain of a site that led to this violation of the world of the rectangle."[73] Rather than the terrain or practical need, Schindler's violation of the 90-degree/45-degree approach is driven by an expressive need to set the structure into motion, to destabilize every static feature of the house and set it on edge.

The Richard Lechner House, also in Studio City, has a plan similar to that of the Kallis House (Figure 3.37). It too spreads out along the landscape, this time at a 100-degree angle. The living room of the Lechner House is perhaps the most expressive and dramatic of Schindler's career. As at the Kallis House, the thin roof plane, here in

FIGURE 3.38. R. M. Schindler, Richard Lechner House, living room (Los Angeles, California), 1946–48. Photograph: Robert C. Cleveland, circa 1951. R. M. Schindler Collection, Architecture and Design Collection, Art, Design & Architecture Museum, University of California, Santa Barbara.

the shape of a pentagon, feels as though it floats on top of the structure, lifting it up to the view and sloping back toward the fireplace (Figure 3.38). The plan is more complex than at the Kallis House. Here, there are two rectangles: a kind of prime or "A" rectangle along the left that contains the kitchen, bedrooms, lawn terrace, and garage; and a second or "B" rectangle on the right that comprises the porch and terrace. The two rectangles come to a head in the living room, where the two shapes overlap to create a third space that combines the two tilted 90-degree rectangles (Figure 3.37). Schindler reinforces the sense in which the two rectangles collide when he shows how the B rectangle bursts through the wall of the A rectangle. This intersection or collision is visibly expressed in the wall of the bedroom, which swings out at 15 degrees from the façade. The line created by this 15 degrees carries through and makes present the lower edge

FIGURE 3.39. R. M. Schindler, Richard Lechner House, living room (Los Angeles, California), 1946–48. Photograph: Robert C. Cleveland, circa 1951. R. M. Schindler Collection, Architecture and Design Collection, Art, Design & Architecture Museum, University of California, Santa Barbara.

of the B rectangle. One is meant to feel how the coordinate systems overlap but do not sync up, as though there is some larger third coordinate system, one that is *not visible* that would bind all of the elements together.

Running down the center of the living room is an imaginary axis that passes from the massive fireplace out through the window to the view of the valley beyond (Figure 3.39). What is unmistakable about the central living space is the sense of friction between it and the various coordinate systems, as though it were part of a larger but unknown set of coordinates. The dominant conflict is that between the 100-degree angle spread of the house with a 50-degree vertex running through the fireplace and the two 90-degree angles of the rectangles—A and B—that form the main body of the house. Schindler draws every feature of the house into the spatial dynamic, including built-in sofas, freestanding furniture, a trellis extending from the fireplace, soffits, the clerestory, and

FIGURE 3.40. R. M. Schindler, Richard Lechner House, presentation drawing (Los Angeles, California), 1946–48. R. M. Schindler Collection, Architecture and Design Collection, Art, Design & Architecture Museum, University of California, Santa Barbara.

a flying beam that cuts across the ceiling. I cannot address all of these elements here, but the plan visualizes how the sofa, pitched at a 15-degree tilt away from the fireplace, and other built-in elements seem to shift and tilt toward the expansive view as though under the invisible pull of heliotropism. As the forms reach toward the light, all the sides of the house allow in different qualities of light. As McCoy brilliantly observes, the "use of clerestories in this house . . . turns every room in the house to all points of the compass."[74] One can further imagine the bodies in the house turning, plantlike, to the light as it changes throughout the day. The overall effect of the complex play of geometry and light suggests that the space is in a peculiar kind of motion, as though it could open and close like a folding fan.

A fan, or a pair of legs. The detailed and imaginative presentation drawing looking back at the Lechner House from the valley outside begins to suggest how the house may be active in the way that a body is (Figure 3.40). There is an unmistakable sense of bodiliness in the drawing, as though we are looking at a splayed set of legs (something not exactly suggested by the actual landscape). Crucially, the sexuality projected in the drawing is ambivalent or doubly coded. From one angle, looking outside in, it takes the shape of a female body; from another angle, inside moving out, it is coded masculine. This doubleness is further epitomized by the drawing, which indicates that the roof is

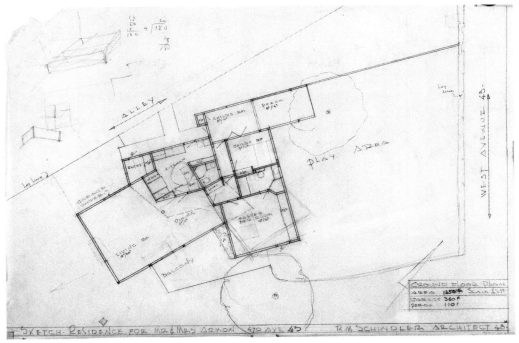

FIGURE 3.41. R. M. Schindler, J. L. Armon House, plan (Los Angeles, California), 1946–49. R. M. Schindler Collection, Architecture and Design Collection, Art, Design & Architecture Museum, University of California, Santa Barbara.

triangular, jutting out, exactly mirroring the shape on the floor in front of the fireplace. But as the early photographs indicate, Schindler modified the jutting form, straightening out the roofline and thereby mitigating the outward and inward thrust evoked by the drawing. Schindler's way of describing this quality emerges with his eroticized account of modern architecture as a whole, reflecting how the new way of living demands "live contact with our neighbors. We have [all] come down to earth. . . . Modern architecture lies down flat on the ground like a kitten who suns itself."[75]

Schindler turned all the complexities of the Lechner House to astonishing use on a significantly smaller scale with his next work, the Armon House in Mt. Washington (1946–49), a small, three-bedroom house with the living spaces arranged on one level (Figure 3.41). Approaching this house from the street, one is presented with what can only be described as a deliberately blank or inexpressive view, the façade once again evoking the fixity of a static right angle. It appears as a white stucco L around a play yard, although there is a hint that not everything is as it seems. The slightly angled roof shape does not line up with the walls below, a disjunction that gets clarified only with

FIGURE 3.42. R. M. Schindler, J. L. Armon House, view from eating nook to terrace (Los Angeles, California), 1946–49. Photograph: Grant Mudford. Courtesy of Grant Mudford.

a larger account of the geometry of the house. To enter the house, one follows the long part of the L and steps inside at the knuckle, where one is given a long diagonal view across to the open, southeast, corner (Figure 3.42). The living space contains various zones within the larger space; to the left are the eating nook and kitchen, and the hall to the left leads to the children's bedrooms. Ahead are the dining room and fireplace, and to the left is the master bedroom, with its own terrace (Figure 3.43).

Recall the initial L shape of the house from the street. The living room and master bedroom also form an L, but it manifestly does *not* align with the first one. The second or "B" L is rotated 15 degrees off-center from the children's wing or "A" L. In other words, there are two Ls overlapping one another, but one is tilted 15 degrees to open up a kind of pizza slice between them. At the Armon House, as at other late works, Schindler not only makes no effort to unify the two grids or coordinates into a seamless image but also flaunts the incongruity between the two shapes. That is, he allows the two grids to overlap without resolving them.

FIGURE 3.43. R. M. Schindler, J. L. Armon House, view to fireplace and terrace (Los Angeles, California), 1946–49. Photograph: Grant Mudford. Courtesy of Grant Mudford.

As at the Lechner House, Schindler introduces a third grid at the Armon House, this one overlapping the line that runs across the fireplace to the bedroom. This line is tilted another 15 degrees to create a 30-degree angle rotation away from the initial L of the children's wing. The only other location where this line is apparent is at the edge of the roof that one sees along the entrance façade. It is crucial to the overall effect that this third set of coordinates is signaled, but not fulfilled, with one's arrival at the house.

The 30-degree line is central to the meaning of the work, and what it suggests is that the space *rotates* or *turns* around an imaginary center, that just like the other more obvious rotational structures from the same moment, the Armon House creates a carousel effect. How? Once one encounters the stepwise addition of 0- to 15- to 30-degree angles, then the next angle, 45 degrees, which is *not visible* but is *implied,* gives one a sense of turning around an invisible center.

Two further moments in the space deserve notice, moments where two, not three, overlapping grids are plainly—even extravagantly—visible. One is the eating nook,

FIGURE 3.44. R. M. Schindler, J. L. Armon House, terrace (Los Angeles, California), 1946–49. Photograph: Grant Mudford. Courtesy of Grant Mudford.

which freely combines the two coordinates (A and B), a fact that is clarified on the plan. The other is the remarkable moment where the two coordinates overlap in the raised terrace (Figure 3.44). Despite, or because of, its deep complexity, the Armon House has received little attention in the literature (with the notable exception of Sheine), in large part because it bears a superficial resemblance to International Style architecture. Or rather, what the Armon House most resembles is a *Schindler house* that is most reminiscent of International Style architecture, the Buck House of 1934 (Figure 3.7 and 3.26). What is so striking is that the Armon House reiterates the basic shape of the Buck House (abutting Ls) but overlaps the two shapes and tilts one slightly away from the 90 degrees, bringing a new sense of movement or rhythm to the same format.

The Tucker House of 1950, located near the intersection of Laurel Canyon Boulevard and Hollywood Boulevard, shares many of the same qualities as the Armon and Lechner Houses, although it is perhaps even less well known than the Armon House.[76] Once again, the façade offers something like a total blank. One enters from the top and steps down into the living room on the main floor (Figure 3.45). The first impression is that

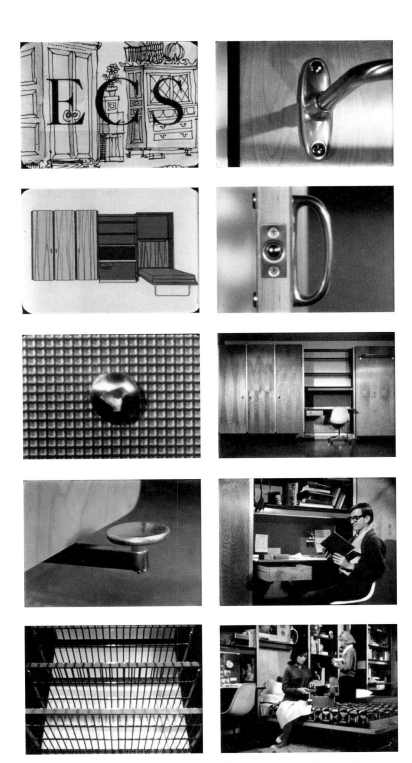

PLATE 1. Charles and Ray Eames, stills from *ECS* (Eames Contract Storage Units), 1961.

PLATE 2. Charles and Ray Eames, still from *Babbage's Calculating Machine or Difference Engine,* 1968.

PLATE 3. Charles and Ray Eames, Eames House, Case Study House No. 8 (Los Angeles, California), 1949. Photograph: Julius Shulman, 1950. Copyright J. Paul Getty Trust. Getty Research Institute, Los Angeles (2004.R.10).

PLATE 4. Craig Ellwood Associates, Smith House, Case Study House No. 16 (Los Angeles, California), 1958. Photograph: Marvin Rand. Marvin Rand Archive, College of Environmental Design Archives, Cal Poly Pomona.

PLATE 5. Charles and Ray Eames, stills from *Konditorei* slide show, 1955.

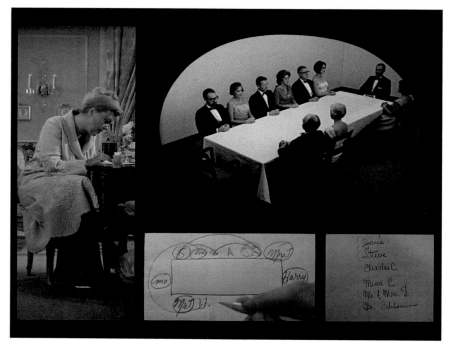

PLATE 6. Charles and Ray Eames, still from "Dinner Party" sequence, *Think*, New York World's Fair, 1964.

PLATE 7. Richard Neutra, Poster Apartments (Los Angeles, California), 1960. Photograph: Julius Shulman, 1964. Copyright J. Paul Getty Trust. Getty Research Institute, Los Angeles (2004.R.10).

PLATE 8. Ray and Charles Eames, stills from *A Communications Primer*, 1953.

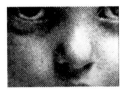

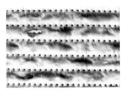
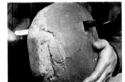

PLATE 9. Charles and Ray Eames, stills from *Bread*, 1953.

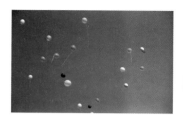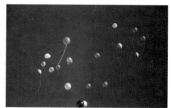

PLATE 10. Charles and Ray Eames, stills from *Movie Sets* slide show, 1973.

PLATE 11. Charles and Ray Eames, *Solar Do-Nothing Machine*, 1957. Designed for the Aluminum Company of America's Forecast Program.

PLATE 12. Charles Eames, stills from "Design Today" lecture, University of Washington Arboretum in Seattle, 1950.

PLATE 13. Charles Eames, stills from "Design Today" lecture, University of Washington Arboretum in Seattle, 1950.

PLATE 14. Charles and Ray Eames, images from *House of Cards*, 1952.

PLATE 15. Ray Eames, stills from *Goods*, 1981. Based on Charles Eames slide show, Norton Lectures, 1971.

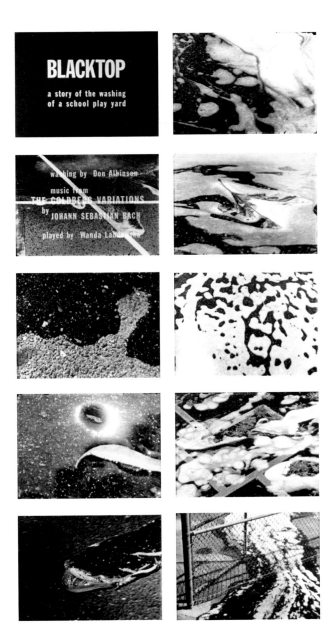

PLATE 16. Charles and Ray Eames, stills from *Blacktop*, 1952.

PLATE 17. Charles and Ray Eames, stills from *Movie Sets* slide show, 1973.

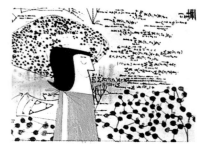

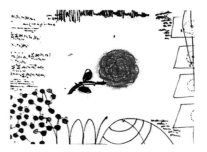

PLATE 18. Charles and Ray Eames, frames from *The Information Machine*, 1957.

the walls seem to shift at oblique angles without any clear rhyme or reason, a quality that Gebhard describes as "planned incompleteness."[77] One finds a sense of relief with the discovery of some spaces arranged along a 90-degree angle, including the living room and the bedroom beyond it. If the farther side of the block—comprising terrace, living room, and bedroom—forms an L, then if one tilts that shape 15 degrees and flips it, one derives another L, the bottom of which is at the top of the plan along the porch and dining room, and the top of which is the outer wall of the bedroom. Just as at the Armon and Lechner Houses, there is a third coordinate system, which was once very prominent but is now mostly lost. In the past it was spelled out by a large wooden pergola that jutted out from the corner of the house and then sliced right through the center of it, a feature clearly visible on the presentation drawing and on the plan (Figure 3.46). There is nonetheless a strong remnant of that third system with the prominent line that cuts across the living room next to the stairs. Consider, finally, the shape of the second bedroom. It is nothing less than an irregular hexagon, as it bears the burden of expressing every coordinate system at play in the house.

Like the Armon House, the Tucker House gets little attention in the contemporary literature because it bears a resemblance to International Style architecture. This may well be a pointed comparison at the Tucker House, as Schindler is taking direct aim at Neutra's International Style aesthetic, which is visible from the patio of the Tucker House. That vantage point offers a clear view onto not one but two houses by Neutra, the Josef Kun House I of 1936 (Figure 3.47) and Kun House II of 1950. (There is no other instance I am aware of where this kind of face-off between Schindler and Neutra occurs.) Schindler, I think, is making a pointed counter to Neutra's designs. The Kun House I comprises three trays stacked on top of one another; the overall shape is one of a rectangle (Shulman's photograph of the house is notable in that it is his first photograph of a Neutra structure). One might say the Kun House is almost obsessively concerned with expressing and reiterating a 90-degree pattern. Schindler takes up that image of patterned order, replays or mirrors it, and subtly but unmistakably upends the stasis of Neutra's design with one of his most dynamic but also compact structures.

The Maurice Ries House of 1950–51 is almost never discussed in the literature, despite the fact that it is relatively intact and in a highly visible location, a few blocks north of Sunset Boulevard right where it meets La Cienega (Figure 3.48). Like the Tucker and Armon Houses, the Ries House does not receive much attention because it bears an unmistakable but also highly unstable resemblance to International Style houses. What is most striking about the Ries House is a very subtle alteration of the line of the fascia, the introduction of a 10-degree angle, an extremely rare instance of this degree of angle as a featured element in Schindler's work. The entrance façade follows the pattern set by the Armon House, where one can subtly but also unmistakably notice that the

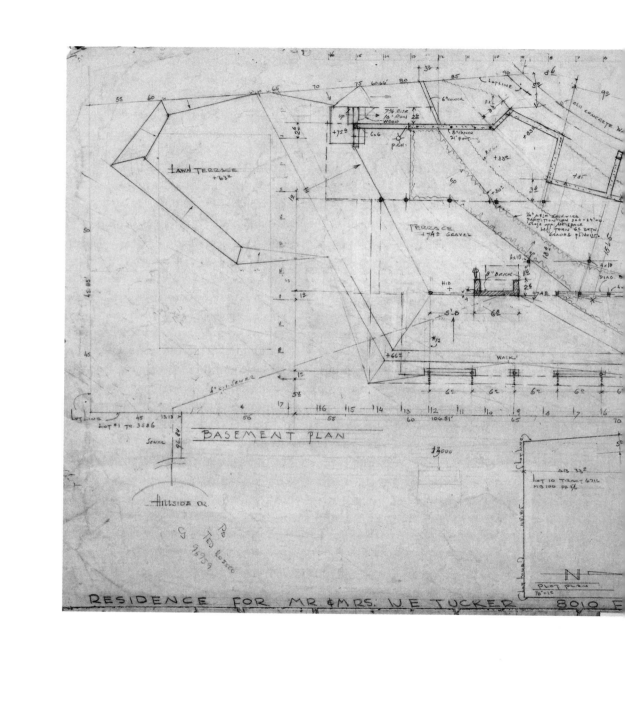

BASEMENT PLAN

RESIDENCE FOR MR. &MRS. W.E. TUCKER 8010 E

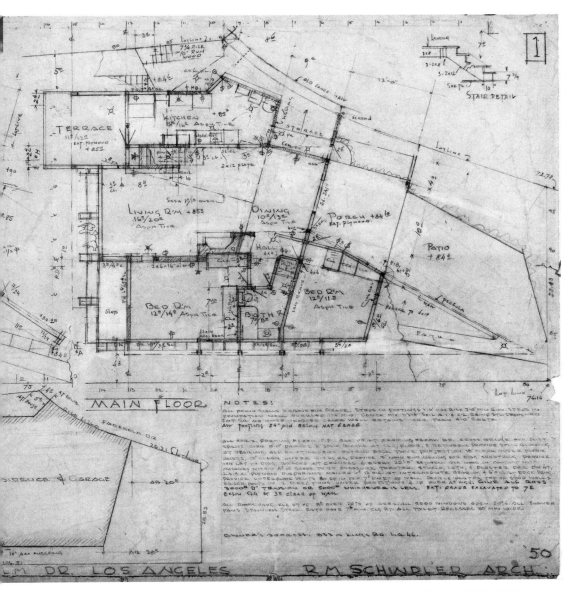

FIGURE 3.45. R. M. Schindler, W. E. Tucker House, plan (Los Angeles, California), 1949–50. R. M. Schindler Collection, Architecture and Design Collection, Art, Design & Architecture Museum, University of California, Santa Barbara.

RESIDENCE FOR
MR ‡ MRS W.E.TUCKER
HOLLYWOOD, CALIF.
R.M. SCHINDLER ARCH
LOS ANGELES, CALIF.   50'

FIGURE 3.46. R. M. Schindler, W. E. Tucker House, presentation drawing (Los Angeles, California), 1949–50. R. M. Schindler Collection, Architecture and Design Collection, Art, Design & Architecture Museum, University of California, Santa Barbara.

roofline is not straight. The roofline shifts away from the seemingly strict 90-degree angle of the rooms below (Figure 3.49). This same 10-degree angle appears again on the other side of the roof, the one facing Sunset, taking the shape of a bent bow, one of Schindler's favored images (it appears on the plans for the Toole House, the Tischler House, the Laurelwood Apartments, and the Skolnik House, among others). There are three 10-degree angles—one to the north, two on the south—but the fourth corner, which one sees to the left of the door upon arrival, is actually tilted at 20 degrees away from the straight line of the rooms below. It is not actually the case that the façade of

FIGURE 3.47. Richard Neutra, Josef Kun House I (Los Angeles, California), 1936. Photograph: Julius Shulman, 1936. Copyright J. Paul Getty Trust. Getty Research Institute, Los Angeles (2004.R.10).

FIGURE 3.48. R. M. Schindler, Maurice Ries House, exterior (Los Angeles, California), 1950–51. R. M. Schindler Collection, Architecture and Design Collection, Art, Design & Architecture Museum, University of California, Santa Barbara.

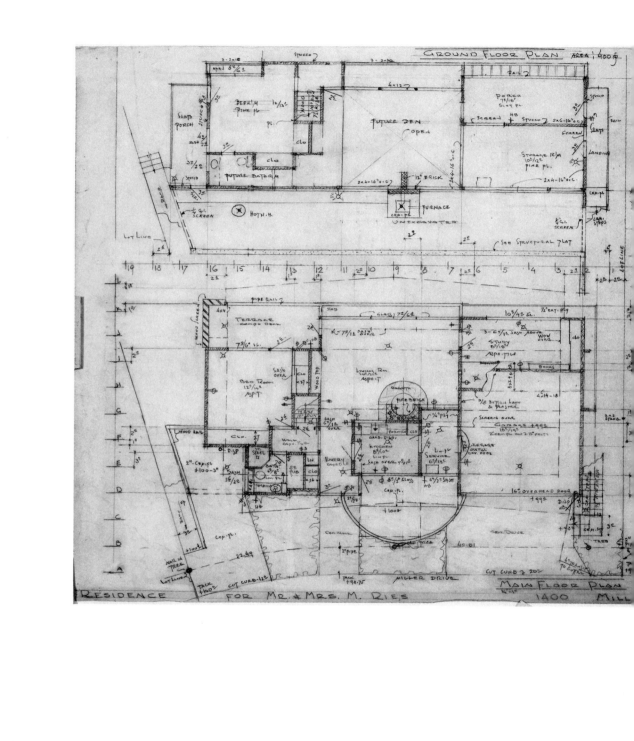

GROUND FLOOR PLAN   AREA 1400 ft

MAIN FLOOR PLAN

RESIDENCE   FOR MR. & MRS. M. RIES   1400   MILL

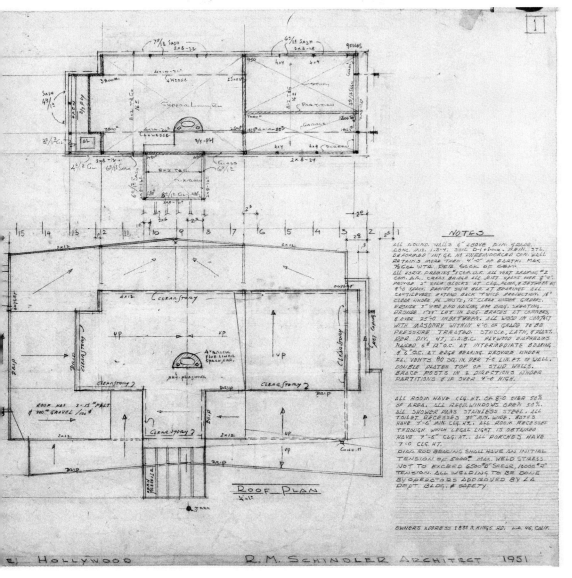

FIGURE 3.49. R. M. Schindler, Maurice Ries House, plan (Los Angeles, California), 1950–51. R. M. Schindler Collection, Architecture and Design Collection, Art, Design & Architecture Museum, University of California, Santa Barbara.

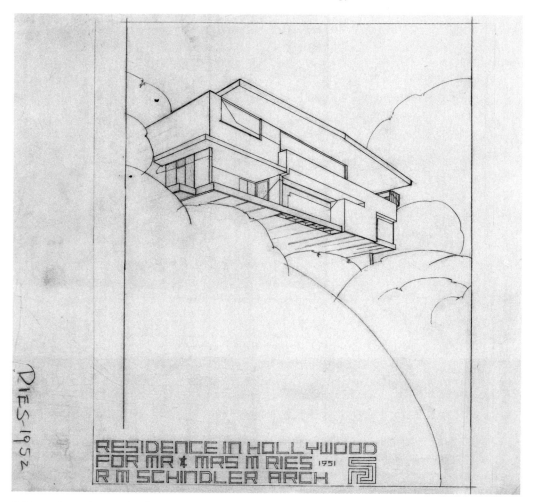

FIGURE 3.50. R. M. Schindler, Maurice Ries House, presentation drawing, southern façade (Los Angeles, California), 1950–51. R. M. Schindler Collection, Architecture and Design Collection, Art, Design & Architecture Museum, University of California, Santa Barbara.

the house is flat; rather, to the left of the entrance is the bathroom, and that room, like the roof above, swings away from the rest of the house at a 20-degree angle (the roofline follows the angle of the bathroom). Bear in mind that the remainder of the house is as solid a rectangle or box as one will find in Schindler's work. It is as though Schindler encourages the use of the four-square rectangle and then, with the flick of a wrist (a 10-degree shift), makes the inert shape come alive.[78] Consider as well the twinned circular forms of the entrance planter and the (unbuilt) fireplace at the center of the plan, repeating the arrangement at the Tischler House (Figure 3.49). Finally, consider the

FIGURE 3.51. R. M. Schindler, Samuel Skolnik House, living room with bar (Los Angeles, California), 1950–52. R. M. Schindler Collection, Architecture and Design Collection, Art, Design & Architecture Museum, University of California, Santa Barbara.

complex play of convex and concave shapes along the exterior of the house (Figure 3.50). There is a great deal to say about the nature of the spatial patterning here, but I would draw attention to one element, the "arrow" shape that leads from the left side of the façade through to the ground floor bathroom clerestory. What this suggests is a sense of movement or velocity from left to right or west to east.

With Schindler's last house, the Skolnik House, completed a few months prior to his death in August 1953, he sets the whole of the structure into revolving motion around the still center. As noted earlier, McCoy describes the living room as "essentially a carousel," while Sheine similarly describes the space as "a dynamic volume not quite containing a number of angled forms which spin around a circular indoor/outdoor fireplace" (Figure 3.51). In a sense, what I have been arguing all along about Schindler's late work is made explicit at the Skolnik House, where the circularity and rotation of the space are put on full display (Figure 3.52). Schindler introduces a new feature at this house: he lowers most of the walls, making the whole house like a giant container for various spinning elements, some clearly part of a set of coordinates, others only evoking an absent system of organization. Above the dining room and the bar area, the ceiling is made of corrugated fiberglass, which, as at the Tischler House, alters the look

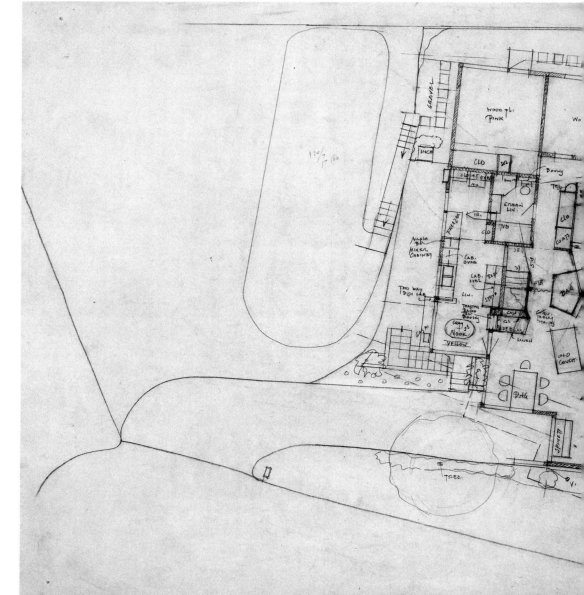

FURNITURE PLAN: RESIDENCE FOR MR. & MRS. S. SKOLNIK   2567 GLENDOWER AVE.

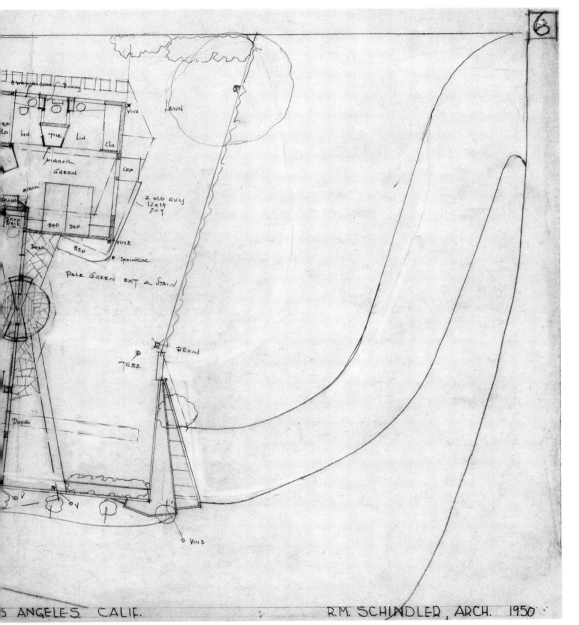

FIGURE 3.52. R. M. Schindler, Samuel Skolnik House, plan (Los Angeles, California), 1950–52. R. M. Schindler Collection, Architecture and Design Collection, Art, Design & Architecture Museum, University of California, Santa Barbara.

FIGURE 3.53. R. M. Schindler, Samuel Skolnik House (Los Angeles, California), 1950–52. Photograph: Hazel Cook. The Architectural Association (AIA), London.

and feel of the interior along the south side. Although there is a remnant of an L-shaped plan, it is as though everything in the space conspires to drag the inert elements into what McCoy calls an architectural "whirlwind." Here Schindler returns to one of his favored images, the bow and arrow, with the arrow piercing the central axis of the plywood bar and the circular indoor/outdoor fireplace.

In a sense we have come full circle. As the Tucker House responds to Neutra, so the Skolnik House responds to Wright (Figure 3.53). As the photograph by Hazel Cook shows, the Skolnik House lies just below Wright's massive or "monolithic" Ennis House of 1923–24. Schindler's response to Wright is highly coded. Where Wright broadcasts an image of mass, defensiveness, and security, a fortress on a hill—one might even imagine boiling oil being poured from its walls—Schindler projects a vision of total openness, of architecture that lives in "contact with one's neighbors," that "lies down flat on the ground like a kitten who suns itself." Schindler always counterposes two worlds, past and present: "static world: earth flat disk" versus "dynamic world: motion-mountains, atoms, elements." The latter is about "development, evolution—change."[79] Schindler creates moving spaces for a form of life where humans, no longer fearing their neighbors, live together as would free-roaming cats, turning, rolling, and sunning themselves in the light that shines on everyone and from all directions.

4

Richard Neutra's Design Theory

Richard Neutra's *Survival through Design* is representative of the full
recognition today of the power of the messages from interior and exterior
design in buildings to pattern general awareness and to affect even
physiological states.
—Marshall McLuhan, "Media Alchemy in Art and Society," 1958

Control is at the center of most of the practices discussed here. Control of the work and
how it is experienced both spatially and temporally is at the very root of architectural
thinking by virtue of the fact that works of architecture enter into the hands of people
other than their creators in ways that are unlike what happens with other media. Both
Neutra and the Eameses sought to retain what can only be described as hyperbolic degrees of control over their work and its reception. Chapters 3, 4, and 5 present the specific nature of Neutra's manic drive to control the whole of the architectural experience.

As I argue throughout, there are at least two different ways to think about control.
The first, associated with the Eameses (but also Schindler, Ellwood, and others), involves
the exertion of control over works as a matter of responsibility (a word the Eameses
use almost obsessively). Because one's works leave one's hands to enter the world and
affect it, potentially for decades or even centuries to come, one should think through
to the end how each work will function, on all levels, spatial and temporal. As it turns
out, the Eameses were as petrified by the prospect of long-term responsibility as they
were obsessed with it. Neutra, by contrast, built his enterprise on creating works that
would retain a sense of his control as though in perpetuity. At its limit, a Neutra work
is never over; an Eames work never begins. Two critical issues are raised by Neutra's
works: First, because they are construed as endless, there is never a definable action,
a clear separation of work and world, that can be evaluated as such. Second, and more
fundamental, the open-ended action that is the work is described as the result of non-
intentional, nonhuman, subconscious forces that the architect merely marshals, never
actually creates, and for which he may never be responsible.

Design in the Nuclear Age

When Neutra published *Survival through Design* in 1954 he intended the title to be taken literally. Humankind risked sudden annihilation unless it came to grips with the alternately liberating and devastating effects of architecture. *Survival through Design*, written throughout the 1940s, catalogs the horrors of the unregulated waste that surrounds us and outlines how the expert designer, by shaping our most intimate spaces, can heal our wounds. Indeed, Neutra granted architects a foundational role in the future survival of the human species. He also suggested that most designers were killing their clients, but because the deadly choices they made were slow acting, no one noticed until it was too late.

Neutra's concern throughout *Survival through Design* is the health of the modern urban dweller's "brains and nerves" (*SD*, 72), which in his view had become diseased. The threat of atomic annihilation seems to haunt every page, but beyond that Neutra intimates that Americans are being irradiated along with the Japanese, only at a slower rate. "With the help of alpha particles and gamma rays, we can influence even the innermost chromosomatic base of the species and cause heretofore unheard-of mutations" (*SD*, 82). The atomic bomb "popularized spectacular dangers of this kind," but "there are many less conspicuous ones" (*SD*, 83). Ultraviolet light, although "seemingly harmless," works on one's nervous system like an atom bomb exploding over a sustained period of time. But Neutra's worry is less about the consequences of a measurable quantity like ultraviolet light than about the unmeasurable—at least by current standards—consequences of the built environment. Through an "infinite number of stimuli," houses, road networks, and cities, Neutra argues, shape and alter the nervous life of the whole community (*SD*, 83). More unsettling for midcentury readers was the idea that the survival of the species as a whole was at stake.

Although Neutra insisted he believed in the idea of the survival of the fittest, at crucial points in *Survival through Design* he turns to decisively non-Darwinian sources for support for his claims, stating, for example, that recent discoveries in biology show that our "inheritable substance itself can be molded," an idea that he expands on in the seemingly innocuous claim that design elements affect the lives of those who use them and the far from innocuous assertion that the chromosomes of the users and those of their progeny are continually being altered. He argues that designers now have "an uncanny leverage on mankind," describing them (half tongue-in-cheek) as a "guild of messiahs" (*NN*, 54, 101). From a certain perspective, *Survival through Design* is an elaborate defense of architects and their innate gift: a sensitivity beyond the capacity of any machine, any measuring device. And the timing of this defense corresponds with the moment when Neutra modified his large-scale ambitions to reform society. From his first book, *Wie baut Amerika?* (1927), to *Survival through Design,* one can trace a drift away from social models based on universal biological principles and a move toward a neurasthenic attention to the details of individual body chemistry.

Even such seemingly core issues as urban planning in its relation to domestic architecture are sidelined in favor of a micrological approach to design effects. Neutra focuses almost exclusively on the permeation of virtually untraceable technological processes into the microbiology of our daily existence. There are "numerous threats in those unheeded by-products" of human invention (*SD,* 84). The most dangerous threats to humanity's existence lie not in the social fabric at large but in the "smallest dose" of ill-conceived design, what Neutra describes as the "multitudinous microdosages of stimuli" (*NN,* 60). "Obscure, seemingly insignificant elements," he insists, "may produce disastrous effects if given sufficient time" (*SD,* 86). Ordinary soot in chimneys, hydrocarbons from kerosene lamps, and microfibers dislodged from wood are just a few of more than "two hundred known carcinogenic substances" that suffuse "the entire urban surroundings of our age" (*SD,* 84). Neutra argues that we are assaulted by our environment at every turn; humanity is suffering under an "avalanche of unasserted so-called progress." That this regress is "unasserted"—no dictator or enemy presence commands us—only makes its danger more deadly.

Neutra's larger claim is that the biology of postwar human beings has undergone a transformation that blunts the sensation of acute but low-level forms of suffering. Even "harsh neon signs" that we pass on the freeway (a favorite motif) are literally "nerve-wrecking to us, whether we know it or not" (*SD,* 85). Although the overt physiological impact of neon signs on the retina may be minimal, the lingering effects of harsh color combinations are slowly and devastatingly depleting the physical and mental reserves of human beings.

Chapter 21 of *Survival through Design* is devoted to a peculiar analysis of the "not consciously recorded" but nevertheless "inexhaustible" effects of odors and tactile sensations on the nervous system (*SD,* 146). Neutra's concern here is specifically the subconscious physiological effects of "integral exhalations" produced by structural and finishing materials. The sites of relaxation are also the sites of threat—our carpets and couches are breaching our delicate sensory defenses. (He muses on a history of architecture "flavored by smells" and not by sight; *SD,* 147.) Todd Haynes's 1995 psychological drama *Safe,* set in the suburbs of Los Angeles, explores a Neutra-like vision of chemical microdosing through the environment. Housewife Carol White (Julianne Moore) is putatively allergic to her environment. She experiences physical symptoms after a renovation of the family's home, and the symptoms spiral until she ends up living alone in a superhygienic pod. Here is some typical dialogue: "Newspapers . . . The ink . . . You know our beautiful new couch? . . . Totally toxic. . . . I can't wear makeup anymore. . . . Burns my eyes. I get sick. . . . So much of it, too, is that we were raised in a chemical place. . . . It *is* in your head. It's in *all* our heads. . . . It ends up in your head because it affects the neurological."[1]

Being raised in a "chemical place," Neutra did not exactly imagine a return to nature, but rather how we might direct chemical exhalations toward more healthy results. In one instance, Neutra makes an extraordinary leap from the "primary comfort of a floating manifold suspension in the uterus" to the resilience of hardwood flooring (*SD*, 150). In Neutra's hands, material exhalations link design to the most primordial events of ontogeny. Neutra suggests that modern urban dwellers prefer hardwood to cement flooring because the almost imperceptible resilience of wood evokes the sensation of uterine suspension. He nonetheless cautions the reader not to neglect the benefits of cement flooring. A more nuanced and precise account of materials, he suggests, would show that cement flooring is in fact more evocative of primordial suspension than wood or tile because less body heat is lost through its medium. People may be misguided in their view that hardwood is more truly evocative of prenatal experience, but they are far from misguided in their belief that that experience orders their taste. In Neutra's view, replicating *"the prenatal experience of shelter"* is the goal of design and construction. Space itself is a "multisensorial product which begins to evolve for us while we are still in the uterus," and the sensation of "floating in the evenly warm liquid medium of the mother's womb is a primary factor molding our later reactions to an outer world" (*SD*, 156). What this argument reveals is a subtle but crucial transformation in Neutra's defense of architectural prefabrication. In his prewar writings Neutra stressed the need for prefabrication for its economic efficiency, environmental sustainability, and social benefits; in his postwar writings Neutra still makes the case for prefabrication but now almost entirely on psychological grounds.[2]

Neutra's psychology is decisively non-Freudian in its emphasis on the preoedipal notion of uterine suspension. His model was a widely known text by Freudian maverick Sándor Ferenczi. In 1923 Ferenczi published *Thalassa: A Theory of Genitality*, a "bioanalytic" treatise that articulates an extreme view of the preoedipal conditions of human development. According to Ferenczi, the purpose of the "whole evolution [of sexuality] . . . can be nothing other than an attempt on the part of the ego . . . to return to the mother's womb, where there is no painful disharmony between ego and environment as characterizes existence in the external world." Ferenczi imagined that all forms of human practice—sex above all—are aimed at the "genital reestablishment of the intrauterine situation."[3] Birth is a "catastrophe," and sex is an effort to reverse the situation but is doomed to repeat it.[4] While the first part of the book describes the ontogenesis of individual life patterns as one of womb lust and overcoming the catastrophe of birth, the second part describes the phylogenic parallel that recurs from primordial times until today. "What if," Ferenczi speculates, *the entire intrauterine existence of the higher mammals were only a replica of the type of existence which characterized that aboriginal piscine period, and birth itself nothing but a recapitulation on the part of the individual of the great catastrophe which at the time of the recession of the ocean forced so many animals . . . to adapt themselves to a land existence, above all to renounce gill-breathing and provide themselves with organs for the respiration of air?*[5]

For Ferenczi, birth trauma itself is a repetition of an even more primordial birth catastrophe: the forced adaptation from an oceanic existence to living on dry land is replayed within individual psychology in the movement from watery womb to a dry outside world. Neutra construed the desert of Palm Springs and the city of Los Angeles itself as both traumatic and reparative places where he could fashion replays or *reversals* of the primordial trauma and thereby provide air for gill-choked masses.

Neutra's fascination with uterine suspension and more generally with neonatal development led him to imagine the pregnant mother as the ur-designer. The "expectant mother holds many lessons for the expectant architect," he notes in his late study "Nurturing Individuality" (*NN*, 39). Mothers are great designers because they bear an "innate gift for individualization" in their "creation of sense-conscious surroundings" (*NN*, 40). The pregnant mother is the super-architect:

> In many respects, the expectant mother is the most sensitive and active of organic beings. The mere potentiality of becoming a mother has endowed females with qualities, emotions, and insights that not even the best male obstetricians can fully understand. Particularly during the later stages of pregnancy, mothers instinctively sense the individualized temperament of their offspring. In effect, they "know" their children before they are born, and can even distinguish them from the others [they have] carried. (*NN*, 39)

Designers, Neutra suggests, are like mothers in that they "know" how their children— their works—will turn out, and, moreover, he urges designers to strive to replicate the experience of birthing, its trauma and joy, narratively through their structures as a way to heal their perpetually convalescing inhabitants.

Neutra's commitment to replicating neonatal experience was at the center of his postwar practice. The uterine principle is illustrated on the cover of the second edition of *Survival through Design* as well as on the cover of *Life and Shape* (1962; Figure 4.1), both of which feature reproductions (a sepia photograph and a colored drawing, respectively) of the spiral stairwell of the Gemological Institute in Los Angeles (1954–55; Figure 4.2).[6] The stairs, the umbilical cord, twist freely in space, hovering over a pond, the uterine fluid. Between the pond and the stairwell appears a circular platform eerily suspended from above, casting a long shadow across the outer surface of the winding structure. The

FIGURE 4.1. Richard Neutra, *Survival through Design,* second edition, cover, 1969. Courtesy of Oxford University Press.

FIGURE 4.2. Richard Neutra, Gemological Institute of America (Los Angeles, California), 1956. Photograph: Julius Shulman. Copyright J. Paul Getty Trust. Getty Research Institute, Los Angeles (2004.R.10).

upright steel disks hovering at the top of the stairs suggest the gripping ends of forceps extracting a baby/inhabitant from the waters below. On the title page of *Survival through Design,* Neutra describes the umbilical stairway as a "striking example of an architecture that stimulates all the senses" and that is "'lived through'" rather than looked at (*SD,* iv).[7]

Neutra was explicit about the traumatic and curative effects that design elements could transmit to infant receivers. In his autobiography he recalls the impact of his early encounters with the four-story stairwell that led to his family home. "The windings and the cold draft are still with me in some dreams." When he suggests that the experience is still "with" him he means it literally—the traumatic sensations of the drafty stairwell are lodged deep inside his psyche, as *engrams.* "What happens to one, *in* one, and around one while ascending a stair—and what of it sticks with us as a strangely lasting memory—is to me a master specimen for what architectural experience means. It's way beyond all that photography or motion pictures can convey" (*LS,* 36). More sensitive than any available recording device, the human body captures all the "microfacts" of the environment and stores them in perpetuity in the recesses of the nervous system. Those effects not only linger deep within the self but also grow and proliferate as traumatic wounds that come to shape one's experience of the world.

While photography and film are unable to capture the unseen effects of the environment that Neutra describes, he nevertheless repeatedly turns to current scientific research to support his claims. Again and again he insists that "only precise physiological experiments *can* prove" the effects of industrial materials on the nervous system. Citing the work of zoologist Frederick Crescitelli, Neutra describes an experiment in which animals were brought to "convulsive action by exposure to a certain sound" (*SD,* 84). What was remarkable about this case was not that the animals reacted violently to a particular sensory stimulus but that the effects continued long after the animals had overtly adapted to the stimulus. Like these animals, Neutra argues, modern urban dwellers are biologically unable to adapt to their human-made environment. They are ill equipped to deal with technological dangers because they rely on outmoded senses developed to respond to natural phenomena. What is terrifying about urban existence is that we cannot sense what is killing us. In the past humans could rely on "minute pain receptors" to warn them of potential dangers (*SD,* 84), but these receptors function only under the impact of natural stimulation. Technologically induced effects do "not cause direct pain," and therefore we are exposed to dangers that we are not alerted to by biological cues. Again and again Neutra insists it is only the architect who is hypersensitive enough to understand and manipulate the wide-ranging effects of design; it is the architect's job to shield and protect clients from an unseen but lethal environment teeming with hazardous waste.

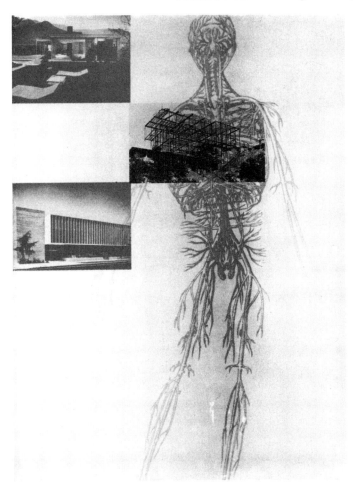

FIGURE 4.3. Richard Neutra, *Survival through Design*, first edition, back cover, 1954. Courtesy of Oxford University Press.

The back cover of *Survival through Design* provides a remarkably literal statement of Neutra's design theory (Figure 4.3). Standing against a white ground, filling up the space from bottom to top, is a diagram of the human nervous system. The sinuous form poignantly overlays the skeleton frame—the term is literalized—of the Lovell House of 1929. The metaphor is clear: architecture provides protection, a kind of armor, for our exposed nervous life. At top left, untouched by the diagram, appears Julius Shulman's famous twilight image of the exterior of the Kaufmann House in Palm Springs (Figure 3.15)—an image of the ultimate security that Neutra's architecture could provide. The argument this image makes—that design can protect and heal our sensory life—poignantly inverts Frank Lloyd Wright's famous description of the pernicious effects of ill-understood machinery on the inner lives of modern human beings in "The Art and Craft of the Machine" (1901):

> Ten thousand acres of cellular tissue, layer upon layer, the city's flesh, outspreads enmeshed by intricate network of veins and arteries, radiating into the gloom, and there with muffled, persistent roar, pulses and circulates as the blood in your veins, the ceaseless beat of the activity to whose necessities it all conforms. . . .
>
> This ten thousand acres of flesh-like tissue is again knit and inter-knit with a nervous system marvelously complete, delicate filaments for hearing, knowing, almost feeling the pulse of its organism, acting upon the ligaments and tendons of motive impulse, in all flowing the impelling fluid of man's own life.[8]

Of course Wright uses this image as a metaphor for the relationship between human beings and machines, but when Neutra inverts it—suggesting that the machine can heal the frail nervous system of a neurasthenic populace—he means it literally.

Positive Trauma

Neutra relies on a mixture of Ferenczi and Freud on trauma to frame his account of affective design. Once humans could no longer rely on basic biological cues for their survival, they became subject to subtle forms of traumatic injury from the environment that challenged the age-old analogy between them and organic formations: "The picture of a slow and steady shaping as with a growing tree, may have to be supplemented" (SD, 228). Neutra focuses on the role "drastic episodes" play in human formation. "The shock of intensive emotion linked to the experience of a single strong stimulation may be a decisive formative agent," he observes (SD, 229). For Neutra, trauma is not simply a wounding or destructive experience but also potentially formative. Above all, architectural forms of shock, by replaying the primordial trauma of birth, allow human beings to master the small-scale traumas of daily life. After the "shock of being born, not into a wonderful natural nest, but into a man-made cradle, an artificial apartment and town, the fantastic receptivity of the impressionable young goes on" (LS, 13). The job of the designer is to re-create the birth trauma as well as the protecting womb. Walking through a Neutra structure is like moving from womb to world over and over again.

Like his contemporary Walter Benjamin (both born in 1892), Neutra hinged his aesthetic on the liberating potential of shock. In "Experience and Poverty," Benjamin appeals to Scheerbart and the Bauhaus, Loos and Le Corbusier to describe the specially evolved nature of the modern traumatized subject. "This much is clear," Benjamin argues. "Experience has fallen in value, amid a generation which . . . had to experience some of the most monstrous events in the history of the world."[9] The old organic metaphors no longer suffice to describe the current state of the human condition. The new "adjustable, movable glass-covered dwellings" are the only appropriate structures to house the new traumatized subject.[10]

For Benjamin, as for Neutra, human beings had to descend into barbarity before a new, transformed subject could emerge. It is a "new, positive concept of barbarism," Benjamin explains, that defines the nature of contemporary existence. The new barbarism "forces man to start from scratch; to make a new start; to make a little go a long way; . . . [to] begin by clearing a tabula rasa."[11] Similarly, Neutra reflects that while "some very negative fixations may thus be produced by what Freud calls trauma," nonetheless, "positive vital experiences can come and be fixed by way of shock" (*SD*, 229). Neutra calls these experiences "positive trauma."[12]

For Neutra, as for Benjamin, shock effects are the only way an architect can defeat the small-scale shocks of everyday life: "One intense delight, like one of mortifying anguish, may become an almost unbeatable competitor to many . . . experiences of the mild habitual kind" (*SD*, 229). Benjamin's suggestion that experiences of the habitual kind have come to an end is more extreme than Neutra's claim, but Neutra nevertheless insists that the architecture of "sudden impact" is more necessary than ever before (*SD*, 229). He literalizes the experience in the abrupt opening of a sliding glass door:

> Here is the value of a wide sliding door opening pleasantly onto a garden. It cannot be measured by counting *how often* and how steadily the door is used, or *how many hours* it stays open. The decisive thing may be a first deep breath of liberation when one is in the almost ritual act of opening it before breakfast or on the first warm and scented spring day. The memories of one's youth and of the landscape in which it was spent, seem composed, to a considerable degree, of this sort of vital recollection. There are in each life certain scattered quanta of experience that may have been small of number or dimension statistically but were so intense as to provide impacts, forever essential. (*SD*, 229)

Whatever Neutra's aversion to abstract divisions between inner and outer, his design theory rests on a broad distinction between ritual and shock. By 1954 he had declared his disinterest in modernist functionalism—new materials, open-plan living, manipulable space divisions—in favor of the rarified experiences of intense bursts of light, air, sound, touch, and smell. He puts the difference succinctly in his autobiography, speaking of the high-tech lighting design at the VDL Research House: "Providing *light* for reading the newspaper was not the primary purpose of this illumination. Rather I saw in it *an emotive stimulant,* changing endocrinal discharges and biochemistry" (*LS*, 266).

For Neutra, it was essential to replace ritualized effects with intense "scattered quanta of experience" that produced irreplaceable "vital recollections." Indeed, he broadly redefined everyday life in terms of a psychosomatic account of nonsensuous environmental toxins. Clients could no longer be left to shape spaces according to their needs because they had become so infected by bad design that they were unable to choose healthy patterns for themselves. With their innate sensitivity and technical capacity to control design elements, architects could subtly jolt clients out of their pathological routines.[13]

McCoy usefully describes the shock of her first encounter with Neutra's work. "A door was opened and I entered," she recalls. "The band of windows in his typical module was so acerbic to the eye that I could stand for minutes tasting the new sharpness."[14] McCoy construes Neutra's module structure as both violent and liberating. This double effect of traumatic healing is a defining trait of Neutra's postwar work. At the Rice House in Richmond, Virginia (1962), for example, when one steps through the massive sliding door onto the balcony hanging over the rocky cliffs above the James River, one becomes instantly aware that one is precipitously suspended over the cliff without the least protective railing (Figure 4.4).[15] Neutra aims to provoke anxious uncertainty from the inhabitant and thereby trigger long-buried mechanisms suggestive of two primordial events: uterine suspension and birth trauma. Once one has become aware of those mechanisms and one's security is ensured, the body will be trained—homeopathically—to deal with the onslaught of daily, low-dosage trauma.

In a late essay on Freud titled "Taking Off the Blinders of Tradition," Neutra describes himself alternately as a depth psychologist and an environmental ophthalmologist. Freud, he argues, could see the "unseen" forces that impinge on the soul, but he was oblivious to "our daily sensorial intake" (*NN*, 13). Having restricted the application of the idea of *Nachträglichkeit* to intersubjective traumas, Freud "did not recognize the sensory assaults to which our systems and psyches are subjected [and which] have a surreptitious, often delayed effect" (*NN*, 15). It is the job of the designer, like a Freudian analyst but now looking *at* the couch on which the patient lies, to "anticipate and avert the many microfacts of environmental damage." Borrowing a phrase from his friend the microbiologist René Dubos, Neutra declares his project a form of "biological Freudianism" (*NN*, 23). If one knew everything about the "various surroundings" of one's "earliest years" of development, one could predict and, more fantastically, avert forms of "self-destructive, sociopathic, or violent behavior." Turning Freud's theory on its head, Neutra declares that it is neither our families nor society that shapes our development; rather, "our environment is our fate" (*NN*, 24).

Like Scheerbart and Taut before him, Neutra goes so far as to equate crime with the delayed effects of living in an unhealthy environment. If human beings continue to "settle for punishing surroundings that . . . debase our emotions, and sap our energies," he asserts, "the pathologies will continue to mount, gradually incarcerating society as a

FIGURE 4.4. Richard Neutra, Walter Rice House (Locke Island, Richmond, Virginia), October 1964. Courtesy of Valentine Richmond History Center.

whole" (*NN*, 24). Neutra literalized his argument about the "sociological ramifications" of the environment in his design for the Orange County Courthouse (1968; Figure 4.5) (*NN*, 66). In his essay on the courthouse, he voices his concerns about the "personal metabolism" of those in the courtroom, as everyone "exudes a different degree of butyric acid, deodorants not-withstanding" (*NN*, 70–71). While this acid is not particularly "toxic," it can nonetheless be "very soporific," and "if more than a couple jurors get drowsy, or fall asleep, an intermission must be called, causing a most cumbersome prolongation of the case, which in turn increases the cost to taxpayers." Neutra acknowledges that this "involvement of public finances with our personal body chemistry may strike you as bizarre," but, he insists, "it is measurably vital" (*NN*, 71). The wider point is clear: if you ignore such "microfacts" as body chemistry in a courtroom, you inevitably ignore the various factors that caused the crime in the first place.

FIGURE 4.5. Richard Neutra, Orange County Courthouse (Santa Ana, California), 1968. Photograph: Julius Shulman. Copyright J. Paul Getty Trust. Getty Research Institute, Los Angeles (2004.R.10).

From Functionalism to Therapeutics

At the time of *Survival through Design* critics noticed a change in Neutra's attitude toward architectural design. Douglas Haskell, writing in 1954, observed how the book signaled a fundamental shift "from early naïve mechanistic functionalism to the psychological, from concern with how architecture goes together to a concern with what it is for, how it affects the user."[16] Harwell Harris offers a vivid picture of Neutra's early functionalism, noting that "for Neutra, *Sweet's Catalogue* was the Holy Bible and Henry Ford the holy virgin." All of Neutra's works, he observes, "had prefabrication in their blood stream" and forecast an "anonymous architecture and anonymous architects."[17] In a 1931 letter to Richard Muetterli, Neutra explained the difference as he saw it between two forms of artistic practice, one based in memory and empathy and the other in dispassionate analysis. "As soon as I observe someone in distress, I try to understand," he wrote, "but my interest in a *general conception of misery* is of a different kind, like my interest in aerodynamics or the construction of a new kind of airplane," adding that "in the field of social-planning, emotional involvement should be carefully avoided."[18] Neutra's self-narrative offers a trajectory for his work, from detached, functionalist concern for social planning to an empathy-driven psychoanalytic expression of "positive trauma." But ultimately the difference between these two accounts is one of emphasis. His underlying commitment was to the *user* of his designs rather than to the autonomy of the structures themselves. It is this sustained address to the user, as either interactive or psychoanalytically treated participant, that instrumentalizes his practice.

Design Plasticity and the New Man

Neutra's early work was dominated by large-scale public projects such as Rush City Reformed, Lehigh Portland Cement Airport, the Ring Plan School, and an elaborate competition design for the League of Nations (which he undertook with Schindler; Figure 3.2). Moreover, Neutra's early domestic architecture was not (at first) construed in terms of emotional cathexis; the Lovell House of 1929, for example, was described by its (initially) unsatisfied clients as "a public museum."[19] Indeed, Neutra grew increasingly concerned with the "directly physiological" notion of architecture, suggesting that too much attention to it would "ruin [his] outlook forever."[20] Instead, he aimed to produce an open-plan, flexible architecture that inhabitants would use in the ways they saw fit. Neutra consistently spoke of the necessity of "elasticity of use," down to the smallest detail.[21] "In our house rooms have no names such as living room, dining room, bedroom," he announced. "Rooms are portions of our great living space and pragmatically elastic." In his 1947 article "The Changing House" for the *Los Angeles Times,* he stressed the necessity of a "ready-for-anything" plan that is "adaptable to almost any living requirements" and "flexible enough to permit all kinds of modifications."[22] On this point, Schindler and Neutra found common ground. "The modern dwelling," Schindler stated in his "Manifesto," "will not freeze temporary whims of owner or designer into permanent features. It will be quiet, flexible background for a harmonious life."[23]

Behind Neutra's and Schindler's ideals of plastic architecture lay Wright's notion of plasticity, advanced in essays like "The Sovereignty of the Individual," which served as the preface to the 1910 Wasmuth edition of his work:

> In America each man has a peculiar, inalienable right to live in his own house in his own way. He is a pioneer in every right sense of the word. His home environment may face forward, may portray his character, tastes and ideas, if he has any, and every man here has some somewhere about him. . . .
>
> It is fair to explain the point, also, which seems to be missed in studies of the work, that in the conception of these structures they are regarded as severe

conventions whose chief office is a background or frame for the life within them and about them.[24]

The mismatch between Wright's ideals and his practice was apparent from the start. Wright had little interest in creating a neutral background for the display of his clients' "tastes," nor did he have much faith in the emergence of the sovereign individual from out of the masses. As Vincent Scully observes, on this score Wright's stated intentions amounted to very little. "The prose of architecture—the background buildings which attempt only a little and are content to serve as neutral settings for any kind of human thought and action—did not interest him," Scully writes. It was Wright's "life-long intention to form human life."[25]

Neutra's prewar work was dedicated to a Wrightian ideal of sovereignty on the side of the inhabitant. The house that Neutra designed in 1937 for Grace Lewis Miller, a practitioner of the Mensendieck method of spinal exercises intended to prevent and correct back problems, was aptly described by its owner (in a letter to the Museum of Modern Art) as a "smart house," one that "lends itself easily for any kind of life, either close, private life, or the gay social life . . . whether there is one or more to dinner; or one or two or a crowd for tea or cocktails; or a bunch of young things, careless of their cigarette butts, for dancing."[26] The spaces were designed in a system of complex layering to make possible expansive multifunctionality. The main room supported functions of living, sleeping, eating, and entertaining and also allowed Miller to use it to perform "functional exercise" with her clients (Figure 4.6).

For Neutra, aesthetic principles of "weightlessness" and "dematerialization" originated in loosely social and political ideals of liberation and freedom. Like other architects in his moment, he construed his structures as promoting new forms of life. Neutra's preoccupation with open planning reached its peak in the early 1940s with his designs for large-scale housing projects for low-income workers. The Channel Heights housing project for shipyard workers near the Los Angeles harbor at San Pedro, funded by the Federal Works Agency and comprising 222 residential structures for 600 families, marked the apogee of Neutra's publicly minded Depression-era program. Supported by a shrewdly managed media campaign, Neutra broadcast far and wide the utopian possibilities of prefabrication. The "prefabricated era is just beginning after many false starts," Neutra told the *Los Angeles Times* in 1941.[27] He trusted that the war economy would forcibly end traditional forms of design and usher in the era of prefabrication. Multifunctionality, made possible by prefabrication, ruled at Channel Heights (Figures 4.7 and 2.5). Houses were situated diagonally, with views of a park on one side and the ocean on the other. Underpasses functioned as surface drains and as "pedestrian communication," as Neutra called it, connecting residential areas and community buildings. The community buildings were masterfully designed with multiple

FIGURE 4.6. Richard Neutra, Grace Lewis Miller House (Palm Springs, California), 1937, 1938, 1939, 1941. Photograph: Julius Shulman. Copyright J. Paul Getty Trust. Getty Research Institute, Los Angeles (2004.R.10).

FIGURE 4.7. Richard Neutra, Channel Heights housing project (Los Angeles, California), 1941. Photograph: Julius Shulman. Copyright J. Paul Getty Trust. Getty Research Institute, Los Angeles (2004.R.10).

functions in mind: the community center functioned as a nursery, the supermarket contained a day-care center, the gardening building became a classroom, the stationery store contained a post office, and the drugstore doubled as a doctor's office.

From Plastic Spaces to Plastic Users

It remains to be seen how one might reconcile Neutra's early commitment to flexible use (open planning and multifunctionality) and his later commitment to a psycho-analytically inflected design. What connects Neutra's seemingly polarized accounts of design pliability and psychological sculpting? It seems that Neutra's identification of architectural openness with user participation conflicts with his later concern to create "organic" structures whose materials, although arranged by the designer into biologically curative ensembles, contain an affective life independent of the designer. If Neutra's early work and writings stress the technological capacities for new forms of liberated experience, technologies that allow for seemingly high degrees of "participation" in the shaping of one's surroundings, then how do those same technologies liberate the *architect's* capacity to manage and shape psychological function?

An important precedent for Neutra's early embrace of an aesthetic of flexibility, plasticity, and multifunctionality was the work of the constructivists in Russia. Although he had limited access to their work, he was acutely aware of their operations through a range of European journals, such as *De Stijl, Vesch/Gegenstand/Objet, Merz,* and *G*. These publications featured current projects of the Russian avant-garde (largely stripped of its political bearings), which were presented to Western audiences as examples of advanced standards for contemporary design. Aleksandr Rodchenko, as the deputy head of the Metfak, or Metalwork Faculty, at the Soviet design school VKhUTEMAS (Higher Art and Technical Studios), poured his energies into the development of objects with "multiple functions which required a creative intelligence to manipulate."[28] These works, including beds, chairs, and storage cases, embodied Rodchenko's ideal of flexible form. Stripped of their social and political context, Rodchenko's works become all-purpose signifiers for "free choice." When Victor Margolin describes Rodchenko's aims as allowing "users [to] realize [the] potential [for action] by interacting meaningfully with the objects rather than relating passively to them," he has effectively turned a communist work into a capitalist product.[29] Rodchenko's design for a collapsible rostrum for the USSR Workers Club exhibited at the Exposition Internationale des Arts Décoratifs et Industriels Modernes in Paris in 1925 "allowed for maximum interactivity with a strong active user who could alter its form according to different needs."[30] As a "virtual volume," Rodchenko's linear frame of struts and planes could unfold to produce a rostrum or movie screen or bench and collapse again into a relatively compact mass.[31] And yet for Rodchenko, there was no question about the kinds of functions his "strong user" demanded.

For Rodchenko, multifunctionality is an expression of enlightenment universality, a point he made about his wood constructions of 1921. The aim is "to show a certain universalism, that from identical forms all sorts of constructions may be constructed of different systems, types, and uses."[32] It is equally an image of total intentionality, everything put to use without remainder, as Rodchenko declares: "NOTHING ACCIDENTAL, UNACCOUNTED FOR." Rodchenko's forms are meant to be readable as expressions of total use, an ideal directly relevant to the work of the Eameses.[33] For Neutra, by contrast, functionality stops at the level of function. That is, there is no sense that the expression of system extends beyond the limits of an item's particular use, and there is no effort to make the functionality of the tool legible to its user. So while everything counts for Neutra—he aims to shape every aspect of his environment to control affective response—it is an intentionality that is neither legible to the inhabitant nor available for understanding (it is chemical reactions that he is organizing). Multifunctionality for Neutra serves to ensnare the subject in a space whose deeper functionality occurs at the level of biology.

It is tempting to historicize Neutra's concerns, to see his early and late work as driven by competing and largely contradictory impulses in response to the changing social and economic climate of the interwar years in the United States. According to Sandy Isenstadt, for instance, by the postwar period, Neutra's "focus had changed from the technology of construction to the technology of perception, a consumer aesthetics."[34] But from a broader perspective there is no conflict between the various phases of his practice. From beginning to end Neutra was devoted to shaping the lives of those who inhabited his structures—the consumer, rather than the site, structure, or form, was his only object. As Barbara Lamprecht rightly notes, "All Neutra houses were to be therapeutic."[35] Stephen Leet elaborates on the idea: "What was unchanging was his belief that the primary responsibility of the architect is to improve and enrich the well-being of architecture's inhabitants. . . . The architect had a professional responsibility to eliminate, or at least ameliorate, the detrimental consequences of poor design and planning."[36] Was it a belief in the architect's responsibility that drove Neutra to imagine structures (for good and ill) as fatally determining the lives of their inhabitants? What kind of responsibility does this amount to? Neutra undoubtedly changed his approach to therapeutic spaces between the time of the Lovell House and that of the Kaufmann House. These were strategic questions—how best and how deeply to shape the lives of the inhabitants.

California Bauhaus

A central source for Neutra's design thinking was Walter Gropius's Bauhaus work. Gropius and Neutra shared a guiding concern for monitoring and controlling the affective qualities of the most minute design details. According to Gropius, "Color and texture of surfaces have an effective existence of their own, sending out physical and psychological energies which can be measured as such."[37] Studying and controlling these "energies" was the basis of the Bauhaus education; at the Bauhaus, "[we] knew and taught that space relations, proportions, and colors control psychological functions."[38]

Gropius's "Modern Theatre Construction," first published in English in February 1928, just weeks prior to his visit with Neutra, bears directly on Neutra's design theory.[39] In this essay, Gropius describes the fate of his unrealized "Total Theater" for Erwin Piscator in Berlin, emphasizing the extreme pliability and plasticity of the structure and how that would allow for new forms of audience participation in performances. Piscator's "utopian demands aimed at the creation of a technically highly-developed, pliable theater-instrument which should to a great degree allow the audience to participate actively in the scene."[40] A few years later, in his Rome lecture on total theater, he notes that the building would be so "adaptable in character" that it could "respond to any imaginable vision of a stage director—a flexible building, capable of transforming and refreshing the mind" (Figure 4.8).[41] The building would be flexible for the *director* in order to "refresh" his audience (needless to say, Gropius offers no discussion of the plays, only of the instrument, as though the meaning is an expression of the medium). The new theater would be "an instrument so flexible" that it could support a seemingly infinite "diversity of purposes."[42] Above all, Gropius is concerned with "drawing spectators into closer relation with stage happenings."[43] Every aspect of the new architecture's technologically inspired flexibility would be aimed at fixing and controlling the spectator's experience. The building would be "so pliant and variable" in order to ensure that the spectator is "brought into the midst of stage events."[44] Architectural pliancy would be the means by which the architect/director could "assault and force the public to participate in the play."[45] If the "precision instrument" is made as "flexible as possible," then the spectator "cannot escape" from the architect's grip. (Gropius describes the arrangement of seats surrounding the circular stage as "pincer-like.")[46] "The goal of this Total Theater," Gropius concludes, "is to overwhelm the spectator. All technical devices serve this goal."[47] Architectural flexibility is in the service of enforced participation. When Neutra speaks, here at a women's university club, of the "plastic purposelessness, passively receptive mind of the infant," he construes the audience as a pliable material to be shaped by the designer.[48] Plasticity is not a relation between inhabitant and environment but rather one between designer (father/doctor), building (mother), and user (infant).[49]

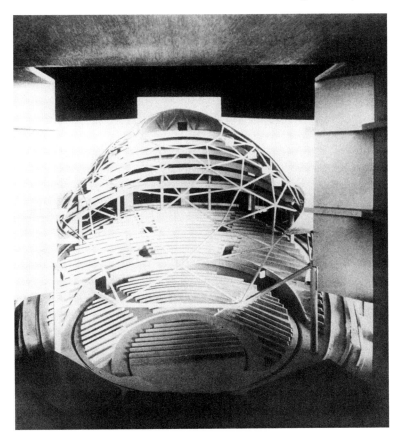

FIGURE 4.8. Walter Gropius, scale model of Bauhaus theater, 1927.

Neutra's Materialism

Neutra's goal was not simply to shape the psychological functions of his inhabitants—an ideal he shared with a multitude of architects—but also to control those functions through only the most diffuse relation to his intentions. For Neutra, control was a result of his careful arrangement of prefabricated materials that contained their own "measureable energies" and not a matter of his intentional shaping of those materials toward a set of desired responses. Throughout his writings Neutra minimizes his aesthetic intentions while granting his materials the form of agency he denied himself. Agency was generated by his materials; thus his desire to incorporate as much of the "neurologically salubrious agents of nature" as possible (*SD*, 195). His belief in the built-in affectivity of his materials, their capacity to generate measurable sensory effects outside his shaping will, describes his basic approach.

Neutra's effort to deny his agency through an "objective" deployment of materials ultimately secured him from the possibility of failure. Or rather, he reconceived failure and success along scientific lines: a good building was one that could potentially be measured for the positive effects it produced for its inhabitants. Likewise, the unhealthy effects of a failed structure could be measured, in principle (what would it be like to measure the effects of a building?). While Neutra invented a secure means to produce architecture, he thereby also made it impossible for his buildings to be evaluated in terms of their meaning. Meaning, for Neutra, was subsumed into hypothetically measurable quantities of energy exchange.

Although Neutra would continue to produce a new architecture and prophesize the coming of its new inhabitant, he severely tempered his social vision after the end of the war. His two major works of the later 1940s—the Kaufmann House in Palm Springs and the Tremaine House in Montecito—lack any ambition for mass-produced functionality. Men and women could no longer be trusted to shape their own lives (however narrowly conceived); now, the subtle "creative guidance" of the designer was necessary to help the newly termed "patient-client" thrive. Through a series of carefully organized shock effects, Neutra would slowly shape his clients into affectively calibrated beings, rescuing them from a life of deadening routine saturated by imperceptible but traumatic shocks.

Near the end of his life, Neutra recalled his brief experience at the Bauhaus and the shared hopefulness of the time that "modern technology could give us humans all we need."[50] He mused about Gropius's ideal as it manifested itself in the faculty housing he designed for the Bauhaus. Gropius emphasized "standardized and identical abodes," Neutra remembered, "accommodating the most diversified people who were certainly not compatible as artists! They were very, very personal and individual in their outlook on art and life." It was only those with a strong sense of self, Wright's "sovereign individual," who "could indeed live in identical dwellings."[51] By 1970, when Neutra wrote this, his idealism had eroded. The Bauhaus was the result of the "wizardry" of Gropius and impossible to repeat. Perhaps the most dramatic shift is marked by his resigned admission that one cannot "frame normed [sic] habitations, or prefab them for quite ordinary families of coal miners or steel workers in Pittsburgh or East Germany!"[52] It is a familiar lament. The world was not ready for the freedoms granted by the architect; rather than make social spaces for a social subject, one could only shelter those individuals who were already free. Neutra chose another option: by focusing his efforts on the microfacts of his environments, he made the ideal of a mass-produced modernism simultaneously impossible and doomed to fail from the start.

5

Functionalism with a Vengeance
Neutra, Soriano, and the Eameses

> We must not forget that "aware and willful" activities are relatively few
> and are directed from the motor areas of the frontal lobe. *Through design,*
> *however, man can . . . extend willful events to his innermost realms where*
> *responses were formerly almost uncontrolled.*
>
> —Richard Neutra, *Survival through Design,* 1954

Ornament and Crime, circa 1950

Early on in *Substance and Function in Architecture,* an oral history of Raphael Soriano's
life and work, Soriano describes his time growing up on the Greek island of Rhodes.
He tells us that his father was "very cruel" to him (*SF,* 12).[1] "He used to beat the hell out
of me," Soriano says. His father's favorite proverb was "Gold that isn't pounded never
shines." Soriano describes how his father would tie his feet together and give them a
"nice *bastonada,*" that is, a "cane stroke [on] the bottom of the feet" (*SF,* 13). After detailing the beatings, Soriano nevertheless insists that his father was not in any way a
"criminal." That's "not the whole truth in life." For Soriano, in fact, it is not the truth at
all. It is not surprising that a son might defend his father against criminal accusation.
However, what is surprising are the terms of his defense. Rather than appealing to a
broader psychological or social explanation for the beatings—that his father was himself abused, that it was part of the culture, that the child had some (misguided) sense
of guilt—he insists that "your behavior depend[s] on your chromosomes." Far from
criminal, his father was naturally carrying out what his genes dictated. His father's
DNA told him to beat his son. Soriano's told him to become an architect.

A few moments later Soriano describes his love of music in strikingly similar
terms. When he was a child, his father taught him to play the violin. "My whole life
revolves around music," he states, but the methods his father employed were (perhaps
not surprisingly) brutal: "If I made mistake on one of the notes, with his bow [he would]
bang on my little fingers" (*SF,* 17). Marlene Laskey, the interviewer, expresses dismay
and adds, "It's interesting that you didn't run away from" music after that. We are

now prepared for Soriano's response. The music, he claims, "was inside my chromo-somes—My mother too loved music, and my brothers. . . . He just cries when he listens to Beethoven and stuff." Beating a child and a child crying when he hears Beethoven are both matters of chromosomes.

In a famous 1958 psychological study of architects that included Soriano, the sum-mary of Soriano begins by stating that he "seeks out punishment; he revels in self-demeaning, self-abusive narrative." Sarnoff Mednick, the psychologist who carried out the study, notes that during his interview with Soriano, the architect was "most ani-mated and excited in his descriptions of being beaten by his father while tied to a couch, being despised by his classmate in college, and being at present penniless." Mednick describes Soriano's behavior as masochistic; it causes him, Mednick argues, to "seek out authority figures before which he can psychologically prostrate himself" (no doubt Neutra was one of those authorities). This pattern, Mednick maintains, is the "most important thing that can be said about him." But it is also the key to his "originality of approach."[2] Soriano saw it as the source of his originality as well, because in his view originality had nothing to do with his agency; rather, all of his actions were the results of biological forces beyond his control.

It was not just that Soriano was committed to extreme forms of behavioral analysis. He believed that science should eliminate every other mode of inquiry. The "biggest problem in our society," Soriano says, is that scientific understanding has been turned into what he calls (again and again) a matter of "personal likes and dislikes." The "deca-dence" of modern society is not in the beatings, in the "criminal" acts, but in the effort to understand them as a matter of social circumstance. "I think this is the tragedy that has occurred in our society today," he states: the tragedy of substituting myth for fact (SF, 342–43).

Not surprisingly, Soriano also saw modern architecture as a matter of chromo-somes. In his interview with Laskey, he offers what he sees as a conclusive defense of modern architecture. He recalls an encounter with a (female) student who was "la-menting at all this mechanization, all this technology." Like his father, he asks her, "What are you afraid of?" And here he enters into a brief Socratic dialogue:

"How did you come here to school?"
    "What do you mean?"
    I said, "What did you do? What transportation do you use?"
    "Oh . . . I have my car, automobile."
    I said, "Really." And I said, "Why didn't you use a horse and buggy?" Yeah. That
hit home, really. And I said, "Do you cook? Do you have an apartment?"
    She said, "Yes."

I said, "Do you have the facilities for cooking? Yes? What kind?"

"I have an electric stove."

I said, "Oh, no. It's best to make fire outside and bring it in and cook it with. . . . You are complaining about all this industrialization, all these mechanical things, disastrous, and yet you're using all of that, which helps you. This is our society. We have to progress. We cannot regress or stay in the same area. This is why we have to think, even in architecture, too. We have to check and evaluate. We discard things that don't serve anymore." (*SF*, 357–58)

What supposedly hit home with this student was the disjunction between her conscious desire for a more "natural" way of life and her actual way of life, one that was saturated with technology. Under scrutiny, her ideal of a natural life dissolved into acceptance of the functionally streamlined life she was living but had refused to recognize.

The logic of the claim was established many years earlier by architects like Loos, who noted that "if technical advance has made it possible to improve the form, then the improvement is always to be used. The flail is replaced by the threshing machine" (*OA*, 122). It is a one-directional logic: the current state of technology should determine the shape of one's house, just as chromosomes determine the patterns of one's behavior. To refuse these facts was a symptom of decadence.

Soriano curtly describes his working procedure (speaking in broken English): "I take tremendous amount of effort to find out the pros and cons and the possibilities" of new technologies. Once he has done the research and is "convinced that it works," "then I use it" (*SF*, 176). Performance and function replace taste or any subjective assessment. This is Soriano's performance theory in a nutshell: "If it works, it's beautiful. . . . If it doesn't work, it's an ugly thing" (*SF*, 344). Soriano's horse-and-buggy argument is a classic of the literature on modernism. His version comes direct from his teacher, Neutra, who borrowed it in turn from his teacher, Loos. In *Survival through Design*, Neutra laments how there is no means of connecting "the half-timbered barn, designed and nailed together as the garage of an American's 'English cottage,' and that other pride of his, the newest model automobile housed in that barn" (*SD*, 60–61). Like Soriano's newly enlightened student, "more and more" people have come to recognize the "ridiculous incongruity of driving *this* car into *that* garage," Neutra writes (*SD*, 61). Once the barn comes to resemble the car (or is simply eliminated), Americans will have finally outgrown their "faked infantilism" and matured into adults. Neutra's goal, like that of many modernists before him, was to convince people that the "continuous improvement toward a machine-made perfection" was identical to improvement toward a fully evolved human subject (*SD*, 54). The central difference between Neutra's machine modernism and the machine modernism of those before him, including that in his own early work, was his idea that in order for people to get used to the presence of the machine, it had to be concealed from them. This practice of *dissimulating machine modernism*—which is anything but a refusal of technology or the machine—came to be called California Modern.

For both Soriano and Neutra, modernism is a battle between performance and myth. For the architect that means removing any trace of *art*. The "arts," Soriano argues, "are purely a mythological thing" (*SF,* 360). That architecture has "degenerated . . . into art, artist. That's it. That's the big tragedy of our lives, is this contaminant called art" (*SF,* 361). The terms, again, are Loosian. It is the "interference of artists" into architecture— the application of ornament where it does not belong—Loos writes, that is the hallmark of cultural degeneration (*OC,* 165). This reactionary "revival of ornament" is respon- sible for impeding the "evolution of mankind" (*OC,* 169). If the artistic "urge to smear" paint on everything is responsible for cultural degeneration, then *"the evolution of cul- ture is synonymous with the removal of ornamentation from objects of everyday use"* (*OC,* 167). Soriano makes the same point in similarly blunt terms: "ornament" has "nothing to do with architecture" (*SF,* 103). "If you carve or paint," you create "confusion and enslavement," Soriano asserts.[3] But when Soriano describes architecture as pure func- tion, he means something very different from what Loos means.

Loos is a functionalist to a point; any work that does not "satisfactorily perform its intended function" cannot, he maintains, be beautiful (*OC,* 63). It is the "first basic condition" of any object considered beautiful that it should "not contravene the rules of practicality." But as Loos is quick to add, this first condition is not the last, because "being functional alone does not make [an object] beautiful. There is more to it than that" (*OC,* 63). The intended function of a building depends on conventions that might have nothing to do with performance. Above and beyond any functional requirements are emotional ones, and those change with the times and with the specific setting and program for any structure.[4] Soriano and Neutra reject Loos's historical and contextual claims; for them, tradition, emotion, and meaning are dissolved under the weight of scientific rationality.[5] "Development depends on liberation from symbolism," Soriano says, while Neutra yearns for a "purely naturalistic approach" that "dispens[es] with supernatural augmentation" and puts an end to "wishful magic and symbolic imagery" (*SD,* 101).[6]

For Soriano and Neutra, criminal degeneration stems from clinging to obsolete ideas. While Loos traces an evolution from the removal of ornament to the achieve- ment of purified classical forms, Neutra traces one from the stripping away of mythical thinking to the achievement of a purified naturalism. Neutra borrows directly from Loos's evolutionary language but refashions it along scientific lines. This is Neutra's reformulation of the Loosian "law" of cultural evolution: *"Gradual increase of functional perfection in design seems to be accompanied by a proportionate decrease of extrafunctional supplementation"* (*SD*, 101). By "extrafunctional supplementation" he means whatever is not a matter of performance, including art, symbol, myth, magic, tradition, and ornament. As evolution unfolds, "supernatural" remnants inevitably fall away. Neutra, unlike Loos, believes that architecture directs the course of evolution. Buildings, rather than humans, stimulate the process of evolution; the inhabitants of these buildings lag behind in an outmoded world of myth. Architecture is meant to serve and to heal a world of stunted subjects.

It is this last point that clearly separates Loos's and Neutra's models of cultural evolution and degeneration. For Loos, evolution is a matter of *education,* of ridding the world of criminal behavior through (elitist) models of good behavior. "To educate someone is to help them leave their primeval condition," Loos explains (*OC*, 184). Indeed, Loos's evolutionary picture is driven by educational advances, not Darwinian mutation. Consider the infamous opening of "Ornament and Crime":

> When a human being is born, his sense impressions are like those of a newborn dog's. In childhood he goes through all changes corresponding to the stages in the development of humanity. At two he sees with the eyes of a Papuan, at four with those of a Germanic tribesman, at six of Socrates, at eight of Voltaire. (*OC*, 167)

Modern forms of education train children to comprehend the stages of human knowledge in a fraction of the time demanded by earlier generations. Everything Voltaire could know about the world was accessible to a modern child at the age of eight. Papuan cannibals, as Loos sees it (through a European supremacist lens), are not criminals because they do not know any better. Modern cannibals are criminal because they do know better (or at least they could). For Loos, the high level of contemporary evolution is the product of "modern nerves," characterized by "immense individuality" and "intellectual strength" (*OC*, 175).

It is true that throughout *Survival through Design* Neutra underscores the role intellect plays in the processing of even the most low-grade design. It is only at an "early evolutionary stage," one that has "not yet reached human levels," that form functions "independent of intellectual cortical appreciation" (*SD*, 116). But his fascination with intellect, what he calls "upper-brain" associations, is strictly a function of his desire to overcome its hold on consumers. With proper knowledge and awareness of upper-brain associations, designers can come to understand how "drastically" they can "operate on such a sociological product as tradition, stiffened as it has become" (*SD*, 241). It is the social dimension of mind, the alterable part of the human subject, that matters to Neutra. If Loos's aim is to reestablish tradition against the rule of the artist-architect, then Neutra's is to show how the inhabitant's empty intellectual clinging to tradition can be broken down and "reconditioned." Neutra does not show the slightest interest in sociological analysis for itself; he is concerned with it only to the extent that it offers a model for the pliability of human nature. Neutra's aim is to convert all social mechanisms, no matter how deeply they run, into potentially malleable elements of environmental design.

Empathy Ballistics

For Soriano, the only question worth asking—whether about a toaster or a building—is "if it works." And if it is an animate thing (like a human), the only question is *how* it works. What complicates answering that question in Soriano's view is the ongoing confusion between function and meaning, fact and myth. There is nothing subtle about Soriano's epic narrative of the battle of science and technology against art. It is precisely in his extremism that he offers a clue to a range of canonical modernist claims. Long before midcentury modern became a marketing tool and the ubiquitous backdrop of "high-class" capitalist goods, midcentury architects developed a highly articulate and logically consistent set of beliefs to provide foundational support for their controversial practices.

During his interview with Laskey, Soriano leafs through a copy of McCoy's seminal *The Second Generation,* the book that brought more attention to his work than any other publication. He then disparages the volume's contents, including the pages on his work. "So what is this?" he asks. "What has it done here that Neutra hasn't done better ten times, hundred times? Imitations of Neutra, badly" (*SF,* 73). The "it" here is the work of the four midcentury architects addressed in McCoy's book: Davidson, Harris, Ain, and Soriano. After dismissing the work of his colleagues, Soriano relates how Neutra's son Raymond came up to him after a lecture and told him, "Raphael, you did what my father wanted to do and never did it" (*SF,* 77).[7] According to Soriano, Neutra was the only "really great" architect he ever encountered. Nonetheless, Soriano describes his own practice as one that "went beyond" Neutra's. By this he means fulfilling the logic of function that Neutra first proposed.[8]

Early on in *Survival through Design* Neutra describes how the natural sciences can explain criminal behavior and, in effect, justify it. Looking back over the advances in naturalism in the nineteenth century, he observes how with proper knowledge of the "laws of heredity and of environmental influence, the weak and unadjustable individual, the criminal, and all the characters on the margin of established society became 'comprehensible'" (*SD,* 33–34). Neutra's criminals, like Soriano's, are products of heredity. But there is one key difference between Soriano's criminals and Neutra's: for Soriano crime is a matter of chromosomes, while for Neutra it is a matter of environmental influence. That is, criminality, as well as morality, is a matter of *architecture*. Neutra rejects the idea that crime is solely a product of one's genes, because that allows the bourgeoisie to be "complacent about unpleasant social realities" (*SD*, 33). Heredity can be "invoked as a neat justification of exploitative practices." On this account, because heredity is fixed at birth, little can be done but to build sufficient prisons and mental hospitals. This view is unacceptable to Neutra, but not for the reasons we might expect. Neutra says next to nothing about the problem of exploitation but instead confines himself almost solely to the problem of design. He aims to replace every instance of hereditary thinking (how genes determine behavior) with environmental analysis (how structures determine behavior). Whether one is healthy or weak, productive or criminal, is a matter of *environment*. But it is not just a matter of environment *versus* heredity; it is also a matter of how environment *shapes heredity itself*.

Neutra embraces the new science of non-Mendelian inheritance, what was called at the time "plasmagene theory." If for Soriano the limits of human behavior and of architectural agency stop at the chromosomes, for Neutra chromosomes are the last barrier to be broken between architect and inhabitant. In chapter 10 of *Survival through Design*, Neutra considers the work of geneticist Tracy Sonneborn (1905–1981), who discovered that "cell plasm genes in protozoa can transmit to a next generation acquired characteristics of . . . higher temperature resistance." Neutra's sense of the consequences of this research for *design* is inordinate; what it suggests to him is that "things are not as fixed as we thought" (*SD*, 83). Through shaped spaces, architects can influence "the future of a species" in far-reaching ways. Alternately, if they fail to understand the role of plasmagene, they can "bring about mutations" more devastating than anything nature can produce (*SD*, 83). Neutra concludes that Sonneborn's research on inherited temperature resistance leads directly to the idea that "through design, we tamper daily with the precious inheritable substance itself" (*SD*, 83). Neutra's claim that the "inheritable substance itself can be molded"—the sculptural analogy is persistent—is closely tied to a more personal consideration: the power to shape the species "adds a great deal to the prestige and significance of design" (*SD*, 83).

Although the fact has gone unremarked, Sonneborn's plasmagene theory was as contentious as Neutra's claims about environmental design. Sonneborn asserted that "there was a gene for each trait and each gene produced a cytoplasmic self-reproducing copy of a part of itself." His view was that there was genetic information contained within cytoplasmic organelles and that this extranuclear information helped to determine hereditary characteristics. Sonneborn outlined an ambitious program for plasmagene. As one of his colleagues described it, Sonneborn believed that "cytoplasm contained some alternative system of genetic determinants . . . even more important than that of the nuclear genes."[9] By emphasizing the cytoplasmic determinates of heredity, Sonneborn suggested that cytoplasm is susceptible to environmental influence in ways that the nucleus is not at all; his goal was to find a "more general system of interactions between genes, cytoplasm and environment."[10] Just as Sonneborn waged a battle against "nucleocentric geneticists," so Neutra waged one against every barrier to environmental influence, including those of chromosomes and DNA.[11] Sonneborn's views clashed with the widespread consensus that, as T. H. Morgan put it in 1926, "cytoplasm may be ignored genetically." In his autobiography, Sonneborn describes his position as "a lifelong critic of what has seemed a blind and erroneous faith in the gene as the source of all heredity."[12] Displacing the gene means affirming the influence of environment on heredity. More controversial, Sonneborn sees his position as driving him into a "closer . . . relation with Lamarckism, with the inheritance of acquired characteristics."[13] This is what Neutra is referring to when he observes how "modern biological research" has "shaken the theory that acquired characteristics, or inflicted impairments, mean nothing to descendants" (SD, 83). (Neutra, hedging his bets, refers not to Lamarck but rather to "early Darwinian days"; SD, 83.) Loos, as we have seen in chapter 1, exhibited a fascination with the discredited ideas of Lamarck. But for Loos, in contrast to Neutra, what mattered was the educational process, how "great" works of art could influence the hearts and minds of those who appreciated them, while for Neutra what mattered was the capacity for forms to unconsciously alter a person's inheritable substance, a power that decisively sidelined normative notions of education.

As Neutra was aware, as early as 1948 Sonneborn was identified with the discredited work of Russian biologist Trofim Lysenko. Lysenkoism was at the center of wide-ranging debate in the Western scientific community at midcentury, and Sonneborn's ideas were construed as congruent with Lysenko's, a fact that damaged Sonneborn's professional credibility. A 1950 article in the *Daily Compass* titled "Is There Any Scientific Basis for the Lysenko Theory?" remarked that Sonneborn's theories were compatible with "the official genetic theories of the Soviet Union."[14] Even though Sonneborn (much later) described Marxism as "evil at the core," he nonetheless strongly supported the Lamarckian view embraced by Lysenko that "the inheritance of environmental effects" is a central factor in heredity.[15]

Showing the impossibility of disentangling acquired and constant characteristics is crucial for Neutra. Bringing Pavlov to bear on human subjects, in chapter 31 of *Survival through Design* Neutra describes how "when we sit down at the *usual* place for the *usual* meal and begin handling spoon, fork, and knife, followed by salivation and swallowing," these activities are accompanied by a "fixed sequence of actions in glands and muscles" (SD, 225). Although he claims in chapter 24 that it is imperative for the designer "to distinguish on all levels" between acquired and constant characteristics, he now argues that "habituation, habit-forming on all organic levels, cannot really be separated from constitutional growth or maturation . . . since growth is not an isolated phenomenon" (SD, 225). Because growth "never occurs in a vacuum" and involves a "manifold interaction with concrete surroundings," there is no way to distinguish between environment and heredity. To make his point, Neutra offers a reflexive model: the "child learns while it grows and grows while it learns. A segregation of acquired habit and sheer growth responses or, in other words, an attempt at theoretical separation of nature and nurture" is impossible (SD, 225–26). But it is not just that Neutra rejects a "theoretical separation" of nature and nurture; he also aims to undermine the existence of nature insofar as it is resistant to architectural will. Neutra rejects any firm distinction between "cultural tradition and innate 'instincts'": as evidence of the questionable nature of such a distinction, he points to the case of a sparrow that was "observed to abandon his natural chirps and to learn canary call notes when reared in a nest with canaries. After some struggle and delay, he imitated their song successfully" (SD, 226). The allegory is obvious. Neutra is telling designers how to create "nests" for inhabitants who, after some inevitable "struggle and delay," will abandon their "natural" attitudes and allow themselves to be "remodeled" by the designer.

To be clear, Neutra is invested not in the primacy of the social, but rather in the capacity of the designer, through a *social theory of biological change*, to alter subjects against their will (but for their own good). Neutra insists, in the boldest terms, that what the "era of brain-physiological research" tells the designer is that he is "perpetually and precariously [an] active conditioner of the race and thus acquires responsibility for its survival" (SD, 224). Indeed, the degree of "good or harm he can do to mankind is staggering" (SD, 245). Far from "catering to" acquired responses, the designer is the "grower of responses and even of the plant itself which can be cultivated to respond" (SD, 244). The message is clear: inhabitants are plants that the architect cultivates with the latest scientific techniques to produce a superior product through genetic modification.

If in chapter 24 Neutra's emphasis falls on the necessity of recognizing the "primary and innate," by chapter 33 he turns his attention squarely to the changing and susceptible aspects of human development, the "vast assortment of acquired conditioned reflexes" that "cannot and will not be set aside" (SD, 245). Challenging Mendelian nucleocentrists, Neutra refers to the work of Friedrich Goltz, who, by systematically removing parts of animal brains, delimited "spheres in which the various sensory nerves deliver their messages, and where the latter are transformed into conceptions and mentally stored."[16] Goltz succeeded in showing that life is maintained "after removal of . . . upper brains," but Neutra is more interested in how his experiments prove the existence of "simplified and . . . predictable psychic material." What Goltz's research reveals is a body of biological fundamentals that one can safely "set aside" in order to focus on the all-important, because alterable, "acquired conditioned reflexes" (*SD*, 245).

Neutra offers his most detailed assessment of primary response in chapter 15, where he addresses Louis Sullivan's notion that form follows function. Asserting that *"function follows form,"* Neutra notoriously reverses Sullivan's terms (*SD*, 116). Form, he argues, is "a primary, a motivating force," one in which "higher brain centers are not involved" (*SD*, 113–14). He observes how humans have "retained the ancient bottom layers" alongside the "impressive top layers to our nervous equipment" (*SD*, 114). And yet the point of this discussion is *not* to explore the imbrication of ancient and contemporary layers of the brain; rather, it is to show how "even imbeciles" do not function at such a low level of animal response. Neutra's aim here is to relegate the "subhuman" and "subnormal" aesthetic responsiveness to a kind of reflex, one that is devoid of significance for the designer. Against the primary aesthetic impulse, Neutra affirms the mix of "purity and impurity," the "indivisible" "neurological entity" that defines *"our stage of development and . . . human* picture of the world" (*SD*, 117, 118). Yet again, this sensible picture of the entwinement of primary and secondary layers gets displaced by Neutra's far more basic fixation on nervous malleability.

Neutra has little patience for the idea of an unacquired, fixed genetic code, because it places a limit on the designer's will. At its most radical, *Survival through Design* can be seen as Neutra's search for a means to turn every "primary and innate" quality into a matter of acquired conditioned reflexes, up to and including the inhabitant's genetic material, a means that he devises by redefining an environment as man-made. He begins with a conventional description of an environment as the "sum total of all stimuli to which a neural system is exposed." Because the architect's primary object is the neural system, "the future development of brain physiology will aid and underscore with factual knowledge the design of a constructed environment" (*SD*, 230). But the neural system, as Neutra is aware, is a product of *nonenvironmental* factors. Neutra observes that no brain is "so plastic" that it can unlearn what shapes it and that much of the brain's development is "irreversible" (*SD*, 228). No matter how plastic the brain is, recesses of it remain resistant to alteration, spaces within the body that remain free of design manipulation. Even though the architect "has appeared to us as a manipulator of stimuli and expert of their workings on the human organism," even though his "technique is really with the organic matter of brains and nerves," there are genetic elements that resist the architect's will (*SD*, 230). Neutra batters this last genetic barrier:

> [The designer's] outer arrangements . . . may further or harm inner physiological developments. This is so except perhaps *where matters seem predestined by heredity.* There it is often *assumed that things are removed from design influence and determined by constitutional equipment and genes.* What seems hereditary, however, is often

influenced by the prenatal, the uterine environment, and the condition of a child-bearing mother is not independent of the situations in which she finds herself for the act of birth. Whether she spends the months of pregnancy in a cave, in a nomadic tent, or in a residence with controlled climate and insulation, whether she has her baby kneeling on two stones or after being wheeled from the labor room into the delivery suite of a modern maternity hospital, briefly encompasses the designer's influential contributions to what may be early death of the infant or *later appear as its inherited constitution*. The limits of these contributions and so the formidable powers of design often seem almost beyond scrutiny. (*SD*, 230–31; emphasis added)

Neutra details how the baby is delivered into a traumatic environmental situation: luminaire lights, the nurse's face mask, the "high-frequency" sound of forty-five yelling babies, the smell of medications, the timed eating, the thermal shocks in the all too "heated, air-supplied man-made room" (*LS*, 273). But what he is interested in is not exactly this primary moment of socialization but rather the nine months *prior to birth*, the time *before* the baby is delivered into the architect's hands.[17]

For Neutra, there are no "predestined" spaces outside the architect's reach. He takes it as a challenge that the inhabitant's genes are "removed from" the influence of design. Neutra's fixation on hospitals and primary educational environments leads him to ponder the prenatal environment and its impact on genetics. The "designer's influential contributions" to the mother's environment, he argues, have effects on the unborn child's development. This influence is so significant that what "later appear[s]" as the child's "inherited constitution" is in fact the inheritance, in part, of the *designer's* intentions (as though the designer inseminated the uterus in some equal measure with the father). While Neutra suggests that this microscopic level of influence seems "almost beyond" scrutiny, it turns out that it is not at all beyond scrutiny and that it is already available for him to consult.

At times Neutra cautions readers about the overly optimistic application of science to design. In chapter 29, after heaping praise on Pavlov's "systematic attempt to accumulate an unprecedented body of verifiable data concerning behavior," he warns readers (citing Ross Menzies) that it "is not justifiable to conclude cavalierly that all conditioning follows the principle of conditioned salivation in dogs" (*SD*, 208). Rejecting what he calls "push button" techniques of nervous influence, Neutra affirms a more subtle *durational* process of empathetic conditioning, what he famously calls "biorealism." The new scientific methods, he observes, must be "tempered and kept under skeptical control." There is, he insists, "little danger . . . that laboratory methods of physiology when applied to design will become burdened." Neutra is not at all skeptical about the prospect of applying laboratory results to design; what concerns him rather is aesthetic speculation unbounded by "systematic experimental observation" (*SD*, 208). The point he stresses in this chapter is the theme of the book as a whole, namely, the dangers of *too little* attention to the latest results of neuroscience.

The real targets of what Neutra calls "design ballistics" are the "INNER DISTRIBU-TIONS OF FORCE AND STRESS within our nervous system" (*SD*, 207). With proper knowledge, nothing in the consumer is beyond the designer's reach. Designers can win their "battle for conquest" against consumers' resistant upper-level brain associations only if they know how to fire their guns accurately. *Survival through Design* is a handbook for those who wish to kill rather than be killed. Society is threatened by a "prolonged guerilla warfare [that] neurotically impedes the organism's activity stream." Designers are at war with the influx of unchecked and unmeasured stimuli, and Neutra's job is to teach them how to ensure that "any and all stimuli and responses possibly militating against [their designs] are not just repressed temporarily but successfully silenced once and for all" (*SD*, 230). Guerrilla warfare—"accidental" environments—must be matched by coldly calculated military operations with scientifically verifiable results. Through experiments that "probe into the operation, measurements, and intensities" of materials, designers can avoid collateral damage and project their "design intention" free of "guesswork" (*SD*, 216). The war will be won with science or not at all.

> If [designers] could grasp more fully all that is involved, the missiles they devise would reach their aims more effectively and their ballistics would be less accidental. They could conquer many a now toughly resistant rampart. They could almost manipulate at will cortical spreads of excitation and inhibition, as well as inductive effects. (*SD*, 217)

Accidental ballistics and guerrilla tactics produce effects beyond the control of the designer. The risk of imprecise attacks is the harm they can cause inhabitants through prolonged effects operating on the subconscious mind and the body. Alternately, a totally measured environment is a form of "preventive medicine." But unlike a pill or a shot, its "full dosage" is "administered every changing minute of the twenty-four-hour day, three hundred and sixty-five days every year, over at least a thirty-year amortization period!" (*LS*, 222) The weapon of choice for breaking down the inhabitant's inner walls is empathy, administered in diffuse and long-acting doses, rather than fast-acting bullets or scattershot imprecision. As Neutra never tires of saying, his plan of attack requires empathy:

> All this is, of course, not done by an unfailing stark and downright push button control technique. Accomplishment will have to come through empathy as through cautiously gathered judgment and the recognition that elements of design are, after

all, somewhat on the order of extremely touchy switches which must be turned on with subtle knowledge in order to elicit the desired processes of response. (*SD*, 217)

To effectively "recondition the sufferer of any maladjustment," one cannot appeal to "brute force such as locking up the cocaine, the opium, or the addict himself." "Police power" tends to "fail here" (*SD*, 241). Empathy warfare "must seep in and find 'volitional' . . . acceptance." As the quotation marks around "volitional" suggest, reconditioned subjects are like addicts resistant to getting sober and will have to be cured against their will. Breaking down the inhabitant's resistant will is the architect's ultimate achievement. "The task of reconditioning us from harmful addictions will be arduous," Neutra reflects, because our "predilections, as they pile upon and against each other, solidify and are hard to dislocate" (*SD*, 109–10). With enough empathetic design the patient can be cured; the "toughly resistant ramparts" of the self will fall, the subject will be sculpted, and the architect can move on to the next house.

As I have argued, one of Neutra's central goals is to show, contra Sullivan, that function follows form, that our lives are a "consequence of shape, of the shapes which surround us."[18] The built environment is a collective fate. Neutra provides an extreme but also typical example of what this view looks like in practice in his account of school design. In *Survival through Design* he takes up a report by D. B. Harmon, a kinesiologist who worked for the Texas State Department of Health. According to the report, a decrease in brightness contrast in an improved classroom produced "stunning" effects: 65 percent of refractive eye difficulties that were "supposedly correctable by glasses only" had disappeared after six months (Figure 5.1, left). "Eliminating muscular strain" resulted in a 47 percent reduction in malnutrition. The students' diets, Harmon insisted, did not change at all. The benefits did not stop there: 40 percent of "chronic infections, nose, throat, and ear ailments, and deficient functions" were "eliminated" strictly by means of "visual hygiene" (*SD*, 310). Further, 50 percent of dental trouble due to "faulty jaw positioning" was attributed to brightness levels—when the lights were adjusted, the dental trouble disappeared (*SD*, 311). "Methodical electric measurement of muscular innervation" of the students guided design solutions, while "anthropometric studies" recorded "habitual strain on the muscular and bone structure of growing children" (Figure 5.1, right). Neutra flatly describes the researcher's invasive scrutiny of the students: "Chemical tests were made on children; quantitative analyses of blood samples, urine, feces, the end products of glandular activity, were statistically compared" (*SD*, 310), and "the disintegration pattern of the basic encephalo-graphic sinus waves" were recorded and measured (*SD*, 311). The students were subjected to an anatomy theater: "Naturally, psychometrics were applied to gauge comparative mental achievement in detail," Neutra notes, as though the subjects were inanimate stuff (*SD*, 311).

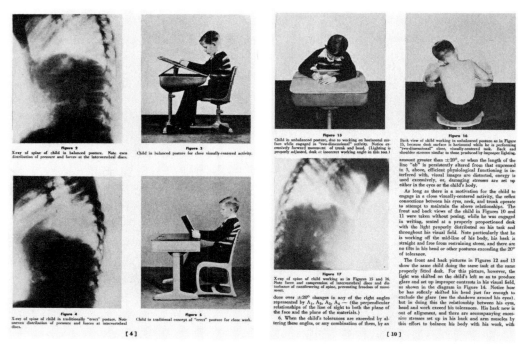

FIGURE 5.1. D. B. Harmon, *The Coordinated Classroom,* Grand Rapids, Michigan, 1951.

Finally, using "biomicroscopic investigations," scientists could pinpoint exactly where "deformations [occurred in] the children who lived and worked" in these spaces (*SD*, 310). All of this fed Neutra's dream of being able to "observe people in an experimental chamber . . . suffering by cumulative irritation" that was "scientifically measurable, within so many minutes, or hours of exposure."[19] We get a glimpse of Neutra's experimental chamber at his 1955 National Charity League Observation Nursery School, one that heavily features one-way glass to enable observers to monitor the children unawares as they play and learn, in order to generate improved outcomes. The school is featured with a series of Shulman photographs at the outset of Neutra's 1962 book *World and Dwelling* (Figure 5.2). The point of all this "science" of design was to persuade architects that it was their responsibility to collect all measurable data about the influence of their shapes on subjects and then deploy those measured shapes in the creation of ideal environments—anything less than that could be viewed as medical malpractice. What has all this to do with California Modern? The look and feel of "California" design—either denigrated or celebrated for its warming up of cold modern—was the package that made the task of human sculpting a more painless procedure.

The parents' council of the Child Guidance Clinic of Los Angeles has protected the peace of many homes. Neutra, in his friendly layout, saves all trees on the campus of the University of Southern California.

Diagnostic nursery seen from court and street corner.

Diagnostic nursery of the National Charity League.

Observation of a child. Face-to-face study helps to form physiognomic judgment.

Play courts with observation booth in the background with one-way glass. Research workers and diagnosticians see, but are not seen.

Play space, sometimes with an intentionally small choice of toys; other psychological tests call for an abundance. "Black windows" in the left background.

A psychiatric observer finishes notes at desk behind the one-way glass, after the children, singly and in groups, have used the play room while she watched.

FIGURE 5.2. Richard Neutra, Child Guidance Clinic (Los Angeles, California), 1954. Photographs: Julius Shulman, in *World and Dwelling* (Stuttgart: Alexander Koch, 1962).

What Was California Modern?

Nothing has proved more fateful for Neutra's reputation than Arthur Drexler's 1982 Museum of Modern Art exhibition and catalog *The Architecture of Richard Neutra: From International Style to California Modern.* Drexler's aim was to revive and defend Neutra's reputation, and his book largely set the terms for what has come to be called mid-century modern. Indeed, the term first gained traction with Cara Greenberg's 1984 *Mid-century Modern: Furniture of the 1950s,* but it was Drexler who established its intellectual framework.[20]

Despite his passing descriptions of Neutra's 1929 Lovell House as an instance of "complexity and contradiction," Drexler does not try to make Neutra over into a post-modern architect *avant la lettre.*[21] Neutra, he writes in the catalog's conclusion, "was without the consciously historicising intentions that now motivate the post-moderns."[22] Drexler views small-scale lyricism as Neutra's alternative to the International Style. Perhaps the clearest evidence of his position is the inordinate space granted in the exhibition to Neutra's pencil, charcoal, and watercolor landscapes and figure drawings (including five portraits, one of a dog, although the Pavlovian dimension goes unregistered) (Figure 5.3). In addition, the first building illustrated in the catalog is Neutra's McIntosh House of 1939, which notoriously features "plywood on . . . closely spaced posts of wood" (Figure 5.4). This house, Drexler writes, "marked a new willingness [by Neutra] to move toward an indigenous 'tradition,'" a return to the indigenous after the failures of internationalism, to post and beam after the disillusionment with steel and concrete.[23] Drexler drives home the point in his conclusion, describing Neutra as "an artist of the keyboard rather than the orchestra: he wrote *ballades,* not symphonies. His first achievement was to 'rationalize' the irrational." Offering only the most perfunctory outline of Neutra's vast commercial and public facilities (which includes virtually no mention of the many schools, churches, community centers, and medical facilities he designed), Drexler unconvincingly refashions Neutra as an architect of "spontaneity and improvisation," of "intuitively free style."[24]

Neutra, for Drexler, serves the purpose of providing an internal opposition to the International Style. Unlike other International Style architects, Neutra is able to "transform his faith in technological modernity into something more substantial." Neutra's "professional optimism," Drexler insists, is only skin deep; "underneath" all the technological and scientific chatter is an "essentially anti-urban, anti-technological sensibility." Expanding on Banham's laudatory description of Neutra's "domestication" of the International Style, one defined by a "sequence of pleasantly romantic houses" in the 1950s (*LA,* 176), Drexler suggests that Neutra's architecture is "more thoughtful, more private, more hesitant" than the "certainties of the twenties allowed."[25]

FIGURE 5.3. Richard Neutra, Milo, drawing, no date. Richard and Dion Neutra Papers (LSC 1179). Library Special Collections, Charles E. Young Research Library, UCLA.

FIGURE 5.4. Richard Neutra, McIntosh House (Los Angeles, California), 1939. HIP / Art Resource, New York.

Drexler's repackaging of Neutra's putative faults (small-scale, suburban, private, woodsy) as virtues had the desired effect of affirming midcentury warmth against early modern austerity. And yet there is not a shred of evidence to support the view that Neutra or his disciples Soriano and Koenig, whom Drexler mentions, were either "anti-technological" or, for that matter, more hesitant and uncertain when it came to scientific and technological fantasies about the domination of nature. If anything, what *Survival through Design,* along with the work of Soriano and Koenig, exemplifies is the increasing lack of uncertainty that defines a certain strain of modernist practice at midcentury. Neutra is not merely speaking metaphorically when he describes his ideal (in 1954) as the "continuous improvement toward a machine-made perfection," nor is it possible to detect hesitation in his definition of the architect as the "active conditioner of the race" who has acquired "responsibility for its survival" (*SD,* 54, 244). Rather than spontaneity and improvisation, it would be more accurate to speak of Neutra's fascination with the *look* of spontaneity and the *feel* of empathy as crucial weapons in his architectural arsenal.

Neutra construed his clients as tradition bound, habituated, and resistant to change, stuck as they were with upper-brain associations. Empathy and "warm" materials—wood, brick, water, landscape, select instances of traditional furniture—were tools he could marshal to achieve a more comprehensive functionalism. While it is accurate to say Neutra was an "artist of the keyboard" rather than the orchestra (as Drexler puts it), it would be wrong to see this as limiting his sense of ambition. Recall that when Neutra reworked Kandinsky's musical metaphor, he emphasized the idea of control of the "physiological keyboard" on which the architect must play (*SD,* 200). The keyboard analogy points to the *directness* of the designer's manipulation of his material (the client's nervous system) rather than to a scaled-down romanticism of the home. Indeed, the scale of artistic control is unprecedented. The point of *Survival through Design* is to provide tools that eliminate all the "reckless guesswork" from design and enable the architect to "foresee" all possible effects and measure them in advance of their deployment on the client (*SD,* 311).

My aim here is not to critique Neutra's excessive sense of control (something that is commonplace within architectural thinking). Nor is it relevant to my argument to weigh in on the fraught question of nature versus nurture in his account. Neutra's manic quality of design control is more a symptom of his seeing intention as a matter of *surefire transmission* rather than fallible communication. Neutra's architectural vision hinges on an idea of intentionality that *denies itself* at the moment of its greatest intensification, that turns every potential instance of expressive meaning into *objective, measurable* realities devoid of any responsibility beyond those associated with (putative) facts. In Neutra's hands as well as in those of his more strictly technologically inclined colleagues, the inviting qualities of California Modern were the external package for an even more radical vision of human sculpting than the expressionist and Bauhaus architects envisioned.[26]

This might seem counterintuitive. Neutra continually implored designers to be responsible for every aspect of their designs, given the vast consequences that built structures have on their environment. But the responsibility he had in mind was that of accepting the veracity of the latest findings of science, rather than of trying to communicate meaning to his clients, thus allowing his works to be understood or misunderstood, felt or unfelt, according to the sensibilities of the receiver. Neutra often referred to "complex responsibilities of design," but those responsibilities could be *settled* through research (*SD,* 311).[27] Architects were responsible both for causing "grossly pathological consequences" and for redressing those consequences of their designs, as though there were no limits on their culpability, but the nature of the obligation was defined by the latest scientific results, not by human significance (*SD,* 311). For Neutra, responsibility meant applying techniques to relieve one of the capacity to make a decision one could be responsible for.

Neutra, the Eameses, and Fate of Scientific Design

Neutra's later work was to an extent a response to that of his younger colleagues Charles and Ray Eames, a fact that has largely escaped notice. At the end of his career, Neutra explicitly attacked the Eameses around the status of scientific design, and it is to the nature of this debate that I turn now. The conflict between Neutra and the Eameses in a sense replays the issues raised in Neutra's conflict with Schindler, although in his critique of the Eameses, Neutra was also taking aim at the wider "affluent society" culture he saw represented in their work.

Charles and Ray Eames left the Cranbrook Academy of Art in Michigan, where Charles had been a design instructor and Ray a student, for Los Angeles in July 1941. Charles started a job in the drawing office of the art department of MGM Studios, a position he held for nine months and that he likely had gotten with help from Katharine Hepburn, who was friends with Charles's client Irene Rich. Irene Rich's daughter, Frances, was a student at Cranbrook Academy, and the Eameses produced drawings for a never-realized guesthouse at Rich's home in Santa Barbara. By September, the Eameses had moved into the Strathmore Apartments, which Neutra had designed in 1937 (Figures 5.5 and 5.6). Comprising eight units in four buildings next to UCLA in Westwood, the apartments are representative expressions of Neutra's 1930s design principles (Figure 5.7). The structure is modular in design, based on a unit of 3 feet by 3.5 inches, determined by the width of the standard steel casement (a width that

FIGURE 5.5. Charles Eames in a Ford convertible outside the Strathmore Apartments, circa 1941.

FIGURE 5.6. Ray Eames on the balcony of the Strathmore Apartments, circa 1941.

FIGURE 5.7. Richard Neutra, Strathmore Apartments (Los Angeles, California), 1937. Photograph: Julius Shulman, 1938, 1939. Copyright J. Paul Getty Trust. Getty Research Institute, Los Angeles (2004.R.10).

also corresponds to the traditional module of Japanese architecture). The Strathmore Apartments were immensely popular and attracted a celebrity clientele that included Dolores del Rio, Orson Welles, Luise Rainer, and Clifford Odets, and later John Entenza. Although it was modular in construction, the structure was not given any expressive weight. As Neutra put it at the time, "It would be far fetched to symbolize in [the] surface" of a structure the nature of its construction; the "exterior [should] give no hint" as to how it is made.[28] In a 1977 interview, Neutra's former colleague Gregory Ain glossed Neutra's disinterest in structure in wholly different terms: "Neutra," he stated, "had absolutely no sense of structure."[29] Neutra's determined lack of interest in structure, a point he shared with Schindler, contrasts sharply with the Eameses' approach, although the conflict goes well beyond any question of structural expressionism.

There is a remarkable set of visual and written records by the Eameses that document their experiences at the apartment complex. In 1948, Ray published an article in *Mademoiselle's Living* under the title "We Live in One of the Newest Houses in California" (Figure 5.8). In it, Ray describes their home as an empty "shell," one that

FIGURE 5.8. Ray Eames, "We Live in One of the Newest Houses in California," *Mademoiselle's Living*, Spring 1948.

imposes "no style on the tenants, but leave[s] them free to create their own surroundings through color, texture, use of area and objects and equipment needed for everyday life and activities" (*EA*, 29). Ray is echoing Neutra's own sentiments here, the idea that the new architecture provides "more and more space for the planning and enjoyment of artistic creation" and offers "peaceful, even vacant backgrounds, non-competitive settings, breathing room, space for the explosion of an art object."[30] And this is precisely how the Eameses used their apartment—as an all-purpose art and design studio. They famously turned their apartment into a furniture workshop, and it was there that they designed some of their most iconic early molded plywood furniture. Ray described their design intention at the time as making "good design . . . available to many people at lower cost" (*EA*, 29). The Eameses turn this idea into their famous motto: to supply "the best to the greatest number of people for the least" (*EA*, 73), an Eamesian reframing of Buckminster Fuller's ephemeralist mantra of "DOING THE MOST WITH THE LEAST."[31]

After living in the apartment for seven years, Charles sent a letter to Neutra in which he reflected on how the apartment building affected everyone who lived there. "The apartments you have developed here have given each [tenant] the opportunity to develop his surroundings in the most expansive way, each feeling that he is living within his own garden, and has complete privacy" (*EA*, 37). Neutra was so touched by the note that he held on to it, and later referred to it as a "love letter" in his autobiography.

At the same moment Charles was writing to Neutra, he and Ray had purchased a plot of land from Entenza, a meadow with eucalyptus trees in the Pacific Palisades overlooking the ocean at the edge of the Santa Monica Bay; it is here that they built their famous house (Plate 3). To get a sense of the innovations at the Eames House, CSH 8, one might compare it with modern houses built prior to it. The first four years of the Case Study House Program were dominated by houses with wood frames and plaster, brick, and wood siding, such as Neutra's Bailey House, CSH 20 (Figure 5.9). This house would have been an immediate point of reference for the Eameses, as not only was CSH 20 built just prior to the Eames House, but it was also built on the same stretch of land, the neighboring plot to the north. CSH 20 was originally a two-bedroom house of redwood and plaster with an L-shaped plan (Figure 5.10). The living room and dining room opened along the south side to a patio shaded by a giant eucalyptus, and the two bedrooms had their own garden spaces to the west. A prefabricated utility core was located at the knuckle of the structure near the entrance. Over the ten years after it was built, the house was expanded three times: two more bedrooms were added as well as a swimming pool along the northern extension.

The most obvious point of contrast between the Bailey House and the Eames House was in the materials. The Eames House was made of steel decking and plaster panels over a steel frame. The frame was built from 4-inch H columns and 12-inch open-web steel beams that were divided into nine bays, each 7.5 by 20 feet; the court had four bays and the studio five. Neutra's materials, by contrast, were traditional: redwood, plaster, brick, and glass, materials that first became dominant in his work with the McIntosh House (Figure 5.4). This is striking because Neutra was, of course, an innovator in the steel-frame house. He famously used a steel frame for the Lovell House (Figure 5.11), but, unlike the Eameses, he did not make this structural technology thematic in the house itself; plaster covered all the major structural elements.

In their original design for their house, the Eameses explored a less emphatic structural format, a bridge form built "between two trusses . . . [to create a kind of] box beam. The structure rested on two steel supports, with the box cantilevering out beyond them, while the house hangs over terraces, and through its raised perch, offers a direct view of the sea" (*MCH*, 54) (Figure 6.6). But when the steel arrived at the meadow, the Eameses had a change of heart and came up with a new plan using the same materials (*EMR*, 306) (Figure 5.12). They had initially wanted to use the largest amount of steel to enclose a modest amount of space, but in the new design they aimed to create the largest enclosure they could with the same materials. The space ended up being

FIGURE 5.9. Richard Neutra, Case Study House No. 20 (Los Angeles, California), 1948. Photograph: Julius Shulman, 1948. Copyright J. Paul Getty Trust. Getty Research Institute, Los Angeles (2004.R.10).

FIGURE 5.10. Richard Neutra, Case Study House No. 20 (Los Angeles, California), 1948. Photograph: Julius Shulman, 1948. Copyright J. Paul Getty Trust. Getty Research Institute, Los Angeles (2004.R.10).

FIGURE 5.11.
Richard Neutra,
Lovell House, steel
skeleton, 1927–29.
*Richard Neutra
1923–50, Buildings
and Projects,*
ed. W. Boesiger
(London: Thames
and Hudson, 1964).

FIGURE 5.12. The Eames House under construction, photographed by Charles Eames in 1949 for *Arts and Architecture.*

much larger, 2,500 square feet for house and studio, more than double the size of the Bailey House (Figure 5.13). "The structural approach," according to Charles, "became an expansive one in that it encouraged use of space, as such, beyond the optimum requirements of living" (*EA,* 39). Both ideas—a "structural approach" and "optimum requirements of living"—were in part a response to Neutra.[32] Neutra long believed that modern housing should be based in what he called "biorealist" principles, the optimum requirements to satisfy biological necessities: "Plans were prepared and experimental studies carried on during a period of two years," he explained, describing his process, "until the most reasonable and economical solution of the problems in hand were decided upon."[33] Neutra, in the beginning, following Bauhaus tenets, worked with a "Minimum Existence Correlation Chart" to determine the most "efficient" solution to parameters of "size, area, cube, cost, and rent."[34] What Neutra's experiments proved is that literal size is unrelated to *perceptual* size. It is perceptual expansion that humans

FIGURE 5.13. Charles and Ray Eames, Eames House (Los Angeles, California), 1949. Photograph: Julius Shulman for *Time*, 1958. Copyright J. Paul Getty Trust. Getty Research Institute, Los Angeles (2004.R.10).

require, not square footage. As he frequently observed, "Physiological . . . spaciousness" is more important than "mere geometrical size."

Another difference between the Eameses and Neutra was that Neutra always thought of his houses as at least potentially objects of industrial production. He had been "anxiously looking forward" to the CSH Program for years, as it was the inception of the "mass production" house (*MCH*, 47). The fascination with the mass-produced is what McCoy is referring to when she describes Neutra's project as one of a "continual search for the typical form and typical detail." He was always in pursuit of "the perfect solution to a detail" (*EMR*, 129). The Eameses, by contrast, rejected the idea of their house as either a type of or a model for mass production. While it is certainly true that the Eames House is emphatic in its use of standardized industrial parts—it is expressly "off the rack"—the Eameses maintained that the actual arrangement was highly "personal," and "whether or not it solves the particular requirements of many families is not important as a case study" (*EA*, 39). These points of divergence between the Eameses and Neutra over materials, spatial concept, and standardization grew wider as the years went on.

Still, in 1950 Neutra was not far from the Eameses' thinking. In a photograph of the Herman Miller furniture showroom taken in that year (Figure 5.14), a large mural of Neutra's home, the VDL Research House (1932), can be seen on the far wall, just beyond an Alberto Giacometti sculpture. The juxtaposition of the sculpture with the mural might reflect the Eameses' experience at Strathmore, with the house as background for the "explosion" of art and furniture. Four years later, the Eameses and Neutra, along with George Nelson, Robert Motherwell, and Richard Lippold, were invited by the West German Foreign Ministry to visit the country as part of a cultural exchange program. A photograph taken by Charles during that trip of Richard and Dione Neutra sitting by themselves at the back of their touring bus (Figure 5.15) perhaps hints at the tensions between the Eameses and Neutra, as it was at this point that significant and formative divergences emerged in their practices.

Charles was hoping to learn more about German folk arts, including games, festivals, music, and especially "mathematics and toys" (*EA*, 138–39). During their short trip, the Eameses assembled materials for an eleven-minute film titled *Two Baroque Churches* as well as for a thirty-two-pass, ninety-six-image slide show of a Munich pastry shop called *Konditorei* (Plate 5). What do pastries, baroque architecture, and modern design have to do with one another? Charles puts it all together: "The pastry is a contemporary example of the Baroque style of architecture of the early eighteenth century in southern Germany, which he calls 'light, humorous, wonderfully thought out, and highly mathematical,'" a pastry, he adds, that he would "like to feed . . . by spoon to today's students of architecture and design" (*EA*, 139). There are several leaps of logic here: baroque, pastry, festival, toys, humor, math, modern architecture. How might one bridge the gaps between these dizzying leaps in scale and content?

FIGURE 5.14. The Eames-designed Herman Miller showroom in Los Angeles in 1950, with mural of Richard Neutra's Van der Leeuw (VDL) Research House, 1932.

FIGURE 5.15. Richard and Dione Neutra in Germany in 1955, at the German Cultural Exchange Program, photographed by Charles Eames.

The Eameses' practice is characterized by five central qualities that I discuss in the remainder of this chapter and again in chapter 6. First is care (Charles's provisional title for his 1970–71 Norton Lectures was "I Care"). What the pastry shop and the baroque church share is a commitment to quality, to loving care down to the least detail, and what Charles wanted to spoon-feed the architecture student is what it looks and feels like to show infinite care for and attention to one's work. The Eameses believed (perhaps naively) that quality is contagious, that care begets more care. The second quality of their work is a clear set of constraints, a necessity if one is to carry out a task to its fullest. The point of *Konditorei* is to show how making a pastry is a precise operation, a process that follows a strict set of rules passed down as "lore" from *Konditormeister* to apprentices. Third, and most difficult to grasp, is the importance of mathematics in the Eameses' work. Although there is a mass of information on display in an Eames film or slide show, what one is supposed to take away from the deluge of images is an underlying pattern, a pattern that tells one something essential about the product. The fourth quality lies in the idea that the play with pattern is itself pleasurable, that there is joy in the manipulation of models. And fifth is the fact that these mini, edible works of art *disappear with use,* making them paradoxically ideal objects for the Eameses, objects that retain lasting value by virtue of their disappearing: they can never be corrupted once they are consumed.

One work that exemplifies all these qualities is the well-known "Dinner Party" sequence from their film *Think* (Plate 6), which was displayed on fourteen large and eight small screens of varying shapes and sizes at the 1964–65 World's Fair in New York City. The sequence stars Joan Shawlee (who appeared in their close friend Billy Wilder's films *Some Like It Hot* and *The Apartment*; Wilder's wife, Audrey, also makes a brief appearance as the vamp). The film is about the use of modeling in everyday life. There is a clear problem that needs to be solved—a table arrangement—and the film shows the viewer the steps used to resolve it. The focus of the vignette is the last step of the process, "manipulating the model." The way the hostess presents various, seemingly infinite, configurations is the way the Eameses conceived of the mathematical formula. And the pleasure here is not in the party itself—not in the *application of the formula,* not in the *product,* as it were—but in the manipulation of the model. The party *is* largely the play with the model (the Eameses notoriously avoided parties). The party is also, like the pastry, ephemeral—nothing, presumably, is left over but memories.

The Eameses were most explicit about the modeling nature of their enterprise in their 1961 exhibition *Mathematica* (Figure 5.16), an exhibition that put them on a collision course with Neutra's approach in the 1960s. In his notes for the exhibition Charles describes "mathematics [as] an abstract model of relationships by which [we] link seemingly unrelated situations" (*EA,* 212). He provides a few key examples:

FIGURE 5.16. Office of Charles and Ray Eames, *Mathematica: A World of Numbers . . . and Beyond,* 1961.

A single grammatical diagram can be a model for several sentences with little else in common. . . .

3 + 2 = 5 is an abstract model for any number of situations that have this characteristic. $x^2/a^2 + y^2/b^2 = 1$ is the model for the ellipse that forms when we tilt a glass of water, or the ellipse that the earth makes [in] its orbit around the sun. . . .

There are men who become so interested in the abstract models themselves that their lives are spent manipulating [models . . .] with no thought or concern for how they may be applied. (*EA,* 212)

While it is certainly the case that the Eameses produced a great deal of work (artworks, furniture, toys, photographs, exhibitions, slide shows, films), indeed a staggering array of work, what was important to them was not multiplicity as such but the idea that multiplicity is underwritten by structure. Jehane Burns Kuhn describes the Eameses' "style" as the capacity for the design "solution" to contain "a diagram of the problem," what Charles describes as a "building [that] models the problem."[35] Kevin Roche attributes the idea to Saarinen and through him to Sullivan. He describes "Eero's philosophy" as "the Sullivan one of the solution being in the problem."[36] (Sullivan observes that "every problem contains and suggests its own solution.")[37] What this motto suggests is that the product is not exactly a finished thing, a solution, but an expression of the elements that make up the problem, a complex variant on structural expressionism.

One of the more striking moments in the simmering dispute between Neutra and Charles came during a 1956 panel discussion chaired by William Wurster at USC, when Charles directed a pointed question at Neutra: "I would like to ask Neutra . . . whether in his book *[Survival through Design]* he suggests a kind of suspicion of science, a suspicion that I do not really think that he has."[38] Neutra retorted, "No." But a few minutes later, he returned to Charles's accusation: "I resent, Charlie, that you more or less implied that I walk around spreading a suspicion against science. . . . I have been very much interested in defining what science has contributed, particularly that observation, curiosity bring results."[39] At first glance, it is hard to imagine what Charles might have been referring to, as Neutra, we know, was utterly obsessed with scientific research. What Charles was pointing to were statements in *Survival through Design* such as that "certain hopes set on science during the last two centuries have proved illusory and the results ambiguous" and that "indeed, despite its spectacular achievements in specialized fields, systematic science does not seem to be applicable to the whole of man's complex affairs" (*SD,* 23), a theme that reappears at the conclusion to the book (chapter 47), where Neutra warns of the abuses of science under fascism. He begins by asserting that the "survival of the race cannot be accomplished well without the use of current and available scientific knowledge." And yet one should question "the implication that the designer . . . can be wholly governed by *scientific attitude* or *methods*" (*SD,* 381). For Neutra, the architect, unlike the scientist, relies on the "intuitive insight often telescoped almost into an instant" (*SD,* 381). Charles most likely had the following passage in mind when he referred to the suspicion of science the book seems to indicate:

> Obviously, art, the art of design, which is a part of the art of living, cannot be replaced by science or technology. While science is proud of . . . its indifference to momentary and personal exigencies, and even to moral issues, the art of design, whether we are concerned with goals or with practical procedure, has none of these far reaching freedoms.
>
> We are touching here perhaps on a crucial issue of our time. The belief that science . . . might . . . do away with "idealistic" ethical norms, with any moral or intuitive bias and with all the arts. . . . It commands less credit today [than in the nineteenth century]. . . . [Scientific] detachment is justifiable only as a means, not as an end in itself. When this truth is forgotten, when scientific attitude absorbs all else, cool indifference together with prolific inventiveness may breed disaster.
>
> Not long ago, totalitarian governments set up their concentration camps for calculated extermination of human beings, and scientists were engaged to practice with

detachment human vivisection. After the Second World War they were tried and executed—obviously not on purely scientific grounds. Atonement is, for example, no scientific concept or procedure, but together with other moral necessities it has not yet been abolished.

> Especially since the advent of the atom bomb, our top-ranking scientists . . . have found it necessary to awaken the world to the fact that something quite different from scientific aloofness is needed to prevent the destruction of humanity. They have begun to speak in the name of universal human brotherhood—which according to diversified anthropological data may not be a scientific concept either. But it is precisely such an insight into the oneness of the human species, its characteristic properties, and its worldwide problems that must guide the work of the designer of our time into a feasible future. (*SD*, 381–82)

Although scientific detachment was justified in the past to protect scientists from political or religious persecution, detachment as a scientific principle brings disaster. Everything that has to do with "ethical norms," with "moral or intuitive" practice, everything involving "the arts," must be construed outside the parameters of science. Every pressing moral issue, including those raised by science itself (like the atom bomb), should be decided on a nonscientific basis. Finally, Neutra notes how even scientists use notions like "universal human brotherhood," a nonscientific concept, to defend humanity against their own inventions.

Charles's criticism of Neutra revolved around three issues: what he regarded as Neutra's conflation of science and technology, Neutra's idea that the root of the scientific attitude is defined by "aloofness" and "detachment," and Neutra's disingenuousness in asserting that intuition, morality, justice, art, and architecture are in fact "beyond science" (*SD*, 383).[40] The first two points are related. For Neutra, science mattered insofar as it delivered results, while the scientific attitude of detachment was inhuman insofar as it treated animate and inanimate with equal indifference. The Eameses, by contrast, radically separated science from any results that might follow from it. Likewise, for them the scientific attitude was valuable precisely insofar as it forestalled the instrumentalizing of people and things. On the last point, Neutra was clear: it is only for "practical purposes" that one acts *as though* morality, justice, and art are phenomena beyond science. That is, it was only as a matter of practical expediency that Neutra assented to the shifting grounds of normative human values; he did not believe conventions are anything but makeshifts that tide humanity over until science provides firmer solutions to our problems. The Eameses, by contrast, whatever their scientific commitments, assumed that the only ground of practice is the tenuous one of human conventions, norms, and values.

Neutra construed aloofness as the defining attitude of a new generation of designers working with large corporations, and he condemned the Eameses' association with IBM on these grounds. He saw the corporation as a soulless machine that turns human beings into abstract numbers on a readout, and he devoted the last fifteen years of his career to the exploration of what he called "biological individuality," individuated human mutations that systematically escape the grasp of corporate designers, with their inhuman play with numbers and figures.

Science, for Neutra, was largely a matter of neuroscience. And when he directed his attack at the Eameses, he used neuroscientific terms to defend his position. An abiding concern of his was to differentiate between recently accumulated layers of the frontal, upper-brain cortex and the deeper subcortical centers, where he believed the deep-seated realities of the "biological common denominator" resided. Much of the confusion of design at the time, he suggested, was a result of architects ignoring the deeper layers of the subcortex and relying too heavily on the superficial layers of the frontal lobe. Although it is hard to see, Neutra's cortex/subcortex distinction maps literally onto his structures, as exemplified in the Bailey and Goodson Houses, which made extensive use of natural materials—wood, brick, water, glass, opulent landscaping—applied to supremely technological structures. While the Strathmore Apartments were stripped down, unornamented, industrial design boxes, the Goodson House of 1948 (Figure 5.17) was woodsy and planar, spreading out into space.

The change of approach from the early austerities of the Strathmore to the California Modern comforts of the Goodson House registers Neutra's belief that what was called California Modern was a ruse. It was the outer layer, the frontal lobe, the inviting surface that would slowly acclimate the resistant consumer to the deep-seated values of modern design. Neutra took the analogy between architecture and the body and brain literally. The general shape of the plan of the Goodson House suggests the body of an upright figure (Figure 5.18). At the top of the plan is the pool or "brain" of the figure. Shulman's photograph taken from the perspective of the diving board looking back at the house (Figure 5.19) suggests how, for Neutra, inhabitants could literally dive into the brain of the structure, going down into the deep end or subcortex, where they would experience the lasting effects of letting go, of a protective bath in the original experience of "intrauterine suspension" (*SD*, 150). The appeal of California Modern is in the warm, domesticated (but often still prefabricated) materials, but for Neutra, those materials were a disguise to introduce contemporary reality into the brains of the still backward-facing, cave-dwelling subcortex of the not-yet fully modern subject.

In *Life and Shape,* Neutra intensifies his critique of the Eameses, attacking what he calls "life-detached abstract speculation [and] self-satisfied electronically managed mathematics" (*LS*, 360). These days, he writes, "statistical numerology has become tops.

FIGURE 5.17. Richard Neutra, Marvin Goodson House, entrance (Los Angeles, California), 1948. Photograph: Julius Shulman, 1950. Copyright J. Paul Getty Trust. Getty Research Institute, Los Angeles (2004.R.10).

Numbers are our 'stop' and 'go' signals, says IBM." This is a reference to the Eameses' *A Communications Primer,* a film in which they explain the stop/go nature of binary code (I consider this film in chapter 6).

> I did not act among a vast regiment of busy readers of regulation bulletins on what was assured by a committee of upstairs sages as this year's or next year's "best for the most"—with these "mosts" and "bests" known to me only by round figures, handed down in interoffice communications. . . . Where is man the *individual?* Is he lost in this progress of the numerical, which sits somewhere in our frontal lobe? . . . Is it perhaps a retreat from total life? (*LS,* 361)

As Neutra was well aware, the Eameses' *Mathematica* was sponsored by IBM, and the Eameses were heavily patronized by the corporation for the rest of their careers. Neutra

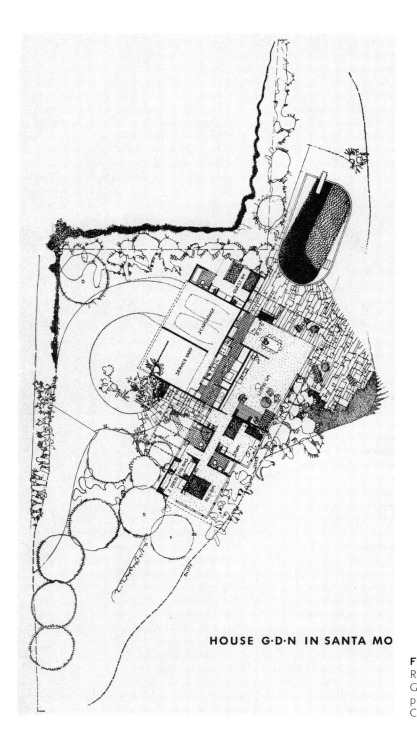

HOUSE G·D·N IN SANTA MO

FIGURE 5.18.
Richard Neutra, Marvin
Goodson House,
plan (Los Angeles,
California), 1948.

FIGURE 5.19. Richard Neutra, Marvin Goodson House, view from pool (Los Angeles, California), 1948. Photograph: Julius Shulman, 1950. Copyright J. Paul Getty Trust. Getty Research Institute, Los Angeles (2004.R.10).

construed the Eameses' idea of the "best for the most for the least" as a quantitative marketing tool, as design by bureaucracy. By contrast, he stressed the individual, specifically the "biological individual" as it was described by Roger J. Williams in a series of influential books.[41] His structures became more and more heterogeneous, increasingly fitted out to a highly specific biological makeup, a quality that Shulman exploited in his increasingly illegible photographs (Plate 7). As Neutra saw it, everyone, looked at closely, is an "individual phenotype," an evolutionary deviant, a genetic mutant who potentially holds the future survival of the species in his or her unexplored DNA. The Eameses, in Neutra's view, were focused on the statistical average, the normative subject, who is slowly eradicating the biologically singular who holds the key to our survival.

Despite all of Neutra's emphasis on the holistic nature of design, on the fusion of world and dwelling, there was, for him, an ultimate barrier to communication. Fearing the dissolution of the self in the Eamesian world of numbers, relations, patterns, and connections, Neutra turned his attention in the end toward the "deviant, peculiar, forward, or specifically valuable individuals" (*LS*, 367), "biological individuals," entities that bear almost no relation to what we generally associate with individuality. These are genetically differentiated individuals, defined by their "stomachs of very different volume, shape, and position, and windpipes of remarkably different diameter, and so many oddities of variation" (*LS*, 304). For the Eameses, the individual is far closer to what we normally think of, a notion of the individual that is not defined by wiring or biology. As Charles insisted during that fateful discussion with Neutra, the new forces of design were converging on the idea of "total responsibility": the "extension of the responsibility of each individual at every level of activity."[42]

Neutra and the Eameses shared the view that architects, unlike other artists, bear a high degree of responsibility because "we impose our creations on society."[43] For Neutra, responsibility meant using the latest findings of the neurosciences and deploying them in the creation of healthful spaces, ones that would ideally shape the inhabitants in perpetuity. Neutra looked beyond conventions, society, politics, culture, and meaning toward some putatively deeper "prehuman" reality, a space that would offer relief from the contingencies of social life. The Eameses followed a similarly extreme route to an alternate outcome. They were so fanatical in their search for design responsibilities that it paralyzed their capacity to create anything that might "impose" on society. This paralysis became a paradoxical form of freedom when the Eameses eschewed the pursuit of product performance and turned to abstract models increasingly detached from the responsibilities that came with imposing their work on the world. Like Schindler, and unlike Neutra, the Eameses knew that the work "has to come to an end": there is a point where one must "call it off" and let the world take over, even if they had unending trouble discovering where that point was (*EA*, 170).

6

Burn after Use
Eames Modeling

And in their inexhaustible desire to learn, they would make daily additions
to this *Encyclopédie grotesque* with further reading and new annotations,
happy at last to be safe from the perils of putting theory into practice, and to
be storing up, with no notion of using it, an archive of misdirected learning.

—René Descharmes, "Le 'Dictionnaire des Idées reçues'
dans l'œuvre de Gustave Flaubert," 1914

In our office . . . our end-product is more often than not in the nature of a
model. We seem to have gotten away with not taking the very last step of
the process.

—Charles Eames, "Film as a Modeling Device," 1975

Charles and Ray Eameses' breakthrough film of 1953, *A Communications Primer* (Plate 8),
describes the process of information transmission in the "age of communication." The
film begins with a diagram that is described as being capable of visualizing "almost
any communication process" (Figure 6.1). The model is based on a threefold schematic
of source, transmitter, and destination, and as the narrator explains, the clear relay of
message to receiver is threatened at almost every turn by noise. "Noise," says the narrator, "is the term used in the communications field to designate any outside force which
acts on the transmitted signal to vary it from the original."[1] Depending on the message,
almost anything can act as noise: sound, motion, the "unpredictable quality" of light
sources, static on a TV monitor, poor sensory equipment.

The film is more about noise, about what gets in the way of communication, than
it is about transmission. Maintaining the strength of an original idea through extreme
levels of interference was, for the Eameses, the key to the problem of mass production.
As Ray observed of mass-produced furniture in 1975, their aim all along had been to
"figure out a way that the hundredth and the five hundredth and the thousandth [prod-
uct] would have the original character" (*EA*, 339). In the *Primer* as in their furniture,
maintaining the purity of the work's "original character"—especially as it arrives in

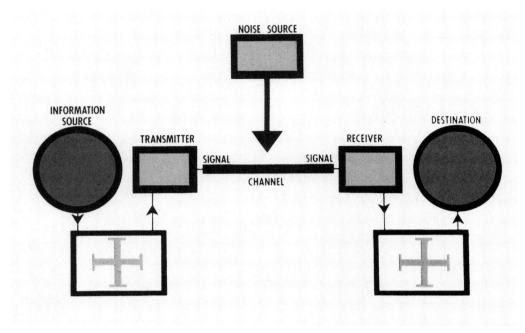

FIGURE 6.1. Ray and Charles Eames, still from *A Communications Primer*, 1953.

the hands of its users—is a guiding concern. Ray records the following note by Charles to this effect: "When the concept is formed it represents about 5 percent of the design effort—the remaining 95 percent of the effort being used to keep the concept from falling apart" (*EA*, 247). If the signal, the idea, can remain at full strength as it passes through a sea of noise, it is either a really crude idea or a powerful one.

The narrator of the *Primer* elaborates how even the simplest technologies are swamped by noise.

> In a typewritten message, the noise source could be in the quality of the ribbon or the keys, and we are all familiar with the carbon copies that keep getting progressively worse. If anything acts on the signal so as to bury it in an unpredictable and undesirable way in the communications system, it is noise.[2]

The film shows layers of carbon-copied text as it quickly devolves into a blurry smudge (Figure 6.2). From the typewriter we move to the telegraph, as a stockbroker at the New York Stock Exchange sends a message to an agent in Los Angeles. Here, there are only two possible messages to be conveyed: "buy" or "sell." The clarity of terms suggests a kind of ideal situation. And yet even here electromagnetism "could distort the signal in such a way as to change 'sell' into 'self.'" How does the stock market neutralize this

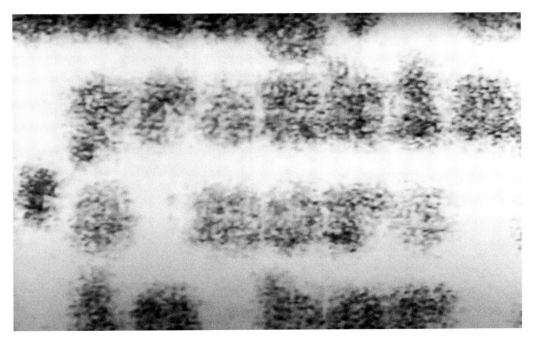

FIGURE 6.2. Ray and Charles Eames, still from *A Communications Primer*, 1953.

threat? Given that there are only "two possible messages, 'buy' and 'sell,' there is sufficient redundancy in the spelling of the words that even if it did read 'self,' the information would still be clear."[3] The message is so primitive that it can handle extreme distortion and still retain its meaning.

In a sense, nothing could be closer to the heart of the Eameses' project than this vision of noise abatement through redundancy. Then again, what makes the exchange of stocks anything but a work of art is its capacity to nullify noise, to make noise fully redundant. For the Eameses, it is essential that their message become intimate with noise. The difference between art and commerce is that answers to an artwork are "*not given in terms of a 'sure thing'*" (*EA*, 136).[4]

The lesson of the *Primer* is not to work with minimum conditions of communication but to work with maximum ones. Writing about the *Primer* to Ian McCallum at the *Architectural Review,* Charles reflects that "if ever an art was based on the handling and relating of an impossible number of factors, this art is architecture" (*EA*, 136). The supremacy of architecture—and the Eameses called everything they did architecture—is its capacity to handle a seemingly "impossible" amount of noise. Exchanging stocks is easy; accurately predicting the market and its futures is the real challenge. On the one hand, the architect is responsible for "calculating and predicting all factors of a problem that can be calculated and predicted" (*EA*, 136). On the other hand, no amount of calculation can free the designer of new levels of responsibility. Tasked with "anticipating relationships . . . yet to be conceived," designers are on the hook for any effects that can be generated by their products (*EA*, 94). New scientific research is exposing ever-deeper layers of responsibility for designers, and Charles is by turns anxious and intrigued that each year "brings discoveries of new human architectural needs we have never suspected" (*EA*, 27).

The Eameses, however, turned the task of anticipation, the management of spiraling chains of causes and effects, the invention of seemingly endless levels of responsibility, into an opportunity to free themselves from traditional notions of production and performance and from the obligation to create works that had clear applications. If it is the case, as Justus Nieland puts it, that the Eames Office ushered in a rising "culture of postindustrial image production and consumption," then by the time they came to make *A Communications Primer*, if not earlier, they had redefined the terms of production and consumption, increasingly short-circuiting the distance between them out of existence.[5]

As soon as Charles raises the issue of the architect's responsibility to calculate everything, he remarks on how this reality forecloses the capacity to build *anything*, or at least anything morally justified. It is "safe to say that in any architectural problem very few of the factors involved have been calculable—relationships of factors are almost impossible to calculate—and most of the factors remain unknown" (*EA*, 136). The aim of the *Primer* is to provide a tool to include "*more* factors" for clear communication and "make calculable the possible results of relationships between combinations of factors" that had never been conceived before (*EA*, 154). Looking back, we might say the *Primer* is designed to exonerate the Eameses from making architecture beyond what they had already built (that is, two houses and a showroom). The *Primer* purposefully multiplies design responsibilities to infinity. The more factors brought into the field of design by the tool, the more "*responsibility* [there is] . . . to use such a tool" (*EA*, 154). The final lines of the narration clarify the sheer density of the decision making provoked by the tools:

> The communication of the total message contains the responsibility of innumerable decisions made again and again, always checking with the total concept through a constant feedback system . . . and though the tool may perform complex tasks, it will never relieve the man of his responsibility, no matter where it occurs, no matter what the technique. Communication means the responsibility of decision, all the way down the line.[6]

Here we can see the true aim of the *Primer* and also what the Eameses hoped to accomplish more generally. For them, new media are to be used not to *solve* complex problems but to *multiply the density of problems and thereby heighten awareness of levels of responsibility*, a potentially endless task that puts the whole enterprise of making things into doubt. By all accounts, the "level of . . . responsibility" their tools generate makes it almost impossible for them or anyone else to use the tools successfully in practice (*EA*, 136). However attractive they thought the *Primer* might be for others in its capacity to visualize patterns of predictability, the Eameses were reticent to build anything lasting beyond their furniture. And by the mid-1950s, even furniture began to look as compromised as architecture in its spiraling of responsibilities.

Charles's 1952 speech to the American Institute of Architects concludes with a long commentary on noise. He describes the basic change in communication engineering from the old method of trying to calculate unpredictable turbulence "on the basis of the predictable turbulence" to a new one that "not only . . . calculate[s] the unpredictable, but . . . calculate[s] it as an element" (*EA*, 108). This new tendency to "calculate the incalculable" is architecturally significant because the "amount of information received in the presence of noise is actually . . . greater than the amount of information received in the presence of less noise" (*EA*, 108). More noise, more information; the more dimensions of unpredictability courted, the higher the conceptual returns.

Charles explores the depths of noise and its abatement in a 1949 design talk in which he launches into an exhaustive list of requirements for making even the humblest objects. Here, his example is a chair. He points to function, height, tactility (to avoid catching a garment), surface materials, bodily comportment (while one eats and when one leans back), surface motion (back and forth), and the relation of the "object to other parts of the room, to the psychological effects of color" (*EA*, 33). He discusses the importance of the chair in the room and its impact on the "conception of space." "We must consider etc., etc., etc." (*EA*, 32). The chair is swamped by design responsibilities. The quality of a design hinges, in Charles's view, on the capacity of the designer to imagine possible uses and effects and to anticipate all those effects in the shape of the product or to eliminate possible effects by making the design function in very particular ways (one cannot stand very well on most Eames chairs). In the famous 1972 "Design Q&A" made for the Louvre, Charles is asked, "Ought form derive from the analysis of function?" His answer is an emphatic yes, but with the crushing proviso that "the great risk here is that the analysis may be incomplete" (*EA*, 284). This really is the point; there *is* no level of analysis that will reach completeness, and that incapacity becomes the solution to a different mode of making, one not driven by performance requirements.

The same "etc., etc., etc." logic runs through a 1951 talk that Charles gave at the University of Colorado, Boulder. Sure enough, we are told that there are "an infinite number of factors not yet measured" in every design problem (*EA*, 94). But it is not one's ability to measure that counts; rather, what matters is the *"degree to which the ultimate performance standards go beyond the solving of the measurable factors,"* as that may *"show the degree to which the artist has functioned"* (*EA*, 94). The artist is a kind of diviner of the mysteries of the calculable. Eames's example (quickly to become a staple) is a cup. The "combinations and relations" of a cup to its user are "infinitely complex" (*EA*, 94). He lists liquid volume, balance (lifted, tilted, on a surface), fluid dynamics, scale, production techniques, and resistance to moisture, corrosion, breakage, heat transfer, and on and on and on. Presumably, this was meant to exhaust the listener, and it certainly has that effect on the reader.

If what this calculation of "factor after factor" for the most modest objects amounts to needs further illustration, consider this brilliant list of twenty questions reproduced in *The India Report* of 1958 (*EA*, 179). That Charles singles out the lota as "perhaps the greatest, the most beautiful" of "all the objects" they saw during their roughly six months in India is to the point. While the "number of combinations of factors to be considered" in the making of lotas is—not surprisingly—"astronomical," some of the noise has been reduced through hundreds of years of streamlining their production (lotas are exactly like tools in this way). The questions that anyone should ask when beginning the process of designing a lota are similar to those one should ask before starting to design chairs and cups:

—The optimum amount of liquid to be fetched, carried, poured, and stored in a prescribed set of circumstances.
—The size and strength and gender of the hands (if hands) that would manipulate it.
—The way it is to be transported—head, hip, hand, basket, or cart.
—The balance, the center of gravity, when empty, when full, its balance when rotated for pouring.
—The fluid dynamics of the problem not only when pouring but when filling and cleaning, and under the complicated motions of head carrying—slow and fast.
—Its sculpture as it fits the palm of the hand, the curve of the hip.
—Its sculpture as complement to the rhythmic motion of walking or a static post at the well.
—The relation of opening to volume in terms of storage uses—and objects other than liquid.
—The size of the opening and inner contour in terms of cleaning.
—The texture inside and out in terms of cleaning and feeling.
—Heat transfer—can it be grasped if the liquid is hot?
—How pleasant does it feel, eyes closed, eyes open?
—How pleasant does it sound, when it strikes another vessel, is set down on ground or stone, empty or full—or being poured into?
—What is the possible material?
—What is its cost in terms of working?

—What is its cost in terms of ultimate service?

—What kind of an investment does the material provide as product, as salvage?

—How will the material affect the contents, etc., etc.?

—How will it look as the sun reflects off its surface?

—How does it feel to possess it, to sell it, to give it? (*EA*, 179)

It feels as though the list could go on ad infinitum. It almost does not matter to the Eameses whether they are designing a lota or planning an airport or a national aquarium, because everything, no matter size or scale, is saturated in noise and saddled with the responsibility for reducing it.

There is a particular kind of genius at play in imagining degrees of design interference and degrees of responsibility that had never been conceived before. Nothing is more striking about the whole body of the Eameses' writing than the depth of their moral commitments, particularly ones that had the perverse effect of attenuating the practice of making things. When Konrad Wachsmann says, "There was a moral in all [their] films" (*EMR*, 137), the moral is really about the immorality of making things that alter the world in unpredictable ways, because "we impose our creations on society."[7] Charles's 1953 lecture course at UC Berkeley was titled "Entropy and Morality" (*EA*, 122). Entropy, following the example of Norbert Wiener, is the scientific term for noise explored in the *Primer*. The principle of entropy in communication "indicates that the probability that a message will increase in accuracy by transmission is zero." Information "can only be dissipated" (*EA*, 122). The morality in question is the response to this entropic situation. Rather than confronting the inevitable "spread" of entropy, human beings tend to divide the world into fictive abstractions of good and bad. Embracing entropy means relativizing moral terms: "Decaying flesh would not seem bad to a vulture" (*EA*, 123). To begin to think in this expanded moral sense would mean taking responsibility not for a vulture's perspective but for the manifoldness of human needs, everything oriented around the human scale (*EA*, 137). This is what Charles means when, in his 1961 report to the U.S. State Department, he speaks of the "*consideration* of the other person's point of view and the effect of the decision on his values" (*EA*, 226). His point is that designers must build into their works an awareness of the "long range effects" of those works on their users (*EA*, 226)—on this, he and Neutra strongly agreed, although they took the point in opposite directions.

Entropy and morality surprisingly emerge as the themes of a short sales film the Eameses made for a sofa designed in 1954. There is a straightforward modernist morality to everything they do. The technique should always "show through the result"—that is, there should never be any mystery to how something is made. But the Eameses' vision goes well beyond the idea that one should "show one's work." This is architecture in the hands of an angry God, what Charles calls "a brutal thing" (*EA*, 305): every decision matters because it stands as a moral act that gives rise to a demandingness that ends up compromising most forms of conventional production. Everything counts, and what counts is vastly more than anyone can reasonably imagine. Film demands a kind of infinite attentiveness of decision, as it represents "the extension of the responsibility of each individual at every level of activity."[8] Every frame bears import: the filmmaker is "really transmitting meaning and all the tricks, and every joke, every color; every tear is sort of pertinent to the meaning" (*EA*, 253). The opening narration of *S73 (Sofa Compact)* states that "more and more the problems of shipping come to be considered as a part of the manufacturer's responsibility" (Figure 6.3). Which means that shipping "automatically becomes the designer's problem" (*EA*, 140).[9] Problems, responsibilities, multiply, and no sofa is safe from newly excavated (or are they projected?) layers of responsibility that require attention. So while the Eameses' mantra is "Take your pleasures seriously"—and their work seems to supply an inordinate amount of "joy" for anemic audiences seeking a way out of boring old boxy modernism—a prime example for them of serious pleasure is the circus, where the "rigors of the discipline" are the source of the pleasure for the performer (*EA*, 328). What the circus represents, I will argue, is an ideal of what the Eameses call "festival arts," a mode of making where production and consumption collapse into one.[10]

If the designer can fully grasp and answer the basic needs inherent in a piece of furniture—and that is a massive *if*—then the work can drift through noise without any loss of concept. Writing of the storage unit, Charles reflects on how the "combination of standard elements can be made to serve an infinite number of uses" without any alteration of the basic idea (*EA*, 75). Get the idea straight, and the work can enter any number of contexts without its meaning being altered: "A chair that works very well in one dining room . . . usually will work in other situations" (*EA*, 210). Charles notes of the Immaculate Heart campus in 1967 that the building could be "scotch taped, nailed into, thumb tacked"; the structure itself could handle "complete changes in program" because the idea of the structure is on some level separable from its physical instantiation (*EA*, 263). Ray clarifies the point: "The idea of structure—what holds up—anything that holds up has to do with structure."[11] This moral idea of form appears in the most unlikely of places, like the *Kaleidoscope Jazz Chair* film of 1959. The twists and turns of the kaleidoscope, the "noise" caused by the lens, do not destroy the idea of the chair, which survives every visual manipulation (Figure 6.4).

Guilt and Responsibility

Toys, sofas, lotas, cabinets, an airport, an aquarium, a religious campus, the seemingly endless supply of imagery generated by the Eames Office—they are all one giant,

FIGURE 6.3. Charles and Ray Eames, still from *S73 (Sofa Compact)*, 1954.

FIGURE 6.4. Charles and Ray Eames, still from *Kaleidoscope Jazz Chair*, 1960.

interrelated problem. As Charles notes in passing during a lecture, if his talk has "meant anything," it is that design is part of a "chain reaction mechanism that can start anywhere and go everywhere, and is commonly related to every problem" (*EA*, 89). Near the end of his life, Charles describes this same reactive connectivity as "eventually everything connects" (*ED*, 266). The quality of a design lies in its capacity to come to terms with that scattered whole, to effect connections where there used to be none. This is what Charles means when he describes the Eames House as a "great web"—the truss rods literalize the image—that both "supports and encloses" the environment (*EA*, 70) (Figure 6.5, Plate 3).

And yet guilt follows the Eameses wherever they go. "If I feel guilty about chickening out of architecture," Charles tells McCoy in 1974, "Eero [Saarinen] was guilty about not giving architecture the careful detailing I could give furniture" (*EMR*, 183). That Charles feels guilty for giving up architecture is clear; he is still talking about it twenty-five years later. Again and again he is asked by interviewers why he doesn't make more buildings after three houses and a showroom. His answer is always the same and highly revealing. To McCoy he says, "In architecture the idea degenerated," while furniture had "a more direct and pleasurable route." McCoy aptly notes that the idea could not "degenerate" at Eames's house because he was "his own client"; by not entering circulation, it could secure itself against misuse (*EMR*, 300). Even so, the continuous stage-managing of the interior space—the now ubiquitously eulogized "good Victorian clutter," as Robert Venturi called it—indicates the persistent (or quixotic) desire to maintain the clarity of the idea over time.

To deflect some of the guilt, Charles points to the significance that furniture holds among modern architectural masters. "For an architect who has difficulty controlling a building because of the contractor and the various forces brought to bear on anything that costs that much money, a chair is almost handleable on a human scale, and so you find great architects turning to chairs: Frank Lloyd Wright, Mies van der Rohe, Le Corbusier, Aalto, Eero Saarinen—any number of them doing it, because this is architecture you can get your hands on" (*EA*, 359). The moral is barely concealed: the "various forces brought to bear" on a building—the noise that potentially distorts the message—should have made architecture more impossible. And if Charles's language here is relatively free of moral sentiment, his more typical formulation reveals a different tone:

> Practicing architecture is a super-frustrating business. You work on the idea, but then standing between you and the event itself are many, many traps to dilute it. The finance committee, the contractor, the subcontractor, the engineer, the facilities guys, the political situation—all of them can really degenerate the concept. Going into furniture or film is a deviation of a sort, but at least we have a more

FIGURE 6.5. Charles and Ray Eames, Eames House (Los Angeles, California), 1949. Photograph: Julius Shulman, 1950. Copyright J. Paul Getty Trust. Getty Research Institute, Los Angeles (2004.R.10).

direct relationship with the end product—better chance to keep the concept from degenerating. . . .

[Architects make furniture so they] can design a piece of architecture you can hold in your hand, that won't get away from you—in concept. (*EA*, 315)[12]

Traps are lurking around every corner; at least with furniture (or one's own house), one *could* be responsible for the product. "It's frustrating to do buildings," Charles notes, "and in furniture . . . it's at least at a scale [one] can control" (*EA*, 276).

The language of degeneration that the Eameses draw on is late Victorian in emphasis. Compare the Eameses' attitude to Henry van de Velde's remarkably similar approach to modern furniture: "My ideal would be to have my projects executed a thousand times, though obviously not without strict supervision, because I know from experience how soon a model can deteriorate through dishonest or misguided handling until its effect is as worthless as the one it was destined to counteract."[13] Degeneration and deviation, deterioration and diminishment, distortion and dilution, dissipation and decay—these ideas (along with noise, entropy, erosion, and oscillation) are *the* core concepts of the Eameses' moral and aesthetic enterprise.[14] All of these notions are summed up for the Eameses in the word "discontinuity," which is one of the poles—along with its opposite, "continuity"—of their moral and aesthetic valuation. "Continuity" is a way of describing a work's special connection to its makers, a connection Charles describes as "not too far removed from the architect's own hand" (*EA*, 188). Early on, Charles reflects on how centuries of building in Germany, the subject of his and Ray's 1955 film *Two Baroque Churches in Germany,* produced "no disunity" between structures—"music, literature, architecture and philosophy were unified"—because they all shared an "attitude" toward life (*EA*, 295). A high degree of "continuity" between art and life obtained in the baroque and Enlightenment eras, according to the Eameses; Benjamin Franklin and Thomas Jefferson were part of the same world as the baroque cathedral.

The original "bridge" plan for the Eames House (Figure 6.6)—it remained in play for five years—"suspended [the house] over the land," which would have allowed it to exist "in a free and independent relationship to its natural environment," exemplifying the Eameses' vision of a structure that would not degenerate in circulation (*EA*, 31). They repeatedly stressed that the house would be "independent of the ground, a point in space looking directly at the mass of the sea." It was in this suspended point in space where the free "development and preparation of ideas" could occur (*EA*, 22). When John Entenza presented the house in 1949 in the pages of *Arts and Architecture* (the house was featured in no fewer than seven of the twelve issues that year), he made its ideational status explicit:

FIGURE 6.6. Charles Eames and Eero Saarinen, Bridge House, first draft of the Eames House, 1945.

> This house represents an attempt to state an idea rather than a fixed architectural pattern, and it is as an attitude toward living that we wish to present it. . . .
>
> Here it is only important to say, and briefly, that we feel that the house must be judged on the basis of its appropriateness to the idea, and that its contributions are things to be derived from it rather than things existing precisely within it.[15]

It is not even an idea but merely an "attempt to state" one. And the idea it aims to express is *itself ideational*, an "attitude" toward living. This is presumably what McCoy means when she inimitably describes the house as "the framework of a structure of an idea."[16] The spiraling expression of hesitation toward the making of a finished product, a kind of parabolic relation to anything existing, marks out the special terrain of Eamesian practice. According to Entenza, it is the idea and the "things to be derived" from it that matter and not the "things existing" in it. Or as Charles put it just after the house was built: "Seeing a situation and the necessity it presents for making a decision is more important than the decision made" (*EA*, 123). Charles makes the point again in his notes to the *Mathematica* exhibition (Figure 5.16), where he lauds those artists and thinkers who have "no thought or concern for how [models] may be applied" (*EA*, 212). The Eameses describe *Mathematica*—their central achievement in exhibition design—as an "introduction to the pleasures of abstract modeling."[17] In the early years of their practice, the Eameses thought in depth about how a model might be applied, which led them to abandon built architecture but not the term *architecture*, which they expanded into a concept that could subsume all of their various practices.

The Morality of Restraint

It is hard to imagine a stronger retort to the contemporary reception of the Eameses than their moral and aesthetic ruminations on the difference between idea and thing.[18] In his remarkable commentary on CSH 9 for *Arts and Architecture*, Charles describes how the house progresses "from idea . . . to reality . . . with a sure sense of concept." What he means by a "sure sense of concept" is that when the house was built it "lacked utterly that sense of stunned surprise that very often confronts those who see their handiwork complete and real for the first time" (*EA*, 60). It is the *lack* of surprise that he values, as though inner and outer were one continuous motion, even if the "outer" here is something less than a fully existing thing.[19] The lack of surprise is the result of a "consistency of idea and purpose which created and carried the whole to completion." The house, Charles concludes, is the "statement of an attitude" (*EA*, 60). All "great original thinkers" are defined by their ideas, rather than by "things existing"; it is the "form of an attitude" that makes them great rather than the things that get made (*EA*, 78).

Nonetheless, when Charles wrote to Peter Blake after living in the house for a few months, he pointed to the "surprises" that "came one by one" as some of the "most pleasant things" about living there (*EA*, 71). The "unplanned" aspects of the house that he celebrated were the changing light and shadows as they played across the architectural form. Reflections! Those cannot be controlled! But it is the form that generates the play of light and shade; that is, the form is *confirmed* by the play, not altered by it. Whatever was "accidental," Charles and Ray went about studying it "for a long time." Light is "of course accidental," he noted in a later talk, before assuring his audience that the "object, however, was not accidental" (*EA*, 91).

One can read everything written on the Eameses and never encounter the fact that they thought centrally about morality (again, of a rather perverse kind). This becomes clearer as their work progresses, and the dominant theme of their later work is the problem of restraint. Finding restraint in a world defined by choice is the path to reestablishing continuity; it is the "horrible freedom" of choice that is the cause of discontinuity. (The Eameses identify Los Angeles with a "you name it—and you can have it" attitude; it is gluttony incarnate, in their view; *EA*, 246.) Restraint is the primary weapon in the battle "against discontinuity." At one point Charles jokes that the use of a "spineless material"—like plastilene and airbrush—by anyone under fifty should be "punishable by death" (*EA*, 244).

Indeed, there is a strong existential tone in the later writings. "Man is totally unprepared for the role of free choicemaker," Charles declares, a point he makes at every opportunity throughout the rest of his career (*EA*, 245). The idea is picked up from Jean-Paul Sartre and the many commentaries on his work at the time. "At bottom," Sartre writes in *Existentialism Is a Humanism*, "what is alarming in the doctrine [of existentialism] . . . is that it confronts man with a possibility of choice."[20] Charles's friend Abraham Kaplan glosses the point by saying that the "limitless freedom of choice in which man's existence consists is thus at the same time a boundless responsibility for what he makes of himself." This "crushing responsibility" is a "dreadful thing." Human beings respond to this responsibility by trying to evade it: "We may seek an escape from it by pretending . . . that we are not really free."[21] Charles makes the point again and again, noting how in contemporary life one is "forced to make many decisions" without the least "restraining effects" of a "common cultural tradition" (*EA*, 245).[22] He clearly longs for an imaginary age when there "was never a real free choice involved" in art and where tradition steered one's least gesture, even if he fully recognizes that the continuous age is over and that we are collectively "doomed to awareness." Far more than that, the Eameses are responsible for affirming a technologically driven hyperawareness, one that stands in significant tension with their moralizing ambitions. The moralism becomes almost hectoring in later writings. In a 1965 speech given in London he laments how "as a race . . . we have never been up against the problem of making a free choice . . . and we are just plain not prepared to make them" (*EA*, 254).

This aspect of the Eameses' project seems a touching relic of the Great Compression, the period between World War II and the later 1960s during which lack of restraint, consumerism, seemed to be a pathological problem in the culture at large rather than what it is now, with the superrich massively exploiting workers; moralizing consumption and restraint for the majority of the impoverished population is not an idea that ought to be revived.[23] Charles's tale of the banana leaf—how the richest and the poorest come together in the end—is perhaps the most dismal of his moralizing parables (*EA*, 306). Reflecting on one of the Eameses' trips to India, Charles notes (here in the mid-1960s) that in many corners of the earth where there is "poverty and deprivation you find that misery is not necessarily the companion of poverty."[24] This fantasy is part of the general existential tenor of responsibility among the American elite in the 1960s. Whatever its purchase was in 1950s American life, by the end of the 1960s it was pure ideology, one that continues to haunt American politics.

"The New Covetables"

If the Eameses' thinking in the 1960s was dominated by ideas of restraint and choice, then in the 1970s it was governed by what they called the "new covetables." New covetables comprise "concepts, ideas" that persist through change "with no degeneration" (*EA*, 280). They are perfect commodities; they are obsolescence perfected. Information, for instance, is "a commodity that isn't diminished by being shared with others" (*EA*, 352), an idea that informs all the Eameses' work. And not surprisingly this free commodity is praised in moral, even religious terms: in Ray's words, information is a pure commodity because "once you have it, it works like the loaves and fishes: you can distribute it without diminishing it" (*EA*, 385). In his Norton Lectures, Charles defines this as one of the qualities of the new covetables: "The nature of the covetable would have to be such that it be like the fishes and the loaves—that you could divide it and it wouldn't in any way deteriorate"; the new covetables are "nondeteriorating."[25]

The idea is borrowed from Buckminster Fuller and his utopian account of ephemeralization. Fuller first refers to the biblical loaves and fishes in 1940 to describe the new "perishables," the model for the Eameses' "goods."[26] Writing of the "leverage principles" first discovered with a fallen tree and put into conscious practice with "gears, pulleys, transistors, and so forth," Fuller notes that it is possible to do "more with less in a multitude of physio-chemical ways." It is this "intellectual augmentation of humanity's survival and success through the metaphysical perception of generalized principles," Fuller writes in the closing line of his chapter titled "Spaceship Earth" in *Operating Manual for Spaceship Earth,* that "Christ was trying to teach in the obscurely told story of the loaves and the fishes."[27] The "real wealth" of society comes from these principles. "You can't exhaust that kind of wealth. It is not physically exhaustible."[28] Fuller construed the difference between technology and the general principles extracted from it as a strict metaphysical divide. The Eameses, by contrast, refused to accept a dualist split between idea and reality. Even if they privileged the idea over its physical manifestation, they did not believe their work was ever reducible to the idea; they did not think it could be extracted from the seemingly endless material processes in which it was bound up.

Like Neutra, the Eameses were obsessed with notions of survival, of conveying meaning to a receiver with minimal loss of signal. In the PBS documentary *An Eames Celebration: The Several Worlds of Charles and Ray Eames* (1975), Charles describes the basis of the exhibition on Franklin and Jefferson that he and Ray were then preparing for the Grand Palais in Paris. They were "both architects," Charles says, "architects of an experiment"; the only question in the end was whether the experiment would work and "survive the wilderness of the Louisiana Purchase and today it's the same question, will the experiment survive the kind of wilderness that we face today."[29] To imagine that Franklin's and Jefferson's questions and the pressing questions of 1975 are the same requires a significant leap in logic. What is the same is only the construal of every problem—social, political, artistic—in architectural terms of survival and death. And so it is not surprising that the Eameses' description of these two founding fathers sounds very much like a self-portrait. Jefferson, for example, they suggest in the book that accompanied the exhibition, had an "unmatched gift for stating a strong conviction, in words simple enough to keep it alive and applicable through changing circumstances."[30] Whether it is "noise" or "wilderness," the problem is the same: the survival of concept in the face of seemingly impossible odds. Minutes later in the documentary, speaking of the national aquarium project, Charles observes that "any kind of activity has its classic description which is all goodness and roses, but in practice, in the day-to-day practice . . . there are little sticky problems that must be overcome if the concept is going to survive." Charles's mind seems to return relentlessly to the problem of survival, as though the idea is under continual threat of dissolution in the hands of an uncaring audience. Architecture is always at war.

"Models of Ideas"

In the 1953 script for "Chair Design Process," planned as an episode for the television show *Discovery*, Charles offers something like a linguistic rendering of the tangled relation between concept and execution in his and Ray's practice in describing the film about the *process* of production rather than the work itself: "Naturally this is a condensed form of an outline of a synopsis of a kind of minimum digest of what actually went on, making a product from the concept stage to the consumer, but certainly it is no special exception" (*EA*, 117). Similarly, the Eameses describe their film *A Metropolitan Overview* (1975) as a "model of a proposed system of how to present information" (*ED*, 202). (Recall too that McCoy describes the Eames House as "the framework of a structure of an idea," as though Eamesian mental knots are contagious.)

Another example is the title the Eameses gave to their groundbreaking collaborative course at the University of Georgia and UCLA in 1953: "A Rough Sketch for a Sample Lesson for a Hypothetical Course." This is a description for a course, for a set of instructions, not for the practical application of the lessons. Yet another example is the title for the 1968 version of *Powers of Ten* (1977), "A Rough Sketch for a Proposed Film Dealing with the Powers of Ten and the Relative Size of Things in the Universe." It is a film that is both a model and *about modeling*, and the language—a kind of infinite delay—suggests the multiple layers of attenuation between model and world. Models compound models. This "rough sketch" itself went through three iterations or format changes: the 1963 "Truck Test," followed by the 1968 film, followed by the "final" model (about modeling), *Powers of Ten*.

Far from marginal, these knotted circumlocutions are expressions of a defining quality of the Eamesian enterprise. If the work could remain perpetually suspended in the state of "rough sketch for a proposal," a kind of model of a model ad infinitum, then the problems of moral responsibility faced by a practicing architect could be temporarily displaced, and if one could make a career out of it, then they would be terminally displaced.[31]

Performance Problems: *Omnibus* 1956

In May 1956 Charles sketched three sets of notes for an upcoming appearance on the CBS television show *Omnibus*. Although the Eameses never actually appeared on the show, his extensive notes provide insight into his basic concerns as a designer. He begins the segment by expressing a familiar sentiment, asserting that everything he and Ray have produced falls "under the heading of architecture" (*EA*, 147). He goes on to describe their house and shows an edited clip from the film *House: After Five Years of Living*, which they had made a year earlier. Charles explains how the design problem of the house is no different from that of a chair, a painting, or a tool. Whatever the object, "it must have a structural concept" (*EA*, 148). One is meant to be struck by the connections drawn between the seemingly disparate aspects of their practice. Ray likewise underscores this in her own notes when she asks the crucial question, "What is it these things have in common?"[32]

Charles is clear that what unites their various practices is not exactly structure but rather a *structural concept,* an elusive but key distinction. In a letter to an executive at CBS, he insists the segment should "make little reference to *things* we have done" and instead show "a great *variety* of things."[33] It is as though the sheer multiplication of products inevitably dissolves them into their "structural concept," a quality that all the things share but also that *no-thing* does.

From the house Charles moves on to the making of kites and brings the viewers over to Ray, who is putting the finishing touches on a toy ornithopter modeled on the Winge-e ornithopter, a Mylar flying toy in the abstracted shape of a bird that Charles was highly impressed by. Charles calls it the "best [toy] I have seen in a long, long time"—he was also an earnest advocate for the Super Ball—and tells viewers that he wished Leonardo da Vinci could have seen it (this is accompanied by on-screen images of Leonardo's kite designs).[34] Charles explains that in "structure our architecture as well as furniture has been likened to kites," and though he cautions viewers not to "take that too literally," he maintains that "it doesn't seem completely unnatural since we are

FIGURE 6.7. Ray Eames, kite collage, from an original design by Charles Eames, tissue paper, 1950. This graphic served as the cover for *Portfolio* magazine, summer 1950.

not only interested in kites but we have used them as problems for students to develop an attitude toward architecture" (*EA,* 148). Charles published a few designs for kites in *Portfolio* magazine in 1950 (*EA,* 76) (Figure 6.7), kites hang on walls of the Eames House, and, at the very end of their career, Charles and Ray produced a kite-making vignette for their film *Polavision* (1977), although the subject is (not surprisingly) *building* a kite, not flying one. Charles describes their work as *like* a kite but not literally so. Kites are not construed as architecture (even in its expanded sense), but they are useful for getting the right "attitude" toward it. But as Charles goes on to explain, kites, unlike toys, are not really like architecture at all.

Charles now turns to what he calls the "kite problem." Kites pose the kind of problem that allows one to definitively assess whether one has succeeded or failed: "It will *fly* or it will *not* fly—I wish more problems could be so beautifully defined."[35] Kites, ornithopters, and model planes are defined by their "critical performance," a fact that offers "priceless experience for developing structural concepts related to performance." Here one detects a breach opened between "structural concepts" and "performance"—the terms are related but nevertheless distinct. The line between performance and concept becomes increasingly absolute for the Eameses, so that by the end of their careers the whole question of performance raised by kites (or built things in general) has become less and less of an issue, as the question of performance is decisively suspended. More pointedly, kites, insofar as they are predicated on nothing but real-world performance, present something like a standing threat to the Eameses' conception of architecture as *modeling*.

In a public lecture delivered six days prior to the scripting of the *Omnibus* notes, Charles defines the current moment as the "age of permanent values." Paradoxically, the conditions for this new age of permanent values emerge as a direct consequence of the "impermanence of its architecture." This paradox is resolved when he describes a permanent value—what he began to call at this moment "goods"—as a value that takes "on other than a physical or monumental aspect."[36] The place where impermanent architecture and permanent values meet is at the level of the model. In the model, architecture and values become something other than strictly physical.

In the *Omnibus* script Charles makes a transition from kites to toys, and this turn signals a shift from the practical and physical to the model and the increasingly immaterial. As Charles insists in the opening of the Eameses' film *Toccata for Toy Trains* (1957), toy trains are not themselves models, but they are akin to models. Part of the appeal of toys, like that of furniture, is their directness of contact, a total transparency of meaning from mind to action to product to use. As Charles puts it in a 1952 letter to Edgar Kaufmann Jr., in the "toy, the line from mind-to-heart-to-hand-to-product, keeps pretty straight, and the influence of materials and the accidentals are seldom resented." At other points it seems as though what is special about toys is how the maker cherishes their materiality. But as Charles's comments in this letter suggest, what is at stake is *not* truth to materials, but rather the straight line that runs from mind to product. Charles is at pains to clarify that toys are *not* like kites. Toys are not invested at all in the question of "critical performance"—that is what makes them special. "BUT the influence of kites . . . on design should not be confused with the influence of TOYS—TOYS are something special," Charles notes (*EA*, 149). No matter how special kites may be, toys are of a different and higher order.[37] Or rather, kites are in the "same category as playing with static electricity, fluid dynamics (building of dams in gutters and streams)" (*EA*, 149). In other words, even here the question of "critical performance"—whether it works or does not work—gets quickly displaced; kites are closer to a form of disinterested play; they can be (almost) subsumed under toys.

Dust, Cake, Bread, Stews, Flowers, Picnics: The Festival Arts

With the introduction of toys, we are edging closer to the Eameses' ideas about the underlying structural basis of their architectural thinking. Toys, Charles writes, "have an influence on our culture . . . but it is an influence of a different kind" from kites. He connects toys with what he calls the "festival arts—masks, floats, cake decorations," what he elsewhere calls "the unsophisticated arts" (*EA*, 148, 230). He includes under this heading (as possible subjects for film) "lettering on architecture, carnival, and festival architecture, the great temporary triumphal arches" (*EA*, 230). Charles lists early Eames films under the heading "Celebration," including here *Traveling Boy, Parade, Blacktop, Toccata for Toy Trains, Tops* (for *Stars of Jazz*), and *Day of the Dead,* which deals with the Mexican celebration of All Saints' Day.[38] Introducing *Day of the Dead* (1957) for his third Norton Lecture, he notes how a Native American mother "scrapes up little things of dust and makes little patterns out of dust. And one thing after another—in the ceremonies, in the ritual."[39] How to make a work out of dust that then returns to dust is the apotheosis of Eamesian art and politics. The political vision is one where production and consumption collapse into each other without priority or remainder. "Ideally you want to turn everybody into Consumer/Producer," Charles says.[40]

Charles's vision of a computer-driven future, on the one hand, and his fixation on traditional images drawn in dust that disappear with a breeze, on the other, reveal his conception of the computer as a tool that can engineer temporary patterns in the way that Native American mothers make drawings in the dirt. This seemingly incongruous ideal—ancient and high-tech, handmade and impersonal—saturates much of the Eameses' imagery. Celebration imagery, often within the seemingly staid universe of science, informed many of their exhibitions, including *Movable Feasts and Changing Calendars* (1973) as well as shows devoted to seemingly unrelated subjects, like *Copernicus* (1972), which was "filled with objects used in Polish Christmas celebrations" (*ED*, 387), and *Isaac Newton: Physics for a Moving Earth* (1973), which was the occasion for a "display of artifacts and images drawn from English Christmas celebrations" of the seventeenth and eighteenth centuries (*ED*, 407) (Figure 6.8).

What is at stake with the festival arts is the immediacy of connection between production and consumption, both collapsed in an ideal of *performance without waste*.[41] The skeletons and skulls made out of candy featured throughout *Day of the Dead* explicitly bring this idea home, but it is also apparent in the early film *Bread* (1953), which concludes with an image of crumbs being ravenously consumed by pigeons (Plate 9). *Day of the Dead* takes as its theme the impermanence of life, the idea that humans, like sugar-candy skulls, dissolve in time, and so one should enjoy life while one can. On this score, it is no coincidence that when the Eameses wanted to show a Claes Oldenburg sculpture in the Herman Miller showroom, they sent the artist a letter in which they specified that "even more appropriate than a soft chair, would be a soft or hard piece of food."[42] Oldenburg assumed that the Eameses might be interested in exhibiting a chair, but the ideal chair would function like food, it would be fully consumed with use.

The third element of the "festival arts," "cake decorations," is celebrated, as we have seen, in the three-screen slide show *Konditorei* of 1955 (Plate 5). The idea of "feed[ing] the pastry by spoon to today's students of architecture" exemplifies not only the quality of care that I describe in chapter 5 but also equally the quality of impermanence (*EA*, 139). The subject recurs throughout the Eamesian oeuvre. As Charles remarks in the third Norton Lecture, "In a Jewish family, whether it's the hamantaschen or the lighting of the candles, a myriad of small things commands the respect of the very young child, things that in themselves have no payoff" (see *EA*, 319). Celebratory or ritual acts around food are, he says, the "real things which make the culture," and he often notes that the "quality of the soup that you get in the restaurant or bread" conveys something essential about the culture (*EA*, 249). From bread and cake, he seamlessly turns to the transient architecture of the New York World's Fair. What you "walk on underfoot, or those thousands of [small] things," stands for the "true measure of the culture" (*EA*, 249). What distinguishes all celebratory acts—architectural or ritual—is that they have "no payoff," meaning also that they *cannot be owned*; the "underfoot architecture" of the city is the "kind of thing no one own[s], but everyone enjoys, . . . fountains, vistas, park."[43] The celebratory arts, *public goods*, are a better model for Eamesian politics than the standard-issue social history of the Eameses as Cold Warriors.

Charles expands on the ritual ideal of total use, a kind of supreme functionalism, in his discussion of traditional Navajo stew, a meal that "is made from nothing but sheep. However, except for wool, hide, and hoofs, it is the whole sheep—the eyes, the brains, the tongue, the bones, and all the insides" (*EA*, 246). The Navajo stew stands on the same terms—a kind of ideal Eamesian work—as cake decoration and consumption.

FIGURE 6.8. Office of Charles and Ray Eames, *Isaac Newton: Physics for a Moving Earth* exhibition, IBM Corporate Exhibit Center, New York City, 1973.

Consider this leap in logic, Charles describing, in one breath, "the Christo experience, or a good birthday cake." Navajo stews, birthday cakes, flowers, and Christo sculptures are the same in terms of their "great value in how the thing disappears and can't be reproduced; it can't deteriorate and grow passé" (*EA*, 363). These items cannot deteriorate because there is nothing left of them after use. It is not too much of a stretch to see this in relation to his and Ray's suggested use of Herman Miller shipping boxes. The 1950 Eames Storage Unit, or ESU, included a pamphlet describing how the shipping carton could be used as a child's playhouse (photographs were made to show the playhouse in practice) (*ED*, 128). To use up everything and leave nothing behind is the standing ideal. In a fascinating moment, Ray spoke of chemical products at the office that would dissolve upon use: "We had cereal bowls that were evaporating dishes, and teacups that were made by the chemical people—a beautiful form." As she explained, it is "necessary to use everything" to achieve beautiful form.[44] In this instance, it is the bowl or cup that collapses into the thing it contains, both disappearing with use. We might now see how Charles could associate stew or shipping materials with "processions, promenades, bowling on the green, war dances, harvest dances, public executions." The crucial point about the festival arts is that "nothing" be "built or made [that] could be allowed to detract from their performance" (*EA*, 246). This is the only viable mode of performance the Eameses could embrace, a *total performance,* where the work disappears in its use.

Along these lines, consider a peculiar moment in the narrative of the film *Something about Photography* (1976), about the then-new Polaroid SX-70 camera. Charles, the narrator (and the first person seen on-screen, lying down as he takes Polaroids of grass), describes the significance of photography as "a most personal procedure." Because through the lens of the SX-70 "viewing is combined with a lens system that can focus from infinity down to ten inches and a system of instant processing where there is no time lag between shooting, seeing the result, and shooting the next picture, then you have no excuse."[45] No excuse for what? There is no grammatical referent, and we are left to wonder who is excusing what. We may presume there is "no excuse" for not using the camera as an "extraordinary personal procedure" (whatever that means). What is special about the Polaroid—a subject of fascination for the Eameses in the 1970s—is the near absolute collapse of idea, sight, shooting, and result, although it is essential to Charles's narrative that the *result* plays little role here; the "next picture" is the real concern, as though one might *not stop* taking pictures and therefore secure an identity of production and consumption without the possibility of remainder. The Eameses' commitment to modeling derives from this ideal. In the absence of a celebratory performance, one could nonetheless make models that remained perpetually and without loss in the state of seemingly total "unselfconsciousness."[46]

In a crucial passage from *The India Report,* Charles sums up the philosophical nature of festival architecture:

> The great opportunity in the occasion is that it involves mood, symbolizing a kind
> of faith and a limited time span—the limited time is important. Cultures need
> occasions when they can be gay, symbolic, moody, colorful, and yet not be held to
> it for all time. The materials of the occasion are even different: they are flowers,
> paper, ribbons, wire, cloth, smoke, color, air, music. None are asked to hold to the
> point of shoddiness—they are gone before they die. . . . Traditional parades were
> great and indecisive modern parades just fall to pieces. (*EA,* 186)

Being "gone before they die" identifies the root quality of the festival arts and under-
lines the logic of the model as well. In the festival, the question of "critical performance" is displaced and in its place appears a mode of consumption and production
that is seemingly *immune to loss.*

This idea helps to make sense of Charles's otherwise peculiar gesture of having the
foyer of the lecture hall for his Norton talks filled with flowers. The audience members
were meant to take one as they passed through the foyer, one flower for each chair,
signaling how the event was to be approached more like a festival and less like a lecture. Flowers, of course, are a signature image for the Eameses. A bouquet of Zeeland,
Michigan, wildflowers adorns the Herman Miller stock certificate. Most famously,
forget-me-nots appear in the closing shot of *Glimpses of the USA* (1959). Flowers are
utterly ubiquitous in their work: they saturate the imagery in *House: After Five Years of
Living;* there is a nosegay in *House of Cards;* there are details of flowers throughout *Think;*
a "Nehru Rose" was featured in the exhibition *Nehru: His Life and His India* (1965); a
wall of flower photographs illustrated the *Fibonacci: Growth and Form* exhibition for the
IBM Corporate Exhibition Center in New York City (1972) (Figure 6.9); and on and on.
The theme of the *Fibonacci* exhibition was a characteristic (but also idiosyncratic) effort to combine imagery related to "seasonal holidays" with "scientific subject matter,"
once again drawing together the celebratory and transitory with the depersonalized and
objective (*ED,* 379). An otherwise obscure remark in which Charles associates flowers
with an image of complete performance by noting, "Flowers. Chinese firecrackers"
(*EA,* 163), illuminates the "nothing permanent" ideal.

Although rarely remarked on, the fact that *Powers of Ten* is organized around the
scene of a picnic (Figure 6.10)—a kind of core Eamesian allegorical event—also suggests the ubiquity of celebratory imagery. The Eameses' frequent use of balloon imagery speaks to this theme as well. The closing shot of their second film, *Parade* of 1952, is
an extended view of a red balloon as it sails through a blue sky, the toys featured in the
film giving way to the real world (a small toy balloon attached to the hand of a wooden

FIGURE 6.9. Office of Charles and Ray Eames, *Fibonacci: Growth and Form* exhibition, IBM Corporate Exhibit Center, New York City, 1972.

FIGURE 6.10. Charles and Ray Eames, still from *Powers of Ten and the Relative Size of Things in the Universe,* 1977.

doll appears to escape, dissolving into the real one seen floating away). Similarly, the final shot of the *Movie Sets* slide show (a work made over the course of twenty years on the sets of Billy Wilder films), features a sea of balloons being released, the stills drawn from Wilder's own circus scene in *Ace in the Hole,* or (as it was renamed by the studios) *The Big Carnival* (Wilder was an assistant on the Eameses' *Parade,* which was made at the same time as *Ace in the Hole*) (Plate 10). The *Herman Miller International* slide show (1967) concludes the same way. The *Tivoli* slide show (1961) and the film *IBM at the Fair* (1964) both end with sequences of fireworks (Figure 6.11), and the film *Smithsonian Institution* (1965) also includes a fireworks display marking the centennial year 1876.

The festival arts are by nature temporary and fleeting, and this quality is desirable for its capacity to refuse clear performance evaluation terms such as those raised by the kite. The question with toys or festival arts is not whether they will work, whether they can be relied on to perform efficiently, but rather whether they are fully consumed in performance. One asks of a kite whether it will fly or not, while flowers, fireworks, and

FIGURE 6.11. Fireworks over the Pacific Coast Highway and Santa Monica Pier, photographed by Charles Eames.

balloons—like the food considered earlier—are intended to disappear with use, their disappearance *registering* their perfected qualitative status.

Model as Product

In an interview with Charles Eames, Owen Gingerich perceptively remarks that many of the Eameses' films "can't be reexperienced." Charles agrees, speaking of the films and exhibition work as falling "into the category of the temporary triumphal arch, which is burned after it is used" (*EA*, 362). To burn the work after use is to suspend questions of use and viability that one would typically ask about works that live on after their moment of creation and, more to the point, after they leave the makers' hands. It is not exactly that the Eameses refuse evaluation but rather that the evaluation of a fleeting performance is *beyond normative notions of dispute,* given that the work gets de-

voured by its users in a specific setting and moment. Charles explicitly indicates how he
feels about evaluation in a document he wrote in the 1970s that opens with the phrase
"When your role is not judgment." Rather than judgment, Charles suggests, what matters is the "seriousness" of the person doing the "deciding."[47] He insists that a decision
is not the same as a judgment and that acknowledging the "seriousness" of a decision
is not just another way of stating the centrality of judgment because he is trying to turn
overt judgment into an unconscious, and continuous, act, to make judgment identical
with the primary Eamesian virtue of "unselfconsciousness."

The theme of burning an object after use emerges again in *The India Report,* where
the Eameses recommend an assignment attributed to Fuller. They ask students to design a "package of services and effects which will be the most essential to salvage from
a city about to be destroyed." This is not about civil defense but a "study of relative
values—what do you take with you when the house burns down?" (*EA,* 183). As the
Eameses' project evolves over the 1960s and 1970s, this thought becomes further radicalized. They increasingly see the world being destroyed through the misuse of the environment, which leads them to regard only ideas, concepts, and goods that are "other
than physical" as valuable, another version of Fullerian "wealth."

One of the manifestations of this permanent value is an account of models stripped
of the necessity, or the desire, for physical application. Charles observes how there are
people so "interested in the abstract models themselves that their lives are spent manipulating old ones and investigating new ones with no thought or concern for how
they may be applied" (*EA,* 230). Of course, what makes this statement so provocative in
connection with the Eamesian aversion to certain kinds of production is that it reveals
that the turn to modeling does not dispense with production. On the contrary, it is accompanied by an even vaster scale of production, only now production is reducible to
modeling, an idea figured in the phrase "The solution is a diagram of the problem."[48]
The Eameses thus feel freer and freer to produce—as the extreme surplus of imagery at
the *Franklin and Jefferson* exhibition, for instance, suggests—at the very moment when
the work is leaving fewer and fewer lasting traces in the world.

Charles makes no clearer statement about the changing nature of his and Ray's
production than when he notes in a 1975 lecture titled "Film as a Modeling Device" how
the "end-product" of the Eames Office is "more often than not in the nature of a model.
We seem to have gotten away with not taking the very last step of the process."[49] The last
step is, of course, to make something based on the model, which would then be available for the kinds of evaluation raised by the kite problem. But despite the Eameses'
obsessive fascination with feedback, they were not interested in it so that they might
bring their models to bear on the world. Instead, they wanted to explore the possibility
of endlessly manipulating models through ceaseless feedback loops.

In a sense, then, the 1957 *Solar Do-Nothing Machine* (Plate 11) epitomizes their ideal work, as well as signaling their growing aversion to "critical performance."[50] Or more exactly, the object as it is memorialized *on film,* rather than its realization as "solar toy," epitomizes their ideal work. As a toy, the work already neutralizes any performance principle—it does nothing—but as the subject of a film its material qualities are further diminished (not erased), and it becomes a model of efficiency without possible application. Calling it a "solar toy" is to construe the work as energy without consumption or as performance without the capacity to fail. The toy itself was dismantled not long after production, and it is not wholly clear how to interpret its finalization in the form of a film given that the film was never intended for public consumption.

Unselfconsciousness

What the Eameses hoped toys and festival arts would express was a pure quality of involvement, care, a total absorption in one's task. In the *Omnibus* script Charles describes this quality as being *"almost completely free from embarrassment and self-consciousness."*[51] The wording is important, as it suggests a kind of literalism in its emphasis on the absence of consciousness. And while the Eameses continually flirted with a literalism of natural expression, with the idea that works *are* natural objects and therefore literally free from consciousness, they never fell into the trap of naturalized automaticity (the word "almost" does a lot of work). Nonetheless, they aimed to ride the increasingly fine line between an absolute or radicalized vision of unselfconsciousness and a relative refusal of effect that made their works *analogous to,* but still fundamentally distinct from, natural objects.

Charles most explicitly addresses a naturalizing literalism in his 1950 illustrated talk "Design Today," delivered at the University of Washington Arboretum in Seattle. Projecting a slide of a Navajo trading post (Plate 12), he notes how it "almost looks like a posed shot." Although at first glance the scene looks like a random or naturally occurring array of objects, its appearing "posed" suggests an underlying order in the chance accumulation and arrangement. The lecture is about how collections, no matter how disparately arranged over time and for varying purposes, retain a sense of identity, what the Eameses describe as a shared "attitude." What Charles thinks brings these seemingly accidentally disposed items together as though they are "posed" is nature itself; nature contains an order hidden within its accidental lines. Charles offers a comparison to this photograph that shows the leaves of a plant, as though that offers the best commentary on the order that permeates the trading post.

> Just because everything was placed here with a certain amount of love, the things themselves have a relationship in the past, a unity which is given it in almost an

overall texture, in a way texture, just as this is texture, the repeated form of the plant, each one like the other, yet each one different and individual, yet hanging together with straight unity. (*EA*, 81)

But to call a trading post "posed" and a leaf "posed" is to say two very different and incompatible things. The trading post can only show unity over time through the application of care if it has been arranged according to someone's aesthetic sensibility. The texture of the trading post is *intentional* (even if that intention is unconscious or precisely because the intention is unconscious), while the "unity" of the plant is not. This conflation of different senses of "posed" is complicated by Charles's discussion of the "consistent attitude" that went into the shaping of driftwood that precedes his remarks on the trading post photograph. The driftwood is a "new and wonderful thing" by virtue of the "unity" of its elements and materials working together (*EA*, 80). As in the case of the trading post, it is the "element of time" that brings out the consistency in the shaping "attitude" (*EA*, 87). Since the unity of the trading post is of an entirely different order from the "unity" of water and wood, the point of drawing them together can only be to suggest that the unselfconsciousness through which the trading post achieves "unity" over time is akin to *nonconsciousness*.

Charles turns from the driftwood, the trading post, and plants to describe a peculiar scene in which a person throws paper into a fire. Once again, he models the ideal work on the fiery dissolution of the product in its making, as though making and consumption could be a *united and almost instantaneous act*. Just before this, Charles shows a slide of Chinese firecrackers, commenting that "the little firecrackers, the lady firecrackers, baby firecrackers, greatly magnified they become something else and something rich in themselves" (*EA*, 81). His point is twofold. First, order or unity becomes visible by virtue of the camera lens. As with the photograph of the trading post, freezing the objects in the frame and magnifying them brings to the surface the kind of unconscious care that goes into their making. Second, firecrackers exemplify the "festival arts" that disappear completely in their performance. From the firecrackers Charles turns to the person who "has the habit of throwing waste paper in the fireplace." He observes that if one consistently "throw[s] enough paper in a fireplace," then "the consistency of that attitude will show up and it doesn't become a bad thing" (*EA*, 83) (Plate 13). It is hard to know what to make of the judgment here (not a "bad thing"). On the one hand, he seems to be suggesting that our intentionality is expressed in the merest gestures, as though, as with the trading post or the firecrackers, our care for the materials drives us to order them in particularly meaningful ways. On the other hand, this is not a judgment at all. Can one badly throw paper into a fire? The job is done if the paper makes it into the fireplace.

Twenty-five years later, Charles describes the central idea that animates the arbore-tum talk, calling it CATCHING A PROCESS IN AN UNSELFCONSCIOUS MOMENT.[52] What he values about the man throwing paper into the fire and a photographer freezing a moment in the evolving nature of the trading post is that they both capture the quality of an ongoing process without stopping that process. Because the process is *ongoing*, any given instance of it that is captured is ipso facto unposed, caught unawares. And if it is the process that matters, then the work made from it could ideally be *dissolved into* it without remainder. The work would be reducible to a "by-product" of the act; it would be a natural extension—or, at the very least, a reminder—of the thing it was.

In the "Design Today" talk Charles points to another instance of an idealized un-selfconscious process in what goes on above the sets of a movie, which he declares is "much more beautiful than what is going on down below," adding that what goes on above is "a real by-product of concentrated effort, as often by-products of any orderly effort are bound to in themselves show a counterpart of order" (*EA*, 82). We are meant to see the connection between the trading post—a by-product of the effort of collecting items for sale—and what is happening above the movie sets, the by-product of film-making. Moreover, the "concentrated" nature of the staged action suggests that the by-product is the expression of *an already quasi-natural or semi-somnambulistic* act. Even so, it remains difficult to equate the relations between filmmakers and their sets and between traders and their shops, on the one hand, with the relation between water and driftwood, on the other. The analogies with the natural world are intensified images for the idea that unconscious acts are more fully expressive than conscious ones. For Charles, all of this is the unconscious expression or by-product of a set of concentrated actions. Moreover, as explicit by-products of a production, they cannot or should not be judged in the way that a standard production would be.

What is most striking about this larger picture of the Eameses' enterprise is their rather perverse aversion to *the product,* as though *consciously intending* something is to automatically compromise its status as meaningful. The paradox of their position emerges clearly in Charles's description of a church under construction in the "Design Today" lecture. In between the discussion of what happens above movie sets and the person who throws paper into a fire, Charles shows the frame of a "church under pro-cess of construction" (Plate 13). He insists that "this building will never look as beau-tiful as it does now." Wanting to keep the process perpetually frozen at the stage of production, to suspend the model (or scaffold) prior to its application, Charles tries to stave off the moment when process becomes product. He notes how he has not "had the heart to go by and see what it looked like after it was put up, but never was the structural purpose of the elements more clear, I am sure, in the building than it was at this stage" (*EA*, 83). What is it to value the "structural purpose" over the actual purpose? What is it to substitute process for product to the extent that the product is always and seemingly necessarily a "degeneration" of the "structural concept"?

A work that is intimately related to the concerns of the arboretum talk is *House of Cards* of 1952. The fifty-four images of this picture deck depict "good things." The deck is described as comprising "familiar and nostalgic objects from the animal, mineral, and vegetable kingdoms" (*ED*, 169). Of particular note, for reasons that will likely be obvious to the reader at this point of my argument, are the images of the "Chinese 'baby' firecrackers," "red-tipped kitchen matches," an "Austrian wax angel," "watch hands" (unattached to any watch), "medicine" (a range of colorful pills), "garden vegetables," a "nosegay of flowers," and a "boar-shaped cookie" (Plate 14). What connects these disparate elements is their quality of impermanence, the fact that their performance value collapses into their use value (swallowed, eaten, melted, burned up, unusable). Even the asterisk (or firework) that appears on the back of the cards and that became the trademark of the Eames Office is an explosive image of transience, or an abstracted flower, captured in passing.

Some of images of "good things" from *House of Cards* recur in *Goods* of 1971, originally shown as *The New Covetables,* a work that perhaps sums up the Eameses' aims better than any other. *Goods* was transferred to film in 1981 by Ray ten years after it was first delivered as a thirty-three-image, three-screen slide show by Charles as part of his Norton Lectures. *Goods* forms the core of the fourth lecture, and the film is the first publicly available extract from the lectures, Charles's most conclusive statement as a designer (Plate 15). *Goods* elaborates on the thought first raised in "Design Today," directly engaging the fundamental difference between the model and "what you do with" it (*EA*, 308).

The film begins with a seemingly casual anecdote about Ray's car being "broken into" and how Charles is most distressed by the fact that the thieves did not steal the most valuable things—they neglected to take the "goods." Searching around the parking lot, he "came upon a bolt of cloth. And this was really distressing, because it was that kind of a bolt of cloth—it was a bolt of wool." That the thieves neglected to honor this good is the real criminal act in Charles's eyes. Ray's car is a scene of celebration, an ideal site where everything is arrayed for festival use: "beautifully wrapped flowers, things to put flowers in, things of food for picnics and stuff. We have a picnic every day at the office" (*EA*, 307).

The film dwells on a variety of "goods," beginning with the bolt of cloth and moving on to hanks of rope, a reel of line, a ball of twine, a keg of nails, reams of paper, boxes of chalk, and finally a cord of wood. Charles lavishes verbal and visual attention on each good, remarking on its qualities, treating all the goods as akin to ur-commodities by noting how in their original states they seem as though they can "go on forever," another variant on Fuller's notion of "wealth." The permanent quality of these commodities embodies the Eameses' paradoxical vision, the idea of a form of production, a perfected commodity, that can be produced and consumed but also remain in an unviolated state of potential, divided like "loaves and fishes: you can distribute it without diminishing it" (*EA*, 385).

Each of the vignettes is interrupted by a transgressive moment of violation, the introduction of noise. Each good is broken into in the way that Ray's car has been at the beginning of the film. The rope is so "perfect" that "you don't want to break into it"; it is always better to "keep it as it is" (*EA*, 307). The ball of twine is special up until the "moment that it's opened up and gotten into." Charles reflects that the phrase "breaking into the keg of nails" is the general term for breaking into any form of goods. A telling aside refers to the goods as an expression of the ideal work, something that disappears entirely with use: "Boxes of candy are thought of as kegs of nails" (*EA*, 308). Most extraordinary, though, is the account of paper: "What you do with a ream of paper can never quite come up to what the paper offers in itself," he says. In its original state—"in itself"—the paper is saturated with a kind of significance, the look and feel of the forest from which it is drawn impressed in its pages. The violation, when it inevitably occurs, is absolute. There is, Charles says, "something about taking out that first sheet that sort of changes it." The fall occurs not with the writing, which is further down the chain of degeneration, but simply with the removal of a sheet from the ream. It is not a coincidence that the cord of wood follows the ream of paper. And exactly as with the paper there is "always that moment when somebody'd eat first—eat into the cord of wood. The first one to take the piece out and it would start to tumble, and before you knew it, the cord of wood was gone" (*EA*, 307–8).

The word "eating" is notable. On the one hand, eating the wood is an image that, like the feast and candy imagery that circulates throughout the Eameses' oeuvre—*Bread,* picnics, cakes, the confections of *Konditorei* (Plate 5) and *Day of the Dead*—literalizes the identification of production and consumption. On the other hand, by eating into the wood, one dismembers it, rendering it inoperative for an always potential, never quite actual, future application, suggesting not the idea of a model suspended before it finds its application but the impossibility of use. Then again, unlike a birthday cake, bread, or a picnic, goods like paper, chalk, and wood continue their lives in the world, and the "in itself" of the thing—already a fictive notion—inevitably degenerates. Better leave the present wrapped, the ream stacked, the wood corded, or else, as with furniture, try your best to calculate the path taken by goods into the world. Anything else must quicken the pace of degeneration.

In her memorial tribute to Ray Eames, McCoy reflects on Ray's "love of packages—packages beautifully wrapped" (*EMR,* 306). She loved wrapped gifts so much that she would sometimes forgo opening them because they would, in her view, lose something about their character, their potentiality, in being used. "I don't know how she would do it, but it would look as though she never opened a gift. Because if she was really taken by the wrapping, the gift would stay there wrapped," Etsu Farfias recalls.[53] For Ray, it seems, it was better if "the package was never opened. It went to the back room to gather dust," McCoy writes. Better to gather dust than be dust.

As Charles notes in the opening narration to *Goods,* goods, like toys, have lost their value in society (he notes how hard it was to find a box of chalks, "sawdust and all"). What he emphasizes in the Norton Lectures is that we live in a world seemingly stripped of the capacity to produce or consume commodities outside a context of self-consciousness or self-expression. We are "doomed to a time of awareness," he says, "self-consciousness" is "irreversible."[54] Whether the fall that occurs between the "in itself" and its worldly application—what gets made with the cloth, the nails, or rope, what gets written on the page, the church that gets built and prayed in (by unbelievers)—is a historical dilemma or something more ontological in nature remains a question, although the nostalgic tone suggests that he sees it as an unfolding reality. Given that modernity is marked by such a heightened degree of self-consciousness, the capacity to break the hold of "discontinuity" between production and consumption is seemingly out of reach.

To *Think* without Thinking

In their practice, the Eameses consistently aim to straddle the line between a kind of absolute or literal unselfconsciousness and the kind of unawareness that comes with the absorptive engrossment in one's activities. The latter quality emerges most clearly in their basic design formula: "He doesn't care, so he produces a terrific thing" (*EA,* 106). Another formulation of the ideal relation between designer and client comes in the question "How do you design a chair for acceptance by another person?" the answer to which is "by not thinking of what the other guy wants" (*EA,* 289). If not thinking is the key to success, then thinking (of an obtrusive kind) is the source of failure. The central danger in making a chair is "trying to introduce our personality or trying to outguess what the other guy's thinking" (*EA,* 289). This is what Charles means when he speaks of the "personality of the designer" as a "barrier between the intended message and the viewer" (*EA,* 206). The barrier between designer and client or user would dissolve in a more transparent situation; in an unselfconscious performance, the person dissolves into the action.

Outguessing is a central issue raised for the Eameses that is registered early on in their fascination with game theory. In a 1952 speech for the American Institute of

Architects, Charles addresses the "business of outguessing the other guy. He thinks that I think, therefore, I think that . . . etc. The duel, it's a basic thing, or, as it gets much more complex, it's the poker hand" (EA, 107). The essential difference for the Eameses between a designer outguessing what a client wants and the capacity of a computer to manage incredibly complex sets of variables is not just that computers do the work of outguessing in a way that is impossible for the designer but, far more important, that it takes the process of guessing out of the hands of the agent, so the agent *cannot perform for another.* Computers disable the capacity to perform for another, as they seemingly automatically detheatricalize the design situation. Fuller puts the same point about the attraction of computers more caustically: "Computers," he says, are "uncorrupted and incorruptible by ignorantly opinionated humans."[55] For the Eameses, computers *almost automatically* take the capacity to perform for another out of the exchange. The human agent still retains—as the last sentence of *A Communications Primer* insists—the "responsibility of decision, all the way down the line." This raises a paradox. What is the difference between the intolerable situation of continually "outguessing" the client and making decisions "all the way down the line"? The problem with outguessing, it seems, is *not* the effort required to readjust plans according to the client's needs but rather how to do so *more securely.* What the designer–computer relation does is take the guessing out of the context of person-to-person interaction (even an attenuated version), making the messy work of addressing complex needs disappear into behind-the-scenes exchanges with an impersonal mechanism. The designer–computer relation effectively detheatricalizes the designer–client interaction by displacing the act of interpersonal guesswork onto an impersonal human–machine relation. The product that results from the human–machine relation is incapable of being driven by the continuous performance demands of the designer–client relation.

There is abundant evidence that Charles was highly sensitized to the problem of performing for another. As he notes in a speech written for the 1964 World's Fair, the one "thing to remember" is if you "are aware of the effect, you have every right in the world of suspecting the intent" (EA, 250).[56] On the other hand, to be *unaware* of the effect, although it is still an intended effect, is to be absorbed with the intent. Charles describes himself as being "hypersensitive" to fakery, noting how he begins to "suspect the intent" of commonplace phrases, as though excessive consciousness haunts the most mundane actions (EA, 276).[57] Because we are all "doomed to a time of awareness," there is "almost nothing that anyone can do without a kind of a side-sight that is always intruding on you, and it's very difficult to screen things out."[58] Theatricality is pervasive; our least gestures, it seems, are haunted or shadowed by an address to an audience (even if none is literally present), an idea for which Charles likely found support in a passage from John Dewey's *Art as Experience* (1934):

If one examines the reason why certain works of art offend us, one is likely to find that the cause is that there is no personally felt emotion guiding the selecting and assembling of the materials presented. We derive the impression that the artist . . . is trying to regulate by conscious intent the nature of the emotion aroused. We are irritated by a feeling that he is manipulating materials to secure an effect decided upon in advance.[59]

As George Nelson glosses this passage, "People don't like to be pushed around—even by an artist" (*PD*, 100). Charles goes beyond merely objecting to obtrusive conscious intent and instead seeks a kind of extreme form of *unconscious intentionality,* one that at times he appears to conflate with natural kinds of automatic behavior.

The Eameses always conceived of toys as a kind of storehouse or repository of pure un-selfconsciousness. But even here in the world of toys, "side-sight" or self-consciousness threatens to unravel the pleasures associated with them. Ever sensitized to the threat of self-consciousness, the Eameses construe the world of contemporary toy making, like everything else, as infected with the disease of self-expression:

When somebody says we want to design a toy or a game which will look as though somebody will have a good time with it, and then a lot of people will buy it . . . now, this is sort of doomed to failure at the beginning. Because as soon as you try to do something that will look as if it will do something, why, the phoniness immediately becomes apparent. (*EA,* 181)

It is as though anything made *with an intent* is suspected of trying for an *effect.* In the past, toys, almost like natural objects, represented seemingly *intentionless* products, objects that took no account of any effect on an audience. The Eameses construe anything made to perform beyond the level of transience as being threatened with intolerable self-consciousness, what they continually lament as personality, originality, uniqueness, and self-expression.

Accidental Agency: Design Perfected

Parke Meek, a longtime member of the Eames Office, describes watching the Oscar Peterson Trio play "Seven Come Eleven" on the television show *Stars of Jazz* at the same time that the Eameses' early film *Blacktop* was screened for TV viewers. Inspired by Peterson's example, the Eameses put together (in a matter of days, as though sheer speed forecloses "side-sight") a first version of their film *Tops* (1957). At the office they tried a range of soundtracks that—rather improbably—all seemed to sync up with the music. "There are just so many accidental places," Meek says, that "things would hit on anything else." But when the film was played on air, the experiment failed, and the synchronization did not come off. Following the Eames formula, Meek notes that "when you try you can't make anything hit."[60]

Meek is repeating the lesson of the earlier film *Blacktop* (1952), which carries the subtitle *A Story of the Washing of a School Play Yard* (Plate 16). The film traces the movement of water over an asphalt schoolyard. As the subtitle suggests, the seemingly random play of water on the surface creates an improbable "story." One might read the story as being about containment and escape, as the water adheres to the painted lines on the playground but, near the end, passes under the chain-link fence, as though it has been set free from confining shapes. At the end, the camera introduces a powerful scaling effect—at one moment we see (mere) water on asphalt, but the next moment, closer up, the densely material ground has become a cosmic vision of the stars—suggesting that what has been freed is our capacity to see. The turning of chance effects into story is made explicit, or rather doubled, with the use of a soundtrack. Charles "synchronized" the film to Bach's *Goldberg Variations* "by reading the optical track for visual clues to see where the music changed tempo" (*ED*, 163). Ray describes the process of transformation from random marks to intentional narrative. "Miraculously," she writes, "many of the [visual] points coincided as if [the music] had been written for the film" (*ED*, 163). Ray turns causality backward by seeing Bach's score as improvised in light of the film made more than two hundred years later (much like the "901" in the film *Babbage*), an idea that is more dramatic than Peterson's capacity to improvise a connection between sound and film or Charles's capacity to read the optical track for musical cues.

Two years after *Blacktop,* the Eameses traveled to Germany as part of a cultural exchange program. In October in Cologne, they attended an infamous performance of John Cage's 1954 prepared piano piece *34'46.776" for two pianists.*[61] Cage's chance-driven works naturally intrigued the Eameses. Charles's account of the performance reveals the lure of quasi-natural art making, in which the artist's lack of intentional control could "miraculously" enact a kind of connection impossible to achieve by design. Speaking of the Cage performance, Charles describes how the audience engaged with the music:

> Cage went, "plinck, plonck, shoonk, choonk, ploonch." And then he slammed
> down the top of the music rack and it went "whamm." And some joker in the crowd
> now said, "Hurray, biffy"—he yells out at Cage. And Cage goes on "clunck." Then
> somebody else hollers and there would be some catcalls. And Cage beaming. Then
> he takes a whistle and blows the whistle. Then the papers go flying and he goes on
> "clunking." And then the guys began stamping their feet, and they started yelling.
> Pretty soon they took a chair and slammed the chair down, and then they started

breaking the furniture, and the people were stamping and they were yelling and Cage was going on "clunking." . . . There was a radio area and I raced backstage at this point, to see if they were taping it, which the idiots weren't. It was the greatest Cage performance. It was a complete shambles, the furniture broken all over the place. . . . And Cage afterwards was out of his mind with pleasure. He said, "You know, the fellow that broke that first chair over that jardiniere, it just couldn't have come at a better moment."[62]

What made this the "greatest" Cage performance was that although the audience did not see it—they were presumably too busy *trying* to make sense out of the music— they were seamlessly involved in the music, as though they were (unconsciously) like Peterson improvising over *Blacktop,* an act not unlike that of the trader at his post. Cage's performance was similar to the *Blacktop* film because it happened by chance and because the responses of the audience members "hit" at precisely the right moments. What remains unclear is whether Charles's interpretation of the success of the performance was the same as, or even related to, Cage's. If for Charles it was about a kind of miraculous, because completely unselfconscious (or unconscious), synchronization between audience and music, then for Cage, who famously "gave up on the notion of communication," no performance could be judged better than another.[63]

It is tempting to see Charles's wish that the performance had been recorded as part of his larger commitment to modeling or rather to the idea that the performance is paradoxically *secondary* to the model. (As it turned out, Charles was wrong—the performance was recorded.) As numerous stories indicate, Charles was an obsessive photographic recorder of events, which suggests that he regarded the photographic (or musical or filmic) record as akin to the event itself rather than its reproduction. In an offhand but revealing description of one of his and Ray's multiscreen productions he describes their purpose as an "outlet for a picture-taking maniac."[64] Indeed, the Eames Office donated eight hundred thousand photographs to the Library of Congress, 5 percent of one of the largest collections in the world. The core of this collection consists of photographs taken by Charles.[65] Once again it is the expansive, seemingly unending, nature of the productive process—constituting a running photographic commentary on seemingly every event in and out of the office—that is the necessary accompaniment to the dematerializing nature of the model. Charles frequently described photographs as exemplary instances of the "new covetables," because they allow one to "have one's cake and eat it too" (*ED,* 434).[66] His equation of cakes and photographs speaks to the core value of transposing technology, with all its suggestions of permanence and mediation, into a transitory and unselfconscious vehicle of communication.

From Toys to Tools to Computers

Charles concludes his *Omnibus* script by telling his audience that to "know so well what you want to accomplish that there is no pressure to be original—this is a desirable state whether one is designing a toy or writing a play or building a chair." But contemporary toy making and furniture, as he had already indicated, were haunted by self-consciousness. Purer even than toys or furniture are *tools,* which, he observes, "are perhaps the most foolproof against the trap of originality" (*EA,* 149).[67] A foolproof means to avoid self-consciousness, to be literally free of pretense, is the impossible limit of the Eamesian enterprise. The primary attraction of the tool is that, like the model, it is essentially expendable and anonymous; further, like Martin Heidegger's *Zuhandenheit,* or ready-to-hand, it can disappear completely in use.[68] Charles notes how office staff "designed and built . . . all the presses and tools and jigs and fixtures that were used in the original production," thereby suggesting three things: that those tools are entirely free of pretense, that their use wholly determines their shape, and that they are expendable after use (*EA,* 167; see also 277, 374). Moving beyond the quest for total control of the product from inception to (mass) production, the Eameses began to seek a mode of production that itself would be collapsible into the tools with which the products were made. As Ralph Caplan describes it, not only are their films "tools," but also a "great many of the films are tools *about* tools."[69]

Not surprisingly, Charles's definition of the tool is peculiar to the Eamesian approach.[70] It is in the making of tools, presumably with *other tools,* that he develops the "attitude" toward every problem, an idea whose evolution in the *Omnibus* script can be traced in the shift from architecture (based in structural concepts) to kites (based in performance) to toys (based on a lack of self-conscious relation to materials) to tools (the unselfconscious means to create architecture) and in the shift from his designing products to his designing tools for products to his finding the right attitude toward designing products in the designing of tools. It is as though the perfect work is the image of the tool to make the work—a theme explored in depth in *Movie Sets* (Plate 17). And although one might conclude that a tool is there to make something, the tools that fascinate the Eameses are, not surprisingly, put totally out of use; they are "a hoard, a treasure." Charles provides a cast of famous characters who covet goods in the right way, by *not using them*: he mentions Walter Huston in *The Treasure of the Sierra Madre,* Julia Child's "basic hoard of knives," Madame Curie's receiving a "gram of radium" as a gift, the "well-kept tool-box, the machinist's tools, the carpenter's tools," and a photographer's store of lenses. While all who possess such goods "may use them," what is more important is having the "treasure."[71] This is a replay of the theme of *Goods*: the quality of the "in itself" nearly always surpasses "what you do with it."

The Information Machine

In 1957, the same year as *Omnibus,* the *Solar Do-Nothing Machine,* the first version of *Tops, Day of the Dead,* and *Toccata for Toy Trains,* the Eameses began their long-term collaboration with the IBM Corporation. Eliot Noyes, consultant director of design at IBM and former director of industrial design at the Museum of Modern Art, brought the Eameses in as consultants, a relationship that lasted until Charles's death in 1978. *The Information Machine or Creative Man and the Data Processor* was their first film for the company (Plate 18); it was also their first commissioned film and first animated film.[72] It is also directly connected with the ideas presented in their first major film, *A Communications Primer.*

The opening line of narration in *The Information Machine* explains that the film is about the ongoing efforts of human beings to "control the environment."[73] Control is a matter of speculation, the capacity to "accurately predict the effect" of a "proposed action." We are, in other words, situated within the world of "kite problems," where what matters is performance and where accurate speculation is haunted by the fact that it is impossible to fully "consider and relate all the factors" in any specific situation, because causes multiply beyond predictable effects. As I have argued, the Eameses were ultimately not that committed to predicting effects; rather, they were interested in how the prediction *might* work (or not) and in remaining at the point where effects—and side effects—could be put off, even intentionally multiplied beyond human control so as to sustain the suspended status of the work between idea and world. The reason they raised the issue of mounting complexity was that it licenses the idea of the necessity of delaying performance. This is part of what it means to define the computer as a "universal model" for which there might be "no thought or concern for how [the models] may be applied" (*EA,* 212).

At this point the narration takes a surprising turn, explaining that the agent most capable of mastering his environment is the artist, the "creative man" of the title. But this is no ordinary artist. The Eameses define artists not as people who have expressive aims but instead as people who can accurately predict the outcomes of actions. They are primitive computers who have specially attuned "memory banks for information" that they can call on when a need arises; they can speculate and predict with high degrees of accuracy. The term "artist" refers to anyone who is unconsciously gifted with the capacity of "relating factors"—we are told that engineers, doctors, scientists, and politicians, as well as architects, are "artists."[74]

The narration then shifts to a description of how numbers play a primary role in the long and ongoing effort to master nature. But numbers no longer serve the artist as they did in the past. The narrative paints a picture of looming chaos as the "science of numerical relationships" cannot keep pace with the "compounding" "complications" of contemporary society. Even the most sophisticated artist cannot begin to comprehend all the factors that have to be taken into account in any attempt to solve even the simplest problem of contemporary society. Enter the electronic calculator and computer to rescue the artist from the chaos of numbers, although it is the artist who sets the "task" and inputs the "data" into the machine; it is "man's decision and his responsibility" to give "direction" to the computer. But if it is the artist who gives the computer direction, the information *itself* is processed in such a way that it is always already "meaningful at the human scale."[75] The computer plays a crucially double role: it is at once free of self-consciousness, able to sort data without getting hung up on meaning, and also a kind of superartist, because it manipulates humanly scaled information, data that are *always already saturated with meaning*. Free of the possibility of having "side-sight," computers embody the ideal qualities of unselfconsciousness, but they are also not natural; the data they crunch are fed into them and shaped by human users. Computer processing, on the Eameses' account, strips data of the stain of self-consciousness while keeping the data humanly meaningful, so that what emerges is an idealized product of human agency.

Computers both model and are models. They are used to create a "model of life," one where "we can see the effect before taking the action," but they also more importantly function to disperse action by multiplying factors. In *The Information Machine,* we learn about models being made of chemical plants, "railroad systems, rocket engines, complete reactors and whole living communities." The Eameses, of course, did not have the least interest in creating any of these objects themselves. Computers for them were "tool[s] for turning inspiration into fruitful prediction," tools that could enable artists to predict outcomes in situations involving highly elaborate and potentially insurmountable amounts of numerical data. In the hands of the Eameses, the computer, like Julia Child's "central hoard," is a "treasure" to contemplate, even if it is never used to make something (an attraction not unlike that of cooking shows—no mess, no mistakes).

The narration concludes in typical Eamesian fashion with a vision of the computer that may seem at odds with the global vision of environmental control that is the main drift of the story. We are told that the "real miracle" of computers remains in their capacity to leave room for the transitory and the ephemeral, the "smallest details" of life, which the narrator calls humankind's "most rewarding wishes." The viewer is presented, yet again, with an image of a flower. The most rewarding wish, in other words, is not a wish for any *thing* but rather a wish for the only kind of permanence that remains inviolable. Or, if one must have something, and the Eameses surely did, it is a model of what it would be like to have a thing more perfect than any object in the world.

Conclusion
Reyner Banham's Neoliberal Aesthetic

California fulfilled Reyner Banham's long-standing dream of not only *un art autre,* but *une vie autre.* All that the northeastern critics construed as thin, disposable, antimonumental, consumer driven, and suburban, Banham saw as the defining terms of a new, and better, way of life. Banham accepted the terms of the architectural establishment but reversed its evaluation. Hollywood film offers the world an image of Los Angeles as providing a "friendly, sexy, adaptable personal environment," a place where everyone lives in "their own habitable bubble of innocence" (Figure C.1). New York, by contrast, is "densely built, overpopulated, low on privacy, violent, serviced by public transport." That Banham does not skip a beat in mentioning violence and public transport together is indicative of his larger criticism of the northeastern design ethos and offers a glimpse of his antistatist politics. Worse still in Banham's view is the fact that New York is the "kind of city that most architects would prefer" (*DC,* 136). The major cities of the United States are the "archaeological remains of a culture that ought to have died when the gizmos came in" (*DC,* 113). *Gizmo* was a relatively new term, invented by the British stationed in Malta during World War II (*x'jismu* is Maltese for "what's its name?"). Banham's fascination with novelty as well as his vision of Los Angeles as the city of gizmos sets him apart from the Eameses. The big cities are "vast unhygienic heaps . . . [of] man-warrens," on which, however, the "only concepts of civilization that we know" were built (*DC,* 113). But that does not rule out the invention of "alternative structures of civilization," such as one built on the "culture of the gizmo" (*DC,* 113–14). Los Angeles, Banham writes in his first article on the city in 1968, "offers radical alternatives to almost every urban concept in unquestioned currency" (*DC,* 68). He first visited "posturban" Los Angeles in 1965 to take part in a symposium at UCLA and took up permanent residence in California beginning in 1976.

Banham's admiration for everything West Coast was seemingly unlimited, and he embraced a consumer culture defined by its "subversive suspicion of the monumental" (*DC,* 57).[1] Like many of his generation, Banham envisioned a future life on the move and affirmed the choices of "untold thousands of Americans who have already shed the dead-weight of domestic architecture and live in mobile homes . . . [that] deliver rather better performance as shelter than do ground-anchored structures costing at least three times as much and weighing ten times more" (*DC,* 96). It was not exactly cities that

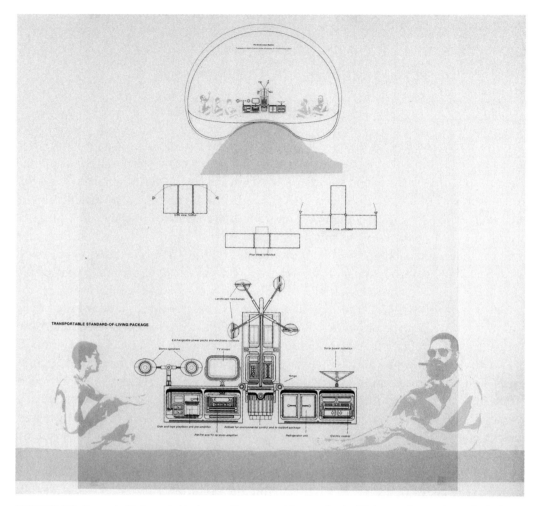

FIGURE C.1. François Dallegret, *Un house. Transportable standard-of-living-package*, also called *The Environment-bubble*, transparent plastic bubble dome inflated by air-conditioning output, 1965. Frac Centre-Val de Loire.

were the problem but rather the fact that cities are made up of buildings: buildings, Banham insists, "are too damn permanent" (*DC*, 96). By contrast, Los Angeles is tear-down at its core: a hub of desirable disposable products, an array of diverse consumer cultures, a seemingly endless circuit of freeways—a cybernetically self-guided utopia (Figure C.2)—serving a mobile culture that generates multicolored sunsets.

Without a doubt Banham's explorations of the city in *Los Angeles: The Architecture of Four Ecologies* of 1971 and in the companion film *Reyner Banham Loves Los Angeles*

FIGURE C.2. Intersection of the Santa Monica and San Diego Freeways. Reyner Banham, *Los Angeles: The Architecture of Four Ecologies* (New York and London: Penguin, 1971). Courtesy of Penguin Books.

of 1972 are among the most influential accounts of Southern California ever produced. But he had worked out the ideas that shaped his view of Los Angeles long before he arrived in the city. Banham's 1955 "A Throw-Away Aesthetic," published in *Industrial Design* in 1960, provides the "methodological framework for many of his later studies," as Penny Sparke rightly notes (*DC*, 90).[2]

At the outset of the essay, Banham states his objections to the canonical picture of modern architecture. By World War I, he argues, modernism had become a codified ideological system whose champions postulated that the arts shared a "common dependence on laws of form that were objective, absolute, universal and eternally valid." This "illusion of a common 'objectivity' residing in the concept of function, and in the laws of Platonic aesthetics," has drastically narrowed the scope and possibilities of functionality (*DC*, 90). As Banham sees it, function needs to be isolated from aesthetics; function is the full realization of the possibilities of technology free of the imposition of empty academic formulas of beauty. "It is basic to [my] whole argument," he writes, "that technology will impinge increasingly on architecture . . . and that technological habits of thought are hostile to architectural habits of thought."[3] Functionality needs to be cleansed of the least trace of artistic habits of mind to ensure the primacy of tech-driven performance.

Following futurists and expressionists like Antonio Sant'Elia, Scheerbart, and Fuller, Banham asserts the primacy of "technological culture" and judges architects as either "pre-technological" (like Le Corbusier) or up-to-the-minute (like those creating prefabricated buildings for the British Consortium of Local Authorities Special Programme, or CLASP).[4] Banham pursues a double program for contemporary architecture: to make every "mental accommodation towards technology" and to push for the "incorporation of the products and usages of technology" into every building.[5] Even though Banham conceives his practice as exemplifying the aims of Schindler and the Eameses, at almost every turn he is at odds with their aims. What makes him think he is aligned with them is that they all embrace the throwaway and the expendable. But his conception of the throwaway is an expression of his deeper commitment to "measurable performance," an idea that is opposed to Eamesian modeling (*DC*, 51).

Banham attacks three "confusions" that have clouded architectural thinking since the 1920s: simplicity, objectivity, and standardization. These confusions are rooted in a false assimilation of technology to aesthetics. Whatever beauty engineered forms produce should be the result of technical requirements, not resistance to them:

> We live in a throw-away economy, a culture in which the most fundamental classification of our ideas and worldly possessions is in terms of their relative expendability. Our buildings may stand for a millennium, but their mechanical equip-

ment must be replaced in fifty years, their furniture in twenty. A mathematical model may last long enough to solve a particular problem, which may be as long as it takes to read a newspaper, but newspaper and model will be forgotten together in the morning, and a research rocket—apex of our technological adventure—may be burned out and wrecked in a matter of minutes. (*DC*, 90)

Banham's model of obsolescence is the rocket that dissolves in flight, as it is for Neutra and Nelson. Like them, he asks, what is the appropriate expression for this new mode of constant change? Whatever that expression might be, it can have nothing to do with the golden ratio, divine proportion, pure form, color harmony, and classical precepts, all of which, in his view, constitute a deceptive and repressive inheritance of the rationalist tradition.

Banham describes the work of H. P. Berlage as providing the most "eloquent expression" of the rationalist school of thought. Math and proportion are for Berlage a "guard against mere passing fashions, a guarantee of permanent value."[6] Berlage quotes Thomas Sheraton at the start of his 1908 *Grundlagen*: "Time alters fashions[;] . . . that which is founded on . . . real science will remain unalterable" (*TD*, 142). Fashion, or impermanence, is pitted against science, or permanence. But, for Banham, even the worst-offending rationalist (like Berlage) speaks an element of truth. So even though Berlage adheres to traditional notions of geometrical perfection, he also seems to grasp the deeper truth of science, the kind of science that explains the success of fashion. Berlage describes the "physiological responses" to architectural "effects"; he sees that proportions are the "cause of the effect [Greek temples] produce even on uneducated minds" (*TD*, 142). As Banham tells it, Berlage instinctively recognizes the biological appeal of fashion, a biological reality he attempts to suppress with his rationalism. Banham's point is that there is a missed opportunity at the heart of the rationalist tradition; there is a real science, one based in pure biological response, simmering beneath traditional scientific assumptions (*TD*, 142).

If truth seeps out along the margins of Berlage's text, then there is another history, a maverick history of modernism, that directly states it. Banham famously ends his *Theory and Design in the First Machine Age* (1960) with an excerpt from Fuller's "flat rebuttal" of the Bauhaus and the International Style, drawn from an unpublished 1955 letter to John McHale. Fuller's letter is a clear inspiration for Banham's argument as a whole. Modern architects are "superficially" wedded to the machine, fitting architecture out with "formalized novelties" instead of relying on traditional "brick assemblage" (*TD*, 326). Modern architects, Fuller continues, have "only looked at problems of modifications of the surface of end-products," end products that are "sub-functions of a technically obsolete world" (*TD*, 326). Machine "garmentation" over a Beaux-Arts body.

Banham, following Fuller, sees the Bauhaus as failing to perform in the ways that its machined surfaces and its public rhetoric about technology proclaim. The Bauhaus commitment to the machine is only skin deep, a machine aesthetic papered over rationalist reality. Banham wants to hold the first machine-age architects to account, to take their machine-age rhetoric—epitomized in the 1923 Bauhaus slogan "Art and Technology: A New Unity"—far more seriously than they took it themselves. That this amounts to a *purification of the aims of the Bauhaus* is made clear by Banham's identification of Fuller's goals with those of Moholy-Nagy at the conclusion of *Theory and Design* (*TD*, 311–19).[7]

Eames, Banham, Performance

Nothing could be more foreign to the Eameses' way of thinking than Banham's notion of the mathematical model as throwaway. Banham describes the current age as one where "a mathematical model is apt to be a mile of punched tape."[8] As disposable as a newspaper or a mechanical system, the mathematical model is exclusively construed as a matter of performance. Charles Eames, in a letter to Banham written in response to the 1960 symposium organized by Banham in the *Architectural Review*, rejects Banham's account of the relation between science and technology. Charles objects to the notion that "science was often equated with efficiency, and that meanings of technology and science were freely interchanged" (*EA*, 208), an idea he attributes to Banham on the basis of H. de C. Hastings's summary of Banham's approach: "Technological habits are scientific and architectural habits aesthetic, hence science and art are in for a tussle."[9] For Charles, this is to confuse the relation between science and world, to mistake technology for science (*EA*, 209).

Charles's challenge to Banham runs far deeper than has been assumed. Banham's approach is driven by his opposition to permanence, which he directly associates with laws, objectivity, and rationalist aesthetics. Banham, in Charles's view, misconstrues the nature of the problem. Charles consistently describes modernity as an era of increasingly "permanent values." And this permanency can be expressed in anything "other than a physical or monumental aspect."[10] Like the Eameses, Banham rejects the monumental, but for him what is crucial is *performance*. The Eameses, by contrast, refuse this impulse, seeking what Charles calls, in his letter to Banham, "NON-technical solutions" to architectural problems (*EA*, 208). The solution is not to implement ever greater efficiency but to discover a set of values immune to the demands for performance. (The Eameses thematize this point in their 1970 film *The Black Ships*, which depicts the Japanese painting grotesque pictures of Americans, the purpose being to underscore how "technology, to [the Japanese], wasn't the principal element in the civilization of a people.")[11] Charles seeks to distinguish between efficiency and architecture rather than between performance and art. Recall how the kite is a performance-driven machine, while a toy, by contrast, is useless. Everything Banham values falls into Charles's category of "kite problems." When Banham's colleague Cedric Price characterizes his own throwaway designs as "short-life toys," what he means is that they maximalize performance; he turns houses into kites.[12]

Desiring Machines

For Banham, Los Angeles is a symbol of triumphant functionality, one that gloriously eschews every academic standard. In "A Throw-Away Aesthetic," Banham lingers on the words of Jean Gregoire, the engineer responsible for front-wheel drive, who speaks of beauty as "the best use of materials according to the current state of technique" (*DC*, 91). Gregoire, Banham notes, favors American cars over Le Corbusier's beloved Bugatti, because their engines are "surrounded . . . by forests of wire and bits and pieces, and designed without a thought for line." Comparing a Bugatti engine and a 1955 Buick V-8 (Figure C.3), Banham observes how the Bugatti conceals its functions under "Platonic ideals of circle and square," while the Buick "flaunts as many accessories as possible . . . with a wild rhetoric of power" (*DC*, 91). Glitter, bulk, three-dimensionality, and a "deliberate exposure of technical means" are Banham's aesthetic and ethical coordinates, which yield the terms that for him define the "popular arts": concealing versus exposure, obscuring versus flaunting.

Articles of popular culture are "not to be treasured, but to be thrown away." Unlike the Bugatti, the dead Buick does not go on making "forlorn claims to be a perennial monument of abstract art" (*DC*, 92). The popular arts bury their dead. Designed for "transitory beauty according to an expendable aesthetic," they serve their purpose and are tossed out.[13] Banham finds support for his antimonumental and throwaway aesthetic in the writings of Italian futurist Sant'Elia. Sant'Elia is the subject of several early articles by Banham, including an extended essay in the *Architectural Review* in 1955. "We no longer believe in the monumental," Sant'Elia writes in his manifesto, and what takes its place is "lightness, transience and practicality" (*DC*, 24). Sant'Elia rejects the "pre-established laws" of architecture, observing that there are "no stock answers, plastic or linear" (*TD*, 135). The alternative to rule-based design, Sant'Elia insists, is a "Futurist architecture" defined by "expendability and transience. Our houses will last less time than we do and every generation will have to make its own." Sant'Elia calls for the "constant renovation of the architectonic environment," a demand Banham

FIGURE C.3. Above: Jean Bugatti, Bugatti Royale Type 41, circa 1931. Below: Buick Century de Luxe Riviera Sedan, 1956. From Reyner Banham, "A Throw-Away Aesthetic," *Industrial Design*, March 1960.

sees as precluding "processes with definite terminations such as a process of perfection must be" (*TD*, 327).

On these terms, even Schindler's work exemplifies an improbable futurism. In Banham's 1979 lecture "Schindler's Architecture—Thick and Thin," his most extensive engagement with the architect, he describes Schindler as the first "honest" modern architect in his acceptance of the demands of stud-and-stucco construction. Rather than "disguising . . . the actual nature of what the building is made of," as classical European modern architecture does, Schindler comes "to terms with building in wood framing." What this means in practice is that Schindler's works in the period between 1928 and 1940 consist of one solid plastic mass divided into a series interconnected volumetric spaces, composed of "volume over volume, volume upon volume, volume against volume." Moreover, the volumes Schindler creates are often dissociated from use, like pure sculpture; they are nonhabitable spaces, what Banham calls "hollow things with air inside." European modernists, by contrast—his prime example is the Rietveld Schröder House of 1924—in their bad-faith commitment to "putting the structure on view" by extensive use of the "thinnest possible membranes" around habitable volumes, deceive the inhabitants of what is often traditional wood construction. It would be wrong to think that Banham, in his defense of wood construction, is abandoning or even revising his futurist demands. By the later 1970s, he affirms wood against the deceptive manipulation of steel and glass, because stud-and-stucco construction is (counterintuitively) composed "mostly of air," as though traditional means of construction, if used the right way to create "hollow things with air inside," exemplify Fuller's ideal of ephemeralization. Far from dismissing the "classical modern European ideal" of structural expressionism, what is at stake for Banham is simply the *truth* of structural expression.[14] Then again, this is not structural expressionism, but more like structural literalism.

Banham's aim is not exactly to analyze the mistakes and subterfuges of modernist machine ideology but rather to purify modernism, to strip machine works of their rationalist ornament and give full expression to technological determinism. This is the moral of *The Architecture of the Well-Tempered Environment* (1969).[15] At the conclusion to the chapter titled "Towards Full Control," Banham describes a wall of air conditioners on an anonymous modern building.[16] What is special about the façade, as Banham sees it, is how the random array of "environmental improvements [by] the householder" comes into "direct conflict with the visual intentions of the architect."[17] The conflict is between the "idealized Machine Aesthetic" of the building façade and the actual machine aesthetic of consumer environmental controls. Architectural intentionality is replaced by individuated agents—what Fuller calls "critical consumers"—who, by acting on their pure desires (assumed to never rise to the level of intent), arrive at a better

FIGURE C.4. I. M. Pei Associates, Kips Bay Apartments, southern façade (New York), 1961. Reyner Banham, *The Architecture of the Well-Tempered Environment* (Chicago: University of Chicago Press).

outcome than any architect might achieve.[18] Outstripping any intended image of the machine is the desire-driven reality (Figure C.4).

The "ethical" "essence" of Brutalism, Alison and Peter Smithson write (at this point they were working closely with Banham), lies in its "attempt to be objective about 'reality,'" its attempt to "face up" to the "urges" of contemporary "mass-production society."[19] A new form of building will emerge that will be determined not just in its parts but in its overall structure by "the whim of the individual occupant, or consumer" (*DC*, 87). Building will be restricted to supplying "a neutral technological frame," "a support of structure and services within which people could express themselves freely" (*DC*, 18). Freedom of expression—that is, the expression of one's biological needs and wants—is basic to Banham's approach at large. The neutral support structure is anathema to architects, because "architects are . . . committed to . . . [a] hieratic culture in which command comes from the few experts at the top and not from the mass of consumers at the bottom" (*DC*, 87). For architects, the "urges" of consumers constitute "an alien culture" (*DC*, 87). They have so far refused to accept that "ultimate command [is] in the hands" of consumers or their delegates in advertising, but now it is time to "ride with the real culture . . . as it exists now" (*DC*, 88). It is in the desire-driven array of air conditioners and not any architecturally intended machine image that one finds the "outward form of the kit environmentally needed to make the high-life of supermarket-America possible."[20] The supermarket is—as he puts it in *Los Angeles*—where those enjoying "the great bourgeois vision of the good life in a tamed countryside" go to shop (*LA*, 238).

Banham's Neoliberalism

Banham described himself as a "Tory Socialist," a position Nigel Whiteley contends is "fully in keeping with the Labour Party's" contemporary "rhetoric about modernization," although hardly in sync with its economic policies.[21] Banham's approach to class is entirely a matter of "class culture," or class*ism,* as he explains in his most explicitly political essay, "The Atavism of the Short-Distance Mini-cyclist" of 1964 (*DC*, 86). To be working-class, for Banham, is about one's likes and dislikes. For Banham, the question of why the working class cannot "be allowed to enjoy Pop culture" is a pressing political concern. He describes a Cold War vision of "divided loyalties," not between labor and capital, but between popular and high culture. For Banham it crucially matters that the working class be able to freely enjoy pop culture, while it does not matter at all whether there remains a working class (he wants to preserve it as a "culture"). Banham puts into the mouth of his friend John McHale what is undoubtedly his own sentiment: "If we go on voting Labour like this we shall destroy our own livelihood" (*DC*, 85). The goal is to preserve working-class culture by holding on to one's money.

Like at the Bauhaus, Banham inherits a vision of class as a cultural phenomenon. His concern is with how working-class *tastes* are being manipulated by the middle class, with how the "rise of the working classes to political power has rested upon someone equipping them with the right kind of responses to social and political situations, manipulative responses" (*DC*, 86). That "someone" is the establishment, largely universities, including university architects; they are the ones who encourage the working class to assume a "traditional . . . middle-class response" toward government (*DC*, 86). Whiteley makes the (mistaken) point perfectly: because the establishment is "controlling the identity" of the working class, it is "in danger of becoming 'culturalized' into middle-class modes of operating."[22] On this account, the working class is uniquely pliable (to the will of the establishment) and uniquely individualist in its free responsiveness to popular culture. Class is an identity formation, a view that surely has political consequences in that it turns political demands into cultural ones and economic positions into conflicting patterns of taste. Banham is not just in step with the growing neoliberal consensus on the centrality of identities and the subordination of class conflict, he is one of its primary designers.

As Banham sees it, the Old World politics of left versus right is over. "Pop is now so basic to the way, and the world we live in," Banham writes in 1964, "that to be with it . . . does not commit anyone to Left or Right, or to protest or acceptance of the society we live in" (*DC*, 89). Rather than protesting or accepting society, Banham's idea is to dispose of it and its permanent mode of expression in cities. In his view, what is imperative is to do away with the "experts"—artistic, educational, political—and let the pure play of "urges" steer the ship to a world where "people could [for the first time] express themselves freely" (*DC*, 87).

Collapsing form and most everything else into function, Banham seeks to replace the architect with the industrial designer. He asks the designer and the critic to assume new roles in the culture; their task is to understand "what will sell" (*DC*, 93). Taking command of "market statistics," they should seek to "predict, introduce an element of control that feeds back information into industry." Staying close to the "dynamics of mass-communication," through surveys, interviews, and empirical studies, the critic would then "sell the public to the manufacturer" (*DC*, 93). Banham sees the critic's task as projecting "the future dreams and desires of people as one who speaks from within their ranks" (*DC*, 93). If the academic distorts the nature of working-class culture, the critic and advertiser apparently have a magic formula that gives them deep insight into working-class needs. Like the earlier advocates of human sculpting, Banham sees the masses as carrying the weight of history, a revolutionary impulse awaiting its release through purified consumption. And as in the earlier utopias, the future is not a product of anyone's intentions but the continuous registration of desires working at the level of biology.

The Lore of the Operation: Eames contra Banham

Banham's fascination with Los Angeles was also a fascination with the Eameses (or rather, with Charles alone). According to Banham, no one "has made so great an impact on the world, both by its products and his personality, as Charles Eames" (*DC*, 103). Banham attended Eames's April 1959 lecture at the Royal Institute of British Architects (RIBA) and quoted it at length in his ambitious and sprawling "Stocktaking" in the February 1960 issue of the *Architectural Review*. Divided into two sections, one that tackles tradition and another that takes on technology, the article reviews the fundamental trends in modern architecture around 1960. At the center of Banham's discussion is the phrase "the lore of the operation," drawn from Charles's lecture, which Banham quotes no fewer than twenty-seven times. As Banham sees it, the lore of the operation is the seemingly infinite capacity for the architectural establishment to direct every technological innovation to reactionary ends. The establishment looks backward, drawing up rules accumulated through past experiences at the expense of staying alert to the novelties of the current situation.

And yet in Charles's view the lore of the operation is central to his whole approach. In his April 1963 talk "Design: Its Freedoms and Its Restraints," Charles elaborates on his response to Banham's 1960 symposium, speaking of the necessity to adhere to operational lore in situations where choices seemed unlimited: "Without the restraining effects of a common cultural tradition, or limitations that come with isolation, or social responsibilities of long standing, or a lore of materials and their appropriate use," the community stands in a desperate situation of choice without guidance (*EA*, 245). Charles describes a "very special example" of an architectural "mess": Los Angeles (*EA*, 245).

> The aesthetic nightmare that is Los Angeles has not happened because Los Angelenos are a less sensitive group than any other in the world. This would happen in the hands of any group freed from the restraints of tradition, and with no new restraints to take their place. (*EA*, 246)

Charles speaks of the "tradition, or lore of an art," as an essential tool for the "artisan [to] bridge those gaps where he lacks sufficient current information upon which to base a decision" (*EA*, 246). Banham's admiration for Los Angeles, by contrast, is predicated on the city's capacity to thrive by *ignoring* the lore of operation. Bypassing tradition entirely, Los Angeles is a model of unrestrained functionality.

Banham considers two phases of operational lore, the classical tradition and what he calls historicist defeatism, associated with the new empiricism and neoliberty. Banham finds little worth salvaging in either the classical or historicist strains of the modern movement. "The most apparently liberated spirits of our time," even though they give the appearance of a radical rejection of academicism, they "will not, in the last resort, renounce the lore of the operation" (*DC*, 51). Once again, surface manifestations of modernity conceal backwardness, a fixation on traditional rules of design.

Banham finds buried within the historicist turn a redeeming moment, as he does in Berlage's work, namely, the "rediscovery of science as a dynamic force, rather than the humble servant of architecture" (*DC*, 51). But even this discovery is lost as soon as it is found. Banham ends the section on tradition with a long quote from Eames's RIBA lecture, which he describes as "a plea for the acceptance of scientific attitudes of mind," by which he means *technology*. Banham does recognize that Charles is, as it were, transfixed by the Medusan gaze of operational lore. Tragically, in Banham's view, Charles is unable to grasp the significance of his own vision. According to Banham, Charles rightly understands that the "real planning, the real architecture, the building of the future" is going to happen with scientific tools, but he stumbles into the tradition trap when he suggests that the future falls "under the head of that great name, architecture, which embraces it" (*DC*, 51). For Banham, this is a major failure of nerve. Architecture is where every great innovation goes to die.

It is with technology that Banham holds out hope that the underlying impulse of Charles's critique of operational lore might be fulfilled. Even if the "operational lore of our whole culture renders domestic architecture practically proof against scientific attitudes," Banham still believes pure science will prevail (*DC*, 54–55). Science and

FIGURE C.5. Peter and Alison Smithson, House of the Future, sitting room, Daily Mail Ideal Home Exhibition, Olympia, London, 1956. John McCann / RIBA Collections.

technology, Banham believes, demonstrate that architecture does "not necessarily imply the erection of buildings" (*DC*, 51).[23] As in "A Throw-Away Aesthetic," Banham takes the automobile as the "standard of comparison for the activities of the architectural profession" (*DC*, 52). He singles out for praise Alison and Peter Smithson's House of the Future of 1956 (Figure C.5), asserting that the Smithsons are alone in seeing that "mass-produced houses would need as high a rate of obsolescence as any other class of mass-produced goods" (*DC*, 53). Banham nonetheless concludes his 1960 survey on a glum note. With every technological advance, the "operational lore of the architectural profession has assimilated prefabrication as a technique," using it to produce small repetitive units and leaving larger structures in the "hands of architects" (*DC*, 54).

"Biological Fundamentals": The Bauhaus Purified

Banham holds out hope for scientific investigation, because among scientists it is at least possible that the conservative "mental disposition" that distorts reality, squeezing it into a narrow channel of preestablished academic forms, can be broken down by objective data. Banham turns for support to the Nuffield Trust, a charitable organization founded in 1939 to coordinate treatment at hospitals operating outside London.

For Banham, the "solid, plodding work" of scientists at the Nuffield Trust that yields the "physiological effects of daylight and color" establishes a firm ground on which to build *un autre* aesthetic. Banham cites the work of his colleague at the trust, Richard Llewelyn-Davies, who had "opened the way to the analysis of supposedly 'soft' social and psychological facts." He quotes Llewelyn-Davies to this effect: "Psychological matters can be assigned numerical values—and statistical techniques make it increasingly feasible to quantify them—they become susceptible to mathematical manipulation. . . . An increasing proportion of the most jealously guarded 'professional secrets' of architecture are already quantifiable."[24] As I have been arguing, to construe "psychological matters" as being "susceptible to mathematical manipulation" reiterates the persistent fantasy of architectural control—affective formalism—that gripped artists and architects from Endell and Taut through Neutra and beyond.

In the 1960 symposium J. M. Richards notes that "as science learns more about human physiological and psychological responses more of the factors that have hitherto been classed as outside science can be regarded as scientific" (Banham declares himself "at one with Richards in this matter").[25] Nothing could be closer, in other words, to the demands of the Bauhaus, and to Neutra, than Banham's insistence that if "a *fully* scientific aesthetic is impossible now . . . it is a thousand-percent more possible than it was thirty years ago."[26] Banham's words mirror those of Kandinsky circa 1920:

> By a scientific aesthetic, I meant one that uses, as the basis and guide to design, observations (made according to the normal laws of scientific evidence) of the actual effect of certain colors, forms, symbols, spaces, lighting levels, acoustic qualities, textures, perspective effects (in isolation or in total "gestalts") on human viewers. . . .
> I maintain that armed with enough information of this kind it should be possible for whoever is responsible for the visual side of a building to produce, say, a church that is more likely to produce a sense of spiritual elation than physical depression.[27]

It is hard to find fault, or comfort, in Banham's suggestion that one can create spaces that have spiritual rather than depressive effects. Does one need science to prove that? Banham's wording is evasive. He writes that this "knowledge" is "manifestly not shared by some church designers at work at present." Does this mean there are designers who do not apply science when they build their churches and are therefore guilty of producing depressing churches?

Although one might get the impression that the aim here is to share some low-grade research with a few lagging designers to prevent any church from projecting a gloomy mood, in fact, Banham wants nothing less than the "fully" scientific aesthetic, that is, a technologically driven form of production that will generate verifiable results through knowledge of the way "colors, forms, symbols, spaces, lighting levels, acoustic qualities, textures, perspective" create sensory experiences. The goal is to seek the "actual effect" of form rather than the effects one might intend, and which might fail to come off or fail to be understood. Banham's vast polemic is not in any way directed *against* the Bauhaus but instead represents an effort to purify its claims by removing any trace of a rationalist-aesthetic packaging. By purging modern architecture of its geometrical bias—the empty abstractions of "operational lore," what Erwin Panofsky calls "fake efficiency"—Banham hopes to reestablish the aims of the Bauhaus and start over with Moholy-Nagy's "biological ABCs."[28]

In the closing pages of *Theory and Design in the First Machine Age,* Banham turns to Moholy-Nagy for a way out of the academic Bauhaus and into a truly scientific variant. Moholy-Nagy "transcends all his predecessors" by virtue of two qualities. First is his "phenomenal command of the non-artistic visual experiences of his time"—as if he were the original pop artist, he is the first to fully grasp the "visual richness of a magazine-culture" (*TD,* 315). Second, and more fundamental, is his replacement of vague *Einfühlung* aesthetics with an understanding of "space as something affecting the sense organs of men by direct physical *Erlebnis*" (*TD,* 318). Banham identifies himself with Moholy-Nagy's vision of "the Biological taken as the guide in everything." This is the concealed truth of the machine aesthetic. Quoting Moholy-Nagy, Banham affirms his mission to "reconquest . . . biological fundamentals" (*TD,* 319).

Biology as Tabula Rasa

Banham's biological reductivism takes a stark turn toward the end of his career, directly intersecting with his libertarian politics. In the closing pages of his last book, *Scenes in America Deserta* of 1982, in a chapter titled "The Eye of the Beholder," Banham reviews the culturalist or normative position that "our responses" to natural beauty "are learned responses, instilled in us by prior experience of man-made images of 'nature' acclaimed as beautiful or artistic, be they great paintings, picture postcards, landscape gardens, or even some classes of maps," and gently satirizes those who believe that "nothing comes between the understandings of those who are pure of heart and the works of the Almighty—or Nature."[29] And yet Banham comes around to exactly this position when he substitutes the seemingly objective eye for the romantic heart. The "rewards of the desert," he contends, are "in the eye of the beholder." And he means it literally. They are "patterns on the rods and cones of the retinas of the eyes that deliver messages to the visual cortex of the brain," that "signal something I had not deemed possible in myself—a pure aesthetic response" (*AD,* 221). But not only had Banham thought pure response possible; he had been arguing for it since the beginning. Bauhaus and Brutalist, the raw desert landscape registers a pure sensation of the tabula rasa.

FIGURE C.6. *This Is Tomorrow* exhibition, Whitechapel Gallery, London, August 1956.

For Banham, then, the New Brutalists are an expression of the Bauhaus purified. Reviewing the 1956 London exhibition *This Is Tomorrow* in the *Architectural Review,* he singles out the work of Group 2 (John Voelcker, Richard Hamilton, and John McHale), whose spaces submerged viewers with jukebox music overlaid with prerecorded sounds of earlier visitors to the exhibition. As in the Georgia Experiment, the show included an olfactory dimension, with perfumes released when spectators activated triggers in the floor (Figure C.6). Banham praises the multisensory effects unleashed by Group 2, commending the designers' use of "optical illusions, scale reversions, oblique structures and fragmented images to disrupt stock responses, and put the viewer back on a tabula rasa of individual responsibility for his own atomized sensory awareness of images of only local and contemporary significance."[30] These artists and architects appealed to the viewers' raw physiology, because it is there on the tabula rasa of sensory awareness that one is able, in Banham's view, to resist rationalist habits of mind. Refusing to rely on "abstract concepts," the New Brutalists generated forms that "resist[ed] classification by the geometrical disciplines" (which the work of Nigel Henderson, Eduardo Paolozzi, and the Smithsons for *This Is Tomorrow* did not). Ultimately, Banham thinks it is possible to do away with artists entirely and have a direct sensory engagement with one's surroundings.

Banham concludes his stocktaking of technology by indulging in a utopian fantasy. It seems possible that at "any unpredictable moment the unorganized hordes of uncoordinated [scientific] specialists could flood over into the architects' preserves and, ignorant of the lore of the operation, create an Other Architecture by chance, as it were, out of apparent intelligence and the task of creating fit environments for human activities" (*DC*, 55). This recalls his ode to the air conditioner in *The Well-Tempered Environment*: the instinctive drives of the tenants, who resemble scientists working toward results in their labs free of all aesthetic impulse, and who, sheerly by desiring to cool their bodies, give rise to a new, purified order. In a sense, of course, this is anything but chance; it is more like a putatively pure biological order given free expression (or an order generated by commodity fetishism). Against any intended order—which is incurably distorted by establishment formulas—biological expressionism is immune to criticism, or evaluation, because it is "true."

Banham stresses the seemingly impossible odds that the technological revolution faces. Operational lore can both withstand and assimilate every obstacle in its quest for total control over mental life. Only a brutal assault on the raw nerve endings— through pop stimuli or the starkness of the desert sand—can possibly break through the encrusted layers of a prehistoric mental fortress. Only when one is forced to deal with pure stimuli can one take "individual responsibility" for one's actions. Banham assures readers he is not taking responsibilities away from architects when he asks them to give up the role of "absolute master of the visual environment" and instead become the arranger of ready-made consumer goods, the "producer of the play, handling a mixed cast of metropolitan professionals and local talent" (*DC*, 100, 101). Indeed, it is only when they surrender this role as master that their "real responsibilities" are clarified. Architects' "responsibilities have increased" precisely in proportion to the extent to which they have become aware of "just how, and how strongly, some desirable and visually fascinating piece of equipment . . . focuses attention and thence organizes the visual and functional space around it" (*DC*, 100). Because gizmos express the purified desires of consumers, architects should simply create settings for gizmos, and the rest will take care of itself. This is precisely where science and advertising merge.

Banham sees the architect's responsibility as needing to learn, scientifically, how people desire. The designer's task is to exercise "choice and background control over the choice of others, to advise, suggest and demand on the basis of knowledge and understanding" (DC, 101). Banham imagines a continuous feedback loop connecting consumer, architect, and manufacturer that enables the creation of perfectly calibrated spaces where every unfulfilled desire is constantly fulfilled. If architects give up on the dream of controlling the total environment, they can nonetheless assert "full control" with a seemingly infinite series of touches and tweaks to the consumer setting.

"You've Got a Friend"

While it has not been discussed in the literature, Banham's market-driven aesthetic is equally a market-driven politics. In one of the more perverse but also most influential assessments of the Case Study House Program, Banham notes in his review of McCoy's *Modern California Houses: Case Study Houses, 1945–1962* that the success of the program is in part due to the fact that it "manipulat[es] the ordinary processes" through which "things [get] built in a free-for-all capitalistic housing market, rather than by a consortium or development group operating under conditions partly shielded from the marketplace" (EMR, 163). To be clear, Banham's aversion is to spaces shielded from the market—above all, unions—*not* the capitalist free-for-all. For Banham, the opposite of the free market is *planning*, which seems to indifferently signal totalitarianism and socialism to him. Opposing both these tendencies is libertarianism. Here is Banham in *Los Angeles*:

> Psychologically, the nub of the matter seems to be that planning, as the discipline
> is normally understood in academic and professional circles, is one of the those ad-
> mired facets of the established Liberal approach to urban problems that has never
> struck root in the libertarian, but illiberal, atmosphere of Los Angeles. (LA, 120)

Banham casually declares that "local libertarians" find "enclosed and planned communities" "unsympathetic" (LA, 124). It is easy to miss the sleight of hand in his identification of a planned community—an economic and social ideal—with enclosure—a moral and aesthetic quality. In any event, whatever aversion California libertarians may have had to "enclosed" communities in 1971—communities with private gates and security guards, for instance—by the end of the decade, alongside the passage of the ultraregressive Proposition 13 in 1978, they became standard.

What Banham thinks a consumer-driven utopia would look like emerges in his

FIGURE C.7. Still of "Brad" from *Reyner Banham Loves Los Angeles*, BBC, 1972.

interview with "Brad, the mobile musician," near the end of *Reyner Banham Loves Los Angeles* (Figure C.7). As Brad tells it, he spent three years "living in a house with a lot of people, it was a commune," but he found he "couldn't do" what he "wanted to do" at times, so he put his upright piano in his van, where he was able to play music and make noise "when he want[ed] to": "So," he says, it is even better than living in a "private apartment"; he has found a way to have "an extremely, extremely private life if I want it to be."[31] For Brad, the ultimate value is "when I want to"—a phrase he repeats no fewer than five times—and this value is, for the most obvious reasons, not compatible with the "commune." And for someone who cherishes privacy, "living alone and independently," so much that he sets up his home in a van, we might be struck by the irony of his singing "You've Got a Friend" as the song that best represents his new vision of freedom.[32] For the viewer, the choice is clear: the commune—socialist, communist, fascist, totalitarian, all the same—or libertarianism; that is, either forced collectivism or freedom.

What becomes of a world of "Brads"? In the concluding pages of *Scenes in America Deserta,* Banham describes the dire situation faced by the Bureau of Land Manage-

FIGURE C.8. Reyner Banham at Silurian Lake, south of Death Valley in San Bernardino County, California, 1981. Photograph: Tim Street-Porter. Courtesy of Tim Street-Porter.

ment in its stewardship of the "fragile ecology that is increasingly over-used" in the Mojave Desert. The BLM is charged with dealing with "innumerable interests, each of whom has one simple and modest claim on the Mojave: they want *all* of it" (*AD,* 196). Tim Street-Porter's well-known photograph of Banham bicycling across the dry bed of Silurian Lake in California's San Bernardino County exemplifies Banham's libertarian ideal of asocial and unobstructed freedom (Figure C.8). Although one might suspect that the response to this negotiation between competing and destructive demands is to reject some of them in the name of protecting the environment, according to Banham, the right response is "benign neglect"; the problem should be "left to solve itself" (*AD,* 196, 197).

The problem is to think there *is* a problem. Not only do free markets take care of themselves, but they apparently take care of the environment as well. Indeed, the "most notoriously endangered" animals, Banham notes (without any evidence), are those "under the direct protection of the National Park Service." The tragedy of the situation is that no one—Banham first among them—"actually wants to see the desert regulated in any way whatsoever" (*AD*, 198). Banham laments a Mojave "under [the] control" of the Park Service (yet another cog in the establishment) and worries that it might become "well-managed" like Death Valley, with its terrifying landscape of "leaflets and maps, prepared parking lots and blacktopped visitor trails and, worst of all, sign-posted scenic overlooks" (*AD*, 199). Apparently, the battle against the signposted views is an imperative. The leaflets represent the slippery slope to statist control: it is "the first step on the road to perdition that is crucial," Banham warns. It is in the desert "where one is free to go where one will, and do what one will, and take the responsibility for the consequences" (*AD*, 198). Responsibility, in other words, is up to the individual and is possible only outside the state. Responsibility flourishes in the free market, outside the constraints of government. Banham may lament the private roads guarding the entrances to Rolling Hills in Palos Verdes (those "planned and enclosed" enclaves), but he unabashedly affirms private spaces: unplanned and free for the winners in the market.

As for Charles Eames, who "taught the whole world a way of seeing," Banham describes him as a variant on "Brad, the mobile musician." Eames is the "grass-roots" American, an instance of the "Mr. Fixit of the nitty-gritty," of the "tradition of the Americans who 'got learned mechanicking down on the farm.'"[33] Eames is a "down-home, do-it-yourself" kind of tinkerer with a "hot-rodder attitude to the elements of building." To say that the Eameses were averse to this kind of kitsch would be an understatement.

Banham might not have been aware that in the 1970s Charles quoted T. W. Adorno's withering critique of the intellectual celebration of common folk in a section titled "They, the People" in his *Minima Moralia,* a book written in Los Angeles in the 1940s (*EA*, 349). The "moment the simple folk are forced to brawl among themselves for their portion of the social product, their envy and spite surpass anything seen among *literati,*" Adorno observes. Countering the kind of grass-roots libertarianism championed by Banham, Adorno argues that the "glorification of the splendid underdogs" is merely a cover for a "glorification of the splendid system that makes them so."[34] For the scholar or artist filled with "guilt-feelings" for being "exempt from physical work," the temptation is to turn those feelings into an "excuse for the 'idiocy of rural life.'" While Charles makes no claims about his commitment to Adorno's sociology, he shares Adorno's hostility to the intellectual fantasy of the architect as "mechanicking . . . down on the farm."

Los Angeles or Mars

No one, in Banham's view, can resist the lure of Los Angeles. Los Angeles makes bitter moralistic midwesterners over into freedom-loving libertarians. Insofar as his book *Los Angeles* bears a thesis, it is about conversion. The "Southern Californians came, predominantly, overland to Los Angeles, slowly traversing the whole North American land-mass and its evolving history" (*LA*, 7).

> They brought with them—and still bring—the prejudices, motivations, and ambitions of the central heartland of the USA. The first major wave of immigration came from Kansas City on excursion tickets after 1885; later they came in second-hand cars out of the dustbowl. . . . In one unnervingly true sense, Los Angeles is the Middle West raised to flash-point, the authoritarian dogmas of the Bible Belt and the perennial revolt against them colliding at critical mass under the palm trees. (*LA*, 7)

Los Angeles is able to overcome the "monolithic Protestant moral tyranny" that defines its midwestern immigrants because those immigrants undergo a conversion. The "Mid-western agrarian culture underwent a profound transformation as it hit the coast, a sun-change that pervades moral postures, political attitudes, ethnic groupings, and individual psychologies" (*LA*, 7). Here and in his conclusion, Banham quotes the work of his friend Ray Bradbury, the popular sci-fi author, whose 1950 collection *The Martian Chronicles* exemplifies the conversion process of the midwesterner (earthling) into a Californian (alien). Like Banham, McCoy writes of "settlers from the East [who] had brought with them the ideal of what a house should be. Wood. It was like the story of Ray Bradbury's about a woman on Mars sending back to earth for her rocking chair" (*EMR*, 207).

According to Banham, Bradbury's "most fundamental" Martian story is "Dark They Were, and Golden-Eyed." As Banham tells it, "The earth-family are subtly transformed, even against their wills, into tall, bronzed, gold-eyed Martians who abandon their neat Terran cities and the earthly cares and duty they symbolize, and run free in the mountains" (*LA*, 8). It is worth pausing to consider Bradbury's tale, as it bears closely on the larger vision of human sculpting. What is most striking is that Banham sees no conflict between Bradbury's environmental conversion narratives and what he takes to be one of the general lessons of Los Angeles. What Los Angeles "emphatically suggests" is that "there is no simple correlation between urban form and social form." Citing Scott's *The Architecture of Humanism*, Banham refers to the "mechanical fallacy," the mistake of thinking "there is a necessary causal connection between built form and human life." What Banham objects to, however, is not this kind of causal connection but rather only the simplicity of it, which is why he can say in the same breath that there are a range of "possible cities" that give expression to "possible forms" of society (*LA*, 219). To each city, with its particular shade of biodiversity, comes a different form. What Banham is interested in is the expression of *possibilities,* free of inherited forms, not the critique of the (specious) connection between form and life.

Indeed, in Bradbury's Mars fantasies the environment *literally* molds and shapes human life in its image. "Dark They Were, and Golden-Eyed" was first published in Bradbury's *Thrilling Wonder Stories* in 1949 (under the title "The Naming of Names") and later reprinted in *A Medicine for Melancholy* (1959) and again in *S Is for Space* (1966). Here is the crucial passage:

> The children ran out in time to see their father hurrying about the garden, pulling up radishes, onions, and carrots from their beds.
>
> "Cora, come look!"
>
> They handled the onions, the radishes, the carrots among them.
>
> "Do they look like carrots?"
>
> "Yes . . . no." She hesitated. "I don't know."
>
> "They're changed."
>
> "Perhaps."
>
> "You know they have! Onions but not onions, carrots but not carrots. Taste: the same but different. Smell: not like it used to be." He felt his heart pounding, and he was afraid. He dug his fingers into the earth. "Cora, what's happening? What is it? We've got to get away from this." He ran across the garden. Each tree felt his touch. "The roses. The roses. They're turning green!"[35]

The architecture itself changes under pressure from the environment.

> He looked with dismay at their house. "Even the house. The wind's done something to it. The air's burned it. The fog at night. The boards, all warped out of shape. It's not an Earthman's house any more." . . .
>
> . . . In the Earthmen's settlement, the Bittering house shook with a feeling of change.
>
> Lying abed, Mr. Bittering felt his bones shifted, shaped, melted like gold. His wife, lying beside him, was dark from many sunny afternoons. Dark she was, and golden, burnt almost black by the sun, sleeping, and the children metallic in their beds, and the wind roaring forlorn and changing through the old peach trees, violet grass, shaking out green rose petals.[36]

For a while Mr. Bittering (really?) refuses to eat the food grown on the new planet and eats only what they kept from the earth "in the deep-freeze." Finally, he relents, with inevitable results.

> He took a sandwich, opened it, looked at it, and began to nibble at it.
>
> "And take the rest of the day off," she said. "It's hot. The children want to swim in the canals and hike. Please come along."

"I can't waste time. This is a crisis!"

"Just for an hour," she urged. "A swim'll do you good."

He rose, sweating. "All right, all right. Leave me alone. I'll come."

"Good for you, Harry." . . .

They leaped into the canal water, and he let himself sink down and down to the bottom like a golden statue and lie there in green silence. All was water, quiet and deep, all was peace. He felt the steady, slow current drift him easily.

If I lie here long enough, he thought, the water will work and eat away my flesh until the bones show like coral. Just my skeleton left. And then the water can build on that skeleton—green things, deep-water things, red things, yellow things. Change. Change. Slow, deep, silent change. And isn't that what it is up there![37]

Harry (no longer Bittering) is baptized by the waters. He is transformed in the Martian canals, undergoing a sea change, or, as Banham has it, a sun change. Harry emerges from the water transformed into a mellow Martian. And when the earthlings (the establishment) return to Mars at the end of the story to "save" the humans stranded there, they cannot find any, only pacified Martians who pity the poor earthlings, who are really the stranded ones but don't know it.

If "Dark They Were, and Golden-Eyed" is the "most fundamental" of Bradbury's Martian stories, then "Ylla" is the "distillation of the essential dream" of Los Angeles (*LA*, 222). If you seek a "prototype of the crystal house of Ylla," Banham writes, "look among the Case Study houses or in the domestic work done by Neutra in the fifties." Banham is referring to the house on Mars/California made of "crystal pillars" by the "edge of an empty sea." The house, like a machine, is where Mrs. K plucks "golden fruits that grew from the crystal walls"; it is a house she cleans "with handfuls of magnetic dust which, taking all dirt with it, blew away on the hot wind."[38] Banham slides between Bradbury's conversion stories and David Hockney's archetypal image of Los Angeles, *A Bigger Splash* of 1967 (*LA*, 221) (Figure C.9). Situated in the text of *Los Angeles* alongside Banham's discussion of Bradbury's stories, Hockney's painting stands as a work of conversion, of the sea and sun change wrought by Los Angeles on its immigrants. The earthling is about to dive into the waters and emerge the liberated Martian. Baptized in the waters of the modern house, one can shed one's earthly ways and become a free consumer of the "good life in a tamed countryside" (*LA*, 220).

Banham/Bradbury's Los Angeles has little in common with the one described by the Eameses. Charles, of course, "came overland" from St. Louis, Missouri, and Ray from Sacramento (both by way of Cranbrook), and no doubt they brought their "prejudices, motivations, and ambitions" along with them. But their motivations did not undergo "a profound transformation" after they hit the coast; instead the "chaos" of Los

FIGURE C.9. David Hockney, *A Bigger Splash*, 1967. Acrylic on canvas, 242.6 × 243.8 cm. Tate Gallery/ London/Great Britain. Copyright David Hockney, Collection Tate. Copyright Tate, London / Art Resource, New York.

Angeles sharpened their already existing moral vision. As the Eameses describe it, they needed the contrast, the "restraint," to clarify their views. No doubt Banham is onto something when he contrasts his vision of Los Angeles with the "general body of official Western culture at the moment, increasingly given over to facile, evasive and self-regarding pessimism" (*LA,* 224). And yet the counter to this self-satisfied pessimism—architect as bioengineer—is equally useless.[39] Charles laments the "horrible freedom" epitomized for him by Los Angeles. To a London audience in 1965, Charles insists that we have "never been up against the problem of making a free choice . . . and we are just plain not prepared to make them" (*EA*, 254). It is the quality of false freedom the Eameses loathe most about Los Angeles; they call it the "you name it—and you can have it" city (*EA*, 246).

By the end of the 1960s the Great Compression was ending, and by the 1970s the Eameses (along with other cultural critics) were stuck in the 1950s critique of the affluent society. To continue to see the problem as a matter of consumption, spectacle, and hierarchy, of how people see and treat one another, rather than how they exploit one another—that is, class society—is to obscure and provide ideological support for prevailing conditions. The affluent society is over, and rank inequality has replaced it, a pattern that has consistently intensified since the late 1960s. And if the Eameses were there to lament the new reality (under outdated terms), Banham was there to celebrate a newly liberated capitalism and to celebrate Los Angeles as its uncontested capital. Banham did not need to look far for a framework for the new reality; it was provided for him by Scheerbart, the Bauhaus, Neutra, and Fuller, all of whom insisted that economic equality had no relation to freedom. And while the path that led from Schindler through the Eameses did not have much to say about capitalism, their shared vision of impermanence and autonomy—of a perfect identification of production and consumption—was also a political vision. Seeing a problem through to the end, imagining the full consequences of an action, models a mode of action that would eliminate the possibility of surplus. This is also a fictional architecture for a fictional place, but it is nevertheless a counter to the fantasy space of a very real neoliberalism, where pure performance means all against all.

Acknowledgments

Looking back, I recall four moments that shaped my sense of modern architecture in California. The first was a graduate seminar taught by David Van Zanten on Frank Lloyd Wright at Northwestern University in 1997. Van Zanten organized two memorable field trips: one to Racine, Wisconsin, site of the S. C. Johnson Administration Building and the equally striking Herbert F. Johnson or Wingspread House of 1938–39; the other to Crow Island School in Winnetka, Illinois. Crow Island School was designed in 1940 by Perkins, Wheeler & Will in collaboration with Eero Saarinen. We collectively turned over child-scaled furniture at the school and noted the names of the designers, Saarinen and Charles Eames.

Second was the fact that I grew up in Los Angeles and began to see it differently when I returned to it after studying Wright. (By complete coincidence, for two stretches of time I lived very close to Schindler's Lovell Beach House and Neutra's Lovell House.) Like others before me, I found Gebhard and Winter's *Architecture in Los Angeles: A Compleat Guide* indispensable, as were Reyner Banham's *Los Angeles: The Architecture of Four Ecologies* and Mike Davis's *City of Quartz*. I attempted to photograph everything modern still standing (or so I thought). I remain grateful to all the many owners who opened their houses to me twenty-five years ago. Over the years I have been welcomed into many homes; I am immensely grateful for the warm welcomes I have received, including invaluable personal narratives.

Third was the fact that my family on my mother's side came to Los Angeles in 1941, Jewish Viennese exiles who managed to create an artistic world alongside so many other immigrants in postwar Los Angeles. It wasn't as if my grandparents knew Schindler and Neutra—they were immersed in a musical scene—but they left me with a strong taste for Viennese cultural traditions that lent itself to my later involvement with the European exile community.

Fourth, in 2007, I read Neutra's magnum opus *Survival through Design*. Here was a highly ambitious vision of design that brought together science, aesthetics, sociology, anthropology, history, philosophy, and psychoanalysis, and seemed to sum up a whole body of thought. For Neutra there was significance behind every feature, down to the smallest details, of the shaped environment. What struck me about Neutra was the sheer determination of his logic and how this contrasted with Schindler's half-pragmatic, half-spiritual approach.

Neutra's extremism was also a normative one for twentieth-century architecture, the clearest exemplification of a mode of thinking that comes down through Jugendstil, the expressionists, and the Bauhaus. But Neutra's was far from the only approach. Schindler, for instance, showed no interest in Neutra's heady mix of "science" and materials. As I slowly came to see, first with Schindler, and then with the Eameses, there stood a powerful counterweight or antidote to the Bauhaus tradition and everything that followed from it.

Numerous friends have made diverse contributions to *Nothing Permanent*. First among those friends, colleagues, and comrades is the *nonsite* team: Charles Palermo, Walter Benn Michaels, Jennifer Ashton, Adolph Reed, Michael Fried, Ruth Leys, Ken Warren, Robert Pippin, Nicholas Brown, Lisa Siraganian, Marnin Young, Elise Archias, Brian Kane, Oren Izenberg, and Bridget Alsdorf. Thanks as well to friends and colleagues at FoSH (Friends of the Schindler House), Judith Sheine and Robert Sweeney, Harriett Gold, Peyton Hall, Kaitlin Drisko, and Leslie Thomas, and to Ian and Guillaume Schindler. This book would be impossible without the constant support and encouragement of Judith. The Neutra family, Dion Neutra and Raymond Neutra, were always generous with their time. Thanks as well to Barbara Lamprecht, Tom Hines, and P. J. Letofsky. Team Eames—Genevieve Fong, David Hertsgaard, Eames Demetrios, Kelsey Williams, and Daniel Ostroff—are the most generous and supportive group one could hope to work with. Thanks as well to Jeannine Oppewall and to Paul Schrader. My thanks to Jocelyn Gibbs, Silvia Perea, and Julia Larson at the Schindler archives at the University of California, Santa Barbara; to Simon Elliott at the Neutra archives at UCLA; to Lauren Bricker and Bob Alexander at the Ellwood archives at Cal Poly Pomona; and to Margaret McAleer at the Eames archives at the Library of Congress. Warm thanks to Lisa Germany Ziegler and to Frank Harmon for their conversations about the life of Harwell Harris.

At Emory University, thanks to Jean Campbell, Lisa Lee, Christina Crawford, Walter Melion, Sarah McPhee, Matthew Bernstein, Andrew Mitchell, and John Lysaker, and to my graduate students Anna McKittrick, Courtney Rawlings, Haley Pierce, Caitlin Glosser, and Catherine Barth. Pieter Martin guided and encouraged this book from beginning to end. Sincere thanks to friends and colleagues Brian Kane, Eik Kahng, Michael Schreyach, Michael Golec, Joel Lande, Gordon Hughes, Daniel Zamora, Anton Jaeger, Alex Ross, Christopher Long, Blake Stimson, Carolyn Yerkes, Preston Smith II, Cedric Johnson, Robin Schuldenfrei, Justus Nieland, Sandy Isenstadt, MJ Devaney, Volker Welter, Robert Somol, Anthony Denzer, Nicholas Olsberg, Pierluigi Serraino, Elana Shapira, and Ralph Ubl. Thanks to Lucia Tripodes and to David Jacobsen and Jonty Nash for an unforgettable ride through the ups and downs of Hollywood filmmaking. I draw continued inspiration from the work of T. J. Clark and Éric Michaud.

My warmest thanks to Mike and Evelyn, Mark and Melody, Barbara and Jeff. I am most grateful of all to my family, Bridget, Nicholas, and Leo: this book is dedicated to them.

Notes

Introduction

1. I consider the nature and problem of intentionality in *Against Affective Formalism: Matisse, Bergson, Modernism* (Minneapolis: University of Minnesota Press, 2013), as well as in a range of other writings.

2. Marcel Duchamp, "The Creative Act" (1957), in *The Writings of Marcel Duchamp*, ed. Michel Sanouillet and Elmer Peterson (New York: Da Capo, 1973), 139.

3. Robert Rauschenberg, quoted in *Readings in American Art, 1900–1975*, ed. Barbara Rose (New York: Praeger, 1975), 150.

4. Maria Gough, "Backyard Landing: Three Structures by Buckminster Fuller," in *New Views on R. Buckminster Fuller*, ed. Hsiao-Yun Chu and Roberto G. Trujillo (Stanford, Calif.: Stanford University Press, 2009), 145. For Gough, the point is not that Fuller was mistaken in his separation of idea and making—he was—but rather that his view reveals him as an intentionalist.

5. Stanley Cavell, "A Matter of Meaning It," in *Must We Mean What We Say?* (Cambridge, Mass.: Harvard University Press, 1969), 227, 226. Cavell was critiquing W. K. Wimsatt Jr. and M. C. Beardsley's "Intentional Fallacy," *Sewanee Review* 54, no. 3 (July–September 1946), 468–88. On Cavell and Anscombe and related matters, see Todd Cronan, "Le Corbusier, Matisse, and the Meaning of Conceptual Art," *nonsite.org*, no. 31 (April 10, 2020), https://nonsite.org. I am indebted to Walter Benn Michaels for drawing my attention to this passage in Cavell as well as for his series of important essays on Anscombe and the visual arts. For Michaels on Anscombe and art, see "'I Do What Happens': Anscombe and Winogrand," *nonsite.org*, no. 19 (May 3, 2016), https://nonsite.org; "Anscombe and Winogrand, Danto and Mapplethorpe: A Reply to Dominic McIver Lopes," *nonsite.org* (October 26, 2016), https://nonsite.org; "'When I Raise My Arm': Michael Fried's Theory of Action," in *Michael Fried and Philosophy: Modernism, Intention, and Theatricality*, ed. Mathew Abbott (New York: Routledge, 2018), 33–47; "Blind Time (Drawing with Anscombe)," *Yearbook of Research in English and American Literature* (2020): 1–12; and "Eyes Wide Shut: Anscombe/Action/Art," *nonsite.org*, no. 32 (September 10, 2020), https://nonsite.org.

6. G. E. M. Anscombe, *Intention* (Oxford: Basil Blackwell, 1957).

7. Paul Rudolph, quoted in John W. Cook and Heinrich Klotz, *Conversations with Architects* (New York: Praeger, 1973), 107.

8. Rem Koolhaas, "The Invention and Reinvention of the City," interview by Paul Fraioli, *Journal of International Affairs* 65, no. 2 (Spring/Summer 2012): 115.

9. Stewart Brand, *How Buildings Learn: What Happens After They're Built* (New York: Viking Press, 1994), 2.

10. I borrow the term *California Modern* from Esther McCoy, a guiding presence throughout this book. It was at Schindler's Kings Road House in 1920, McCoy notes, that the "hallmarks of California modern architecture" were first established. Esther McCoy, "R. M. Schindler," unpublished manuscript, n.d., 25, Esther McCoy Papers, 1876–1990, bulk, 1938–89, Box 15, Folder 3: Drafts and Notes, R. M. Schindler, 1950s, Archives of American Art, Smithsonian Institution.

11. Charles and Ray Eames, *An Eames Anthology: Articles, Film Scripts, Interviews, Letters,*

Notes, Speeches, ed. Daniel Ostroff (New Haven, Conn.: Yale University Press, 2015), 224; hereafter cited in text as *EA.*

12. Ralph Caplan, "Making Connections: The Work of Charles and Ray Eames," in *Connections: The Work of Charles and Ray Eames,* ed. John Neuhart and Marilyn Neuhart (Los Angeles: UCLA Art Council, 1976), 15. Caplan goes further, stating that "nothing anyone has ever said or written comes closer to describing the pattern of the Eames design practice, which might be defined as the art of solving problems by making connections" (15).

13. "Dormitory in a Nutshell: ECS," *Interiors,* November 1961, 144.

14. For further discussion on this topic, see Todd Cronan, "Why Architecture Matters as Art as Never Before: Le Corbusier, Tony Smith and the Problem of Use," *nonsite.org,* no. 21 (July 17, 2017), https://nonsite.org. Still the basic source on this question is Philippe Boudon's *Lived-in Architecture: Le Corbusier's Pessac Revisited,* trans. Gerald Onn (Cambridge: MIT Press, 1972).

15. Hugh Stubbins, "Thoughts on Architecture," in *Hugh Stubbins, Architecture: The Design Experience,* ed. Susan Braybrooke (New York: John Wiley, 1976), 15.

16. Charles Moore, quoted in Cook and Klotz, *Conversations with Architects,* 243.

17. Charles Eames, quoted in Ralph Caplan, "The Messages of Industry on the Screen," *Business Screen,* April 1960, 50. In his 1955 essay "High Time to Experiment," the Eameses' friend and collaborator George Nelson, following Sergei Eisenstein, identified film as exemplifying connections: "A particularly interesting characteristic of film is that it is better at dealing with relationships than with isolated facts. Actually, a film *is* a relationship—the picture strips of which it is composed have no meaning by themselves. This most modern of media happens to fit like a glove the most important of all problems in education: development of the individual's capacity to establish connections between isolated phenomena." George Nelson, *Problems of Design* (New York: Whitney Library of Design, 1957), 81; hereafter cited in text as *PD.* The Eameses' view of relations in film was even more ontologically extreme. As Charles frequently pointed out, the main body of their film work consists of sequences of still photographic images. In that sense, the relations among the filmic elements are more complicated than the relations in continuous film strips.

18. Caplan, "The Messages of Industry," 50. As Ray Eames and John and Marilyn Neuhart put it, for Charles film was a "method for getting lots of information across in a very short time to an audience whose concentration he could control and focus." John Neuhart, Marilyn Neuhart, and Ray Eames, *Eames Design: The Work of the Office of Charles and Ray Eames* (New York: Harry N. Abrams, 1989), 192; hereafter cited in text as *ED.* What was at stake was the focus, and control was a way to create a situation that lent itself to focus. So even if the Eameses were pessimistic about the availability of the right kinds of settings to convey ideas, it was still ideas they hoped to convey, not effects.

19. Charles Eames, quoted in Paul Schrader, "Poetry of Ideas: The Films of Charles Eames," *Film Quarterly* 23, no. 3 (1970): 12, 14.

20. Charles Eames, interview by Studs Terkel, October 1, 1965, Chicago, Studs Terkel Radio Archive, https://studsterkel.wfmt.com.

21. Charles Eames, remarks in *An Eames Celebration: Several Worlds of Charles and Ray Eames,* directed by Perry Miller Adato (New York: WNET, 1975).

22. Eames, quoted in Schrader, "Poetry of Ideas," 14.

23. Richard J. Neutra, "Tribute to a Photographer: Julius Shulman," *AIA Journal* 51 (1969): 162. It is unfortunate that the complex relationship between Neutra's work and Shulman's photography is frequently reduced to formulas like "Shulman proved to be the master at creat-

ing images that conveyed an almost palpable feeling of the 'good life' in California." Alice T. Friedman, "Palm Springs Eternal: Richard Neutra's Kaufmann Desert House," in *American Glamour and the Evolution of Modern Architecture* (New Haven, Conn.: Yale University Press, 2010), 87. I discuss the pervasive effort to reduce architectural photography to visual culture or reception issues—self-promotion, publicity, consumption, and lifestyle—in chapter 3.

24. Julius Shulman in 1992, quoted in Simon Niedenthal, "'Glamourized Houses': Neutra, Photography, and the Kaufmann House," *Journal of Architectural Education* 47, no. 2 (November 1993): 107.

25. Shulman, quoted in Niedenthal, "'Glamourized Houses,'" 108. Niedenthal rightly observes that "for Neutra, the design conception was complete not when conceived, or built, but when photographed and reexperienced" (108).

26. Neutra's fleeting admission of the superiority of photography to his own medium seemingly has only the most tangential relation to his larger vision of architectural meaning. Neutra's late affirmation of Shulman's significance stands in marked contrast to his overt claims about the superiority of architecture over film. And yet around this same moment, Neutra brilliantly drew on photographic metaphors to describe Frank Lloyd Wright's Fallingwater (an inspiration, Neutra said, for his work in Guam). "Compared to that heroic dramatization of nature, which he brought into intimate scale with human experience, Niagara Falls seemed scaleless and scattered in its effect. Like a great polished lens, Wright's structure had focused, fused, and refracted the native radiance of its natural setting, making human consciousness part of the spectrum." Richard Neutra, *Nature Near: Late Essays of Richard Neutra*, ed. William Marlin (Santa Barbara, Calif.: Capra Press, 1989), 166; hereafter cited in text as *NN*. In this instance, Neutra construed architecture as a framing device, one that brings scale, fusion, and focus to the seemingly limitless expanse of the natural world.

27. Neutra dedicated the 1969 edition of his book *Survival through Design* to Wright.

28. Frank Lloyd Wright, *Collected Writings*, vol. 2, *1930–1932*, ed. Bruce Brooks Pfeiffer (New York: Rizzoli, 1992), 333.

29. Richard Neutra, "Mural Conceptualism" (1939), *Architectural Forum* 72, no. 2 (February 1940): 94. Neutra republished this essay, or sections of it, several times.

30. Richard Neutra, "The Senses and the Setting," 1967, 14, Richard and Dion Neutra Papers (LSC 1179), UCLA Library Special Collections, Charles E. Young Research Library, University of California, Los Angeles. Claire Zimmerman discusses the relation between photographic representation and the "on-site" experience of architecture, describing how architectural photographs "privileged visual perception over other sensory modes, imposing a viewing regimen that subtracted many of architecture's specific attributes." Claire Zimmerman, *Photographic Architecture in the Twentieth Century* (Minneapolis: University of Minnesota Press, 2014), 123. Curiously, when she addresses Neutra's positive appraisal of Shulman's work, she dismisses his desire to create an "intensified visual document" that might be "correlated to bodily experience" because he failed to provide adequate "anchors or relays between these two affects" (228). On this score, by rejecting efforts at multisensory representation, Zimmerman divides media in ways that reify rather than draw the senses together. Writing of the photography of Ludwig Mies van der Rohe's Tugendhat House, she notes how "architectural abstraction might be explored and developed in a two-dimensional mode, with cool, unchanging photographs leaving their built counterpart alone and in peace to fight the messy battles of budget shortfalls, good or poor construction, inhabitation, aging, and other trials of history" (124). As I have been arguing, Neutra and the Eameses were attracted to the photographic medium precisely for its capacity to

abstract from contingencies (this was not an "imposition" but an achievement). Zimmerman is saying two things: that photographs adhere to a "different visual model" from the "on-site" experience of architecture and that this optical orientation results in an imposition on lived experience (124). The first point (the difference between photograph and world) is truistic; the second (Zimmerman's central claim) requires that viewers and critics ignore the first point and reify differences between media and between the senses.

31. Richard Neutra, "The Photographer and Architect," in *Photographing Architecture and Interiors,* by Julius Shulman (New York: Whitney Library of Design, 1962), vii.

32. Esther McCoy, *Piecing Together Los Angeles: An Esther McCoy Reader,* ed. Susan Morgan (Valencia, Calif.: East of Borneo, 2012), 183; hereafter cited in text as *EMR*.

33. Jacques Derrida, "Signature Event Context" (1972), in *Limited Inc,* trans. Samuel Weber and Jeffrey Mehlman (Evanston, Ill.: Northwestern University Press, 1988), 1, 3.

34. Derrida, "Signature Event Context," 8. Recall Stubbins's language of nursing concepts, cutting off the umbilical cord from a work, and buildings as abandoned offspring.

35. McCoy, "R. M. Schindler," 4.

36. Derrida, "Signature Event Context," 10.

37. These are issues connected to fantasies of what I call "affect machines" and "surefire effects" in chapter 1 of *Against Affective Formalism*. On the surefire, also see my response to critics in "Against Affective Formalism: Matisse, Bergson, Modernism," *nonsite.org,* no. 16 (June 22, 2015), https://nonsite.org.

38. R. Buckminster Fuller, "'S a House, Darling," in *Nine Chains to the Moon* (1938; repr., Carbondale: Southern Illinois Press, 1963), 11.

39. R. Buckminster Fuller, introduction to *Expanded Cinema,* by Gene Youngblood, 50th anniversary ed. (New York: Fordham University Press, 2020), 29, 26.

40. R. Buckminster Fuller, "Patrons of Art: Death and Life," in *Nine Chains to the Moon,* 113.

41. Fuller, *Nine Chains to the Moon,* 364, 144.

42. R. M. Schindler was prescient in his criticism of Fuller. In his 1934 essay "Space Architecture," he observed that Fuller's Dymaxion house was not as "ephemeral" as Fuller claimed; rather, "it is born of a sculptural conception. Its structural scheme is akin to the one of the tree. . . . The 'room' they enclose is not an aimful space conception but a byproduct without architectural meaning." R. M. Schindler, "Space Architecture" (1934), in *R. M. Schindler: Architect, 1887–1953,* ed. August Sarnitz (New York: Rizzoli, 1988), 51.

43. Beatriz Colomina, "Enclosed by Images: The Eameses' Multimedia Architecture," *Grey Room,* no. 2 (Winter 2001): 24. In contrast to Colomina, Eric Schuldenfrei rightly notes that "what was important to the Eameses was not the message within a specific image, but how the image contributed to a precise argument when juxtaposed with the other images." Eric Schuldenfrei, *The Films of Charles and Ray Eames: A Universal Sense of Expectation* (New York: Routledge, 2015), 26. Colomina not only shows no interest in the "messages" but also does not offer a sense as to what they might be.

44. Colomina, "Enclosed by Images," 12, 13.

45. Colomina, "Enclosed by Images," 24–25.

46. Colomina, "Enclosed by Images," 13.

47. Colomina, "Enclosed by Images," 25.

48. Reinhold Martin, "Fuller's Futures," in Chu and Trujillo, *New Views on R. Buckminster Fuller,* 185–86.

49. Martin, "Fuller's Futures," 187.

50. I take up the problem of spectatorial aesthetics, especially within theoretical texts that explicitly criticize this mode of address, in *Against Affective Formalism.* I consider the long-standing fantasy of "mode of perception" in "Wölfflin and the Promise of Anonymity," review of *Principles of Art History: The Problem of the Development of Style in Early Modern Art,* by Heinrich Wölfflin, *caa.reviews,* May 11, 2018, http://www.caareviews.org.

51. R. Buckminster Fuller, "Teleology," in *Nine Chains to the Moon,* 49.

52. R. Buckminster Fuller, "Genius and Talent," in *Nine Chains to the Moon,* 104–5.

53. Thirty-five years after creating the Lovell House, Neutra visited the new owners of the property, the Toppers, and did not approve of certain details of their decor. He subsequently sent them detailed written instructions about how to rehang a picture in the upstairs study: "The water color should be taken out of the frame and off the mat and mounted on thin plywood projected two inches off the wall on four recessed wooden blocks so that the painting floats freely from the wall, which goes through. An additional frame is necessary unless glass is desired in which case a *very* thin chrome frame could be used." My thanks to Josh Gorrell for sharing this letter with me.

54. Hugh Kenner, "Modeling the Universe," in *Bucky: A Guided Tour of Buckminster Fuller* (New York: William Morrow, 1973), 91.

55. The October 1955 issue of *Domus* featured a flexible shelving/table system for mass production designed by Angelo Mangiarotti and Bruno Moarassutti for Fratelli Frigerio that was itself modeled on the furniture designs of the Eameses. See *Domus* 311 (October 1955): 44–48.

56. Schrader, "Poetry of Ideas," 7, 8, 9, 14. The phrase appears eight times in this article.

57. "Credibility" is a term the Eameses used frequently; see *EA,* 193–94, 257, 291, 313, 330, 362.

58. A visual point made by Eames Demetrios; see *Eames: Beautiful Details,* ed. Gloria Fowler and Steve Crist (Los Angeles: AMMO Books, 2014).

59. Ralph Caplan, "Making Connections: The Designer as Universal Joint; Object Lessons in the Work of Charles and Ray Eames," in *By Design* (New York: St. Martin's Press, 1982), 205.

60. This phrase was likely first uttered in an interview that Charles did during the "Making Connections" Aspen Design Conference in June 1978. The passage is most often quoted from *ED,* 266. Compare it with Ray's claim that "I don't know how to separate anything." Ray Eames, oral history interview, July 28–August 20, 1980, Archives of American Art, Smithsonian Institution. It is possible that Charles had economist Barbara Ward's words in mind when he made this comment. Ward was an important figure at the 1972 United Nations Conference on the Human Environment, held in Stockholm, where Fuller's ideas played an important role. That event was "the beginning of the realization that everything connects," and Ward offered a crucial warning about this ecological picture: if "everything is important you can get to a position where nothing is important. If everything connects with everything you can end up going round and round and round and round." Quoted in Geoffrey Lean, "If Everything Is Important, Nothing Is Important," *New Scientist,* June 26, 1975, 704.

61. The Eameses discuss Babbage's work in *A Computer Perspective,* ed. Glen Fleck (Cambridge, Mass.: Harvard University Press, 1973), 12–19, 140–41. For a brilliant commentary on the legacy of Babbage, one that is analogous to the issues explored by the Eameses, see Hugh Kenner, *The Counterfeiters: An Historical Comedy* (Indianapolis: Indiana University Press, 1968).

62. R. Buckminster Fuller, quoted in Alden Hatch, *Buckminster Fuller at Home in the Universe* (New York: Delta, 1974), 153, 155. This is what Kenner describes as "the eye of vision sees

systems of connectedness; this may not *be* that, but it has the same structure." Hugh Kenner, *The Pound Era* (Berkeley: University of California Press, 1971), 33.

63. The issue is more complex than this. The Eameses did in fact continually flirt with Fuller's natural geometry, a point made explicit, for instance, in their 1972 exhibition *Fibonacci: Growth and Form* (*ED*, 378–79).

64. No doubt the Eameses were thinking of Fuller's notion of continuous man, a concept that first appeared in print in an essay by that title in Fuller's *Ideas and Integrities: A Spontaneous Autobiographical Disclosure* (New York: Collier, 1963), 278–301.

65. Charles Eames, Norton Lecture no. 5, March 29, 1971, audio recording, Work of Charles and Ray Eames, Manuscript Division, Library of Congress.

66. See also Charles Eames, "On Reducing Discontinuity," *Bulletin of the American Academy of Arts and Sciences* 30, no. 6 (March 1977): 24–34. I owe a debt of thanks to Michael Golec for pointing out the difference between continuity and nondiscontinuity in the Eameses' work.

67. Charles Eames, remarks in *An Eames Celebration*. In his 1965 interview with Studs Terkel, Charles attributed this idea to Jacob Bronowski. Here is the relevant passage from Bronowski's work: "All science is the search for unity in hidden likenesses. . . . What struck [Newton] was the conjecture that the same force of gravity, which reaches to the top of the tree, might go on reaching out beyond the earth and its air, endlessly into space. Gravity might reach the moon: this was Newton's new thought. . . . In Newton's sentence ["I found them answer pretty nearly"] modern science is full grown. It grows from comparison. It has seized a likeness between two unlike appearances. . . . The progress of science is the discovery at each step of a new order which gives unity to what had long seemed unlike." Jacob Bronowski, *Science and Human Values* (New York: Messner, 1956), 23, 26. As Bronowski makes clear, Newton was describing a hidden order, not creating one.

68. While Fuller endorsed a hard split between mind (principles) and brain (matter) and saw every materialization as an expression of immaterial principles, for the Eameses the pursuit of relations could only be extracted from a particular context of making. From his earliest writings Fuller described the ontological difference between empirical connections and underlying structure as the difference between brain and mind. This is what Fuller means when he says that "at the very instant an absolutely straight line might be attained, it would physically cease to exist, and become what it originally was: non-physically-demonstrable because conceived in the mind, which, alone, can conceive perfection." Fuller, "Genius and Talent," 105. His prioritization of principles over reality discloses his transcendental commitments: "Principles are more of a reality than the qualities they produce." Fuller, quoted in Kenner, *Bucky*, 120. Fuller offers his most extensive commentary on the difference between mind and brain in *Intuition* (New York: Doubleday, 1972).

69. The basic reference book on the CSH Program is still Esther McCoy, *Modern California Houses: Case Study Houses, 1945–1962* (New York: Reinhold, 1962); hereafter cited in text as *MCH*. See also Elizabeth A. T. Smith, ed., *Blueprints for Modern Living: History and Legacy of the Case Study Houses* (Cambridge: MIT Press, 1989); Elizabeth A. T. Smith, *Case Study Houses: The Complete CSH Program, 1945–1966*, ed. Peter Goessel (Cologne: Taschen, 2002); Ethel Buisson and Thomas Billard, *The Presence of the Case Study Houses*, trans. Jasmine Benyamin (Basel: Birkhäuser, 2004).

70. Beatriz Colomina, *Domesticity at War* (Cambridge: MIT Press, 2006), 31. Colomina's analogizing of the house to a storage system is meant to be deflationary, to reduce the house to a "consumable image."

71. Craig Ellwood, "On Form and Function," *Zodiac* 4 (1959): 160.

72. Ellwood, answer to a questionnaire, "Fields of Practice: Residential Design," *Progressive Architecture*, March 1959, 95.

73. Ellwood became acquainted with the Eameses when he served as the cost estimator on the Eames and Entenza CSH projects. As Neil Jackson remarks, nearly all the work that came out of Craig Ellwood Associates between 1948 and 1950—including the Bobertz, Andersen, Steinman, Epstein, Zimmerman, Hale, and Zack Houses, as well as CSH 16, the Brettauer Apartments, and the Natham Stores—Ellwood "had picked up from Charles Eames and Eero Saarinen while [he was] working for Lamport, Cofer, Salzman." Neil Jackson, *California Modern: The Architecture of Craig Ellwood* (New York: Princeton Architectural Press, 2002), 60.

74. As Ernie Jacks of the Ellwood office observed of Ellwood, it was the connections and the detailing that were most centrally on his mind: "I think his inventiveness lay in detailing. Because there would be a family of details for a certain sort of construction system. I also felt like he was very creative when it came to marrying a vertical steel structure with a horizontal wood structure." Quoted in Jackson, *California Modern*, 49.

75. I do not intend to weigh in on the fraught and important issue of accreditation at Ellwood Associates. I assume that, as at the Eames Office, there was a high degree of fluidity, as well as tension, among the firm's various members.

76. Jackson, *California Modern*, 98, 99. As Jackson notes, "Ellwood dominated the [Case Study House] program from 1952 to 1958" (139), and of "all his Case Study Houses [No. 18] received the widest exposure" (97).

77. Ellwood celebrated the house's manifesto character, declaring, "This is the first use of rectangular steel tubing as beams and is probably the first application of a modular steel frame with prefabrication methods." Craig Ellwood Associates, "Case Study House 18," *Arts and Architecture*, April 1957, 18.

78. Ellwood's introduction of the house in February 1956 reads as a manifesto for prefabrication. In "ten or fifteen years houses will be built from pre-cut and prefabricated components. . . . Catalogs will offer a choice of metal, wood or plastic structural frames. . . . There will be a great variety of prefabricated, pre-finished modular panels, and these, too, will be bolted simply into place." The future of prefabrication had arrived. The "great variety of panel materials now available permits a multiplicity of combinations so that with one floor plan in a 100-unit tract no two streetside facades need be the same." Craig Ellwood, "Project for Case Study House 18," *Arts and Architecture*, February 1956, 20.

79. Ellwood, "Project for Case Study House 18," 20. As Ellwood continually stressed, what was special about the house was how "one detail, one connection, handles all exterior wall conditions." Craig Ellwood, "Case Study House No. 18," *Arts and Architecture*, November 1957, 19.

80. In her book on Ellwood, McCoy uses similar language to make the decisive point: "One jointing detail allows the columns to receive doors, fixed glass, windows, sliding glass doors, or solid panels." Esther McCoy, *Craig Ellwood: Architecture* (New York: Walker, 1968), 24. Jackson similarly notes how the "separation of the walls from the structural frame further allowed flexibility both in terms of design and in the choice of materials for the infill panels, which might be metal, wood, glass or plastic." Jackson, *California Modern*, 99.

81. Craig Ellwood Associates, "Case Study House No. 18," *Arts and Architecture*, March 1958, 26. A note beneath the sections indicates that the "details and design" were copyrighted in 1955 by Ellwood, and Ellwood insisted that the system was in fact first developed in 1950. The description first appeared in Ellwood's "Project for Case Study House 18" in the February 1956 issue of

Arts and Architecture. Henry Salzman, the contractor on many of the CSHs, including Ellwood's CSH 16, was more pragmatic in his assessment of the possibility of a universal connection. According to Salzman: "New sections will come when a thousand houses are planned at one time. A section will then be worked out that makes sense. When you use I-beams or H-columns in a house today the finishing details are always a problem around the H or the I—it's touchy to close in around a wide flange beam. An ideal situation would be a webbing running horizontally. A box beam is needed that is the same width as the columns; then the beams won't have to run in and out of a flange" (*MCH*, 70–71). Salzman may have been thinking here of the Eames House, which used open web joists to take the connections from the columns.

82. Esther McCoy, *The Second Generation* (Salt Lake City: Gibbs M. Smith, 1984), 22. The hinge plan—one wing shifted by a 100-degree angle from the main bar—introduced at the Thomas Mann House of 1941 was repeated in a series of smaller houses, including the Floyd D. Crosby House of 1946, the Sam Taylor House of 1947, Davidson's own house of 1947, and the Madeline Goss House of 1948. Although it is beyond the parameters of this discussion, Schindler's extensive use of eccentric angles after 1945 might have been inspired in part by Davidson's wartime work.

83. J. R. Davidson, quoted in McCoy, *The Second Generation*, 15.

84. McCoy, *The Second Generation*, 28.

85. McCoy, *The Second Generation*, 28.

86. McCoy, *The Second Generation*, 28.

87. As McCoy observes, with posts typically spaced at intervals of 9 feet in one direction and 21 feet in the other, Davidson was forced to incorporate more and more half walls to define his spaces, usually in the form of bookcases, shelving, cabinets, and bars.

88. Peter Blake, "Craig Ellwood," *Zodiac* 4 (1959): 164. In his preface to McCoy's book on Ellwood, Blake characteristically rejects the Miesian notion that "God is in the details," stating that the "ultimate test of architecture must be the sum of its parts: the spaces formed by the many parts as they go together." Ellwood's "ultimate reputation," Blake concludes, "will rest on the spaces he has made with the parts." Peter Blake, preface to McCoy, *Craig Ellwood*, 6.

89. "House by Craig Ellwood," *Arts and Architecture*, October 1952, 31.

90. Richard Neutra, "Wider Planning If We Want to Survive," in *World and Dwelling* (London: Alec Tiranti, 1962), 26.

91. "The New Case Study House," *Arts and Architecture*, June 1953, 26.

92. "Space-Frame-Game," *Architectural Review* 127, no. 758 (April 1960): 222.

93. David Gebhard and Robert Winter, *An Architectural Guidebook to Los Angeles*, rev. ed. (Salt Lake City: Gibbs M. Smith, 2003), 40.

94. Peter Blake, *No Place Like Utopia: Modern Architecture and the Company We Kept* (New York: W. W. Norton, 1996), 112, 114.

95. Arthur Drexler, "Unframed Space: A Museum for Jackson Pollock's Paintings," *Interiors*, January 1950, 90.

96. The question of whether "universal space" bears centrally on Mies's intentions is beyond the scope of my argument, but it is worth noting that the issue has generated considerable disagreement. Mies, for instance, noted that the glass and steel of the architectural envelope are "immortal," while the flexible nature of interior spaces means that they inevitably change and die away, a point Paul Heyer makes when, in a gloss on "universal space," he explains that "Mies creates a flexible space capable of continual modification and thereby designed to counteract ob-

solescence." Paul Heyer, *Architects on Architecture: New Directions in America*, new and enlarged ed. (New York: Walker, 1993), 33. When designing the Illinois Instliute of Technology, which was to be built over a long period of time, Mies said his aim was to "decide on something that would not change, that would not be out of date by the time we had finished." Ludwig Mies van der Rohe, interview in Heyer, *Architects on Architecture*, 30. With a "variable ground plan," Mies further explained, "the building lasts much longer than its function." As Daniel Abramson critically observes of this claim, "Obsolescence's flux [was] absorbed within the perfect, fixed frame." Daniel M. Abramson, *Obsolescence: An Architectural History* (Chicago: University of Chicago Press, 2016), 85. To complicate matters further, as Colin Rowe persuasively argues, there is a distinction to be made between Mies before and after his arrival in Chicago. Rowe contends that Mies's "old [German] column had offered a minimum of obstruction to a horizontal movement of space; but the new [Chicago] column presents a distinctly more substantial stop." Colin Rowe, "Neo-'Classicism' and Modern Architecture II" (1956–57), in *The Mathematics of the Ideal Villa, and Other Essays* (Cambridge: MIT Press, 1976), 145. There is far more to say on this subject, but this will have to suffice to suggest the kinds of problems raised by attempts to interpret Mies at midcentury. I will further add, as I noted previously, there remains a significant difference between the "immortality" that Mies pursued and Ellwood's Miesian variant. Ellwood's version of Mies is at once "immortal" in its pursuit of an enclosed totality and, as Gebhard observed, "cardboardy" and "fragile."

97. Ellwood, "Case Study House No. 18" (1957), 19.

98. Craig Ellwood, "On the Future of Architecture," *Zodiac* 4 (1959): 160.

99. In his commentary in the *Arts and Architecture* spread, Entenza reflected that the architecture was "based upon the system utilized" and that "the visual organization properly reflects this system." Unlike all previous prefab systems, this frame did *"all* the work," allowing for "flexibility not otherwise possible by setting no limitation as to the selection of wall material." "Case Study House No. 18," *Arts and Architecture*, June 1958, 22, 24.

100. Jackson, *California Modern*, 26.

101. Konrad Wachsmann and Walter Gropius, "'House' in Industry: A System for the Manufacture of Industrialized Building," *Arts and Architecture*, November 1947. This issue also contained features on the two other CSHs that shared the same plot of land with the Eames and Entenza Houses: Neutra's CSH 20, the Bailey House, and another CSH 18 (there were two of them) by Rodney Walker.

102. Wachsmann and Gropius, "'House' in Industry," 28. For a discussion of the development of the wedge connector, see Gilbert Herbert, *The Dream of the Factory-Made House: Walter Gropius and Konrad Wachsmann* (Cambridge: MIT Press, 1984), 249, 275. As I have noted, Ellwood's CSH 16 was described as a fulfillment of the house as erector set.

103. Wachsmann and Gropius, "'House' in Industry," 30.

104. Wachsmann had first devised the connector in 1941 and obsessively revised it until 1945, when he filed the patent on it. William Wurster tersely summed up Wachsmann: "Interested in technical joints—don't regard him as an architect." Quoted in Pierluigi Serraino, *The Creative Architect: Inside the Great Midcentury Personality Study* (New York: Monacelli Press, 2016), 75.

105. Eero Saarinen, *Eero Saarinen on His Work* (New Haven, Conn.: Yale University Press, 1962), 28. For further information on the gasket, see Antonio Román, *Eero Saarinen: An Architecture of Multiplicity* (New York: Princeton Architectural Press, 2006), 169.

106. Esther McCoy, *Richard Neutra* (New York: George Braziller, 1960), 16.

107. Fuller, quoted in Kenner, *Bucky*, 171.

108. Esther McCoy, oral history interview, June 7–November 14, 1987, Archives of American Art, Smithsonian Institution. While Neutra was an admirer of Mies's architecture and it was Mies who invited him to lecture at the Bauhaus, Neutra's assessment of Mies's designs for IIT was mixed. Writing of Crown Hall in *Architectural Record* in 1956, Neutra stated his concerns about the potentially static nature of universal space. It was only when he began to see Mies's "big" space in constant motion that he could affirm it. "Against this regularity [of the bay system] the tracery of the locust leaf shadow patterns is a subtle overlying texture," he noted. Richard Neutra, "Remarks on Mies van der Rohe," *Architectural Record* 120, no. 2 (August 1956): 136.

109. Looking back on his career, Ellwood realized he had come to reject the notion that one space "flows into the other," affirming instead the "privacy" of spaces through a variety of enclosures. Craig Ellwood, interview by Shelley Kappe, in "Charles Eames / Craig Ellwood / César Pelli (November 23, 1976)," SCI-Arc Media Archive, https://www.youtube.com.

110. Pierre Koenig, quoted in Neil Jackson, *Pierre Koenig: A View from the Archive* (Los Angeles: Getty Research Institute, 2019), 39.

111. At its most inelegant, the central I beam that traverses the dining and living areas at Koenig House 1 (1950) punctures the beech plywood siding on the west wall but does not continue beyond the steel frame on the other side of it. This creates a mixed visual message, as though the beam continues but it also clearly stops just beyond the line of sight.

112. Jackson, *Pierre Koenig*, 46. In 1963 Neutra solicited Koenig to be his associate and move into Neutra's offices in Glendale, California. This further establishes that Neutra, Soriano, and Koenig had shared concerns.

113. In their book on Koenig, James Steele and David Jenkins describe the pavilion as a "microcosm of Koenig's principles" that "demonstrates the value he places on the honesty of exposed structure." It is hard to know what the latter phrase means in Koenig's case, as he decisively rejected the pattern established by Eames and Ellwood Associates making the connection a programmatic statement of purpose. James Steele and David Jenkins, *Pierre Koenig* (London: Phaidon, 1998), 114.

114. I owe a debt of thanks to Anna McKittrick for drawing my attention to this passage, one that intersects with the Eameses' larger fixation on design constraints.

115. Ellwood, interview by Kappe.

116. Charles Eames, "Film as a Modeling Device," lecture, American Iron and Steel Institute, Atlanta, April 17, 1975, 1, Work of Charles and Ray Eames, Manuscript Division, Library of Congress.

117. The Eameses were on friendly terms with Schindler and Neutra. As Ray described it in a 1980 interview: "Early on we had seen Neutra and, of course, we admired him very much. Charles always said his greatest contribution was not these special houses but the fact that he was producing these drawings, sets of drawings, and then refining those drawings, and refining those so that they were . . . a way that the anonymous contractor could use and build houses. The same way with Schindler." Eames, oral history interview, July 28–August 20, 1980. In other words, the Eameses regarded both Schindler and Neutra as creators of *drawings* rather than built structures, which matches the Eameses' own self-description. Soriano worked briefly in Schindler's studio and came to an unsparing conclusion, one that points to the fault lines within the seemingly close-knit world of California Modern: "I couldn't stand Schindler," Soriano told

an interviewer in 1985, adding that Schindler's work was "very personal, very sculptural. . . . And I was just the opposite. I wanted to structure the thing objectively, not sculptural." Raphael Soriano, *Substance and Function in Architecture,* interview by Marlene L. Laskey (Los Angeles: Oral History Program, University of California, 1988), 78; hereafter cited in text as *SF.* (Laskey interviewed Soriano in July 1985.)

118. R. M. Schindler, "Directory of Contemporary Architecture, USC" (1949), in Sarnitz, *R. M. Schindler,* 69. When Schindler introduced the idea in a 1943 article, he described it as "a new building material for unlimited use—the PREFABRICATED 'PANEL-POST' UNIT." He did not, it is worth underscoring, mention exchangeable wall panels of different materials. R. M. Schindler, "Prefabrication Vocabulary," *California Arts and Architecture,* June 1943, 33. Judith Sheine describes it as "a skeleton system of posts with nonstructural interchangeable panels, composed on a module, allowing for greater openness and flexibility." Judith Sheine, *R. M. Schindler* (London: Phaidon, 2001), 94.

119. R. M. Schindler, "Architecture: If We Speak of Civilization . . . ," undated, and "American Standard of Living," 1942, unpublished lectures, R. M. Schindler Papers, Architecture and Design Collection, Art, Design & Architecture Museum, University of California, Santa Barbara.

120. Esther McCoy, *Schindler in California,* audio recording (London: World Microfilms, 1980). As McCoy was aware, the structural frames in this house actually defined the spatial qualities of the interior space. That is not to suggest that they were the same; rather than collapsing structure and space, Schindler aimed to relate them and disarticulate them at once, as though to emphasize the proximity and distance between what he called at the time "shelter" and "playground."

121. McCoy, *The Second Generation,* 14.

122. Harwell Hamilton Harris, memorial note for Schindler in *Arts and Architecture,* May 1954, 36.

123. Charles Eames visited Harris at his Fellowship Park House and studio—itself modeled on the Schindler House—in 1940. See Harwell Harris, *The Organic View of Design,* interview by Judy Stonefield (Los Angeles: Oral History Program, University of California, 1985), 137. (Stonefield interviewed Harris in August 1979.)

124. Here, and throughout my discussion of the work of Schindler, I am deeply indebted to the work of Judith Sheine. In this instance, a personal communication helped me to extrapolate Harris's point.

125. R. M. Schindler, "Building Descriptions," n.d., n.p., R. M. Schindler Papers, Architecture and Design Collection, Art, Design & Architecture Museum, University of California, Santa Barbara. At the Von Koerber House in Hollywood (1931–32), Schindler responded similarly to a local ordinance requiring the use of red clay tile roofing, spreading the curved tiles over the roofs, down the sides of the house, and into the interior, covering the immense entry hall and fireplace.

126. See Sheine, *R. M. Schindler,* 178–81. Moreover, Schindler took the economic and site exigencies as license to use "different materials on the four sides." Quoted in Sheine, *R. M. Schindler,* 180.

127. The most extreme variant on this idea appeared with the 1934–35 Kaun Beach House in Richmond, California. There Schindler covered the whole of the house in horizontal bands of green rolled roofing. As Sheine rightly notes, although the stated excuse was cost savings, the design's "similarity to the horizontal concrete and redwood banding of the 1925 How house is obvious." Judith Sheine, *R. M. Schindler: Works and Projects* (Barcelona: GG, 1998), 126.

128. Schindler, "Building Descriptions," n.p.

129. Lionel March, "'Proportion Is an Alive and Expressive Tool,'" "Log House, *Urhutte* and Temple," "Dr. How's Magical Music Box," and "The Translucent House," in *R. M. Schindler: Composition and Construction*, ed. Lionel March and Judith Sheine (London: Academy Editions, 1993). See also March's "R. M. Schindler: Kings Road and How Houses," *GA Houses: Residential Masterpieces* (Tokyo: A.D.A. Edita, 1999); and "Rudolph M. Schindler: Space Reference Frame, Modular Coordination and the 'Row,'" *Nexus Network Journal* 5, no. 2 (2003): 51–64.

130. In a typical instance of his style-based approach, Gebhard, writing of Schindler's seemingly eccentric Packard House (1924), describes it as "quite arbitrary in its exterior geometry." David Gebhard, *Schindler*, 3rd ed. (San Francisco: William Stout, 1997), 37. As Jin-Ho Park and Joung-Lan Park observe, this claim is "inaccurate," given that all of Schindler's "geometric decisions" concerning the house "were rationally determined." Jin-Ho Park and Joung-Lan Park, "The Underlying Geometry in Rudolph M. Schindler's Packard House," *Journal of Asian Architecture and Building Engineering* 12, no. 1 (May 2013): 13.

131. R. M. Schindler, "Lecture 6: Planning," Church School of Arts Lecture Series, Chicago, 1916, n.p., R. M. Schindler Papers, Architecture and Design Collection, Art, Design & Architecture Museum, University of California, Santa Barbara. As Sheine observes, these lecture notes "lay out the themes for much of Schindler's future writings and work." Sheine, *R. M. Schindler* (2001), 280n1. It was Sheine who first discovered the Church School lectures in 1999. In a footnote in March and Sheine, *R. M. Schindler: Composition and Construction*, March mentions that H. Toler Booraem's articles on the musical ideals in architecture published in *Architectural Record* in 1895 may have influenced Schindler's thinking, a suggestion supported by a note in the Church School lectures (although March was unaware of the note when he made his observation).

132. Gregory Ain, who worked for Neutra alongside Harris in Schindler's studio in the late 1920s, went on in the early 1940s to work in the Eames Office. Ain, along with McCoy, marks an important point of transition between Schindler and the Eameses, and Ain took his cue explicitly from mathematics. McCoy sees Dunsmuir Flats (1937) as Ain's most successful work (and he himself did as well), describing the complex as a "mathematical game." McCoy, *The Second Generation*, 96. Ain referred to Dunsmuir as a reflection of what he learned as a "math major. . . . I like to put things into an equation." Quoted in Anthony Denzer, *Gregory Ain: The Modern Home as Social Commentary* (New York: Rizzoli, 2008), 81. Denzer emphasizes how the photographic record was retouched to make it appear to correspond to the ideal plan, suggesting that the building was not the "perfectly planned mathematical game that Ain might have wished to portray" (82). What is at stake here is less the reality of the achievement than the peculiar intention to conceive architecture in mathematical terms. Taking Schindler's El Pueblo Ribera Court (1923) as his model, Ain made the difficult site conditions—the lot was roughly an isosceles trapezoid—a key to the Dunsmuir plan. Rather than taking his cue from the street line or sidelines, he took the alley line as his source, creating a sawtooth pattern in which each unit was offset 6 feet in plan from the last.

133. From the beginning Schindler rejected an architecture of permanency; his standard figure for it was the cave. In the opening of his 1912 manifesto, he asserted, "The cave was the original dwelling. A shallow abode pile was the first permanent house." R. M. Schindler, "Manifesto" (1912) and "Contra" (1932), in Sarnitz, *R. M. Schindler*, 42, 50.

134. R. M. Schindler, "A Cooperative Dwelling," *T-Square*, February 1932, 21.

135. Michael Darling considers this quality in "The Vulnerable Architecture of R. M.

Schindler," in *The Architecture of R. M. Schindler,* ed. Elizabeth A. T. Smith and Michael Darling (New York: Harry N. Abrams, 2001), 174–213.

136. R. M. Schindler, "Furniture and the Modern House: A Theory of Interior Design" (1935), in Sarnitz, *R. M. Schindler,* 54.

137. As assistant on Wright's Hollyhock House, Schindler contributed to an iconographic program that reflected on the dramatically volatile geological patterns of Southern California. See Neil Levine, "Building against Nature on the Pacific Rim," in *The Architecture of Frank Lloyd Wright* (Princeton, N.J.: Princeton University Press, 1996), 113–48.

138. Frank Lloyd Wright, quoted in Arthur Drexler and Thomas S. Hines, *The Architecture of Richard Neutra: From International Style to California Modern* (New York: Museum of Modern Art, 1982), 49. I address Drexler's account of California Modern in chapter 5.

139. Harwell Hamilton Harris, foreword to *Vienna to Los Angeles: Two Journeys,* by Esther McCoy (Santa Monica, Calif.: Arts and Architecture Press, 1979), 11.

140. Harris, foreword, 11.

141. Frank Lloyd Wright, *Autobiography* (New York: Duell, Sloan and Pearce, 1943), 274.

142. R. M. Schindler, "Visual Technique" (1952), in Sarnitz, *R. M. Schindler,* 67.

143. "Lovell House—we are in the middle of it," Dione Neutra wrote in April 1928. Dione Neutra, comp. and trans., *Richard Neutra, Promise and Fulfillment, 1919–1932: Selections from the Letters and Diaries of Richard and Dione Neutra* (Carbondale: Southern Illinois University Press, 1986), 171.

144. Walter Gropius, "Sociological Premises for the Minimum Dwelling of Urban Industrial Populations" (1929), in *Scope of Total Architecture* (New York: Collier, 1970), 98.

145. Ludwig Mies van der Rohe, quoted in Thomas S. Hines, *Richard Neutra and the Search for Modern Architecture* (Berkeley: University of California Press, 1982), 96.

146. Neutra took his first step in establishing a U.S. Bauhaus in April 1931, when he, along with his students Ain and Harris, formed the American chapter of the Congrès Internationaux d'Architecture Moderne (CIAM). Under Neutra's direction, the group had developed plans for low-cost housing to be presented at the third CIAM conference, held in Brussels in 1930. The general theme was rational planning, and the discussion centered on Gropius's query "Low-, mid-, or high-rise building?" Neutra used almost identical terms in his CIAM 3 contribution, titling his presentation "High-, Mid- and Low-Rise Building in American Circumstances." All of Neutra's early projects fed into his large-scale plan for Rush City Reformed: office towers linked by bridges, a twenty-story apartment block on the beach, row housing with a community center, and the Diatom series of modular houses. In this scheme, Ain was responsible for the beach apartment building and a prison. McCoy describes the effort as "one of the most vital and concentrated student projects ever attempted in the United States." McCoy, *The Second Generation,* 87.

147. Ludwig Mies van der Rohe to G. W. Farenholtz, quoted in Richard Pommer, "Mies van der Rohe and the Political Ideology of the Modern Movement in Architecture," in *Mies van der Rohe: Critical Essays,* ed. Franz Schulze (New York: Museum of Modern Art, 1989), 108.

1. The Medium Has No Message

1. Adolf Loos, *On Architecture,* ed. Adolf Opel and Daniel Opel, trans. Michael Mitchell (Riverside, Calif.: Ariadne Press, 2002), 33; hereafter cited in text as *OA.* All translations from Loos have been modified to fit the original, *Sämtliche Schriften,* Wikisource, accessed October 18, 2022, https://de.wikisource.org/wiki/Adolf_Loos. I briefly consider Loos's notion of intended effects in *Against Affective Formalism,* 35.

2. Richard Neutra, *Survival through Design* (New York: Oxford University Press, 1954), 179; hereafter cited in text as *SD*.

3. Adolf Loos, *Ornament and Crime: Selected Essays*, ed. Adolf Opel, trans. Michael Mitchell (Riverside, Calif.: Ariadne Press, 1998), 46; hereafter cited in text as *OC*.

4. That is also why repeating past forms could consist of altering the look of those forms in view of "technical advances." As Loos noted, if it is possible to improve a form, then technical "improvement is always to be used" (*OA*, 122).

5. Loos did not reject the existence of natural feelings associated with certain structures, but whatever those were he construed them as occurring at such a low and generalizable level as to be insignificant. Because he could not be responsible for those automatically generated feelings, they were not part of his architectural expression.

6. Loos's evaluative criticism was derived in part from the model of judgment in Kant's third critique, such as in section 8, where Kant states there is "no rule" by which one can be "compelled to recognize anything as beautiful." Our judgment can be swayed, but only "with our own eyes." One "*imputes* agreement to everyone" not because everyone will agree with one's judgment but because, in Kant's view, everyone ought to. Immanuel Kant, *The Critique of Judgement,* trans. James Creed Meredith (Oxford: Clarendon Press, 1952), 56. As Robert Pippin has argued, Kant's peculiar vision of the "subjective validity of judgments of taste" rests on the assumption of a practical normativity within all reflective judgment. On this account, the beautiful's claim on us rests on an unusual social norm: our collective appreciation of the purposiveness of nature. See Robert B. Pippin, "The Significance of Taste: Kant, Aesthetic and Reflective Judgment," *Journal of the History of Philosophy* 34, no. 4 (October 1996): 549–69. Loos was explicit regarding his debt to Kant. In his essay on Josef Veillich he credited Kant with the conceptual invention of the *Raumplan*: "That is the great revolution in architecture: the *spatial* solution of the ground plan. Before Immanuel Kant, mankind could not think spatially and architects were compelled to make the WC as high as the ballroom" (*OA*, 189).

7. I explore a related set of issues around the inside/outside logic of Le Corbusier's approach in "Le Corbusier, Matisse, and the Meaning of Conceptual Art."

8. Éric Michaud, "La Fin de l'iconographie (une nouvelle rhétorique du sensible)" (1979), in *La Fin du salut par l'image et autres textes* (Paris: Flammarion, 2020), 87–89, my translation.

9. August Endell, "The Possibility and Goal of a New Architecture," in *Architectural Theory,* vol. 2, *An Anthology from 1871 to 2005,* ed. Harry Francis Mallgrave and Christina Contandriopoulous (New York: John Wiley, 2008), 98.

10. August Endell, "The Beauty of Form and Decorative Art," in *Form and Function: A Source Book for the History of Architecture and Design, 1890–1939,* ed. Tim Benton, Charlotte Benton, and Dennis Sharp (London: Open University, 1975), 21.

11. Hermann Obrist, "Dekorative Kunst," *Illustrierte Zeitschrift für angewandte Kunst* 3 (February 1900): 189–90, my translation.

12. Henry van de Velde, "The New Ornament," in Mallgrave and Contandriopoulous, *Architectural Theory,* 2:116. For a largely uncritical assessment of van de Velde's metaphysics of line, see Barbara von Orelli-Messerli, "The Line as Force: Henry van de Velde's Scientific Approach to Artistic Problems," in *Spatiotemporalities on the Line: Representations-Practices-Dynamics,* ed. Sebastian Dorsch and Jutta Vinzent (Berlin: De Gruyter, 2017), 119–40.

13. Henry van de Velde, *Kunstgewerbliche Laienpredigten* (Leipzig: Seemann, 1902), 188, my translation.

14. Frank Lloyd Wright, *Collected Writings,* vol. 1, *1894–1930,* ed. Bruce Brooks Pfeiffer (New York: Rizzoli, 1992), 41, 123.

15. Walter Gropius, "The Theory and Organization of the Bauhaus" (1923), in Benton et al., *Form and Function,* 124.

16. Walter Gropius, *Apollo in the Democracy: The Cultural Obligation of the Architect* (New York: McGraw-Hill, 1968), 148.

17. Robert Hurley, "Introduction to Lyotard," *Telos,* no. 19 (Spring 1974): 126.

18. Thomas Mann, "Tristan" (1903), in *Death in Venice, and Other Stories,* ed. and trans. Jefferson S. Chase (New York: Penguin, 1999), 28.

19. Mann, "Tristan," 22.

20. Paul Valéry comes to remarkably similar conclusions in his study of ceramics. See Paul Valéry, "On the Pre-eminent Dignity of the Arts of Fire," in *Degas, Manet, Morisot,* trans. David Paul (Princeton, N.J.: Princeton University Press, 1989), 169–72. I consider the latter in *Against Affective Formalism,* 232–36.

21. In "The Principle of Cladding" (1898), Loos observed that whatever the "effect he wants to arouse in the observer," it derives from two sources: the "materials used and the form." He would later expand his sources to include the character of the place, "its soil and air" (*OA,* 42, 65).

22. For a critical assessment of the broad architectural foundations of affective formalism around the turn of the last century, see my review of Zeynep Çelik Alexander's *Kinaesthetic Knowing: Aesthetics, Epistemology, Modern Design* in *Art Bulletin* 101, no. 4 (Winter 2019): 154–57.

23. Wassily Kandinsky, "A New Naturalism?," in *Complete Writings on Art,* ed. Kenneth C. Lindsay and Peter Vergo (New York: Da Capo, 1994), 480–82; *Complete Writings on Art* is hereafter cited in text as *WA.*

24. Wassily Kandinsky, "Line and Fish," *Axis* 2 (April 1935): 6.

25. This interpretation is at odds with Lisa Florman's recent account of Kandinsky's late 1920s works, in which she argues that the skeletal armature of *Levels* (a 1929 work closely related to *Each for Himself*) functions to provide "various components, whatever their differences, with a common frame of reference, thereby lending them a degree of commensurability." "Diversification," she asserts, "is accompanied by a pronounced effort not only to integrate those individual heterogeneous elements into the composition as a whole, but also to make evident their interrelatedness." Lisa Florman, *Concerning the Spiritual and the Concrete in Kandinsky's Art* (Stanford, Calif.: Stanford University Press, 2014), 127. Kandinsky's title, *Each for Himself,* stresses the heterogeneity of the elements, the individuated and separable beings, that make up the whole.

26. Kandinsky, "Line and Fish," 6.

27. Neutra, *World and Dwelling,* 33.

28. Graham Harman, *The Quadruple Object* (Winchester, England: Zero Books, 2011), 103.

29. Arnold Schoenberg, *A Schoenberg Reader: Documents of a Life,* ed. Joseph Auner (New Haven, Conn.: Yale University Press, 2008), 89.

30. Again, this puts my account at odds with Florman's Hegelian understanding of Kandinsky's purposes. Hegel, from the opening of his *Lectures on Fine Art,* explicitly in contrast to Kant, construed artworks as separate from and superior to the natural world.

31. Like Kandinsky, new realist philosophers, whatever their aversion to affect theory, maintain a similar bad-faith commitment to affect. New realists reject the idea of viewing objects

through the lens of human subjectivity, but they nonetheless—like Kandinsky—project subjectivity onto everything in the world, thus suggesting that, as Kandinsky puts it, "things bear agency." Once an object becomes a subject, the necessary next step—the one with political consequences—is to either downgrade or deny the existence of the subject that makes that projection. Things bear agency to the precise degree that human agency is found wanting. From my perspective, whether the subjects are particular (as in affect theory) or collective (as in new realism) is beside the point because both Kandinsky and the realists refuse to consider the finite but essential role of the subject in artistic production. As Andrew Cole has observed, the effort of realism may be to "decenter the human, but . . . as a way of *thinking*—it expands the human into all relations." Andrew Cole, "Those Obscure Objects of Desire: The Uses and Abuses of Object-Oriented Ontology and Speculative Realism," *Artforum* 53, no. 10 (Summer 2015), https://www.artforum.com.

32. See Thomas S. Hines, "Then Not Yet 'Cage': The Los Angeles Years, 1912–1938," in *John Cage: Composed in America,* ed. Marjorie Perloff and Charles Junkerman (Chicago: University of Chicago Press, 1994), 65–99.

33. John Cage, "A Composer's Confession" (1948), in *John Cage, Writer: Previously Uncollected Pieces,* ed. Richard Kostelanetz (New York: Limelight, 1993), 31.

34. John Cage, with Daniel Charles, *For the Birds: John Cage in Conversation with Daniel Charles* (Boston: M. Boyars, 1981), 74–75; John Cage, "An Autobiographical Statement" (1989), in *John Cage, Writer,* 239.

35. Cage, *For the Birds,* 220–21.

36. John Cage, "Autobiography," in *Conversing with Cage,* ed. Richard Kostelanetz (New York: Limelight, 1988), 8.

37. I am referring to the basic distinction described by Quentin Meillassoux in *After Finitude: An Essay on the Necessity of Contingency,* trans. Ray Brassier (New York: Continuum, 2008).

38. Douglas Kahn, *Noise, Water, Meat: A History of Voice, Sound, and Aurality in the Arts* (Cambridge: MIT Press, 1999), 161–99.

39. Kandinsky warns of a potential hurdle. If the picture contains figurative elements, then a line can still be understood "as a means of delineating an object." The viewer and the painter must give up the desire to see lines as having "the purpose of indicating an object." Only when they are emancipated from their servitude to objects can lines be experienced "exclusively [in terms of their] purely pictorial significance" (*WA,* 247).

40. Billy Klüver, "Notes for John Cage," quoted in William Fetterman, *John Cage's Theatre Pieces: Notations and Performances* (New York: Routledge, 1996), 136.

41. Wassily Kandinsky, "Questionnaire," *Experiment* 8 (2002): 158.

42. Kandinsky, "Questionnaire," 159.

43. Many of these kinds of studies have been conducted to analyze seemingly interchangeable popular phenomena. See, for instance, Arthur P. Shimamura and Stephen E. Palmer, eds., *Aesthetic Science: Connecting Minds, Brains, and Experience* (Oxford: Oxford University Press, 2012); or Jonah Lehrer, "The Neuroscience of Music," *Wired,* January 19, 2011, https://www.wired.com.

44. Manfredo Tafuri, *The Sphere and the Labyrinth: Avant-Gardes and Architecture from Piranesi to the 1970s,* trans. Pellegrino d'Acierno and Robert Connelly (Cambridge: MIT Press, 1990), 129. Tafuri mistakenly claims that it was with Kandinsky's 1920 program that Gropius's educational ideas began to change, but the "new themes" go back at least to 1914. Tafuri's cri-

tique of the "worn-out populism" of the Berlin avant-garde—including the Crystal Chain, the Arbeitsrat, Novembergruppe, and early Bauhaus—remains stuck within the terms of the same avant-garde. The problem, as Tafuri sees it, is a depoliticized reconciliation of "collectivity and technology," what became, under international constructivism, the *ideology of highly mechanized work*" (131, 148). Here he follows Benjamin's technomedia fetishism, as though technology bears political import of its own accord, a view that, as I am arguing, is indebted to the very claims—to Scheerbart, Taut, and the Bauhaus—that Tafuri putatively aims to reject.

45. Bruno Taut, "A Necessity," in *German Expressionism: Documents from the End of the Wilhelmine Empire to the Rise of National Socialism,* ed. Rose-Carol Washton Long (Berkeley: University of California Press, 1993), 125, 126.

46. Paul Scheerbart, *Glass Architecture,* ed. Dennis Sharp, trans. James Palmes (New York: Praeger, 1972), 41, translation modified.

47. Buckminster Fuller, "Chronofile," in *The Buckminster Fuller Reader,* ed. James Meller (Harmondsworth: Penguin, 1970), 19.

48. Walter Benjamin, "Experience and Poverty" (1933), trans. Rodney Livingstone, in *Selected Writings,* vol. 2, *1927–1934,* ed. Michael W. Jennings, Howard Eiland, and Gary Smith (Cambridge, Mass.: Belknap Press, 1999), 733–34.

49. Benjamin, "Experience and Poverty," 734.

50. Paul Scheerbart, quoted in Wolfgang Pehnt, *Expressionist Architecture,* trans. J. A. Underwood and Edith Küstner (New York: Praeger, 1973), 74. When Herman Muschamp cited the phrase, he noted that "for three years . . . the SS operated its torture chamber in complete secrecy behind [Erich] Mendelsohn's crisp glass facade." Herman Muschamp, "How Buildings Remember" (1989), in *Hearts of the City: The Selected Writings of Herman Muschamp* (New York: Alfred A. Knopf, 2009), 41.

51. Bruno Taut, quoted in Rosemarie Haag Bletter, "Bruno Taut and Paul Scheerbart's Vision: Utopian Aspects of German Expressionist Architecture" (PhD diss., Columbia University, 1973), 218.

52. Adolf Behne, "Gedanken uber Kunst und Zweck, dem Glashause Gewidmet," *Kunstgewerbeblatt* 27, no. 1 (1916): 4, my translation.

53. Adolf Behne, *Die Wiederkehr der Kunst* (Leipzig: Kurt Wolff, 1919), 12, my translation. Behne's reference to "exhibiting, selling and storing away" was an attack on art dealers, specifically Herwarth Walden, whose Jewish ancestry was not lost on the critic.

54. Behne, *Die Wiederkehr der Kunst,* 65, my translation.

55. Detlef Mertins, *Modernity Unbound: Other Histories of Architectural Modernity* (London: Architecture Association, 2011), 17, 91. In an important analysis of Behne's 1920s work, Frederic J. Schwartz acutely observes how for Behne the "mere presence of *sachlich* objects and environments" will "unleash and lead the human subject in an enlightened path." Frederic J. Schwartz, "Form Follows Fetish: Adolf Behne and the Problem of *Sachlichkeit,*" *Oxford Art Journal* 21, no. 2 (1998): 55. According to Schwartz, Behne's project wavered "between the attempt to subordinate objects to social processes and the attempt to 'bring material to life'" (55), but I would argue that the attempt to bring material to life dominated Behne's project. Schwartz believes that Behne's work was "deeply unstable" owing to the insecurity of the "discursive structures" under which he was laboring (72). That is, Behne's position is more expressive of the historical tensions of his moment than of any intentional privileging of object agency. On this account, Schwartz asserts, Behne's problems "were not so much a failure as a faithful mirror of the confusion about the subject of architecture at the time" (75). My position, which I sketch out

here, is that Behne's practice—as well as that of his expressionist and Bauhaus colleagues and associates—was far more consistent with the aims of his generation than Schwartz appreciates. Those aims, I contend, are less "fragmented, incomplete and pulled in various discursive and institutional directions" (74), and far more intentional, than some might wish them to be.

56. Scheerbart, *Glass Architecture*, 67.

57. Erich Baron, "Aufbau," in *The City Crown*, by Bruno Taut, trans. and ed. Matthew Mindrup and Ulrike Altenmüller-Lewis (Burlington, Vt.: Ashgate, 2015), 122.

58. Commentators are quick to disavow Mies's ties to Taut and the Arbeitsrat für Kunst. Richard Pommer, for instance, describes Mies as going "out of his way to demonstrate his distance from the ideals of the *Arbeitsrat* circle" in his early designs for *Frühlicht*. According to Pommer, in the Glass Skyscraper project Mies explicitly eliminated "all the social functions, ecstatic overtones, symbolic forms . . . in order to fix on the steel framework and the play of reflections in the faceted glass. Mies had chosen the most charged symbols as models in order to bring out by contrast his reduction of the building to its structural and material elements." Pommer, "Mies van der Rohe," 103. But as Colin Rowe rightly notes, what is striking about Mies's glass tower is that it carries an "implicit social criticism" precisely where other similar works are "devoid of ideological overtones." Colin Rowe, "Chicago Frame" (1956), in *The Mathematics of the Ideal Villa*, 106.

59. Bruno Taut, *Alpine Architecture*, ed. Dennis Sharp, trans. Shirley Palmer (New York: Praeger, 1972), 123.

60. Taut, *Alpine Architecture*, 126.

61. Taut, "From *YES!—Voices of the Workers Council for Art*," in *Voices of German Expressionism*, ed. Victor H. Miesel (Englewood Cliffs, N.J.: Prentice Hall, 1970), 175.

62. Walter Gropius, quoted in Reginald Isaacs, *Gropius: An Illustrated Biography of the Creator of the Bauhaus* (Boston: Bulfinch, 1991), 64.

63. Baron, "Aufbau," 118, 122. I address Scheerbart's aesthetic of violent purification in "The Meaning of Pain: Paul Scheerbart's *Lesabéndio: An Asteroid Novel*," *Radical Philosophy* 185 (May/June 2014): 64–65.

64. Gropius, quoted in Isaacs, *Gropius*, 64.

65. Taut, *Alpine Architecture*, 125–26. Utopia, Taut believed, could be achieved through work; work could set one free. Rosemarie Bletter describes this idea (without irony) as a kind of "occupational therapy": by averting boredom, work averts war, and work itself is transformed into a "living symbol of peaceful social cooperation." Bletter, "Bruno Taut and Paul Scheerbart's Vision," 436–37. Mertins, commenting on Benjamin's discussion of Sigfried Giedion's aesthetics of labor, writes (in an equally problematic but more theoretical turn of phrase) of "construction— *bauen*— . . . as a kind of direct bodily production of labor, a potentially unmediated, collective physiological event in which dream-consciousness comes to realization as 'traces in thousands of configurations of life.'" Mertins, *Modernity Unbound*, 108.

66. See, for instance, Kai Konstanty Gutschow, "The Culture of Criticism: Adolf Behne and the Development of Modern Architecture in Germany, 1910–1914" (PhD diss., Columbia University, 2005), 225–72. See also Tafuri, *The Sphere and the Labyrinth*, 122–25.

67. Iain Boyd Whyte, ed. and trans., *The Crystal Chain Letters: Architectural Fantasies by Bruno Taut and His Circle* (Cambridge: MIT Press, 1985), 3.

68. Bruno Taut to Max Taut, quoted in Matthew Mindrup and Ulrike Altenmüller-Lewis, "Introduction: Advancing the Reverie of Utopia," in Taut, *The City Crown*, 18.

69. Adolf Behne, "Rebirth of Architecture," in Taut, *The City Crown*, 137.

70. Friedrich Nietzsche, *Thus Spoke Zarathustra: A Book for Everyone and Nobody,* trans. Graham Parkes (Oxford: Oxford University Press, 2005), 43.

71. Nietzsche, *Thus Spoke Zarathustra,* 52.

72. Baron, "Aufbau," 117.

73. Baron, "Aufbau," 122.

74. Bruno Taut, *Modern Architecture* (London: The Studio, 1929), 9.

75. Bruno Taut, statement for the "Exhibition of Unknown Architects" (1919), in *The Architecture of Fantasy: Utopian Building and Planning in Modern Times,* by Ulrich Conrads and Hans G. Sperlich, trans. and ed. by Christiane Crasemann Collins and George R. Collins (New York: Praeger, 1962), 138.

76. Behne, *Die Wiederkehr der Kunst,* 67–68, my translation.

77. Matthew Mindrup addresses this aspect in his introduction to the English edition of *The City Crown*: "The key to the success of the *Kristallhaus* . . . was based upon a faith in *Gemeinschaft* unified by a common spirituality: a fusion of Christianity and socialism that Taut called 'social commitment.'" Mindrup and Altenmüller-Lewis, "Introduction," 18.

78. Taut, *The City Crown,* 83, translation modified.

79. Baron, "Aufbau," 121.

80. Lisbeth Stern, "Stadtkrone," quoted in Mindrup and Altenmüller-Lewis, "Introduction," 21.

81. Walter Gropius, "Program of the State Bauhaus in Weimar," in *Bauhaus: Weimar, Dessau, Berlin, Chicago,* by Hans M. Wingler, ed. Joseph Stein, trans. Wolfgang Jabs and Basil Gilbert (Cambridge: MIT Press, 1978), 31.

82. Baron, "Aufbau," 116.

83. The English-language translation of *Von Material zu Architektur* was László Moholy-Nagy, *The New Vision: Fundamentals of Bauhaus Design, Painting, Sculpture, and Architecture,* trans. Daphne M. Hoffmann (New York: Dover, 2005), 12.

84. Moholy-Nagy, *The New Vision,* 200.

85. Frederic J. Schwartz, "Utopia for Sale: The Bauhaus and Weimar Germany's Consumer Culture," in *Bauhaus Culture: From Weimar to the Cold War,* ed. Kathleen James-Chakraborty (Minneapolis: University of Minnesota Press, 2006), 120.

86. Schwartz, "Utopia for Sale," 131.

87. Sigfried Giedion, *Mechanization Takes Command: A Contribution to Anonymous History* (Oxford: Oxford University Press, 1948), 130, 126, 123.

88. Walter Gropius, "The Development of Modern Industrial Architecture" (1913), in Benton et al., *Form and Function,* 54.

89. Gropius, "The Development of Modern Industrial Architecture," 53.

90. Moholy-Nagy, *The New Vision,* 8.

91. In 2019, MoMA reconceptualized its patterns of exhibition by including more diverse artistic representatives. Unfortunately, the rehang did little to examine the ideological commitments of the artists or the movements on display. So for MoMA, and the professional managerial class, it is progress to include Grete Schütte-Lihotzky's "tiny kitchen" (*Frankfurt Kitchen,* 1926–27), whereas for the less fortunate, the dream of minimum existence—a program of austerity—has become a far from glamorous reality, one that the Bauhaus provided ideological support for. Schütte-Lihotzky, of course, as opposed to the Bauhaus artists, was a serious leftist political actor, imprisoned during World War II for her involvement in the Communist

Party Resistance in Austria. As Peter Chametzky has observed (in conversation), there may be a sliver of cruel irony in the fact that Schütte-Lihotzky's early involvement in the ideology of minimum existence provided not just ideological but perhaps even technological support for her own imprisonment.

92. Gropius, "Sociological Premises," 98.

93. Gropius, "Sociological Premises," 98–99.

94. Gropius, "Sociological Premises," 95–96.

95. Paul Overy, *Light, Air and Openness: Modern Architecture between the Wars* (New York: Thames and Hudson, 2007), 95.

96. Johannes Itten, quoted in Magdalena Droste, *Bauhaus, 1919–1933* (Cologne: Taschen, 2002), 32.

97. "The Masters and Students of the Weimar Bauhaus to Henry Ford, William Randolph Hearst and others," trans. Lyonel Feininger, in *The Bauhaus: Masters and Students by Themselves,* ed. Frank Whitford (Woodstock, N.Y.: Overlook, 1993), 153.

98. Walter Gropius, quoted in Nicholas Fox Weber, *The Bauhaus Group* (New York: Alfred A. Knopf, 2009), 39. Anni Albers—a rare Jew among Bauhaus colleagues—described her Jewishness as "that stone around my neck" and referred to other Jews as having "that dark side." Quoted in Weber, *The Bauhaus Group,* 359.

99. Arnold Schoenberg to Wassily Kandinsky, April 20, 1923, in *Letters,* ed. Erwin Stein, trans. Eithne Wilkins and Ernst Kaiser (Berkeley: University of California Press, 1987), 88.

100. Ise Gropius, quoted in Rebecca Watson, "Growing Up in the Bauhaus," *Financial Times,* April 5, 2019, https://www.ft.com.

101. Moholy-Nagy, *The New Vision,* 30.

102. See, for instance, Elaine S. Hochman, *Architects of Fortune: Mies van der Rohe and the Third Reich* (New York: Weidenfeld & Nicolson, 1989). I do not in the least mean to suggest that Mies's career is reducible to fascism. Unlike others at the Bauhaus, Mies may truly have been a political opportunist. That is, his biological and economic commitments were ultimately less sincere than his aesthetic ones.

103. Ludwig Mies van der Rohe, quoted in Franz Schulze, *Mies van der Rohe: A Critical Biography,* rev. ed. (Chicago: University of Chicago Press, 2012), 153.

104. Adolf Behne, quoted in Winfried Nerdinger, "Bauhaus Architecture in the Third Reich," in James-Chakraborty, *Bauhaus Culture,* 139.

105. R. M. Schindler, "The Radical Looks at His Own House," 1930, n.p., R. M. Schindler Papers, Architecture and Design Collection, Art, Design & Architecture Museum, University of California, Santa Barbara.

106. Meyer's political commitments during his tenure at the Bauhaus are the subject of ongoing debate. For a nuanced picture of Meyer's mixed (or naive) politics, see Eva Forgács, *The Bauhaus Idea and Bauhaus Politics,* trans. John Bátki (Budapest: Central European University Press, 1991), 159–81.

107. Hannes Meyer, quoted in Hideo Tomita, "Hannes Meyer's 'Biological' Concept and Its Loosening Influence on Form," *Journal of Asian Architecture and Building Engineering* 7, no. 2 (2008): 183.

108. Mies to Farenholtz, quoted in Pommer, "Mies van der Rohe," 108.

109. John Willett, *Art and Politics in the Weimar Period: The New Sobriety, 1917–1933* (New York: Pantheon, 1978), 225.

110. Barry Bergdoll, "What Was the Bauhaus?," *New York Times*, April 30, 2019, https://www .nytimes.com.

111. Juliet Koss, "Bauhaus Theater of Human Dolls," *Art Bulletin* 85, no. 4 (December 2003): 728.

112. From the beginning Kandinsky insisted on the diversity of forms and its dissociation from a more stable underlying content. So while there are *"many different, equally valid forms,"* these forms are merely the *"external expression of inner content"* (*WA*, 237).

113. Exceptions can and should be made to this general claim. It is not clear that Paul Klee, for instance, assented to the biological commitments of his colleagues. And as I have also suggested, Mies was less than fully faithful, at least after 1928, to Bauhaus dogma on biology and environment.

114. Gary Indiana, "A Strange Bird: Paul Scheerbart, or The Eccentricities of a Nightingale," in *Glass! Love!! Perpetual Motion!!!: A Paul Scheerbart Reader,* ed. Josiah McElheny and Christine Burgin (Chicago: University of Chicago Press, 2014), 158.

115. Behne, *Die Wiederkehr der Kunst,* 65, my translation.

116. Adolf Behne, "Unknown Architects" (1919), in Washton Long, *German Expressionism,* 202.

117. Behne, "Unknown Architects," 202. Baron quoted Walt Whitman to the same effect: "Were you looking to be held together by lawyers? Or by an agreement on a paper?" He went on to inveigh against "empty parliament formulas, newspaper headlines and book titles." Baron, "Aufbau," 119, 121.

118. Adolf Behne, quoted in Pommer, "Mies van der Rohe," 110.

119. It is as though Lenin's *"Left-Wing" Communism: An Infantile Disorder* of 1920, an attack in part on the German Communist Party's commitment to "no compromise," was written in response to Bauhaus media politics.

120. Walter Gropius, "New Ideas on Architecture" (1919), in *Programs and Manifestoes on 20th-Century Architecture,* ed. Ulrich Conrads (Cambridge: MIT Press, 1971), 46.

121. Walter Gropius, quoted in Forgács, *The Bauhaus Idea,* 19.

122. Gropius, "New Ideas on Architecture," 47. In his first entry in the Glass Chain correspondence—alongside his comrades Gropius and Behne—Taut similarly wrote, "Let us consciously be 'imaginary architects'! Away with individualism. . . . Let us not inquire about the maker's identity but rejoice instead, that in the far distance, independent of us, the idea lives on." Quoted in Forgács, *The Bauhaus Idea,* 21.

123. Mies to Farenholtz, quoted in Pommer, "Mies van der Rohe," 108.

124. Taut, *Modern Architecture,* 171.

125. Walter Benjamin, "Surrealism: The Last Snapshot of the European Intelligentsia," in *Reflections: Essays, Aphorisms, Autobiographical Writings,* ed. Peter Demetz, trans. Edmund Jephcott (New York: Harcourt Brace Jovanovich, 1978), 189.

126. Living in a glass house, Benjamin affirms, is a mode of "moral exhibitionism," one he insists we "badly need." Benjamin, "Surrealism," 180. Benjamin, prescient as always, has had his wish fulfilled: moral exhibitionism might best describe the nature of academic politics today.

127. Benjamin, "Surrealism," 189.

128. It was the scaffolding erected at the Bon Marché, Le Corbusier suggested, that was the inspiration for the scale and shape of his *immeubles-villas.* Le Corbusier, "Pavillon de l'Esprit Nouveau," in *Œuvre complète,* vol. 1, *1910–1929,* ed. Willy Boesiger and Oscar Stonorov (Zurich: Editions Girsberger, 1943), 98.

2. Not Learning from Los Angeles

1. Henry-Russell Hitchcock, "An Eastern Critic Looks at Western Architecture," *California Arts and Architecture*, December 1940, 40.

2. Hitchcock, "An Eastern Critic," 40.

3. Henry-Russell Hitchcock, "Richard J. Neutra," in *Modern Architecture: International Exhibition* (New York: Museum of Modern Art, 1932), 158.

4. Hitchcock, "Richard J. Neutra," 159.

5. Hitchcock, "Richard J. Neutra," 160.

6. Hitchcock, "An Eastern Critic," 41.

7. Hitchcock, "An Eastern Critic," 41.

8. Henry-Russell Hitchcock, preface to Gebhard, *Schindler,* 7.

9. Hitchcock, preface, 8.

10. Talbot Hamlin, "The Trend of American Architecture," *Harper's Magazine,* January 1942, 164–71. Hamlin's comments are excerpted in "Exhibition of California Houses Opens at Museum of Modern Art," press release for *Five California Houses,* Museum of Modern Art, New York, March 17–April 18, 1943, https://www.moma.org.

11. Museum of Modern Art, *What Is Modern Architecture?* (New York: Museum of Modern Art, 1942), 23. The quoted statement appears in the caption to a photograph of John Funk's 1939 Heckendorf House, among the houses most featured in the 1940s at MoMA. The catalog also features Harris's Hawk House and Neutra's VDL House and Bell Experimental School of 1935.

12. David Gebhard, "Architecture in Los Angeles," *Artforum* 2, no. 12 (Summer 1964): 10.

13. Anthony Denzer has done remarkable work on Ain's political commitments. See his "Community Homes: Race, Politics and Architecture in Postwar Los Angeles," *Southern California Quarterly* 87, no. 3 (2005): 269–85; and "Gregory Ain: Under Surveillance," in *Notes from Another Los Angeles: Gregory Ain and the Construction of a Social Landscape,* ed. Anthony Fontenot (Cambridge: MIT Press, 2022), 181–91.

14. "Exhibition of California Houses."

15. Harwell Harris's Hawk House and Gregory Ain's Byler House both appeared in the 1941 MoMA exhibition *The Wooden House in America.*

16. I consider Neutra's turn to an explicit thematics of wood in chapter 5.

17. Elizabeth Mock, ed., *Built in USA: 1932–1944* (New York: Museum of Modern Art, 1944); Elizabeth B. Mock, *If You Want to Build a House* (New York: Museum of Modern Art, 1946).

18. Mock, *Built in USA,* 14.

19. Mock, *Built in USA,* 23, 25.

20. Mock, *Built in USA,* 25. Mock similarly concluded *If You Want to Build a House* by affirming that good design is "not just a matter of personal advantage, but of social responsibility" (93).

21. Mock, *Built in USA,* 25.

22. Sigfried Giedion, *Architecture, You and Me: The Diary of a Development* (Cambridge, Mass.: Harvard University Press, 1958), 125; hereafter cited in text as *YM.*

23. Giedion was not referring to Frank Lloyd Wright's Los Angeles work. Writing of that work, Giedion inimitably described it as "fortress-like seclusion, the expression of an embittered and angry genius opposing a hostile world." Sigfried Giedion, introduction to *Richard Neutra, 1923–50: Buildings and Projects,* ed. Willy Boesiger (1950; rpt., New York: Praeger, 1964), 8.

24. Henry-Russell Hitchcock, in "What Is Happening to Modern Architecture? A Symposium at the Museum of Modern Art," *Bulletin of the Museum of Modern Art* 15, no. 3 (1948): 9.

25. Giedion, introduction, 9.

26. Giedion, introduction, 10. Architects, in Giedion's view, must pass "through the needle's eye of modern art" to authentically express the emotional reality of the current day. To realize their role as the "builders of contemporary life" and not just of functional forms, architects must make contact with the unconscious space conception of modernity. This unconscious reality is directly engaged by artists, specifically by painters. Painting, Giedion insists (following André Breton's claims in the "First Surrealist Manifesto"), is "intimately related to man's direct projection of what flows in the subconscious mind" (*YM*, 127).

27. Giedion, introduction, 10.

28. Giedion, introduction, 10.

29. Giedion, introduction, 9.

30. Giedion, introduction, 10.

31. It would be wrong to suggest, as Reyner Banham does, that Giedion imposed a "Zone of Silence" on expressionist architecture, on work made between 1910 and 1926. Reyner Banham, *Design by Choice*, ed. Penny Sparke (New York: Rizzoli, 1981), 20; hereafter cited in text as *DC*. While it is true that Giedion rarely cited Scheerbart and Taut in his genealogies, he was a crucial figure in legitimating their position. For a discussion of the personal and theoretical relations between Behne (who coined the phrase "human sculpting") and Giedion from a sympathetic perspective, see Detlef Mertins, "Transparencies Yet to Come: Sigfried Giedion and Adolf Behne," *A + U* 10, no. 325 (October 1997): 3–17.

32. Sigfried Giedion, *Space, Time and Architecture: The Growth of a New Tradition* (Cambridge, Mass.: Harvard University Press, 1941), 705.

33. Alfred Barr Jr., in "What Is Happening to Modern Architecture?," 8.

34. Joseph Rosa, *A Constructed View: The Architectural Photography of Julius Shulman* (New York: Rizzoli, 1994), 102.

35. Willett, *Art and Politics in the Weimar Period*, 225.

36. Neutra's FBI file is sixty-nine pages long, and Ain's and his colleague Garrett Eckbo's are both well over two hundred pages. A detailed assessment of those files deserves close analysis in another context. See, above all, Denzer, "Gregory Ain."

37. Reyner Banham, *Los Angeles: The Architecture of Four Ecologies* (New York: Harper & Row, 1971), 238; hereafter cited in text as *LA*.

38. Vincent Scully, *Louis I. Kahn* (New York: George Braziller, 1962), 18–19.

39. Vincent Scully, *Modern Architecture, and Other Essays*, ed. Neil Levine (Princeton, N.J.: Princeton University Press, 2005), 67; hereafter cited in text as *MA*.

40. For a useful survey of the controversies around the plan and architecture, see Vikramaditya Prakash, *Chandigarh's Le Corbusier: The Struggle for Modernity in Postcolonial India* (Seattle: University of Washington Press, 2002).

41. Arthur B. Gallion and Simon Eisner, *The Urban Pattern: City Planning and Design*, 6th ed. (New York: John Wiley, 1993), 548. Both Gallion and Eisner worked at the University of Southern California's School of Architecture.

42. Gallion and Eisner, *The Urban Pattern*, 549.

43. Gallion and Eisner, *The Urban Pattern*, 125.

44. Scully corrected the mistake in the *Perspecta* version of the essay.

45. Mock, *Built in USA*, 22.

46. See Lisa Germany, *Harwell Hamilton Harris* (Austin: University of Texas Press, 1991), 97–105. By 1945 Harris was among the most publicized modern architects working in the United

States, a fact made evident by a string of MoMA publications—*What Is Modern Architecture?*, *Five California Houses, Built in USA, If You Want to Build a House*—and also in George Nelson and Henry Wright's best-selling *Tomorrow's House: A Complete Guide for the Home Builder* (New York: Simon & Schuster, 1945), where Harris's work was featured more than that of any other architect except Edward Durell Stone (with no fewer than fourteen photographs of his work). Nelson and Wright's book was published under the auspices of *Architectural Forum*, which was a major vehicle for Harris's work, featuring it in at least one issue every year beginning in 1935. In 1935 and again in 1940, in feature articles, the magazine's editors declared Harris's first house—the Lowe House—"one of the best houses they had ever seen."

47. The last phrase appears in Scully's related critique of works by Stone, Minoru Yamasaki, and Eero Saarinen (*MA*, 36).

48. [George Nelson], "Fuller's House," *Fortune*, April 1946, 167–72, 174, 176, 179. The Dymaxion house's geodesic-dome framing system was subsequently published with Nelson's guidance in *Architectural Forum* in 1951.

49. Nelson and Wright, *Tomorrow's House*, 206.

50. George Nelson, "The Furniture Industry," *Fortune*, January 1947, 178.

51. George Nelson, quoted in Stanley Abercrombie, *George Nelson: The Design of Modern Design* (Cambridge: MIT Press, 2000), 91.

52. Still the best book on this subject is Ralph Caplan, *The Design of Herman Miller: Pioneered by Eames, Girard, Nelson, Probst, Rohde* (New York: Whitney Library of Design, 1976).

53. George Nelson, in "What Is Happening to Modern Architecture?," 12.

54. Nelson, in "What Is Happening to Modern Architecture?," 13.

55. Fuller was a central figure for the circle around Neutra and the Eameses by the 1930s, well before his discovery by John McHale, Banham, and the Independent Group. Anthony Vidler describes "John McHale's discovery of Richard Buckminster Fuller in 1955 and the full-blown Bucky Fuller revival of the 1960s" in "What Happened to Ecology? John McHale and the Bucky Fuller Revival," *Architectural Design* 80, no. 6 (November/December 2010): 24–33. It is also true that the terms of Fuller's different receptions overlap to a large extent, a point I explore in the Conclusion.

56. See George Nelson, *The Industrial Architecture of Albert Kahn* (New York: Architectural Book Publishing, 1939).

57. George Nelson, "The End of Architecture," in *George Nelson on Design* (New York: Whitney Library of Design, 1979), 35–43. For an important discussion of Nelson's late work, see John Harwood, "The Wound Man: George Nelson and the 'End of Architecture,'" *Grey Room*, no. 31 (Spring 2008): 90–115.

58. As Nelson observed in 1947, the typical producer "has no control over anything or anybody, either the design of his product or its retail price, either the man who sells it or the woman who buys it" (*PD*, 89).

59. See also Nigel Whiteley, "Toward a Throw-Away Culture: Consumerism, 'Style Obsolescence' and Cultural Theory in the 1950s and 1960s," *Oxford Art Journal* 10, no. 2 (1987): 3–27; Abramson, *Obsolescence*, 65–67. What is striking about Abramson's important study is its virtual silence on the question of obsolescence in the United States in the 1950s (Abramson touches on Nelson's article in a two-page section titled "Postwar America").

60. R. Buckminster Fuller, *Education Automation: Freeing the Scholar to Return to His Studies* (1962; repr., Garden City, N.Y.: Anchor Books, 1971), 42. As I argue in my Conclusion, Fuller's "critical consumer" is essential to Banham's account of architecture.

61. Fuller, *Education Automation*, 42, 48.

62. Nelson may have been responding in part to an editorial on obsolescence published by Neutra several years earlier. In "Remedy for Obsolescence—Rational Design," which appeared in the September 1941 issue of *Housing*, Neutra argued that while "bombs dropped from planes" were destructive, the real danger was "sped-up progress and change of many living conditions." Like Nelson, Neutra saw bombs as exemplifying obsolescence; they were "miracles of up-to-dateness." The houses they turned into "junk heaps" were junk before the bombs landed on them. What was needed was "all the vision we can muster" to design a structure over time that would retain its value the way a bomb seamlessly fulfilled its function in a second. The "brains and vision" that went into weaponized obsolescence, that enabled "guns, bombs, and armed speed boats" to destroy their targets and leave nothing behind and so fully retain their value in their use, could be marshaled to produce homes. It was not that Neutra wanted to compete with bombs; rather, he wanted to create something *more lasting* than them. But the problem was the alarming rate of change of industrial society, what Neutra called the *"period of quick obsolescence!"* (10). His aim was to remedy this situation by creating structures that would endure. Nelson's approach was not to remedy obsolescence but to perform it better, faster.

63. George Nelson, "How to Kill People: A Problem of Design," *Industrial Design*, January 1961, 52, 53. See also Harwood, "The Wound Man." Nelson's critique of postwar weaponry focuses on the loss of connection between producer and consumer resulting from the rise of "anti-human values." George Nelson, "People-to-Product Relationship," *Industrial Design*, May 1962, 54. At its lowest point, Nelson's critique of affluent society becomes a parodic and pathetic defense of ruling-class ideology. That he occupied a supremely entitled position is apparent in his reference to the "endless babbling about our standard of living." George Nelson, interview by Studs Terkel, January 16, 1962, Chicago, Studs Terkel Radio Archive, https://studsterkel.wfmt.com. Nelson concluded a 1962 talk delivered in Milan alongside Charles Eames with an account of the military–industrial complex as an example of "production without consumption," a degraded and ironized version of the obsolescent ideal of a perfect match between production and consumption: "He dreams of production without sale, of products without consumers. This beautiful insane dream begins with a full automation factory, and ends with the scrapheap. Do you want to know who will pay? The government. If you think this dream is insane, I would agree, but I must add that we are spending more than forty-five billion dollars this year for products which will soon be destroyed, or will lose their usefulness almost immediately upon completion. Not bad, for an insane dream. This work, which calls itself 'defense-work' is what every industrialist is looking for. It is good work. The profit is assured. The products are beautiful and the feelings aroused are those of patriotism." In the remainder of his bathos-ridden talk, Nelson declaimed "millions and millions of new American homes" whose "symbol of death disguised as life has never been surpassed. Have you ever seen the malls in American cities? They are all the same, all nightmares." George Nelson, "A Milano, promossa da de Padova, una conferenza," *Stile Industria* 40 (December 1962), ix, my translation. Nelson's pessimism is the flip side of his utopian futurism, a duality that reflects the terms presented by Buckminster Fuller in *Utopia or Oblivion: The Prospects for Humanity* (New York: Bantam Books, 1969).

64. George Nelson, "The Office Revolution" (1977), in *George Nelson on Design*, 153–54.

65. George Nelson, "The Future of Packaging" (1968), in *George Nelson on Design*, 133.

66. Buckminster Fuller, quoted in Kenner, *Bucky*, 205.

67. Kenner, *Bucky*, 205.

68. Nelson was responsible for parts 1, 2, 4, and 7 of the Georgia Experiment, and the Eameses

for parts 3, 5, 6, and 8. The Eameses subsequently made parts 3 and 8 into the film *A Communications Primer*, and they used parts 5 and 6 to create the film *Calligraphy* (combining the French film *La Lettre* and an animated sequence by UPA for CBS).

69. This idea, that a moment of transparent communication between subjects is possible, rare though it might be, is a Fullerite fantasy. This idea would abolish communication, dissolving it into something like telepathy, a position that Fuller came to inhabit more and more. Fuller's most elaborate telepathic fantasies emerge in his 1970 introduction to Youngblood's *Expanded Cinema*, 15–35.

70. In 1986, Hugh De Pree, CEO and president of Herman Miller after 1962, reflected back on Nelson's forty-year tenure at the company. What is striking about his reflections is his sense that Nelson was increasingly unable to finish a product, an attitude that mirrors but also differentiates itself from the Eameses' later attitude toward production. Nelson and the Eameses, while close early on, had a falling out sometime in the 1960s and rarely worked together from that point forward. According to De Pree, Nelson "thought so clearly, so easily, so quickly about so many subjects, that it was difficult for him to bring projects to completion. He seemed to lack discipline, especially during the waning years of our relationship. 'He had all the talents,' it has been said, 'but the talent to use them.' . . . Often our agenda would be set aside, and George would express some vision of a solution to our urban blight, or to a political crisis. It was fascinating but frustrating. I once suggested he give up his office and do nothing but write, since that seemed to be the only work he would complete. A long period of silence followed that nearly broke our relationship." Hugh De Pree, *Business as Unusual: The People and Principles at Herman Miller* (Zeeland, Mich.: Herman Miller, 1986), 46.

71. Nelson, *George Nelson on Design*, 177.

3. Between Culture and Biology

1. Richard Neutra, *Life and Shape* (1962; repr., Los Angeles: Atara Press, 2009), 192; hereafter cited in text as *LS*.

2. Every space is "plural," Neutra observes in his unpublished book "Man into Cosmos." This plurality is a product of the fact that "every individual has its own space-world as a complex function of its own nerves and muscles." Richard Neutra, "Man into Cosmos," n.d., h8, Richard and Dion Neutra Papers (LSC 1179), UCLA Library Special Collections, Charles E. Young Research Library, University of California, Los Angeles.

3. Neutra adds that it is the southerner who truly wields the deepest "power of assimilation" (*LS*, 309).

4. R. M. Schindler, "About Lighting" (1926), in Sarnitz, *R. M. Schindler*, 45.

5. R. M. Schindler, "Modern Architecture: A Program" (1912), in Sarnitz, *R. M. Schindler*, 42.

6. The plans were exhibited alongside notable entries by Le Corbusier, Hannes Meyer, and Hans Wittmer.

7. They were on familiar terms throughout the 1930s, and often delivered lectures on modern architecture on shared programs, but there is little to suggest their friendship survived after 1932. Schindler and Neutra met again by chance encounter in 1953, a few months before Schindler died, when they shared a hospital room and briefly renewed their friendship.

8. Richard J. Neutra, "Points of View: Pro," *Southwest Review* 17, no. 3 (Spring 1932): 350–52; R. M. Schindler, "Contra," *Southwest Review* 17, no. 3 (Spring 1932): 353–54. Further citations of the latter essay refer to page numbers in the version reprinted in Sarnitz, *R. M. Schindler*.

9. Schindler, "Modern Architecture," 42.

10. See Karl Kraus, *Werke,* vol. 3 (Munich: Kösel-Verlag, 1965), 341. Schindler, like Kraus, inverted Loos's qualitative distinction between building and art, and while Loos would agree with Schindler's assertion that "ninety-nine percent of all buildings erected cannot be classed as 'architecture,'" Loos would see that as a defense of building against architecture. Schindler, by contrast, affirmed architecture against building. Most buildings, he said, are "as useful as newspaper editorials, which are just as far from being literature." R. M. Schindler, "American Scene," n.d., n.p., R. M. Schindler Papers, Architecture and Design Collection, Art, Design & Architecture Museum, University of California, Santa Barbara. Loos considers the distinction between buildings and art in "Architecture," in *On Architecture,* 73–85.

11. R. M. Schindler, "Church School Lectures," quoted in Sheine, *R. M. Schindler* (2001), 88.

12. R. M. Schindler, "Shelter or Playground" (1926), in Sarnitz, *R. M. Schindler,* 46.

13. Schindler, "Contra," 50.

14. R. M. Schindler, "Deflating the Slogan," n.d., n.p., R. M. Schindler Papers, Architecture and Design Collection, Art, Design & Architecture Museum, University of California, Santa Barbara.

15. Schindler, "Space Architecture," 51; Schindler, "Contra," 50.

16. Schindler, "Modern Architecture," 42.

17. Schindler, "Shelter or Playground," 46.

18. Schindler, "Furniture and the Modern House," 56.

19. Frank Lloyd Wright, "Ausgeführte Bauten und Entwürfe," in *Collected Writings,* 1:107.

20. Schindler, "Modern Architecture," 42.

21. Schindler, "Notes on Architecture (1914–1919)," in Sarnitz, *R. M. Schindler,* 42.

22. Schindler, "Contra," 50.

23. March, "Log House, *Urhutte* and Temple," 106. March's mathematically driven analysis has inspired a series of important essays on Schindler's works by Jin-Ho Park, including "Rudolph M. Schindler: Proportion, Scale and the 'Row,'" *Nexus Network Journal* 5, no. 2 (2003): 65–72; "Space Architecture: Schindler's 1930 Braxton-Shore Project," *Architectural Research Quarterly* 7, no. 1 (2003): 51–62 (with Lionel March); "An Integral Approach to Design Strategies and Construction Systems: R. M. Schindler's 'Schindler Shelters,'" *Journal of Architectural Education* 58, no. 2 (2004): 29–38; "Numerical Properties of Rudolph Michael Schindler's Houses in the Los Angeles Area," *Mathematical Intelligencer* 28, no. 1 (2006): 40–49; "R. M. Schindler's Theory of Space Architecture and Its Theoretical Application to His Space Development of 1945," *Journal of Architecture* 11, no. 1 (2006): 37–54; "The Interplay of Modular Idea and Symmetry in Rudolph M. Schindler's Housing," *Journal of Asian Architecture and Building Engineering* 11, no. 2 (2012): 335–42; "The Underlying Geometry in Rudolph M. Schindler's Packard House" (with Joung-Lan Park); "'House Growing Out of Site': The Case of Rudolph M. Schindler," *Journal of Asian Architecture and Building Engineering* 14, no. 3 (2015): 513–20; and "On Proportional Design and Diagonal Planning in R. M. Schindler's Beach House of 1936/38 for Anna Olga Zacsek," *Journal of Asian Architecture and Building Engineering* 19, no. 2 (2020): 166–75 (with Su-Jung Ji). I address some controversial aspects of Park's account in the last section of this chapter.

24. Elizabeth A. T. Smith, "R. M. Schindler: An Architecture of Invention and Intuition," in Smith and Darling, *The Architecture of R. M. Schindler,* 29.

25. Schindler, "Furniture and the Modern House," 56.

26. See David Gebhard, "Ambiguity in the Work of R. M. Schindler," *Lotus* 5 (1969): 106–21; Esther McCoy, "The Office of R. M. Schindler" (1967), in *EMR,* 102–13; August J. Sarnitz,

"Integrity and Ambiguity," in March and Sheine, *R. M. Schindler*, 76–87; March, "Log House, *Urhutte* and Temple," 106.

27. Schindler, "Contra," 50.

28. Neutra, "Points of View: Pro," 352.

29. Richard Neutra, remarks in William Wurster, Abraham Kaplan, Edgardo Contini, Charles Eames, and Richard J. Neutra, "Converging Forces on Design, Part 1," *Journal of Architectural Education* 12, no. 1 (Fall 1956): 13. As I discuss in chapter 5, Neutra's talk was preceded by one from Charles Eames.

30. The academic literature on Shulman is all but exclusively devoted to questions of consumption, publicity, and lifestyle. In his essay "'Glamourized Houses,'" Simon Niedenthal largely follows this pattern, although his essay contains important observations about the role of photography in Neutra's work. He notes up front that "if Shulman's image has indeed become an object of uncritical devotion, it is not because of the way in which the photograph functions as architectural communication, as an expression of Neutra's design intent; in fact, evidence in the Neutra archives at UCLA suggests that any number of other photographs of the Kaufmann house would be better suited to that task." Simon Niedenthal, "'Glamourized Houses': Neutra, Photography, and the Kaufmann House," *Journal of Architectural Education* 47, no. 2 (November 1993): 101. Niedenthal's subject is not the architect's intent but rather the print afterlife of the famous image. He remarks (unconvincingly) that Shulman's tastes "had less to do with architectural communication" and more to do with romantic lifestyle imagery (106).

31. "Interview with Richard J. Neutra," *Transition* 29 (1967): 31.

32. Richard Neutra, "Restlessness and Tranquil Security," in *Building with Nature* (New York: Universe Books, 1971), 221.

33. In addition, he designed the Adelup and Umatac Schools in Guam in 1952 and produced a range of highly influential designs in and around Los Angeles (including Kester Avenue Elementary School, 1951; Alamitos Intermediate School, 1957; UCLA Kindergarten and Elementary School, 1957; and Palos Verdes High School, 1961) as well as the 1961 Ring Plan School in Lemoore, California. His work on the East Coast included Mellon Hall at St. John's College in Annapolis, Maryland (1958).

34. Richard Neutra, *Mystery and Realities of the Site* (Scarsdale, N.Y.: Morgan and Morgan, 1951), 24.

35. Richard Neutra, *Life and Human Habitat / Mensch und Wohnen* (Stuttgart: Alexander Koch, 1956), 20–21.

36. Neutra, *Mystery and Realities of the Site*, 24.

37. Gebhard, *Schindler*, 75. Gebhard's provocative and groundbreaking analyses of Schindler's work are saturated with Venturi-inspired pronouncements on conflict and contradiction. This largely style-based approach distorts the basic premises of Schindler's architecture, although it did serve to bring Schindler directly into contemporary consciousness in the later 1960s and beyond.

38. Gebhard, *Schindler*, 116.

39. McCoy, "R. M. Schindler," 31. Judith Sheine seems to counter Gebhard's claim when she writes that for Schindler, unlike Loos, "there should be no separation of the interior from the exterior environment." But the latter point is about the internal structure of the work, not its relation to the world around it. Sheine, *R. M. Schindler* (2001), 85.

40. R. M. Schindler, "All Slogans Based on Ideas of Construction Are from Yesterday," n.d.,

n.p., R. M. Schindler Papers, Architecture and Design Collection, Art, Design & Architecture Museum, University of California, Santa Barbara.

41. Schindler, "About Lighting," 45.

42. Schindler, "Furniture and the Modern House," 55.

43. Schindler, "Shelter or Playground," 47. Neutra's last book, published in 1971, is characteristically titled *Building with Nature.*

44. R. M. Schindler, "Reference Frames in Space" (1946), in Sarnitz, *R. M. Schindler,* 59.

45. Schindler, "Reference Frames in Space," 59.

46. Schindler established a 4-foot "reference frame" as early as 1921 and deployed it in virtually every structure he planned or built throughout the rest of his career.

47. Schindler, quoted in Sheine, *R. M. Schindler* (2001), 96.

48. Schindler, "Shelter or Playground," 46. The phrase "simple weave of materials" appears in Schindler, "Furniture and the Modern House," 53.

49. Schindler, "Furniture and the Modern House," 53.

50. Schindler, "Shelter or Playground," 46.

51. Schindler, "Furniture and the Modern House," 56.

52. Schindler, "Furniture and the Modern House," 53.

53. McCoy, "R. M. Schindler," 27.

54. Schindler, "Furniture and the Modern House," 56.

55. Schindler, "Furniture and the Modern House," 56.

56. This is the final line of Schindler's "Space Architecture," 51.

57. Schindler, "Modern Architecture," 42.

58. Here is the quote in full: "Once an architect begins to worry about tying things down and about correct spacings he arrives only at formal harmonies, and these have little to do with living." R. M. Schindler, quoted in Esther McCoy, *Five California Architects* (New York: Praeger, 1960), 173–75.

59. R. M. Schindler, quoted in Sheine, *R. M. Schindler* (2001), 147. Judith Sheine observes eight characteristics of Schindler's plaster-skin work: abstract interlocking volumes devoid of decoration (the 1920s work, by contrast, often included integrated decorative elements); exterior surfaces molded out of one material (typically stucco); minimal light/dark contrast (whereas at the Kings Road and How Houses Schindler played material against material—concrete, for instance, against redwood); numerous corner windows; façades that read as volumes that move in and out, often creating a sense of deep space across them; complex, interlocking shapes formed by stucco volumes, often with thin planes extending from them that turn up or down or go around corners; interior surfaces covered in plaster, with plywood built-in furniture; and interior stucco, plaster, and plywood stained or painted in natural colors like tan, gray, and green (Schindler was largely averse to white walls).

60. McCoy's writings are largely, and blissfully, free of any stylistic bias, and her account of the "cube" here does not rise to a stylistic assertion. McCoy rightly sees this as broader inheritance of Cézannian conceptions of space: "Cézanne's discoveries in space, which were to have an ultimate effect upon architecture." McCoy, "R. M. Schindler," 9. August Sarnitz is surely correct, writing against Gebhard's style-based approach, that it is impossible to ascribe any *specific* architectural style to Schindler's work, be it "De Stijl, Cubism, International Style, and Streamline Modern, or whatever." Sarnitz, *R. M. Schindler,* 24. Nonetheless, as McCoy makes

clear, broad analogies between Schindler's aims and those of modern art are far from beside the point.

61. McCoy, "R. M. Schindler," 28.

62. David Gebhard, "Late Designs 1944–53," in March and Sheine, *R. M. Schindler*, 253.

63. McCoy, *Five California Architects*, 192.

64. Ellen Janson, *Poems* (Hollywood, Calif., 1952), n.p.

65. Gebhard, "Late Designs 1944–53," 254.

66. R. M. Schindler, quoted in McCoy, *Five California Architects*, 191.

67. Sheine, *R. M. Schindler* (2001), 58.

68. McCoy, "Schindler at Work: An Appreciation," in March and Sheine, *R. M. Schindler*, 259.

69. Schindler, "Visual Technique," 67.

70. Sheine, *R. M. Schindler* (2001), 215.

71. Park and Park, "The Underlying Geometry in Rudolph M. Schindler's Packard House," 12. If these authors insinuate the significance of the device, that claim was made explicit in the exhibition *The New Creativity: Man and Machines*, curated by Sylvia Lavin in 2015 at the MAK Center for Art and Architecture. This show exemplified the ubiquitous medium/message claims discussed in chapter 1. The point of the exhibition was to look at creative practices in relation to the "technical complexes that support and constrain them," with a heavy emphasis on the latter. In one display, a Plan Hold drafting machine was placed atop the plans for Schindler's Kallis House, suggesting that the shape of the house was "generated" by the machine. According to the exhibition, Schindler was an early adopter of the idea that works are "produced by systems rather than people." See "Announcements: The New Creativity: Man and Machines," *e-flux*, June 7, 2015, https://www.e-flux.com.

72. Schindler, quoted in Sheine, *R. M. Schindler* (2001), 216.

73. Gebhard, "Late Designs 1944–53," 255.

74. Esther McCoy, "Richard Lechner House: Studio City," unpublished manuscript, n.d., 1, Esther McCoy Papers, 1876–1990, bulk, 1938–89, Box 15, Folder 3: Drafts and Notes, R. M. Schindler, 1950s, Archives of American Art, Smithsonian Institution.

75. R. M. Schindler, "Talk on Architecture" for "Creative Class," June 4, 1938, n.p., R. M. Schindler Papers, Architecture and Design Collection, Art, Design & Architecture Museum, University of California, Santa Barbara.

76. In a 1993 essay, Gebhard describes the Tucker House as being among those of Schindler's works that have "attracted the most comment," a sentiment that can only reflect Gebhard's own early interest in Schindler and his relation to the Intentional Style in the 1960s. Gebhard, "Late Designs 1944–53," 255.

77. Gebhard, "Late Designs 1944–53," 255.

78. Consider too the circular form near the entrance of the Ries House. From an early perspective drawing one can determine this was intended to be a large planter, and while this planter wall was never made, a curved walkway in front roughly follows the lines on the plan. This large sweep was supposed to be doubled inside the house by a fireplace, which also was never built.

79. R. M. Schindler, "The House You Want to Live In," lecture, 1928, n.p., R. M. Schindler Papers, Architecture and Design Collection, Art, Design & Architecture Museum, University of California, Santa Barbara.

4. Richard Neutra's Design Theory

1. *Safe,* directed by Todd Haynes (New York: Sony Pictures Classics, 1995), ellipses in original script. Haynes's point is not about a (classed) neurasthenic culture but about the social fixation on cures; he is, he says, "on the side of the disease and not the cure." In other words, what looks like satire is actually much closer to Neutra's own view than it might at first appear. To be clear, Haynes thinks of disease as a metaphor for the fragility of identity formation, its being threatened on all sides in suburban America, a view that is not that different from Neutra's more literal sense of the effects of the ongoing and subliminal threats of an affluent society on a helpless subject. Todd Haynes, interview by Alison MacLean, *BOMB Magazine,* July 1, 1995, https://bombmagazine.org.

2. Sandy Isenstadt observes the "shift in [Neutra's] justification for characteristic modern forms" from functionalism to one "legitimized on psychological grounds." Isenstadt is perhaps more ambivalent when it comes to Neutra's scientism. He cites Neutra's claim with respect to visual stimuli that "at however minute a level, 'continuous, *smooth and even* distribution of stimuli,'" such as produced by linoleum, smooth walls, flush cabinetry, glass, and views onto natural panoramas "across a surface lead to relaxation," but he leaves it to the reader to evaluate the status of that claim. Sandy Isenstadt, "Richard Neutra and the Psychology of Architectural Consumption," in *Anxious Modernisms: Experimentation in Postwar Architectural Culture,* ed. Sarah Williams Goldhagen and Réjean Legault (Cambridge: MIT Press, 2001), 98, 106. Isenstadt cites J. J. Gibson's notion of "abstract constituents of vision" as support for Neutra's notion that continuous spaces can manage a healthy relay between interior and exterior view.

3. Sándor Ferenczi, *Thalassa: A Theory of Genitality,* trans. Henry Alden Bunker (New York: W. W. Norton, 1968), 18, 26.

4. Otto Rank, inspired by Ferenczi's example, had a profound impact on Neutra's aesthetics. According to Sylvia Lavin, Rank shifted "away from the primacy of the oedipal complex" in Freud and toward "the role of the mother in infantile psychological development." Sylvia Lavin, *Form Follows Libido: Architecture and Richard Neutra in a Psychoanalytic Culture* (Cambridge: MIT Press, 2004), 54. As René Girard argues, Freud and Rank share a philosophical foundation based on individual rather than social psychology. Rank and Freud, Girard observes, "never start out from the relation, but always from the isolated individual." René Girard, "Discussion avec René Girard," *L'Esprit* 429, no. 11 (November 1973): 542. Mikkel Borch-Jacobsen, following Girard, offers a deconstructive account of Rank's *The Trauma of Birth.* For Borch-Jacobsen, there is no primal event of birth, because birth is "not an event at all, since it is the advent of the subject, *before* any event." Mikkel Borch-Jacobsen, *The Freudian Subject,* trans. Catherine Porter (Stanford, Calif.: Stanford University Press, 1988), 277. These are obviously complex matters that cannot be fully addressed here. Suffice it to say that the stakes of a relational model against Neutra's "biological individuality" are relevant to my claims throughout.

5. Ferenczi, *Thalassa,* 45, emphasis in original.

6. I discuss the Gemological Institute's stairwell (while descending the stairs) in the 2019 film *Neutra: Survival through Design,* directed by P. J. Letofsky.

7. Neutra states later in the book that while the "somesthetic" experience of the uterus is multisensorial, it decisively lacks "visual responsiveness" (*SD,* 256). As he puts it in a later essay, "Never are we 'all eye,' as the Impressionists averred" (*NN,* 97).

8. Frank Lloyd Wright, "The Art and Craft of the Machine" (1901), in *Frank Lloyd Wright: Essential Texts,* ed. Robert C. Twombly (Princeton, N.J.: Princeton University Press, 2009), 65–66.

9. Benjamin, "Experience and Poverty," 731.

10. Benjamin, "Experience and Poverty," 733.

11. Benjamin, "Experience and Poverty," 732. I address aspects of Benjamin's politics in "The Meaning of Pain."

12. Richard Neutra, quoted in Lavin, *Form Follows Libido*, 87.

13. In her analysis of Neutra's late work, Lavin considers some of the issues raised by his theory of trauma. She focuses on the implicit and explicit ties between Neutra and the "age of psychoanalysis." Relying on that vague overarching label, she examines Neutra's attempt to create an empathetically oriented architecture. Lavin's broad psychoanalytic brush flattens the various phases of Neutra's practice and blandly affirms Neutra's own commitments to "empathy." In her general description of the difference between psychological architecture and its postwar revision, Lavin fails to provide a specific characterization of the former, merely stating that in it Neutra was focused on "symbolically and programmatically curative building types" (such as asylums and hospitals), while in the second phase he embraced a "new therapeutics that opened the house to a wide array of projections that psychologized an emerging domestic environment." Lavin, *Form Follows Libido*, 47. In other words, for Lavin, architecture is affective *tout court*. More generally, her guiding claim that Neutra's approach has "nothing to do with the discourses on function and structure normally associated with modernism" (50) is unsustainable (a point I consider in chapter 5). Lavin is right to suggest that Neutra's early critics "deflect focus away from his interest in form and its effects" (13), but her embrace of affective fantasies ultimately obscures and authorizes Neutra's most extravagant claims.

14. McCoy, *Vienna to Los Angeles*, 72.

15. Barbara Lamprecht notes of this house that "Neutra managed to dispense with any kind of railing beyond the L-shaped, two-inch-deep reflecting pool lined in dark anodized aluminum that embraces the upper terrace." Barbara Lamprecht, *Richard Neutra: Complete Works*, ed. Peter Gössel (New York: Taschen America, 2000), 436. The same year that Neutra designed the Rice House, Walter Gropius similarly considered the psychosomatic effects of open railings. "Standing high up on a balcony with an open railing, many of us experience a sensation of dizziness. Such dizziness stops immediately, however, when cardboard or paper is hung on that open railing which, giving the eye support, reestablishes our equilibrium through the *illusion* of safety, though of course nothing has been added for greater physical safety." Walter Gropius, *Apollo in the Democracy: The Cultural Obligation of the Architect* (New York: McGraw-Hill, 1968), 149.

16. Douglas Haskell, "Planning Our Plans," *Saturday Review*, February 20, 1954, 15–16.

17. Harris, foreword to McCoy, *Vienna to Los Angeles*, 8–9. Stephen Leet helpfully describes Neutra's turn from a "tempered optimism of the 1930s" to postwar resignation in the face of the "insurmountable obstacles to industrialized building in the United States," a turn that resulted in Neutra's "increasingly critical [view] of the deleterious effects of industrialization generally." Stephen Leet, *Richard Neutra's Miller House* (New York: Princeton Architectural Press, 2004), 172.

18. Richard Neutra to Richard Muetterli, 1931, in Neutra, *Richard Neutra: Promise and Fulfillment*, 190, 221.

19. McCoy, *Vienna to Los Angeles*, 69.

20. Richard Neutra, quoted in Hines, *Richard Neutra*, 93.

21. Neutra, quoted in Hines, *Richard Neutra*, 114. In Neutra's words, "Everything had to double for something else to yield increase and elasticity of use" (*LS*, 267).

22. Richard J. Neutra, "The Changing House," *Los Angeles Times,* June 22, 1947, E6. The caption on the photograph accompanying the article reads "FLEXIBLE."

23. Schindler, "Manifesto," 42.

24. Frank Lloyd Wright, "The Sovereignty of the Individual" (1910), in *Frank Lloyd Wright: Essential Texts,* 119, 128.

25. Vincent Scully, *Frank Lloyd Wright* (New York: George Braziller, 1960), 11.

26. Grace Lewis Miller, quoted in Hines, *Richard Neutra,* 121.

27. Neutra, quoted in Hines, *Richard Neutra,* 178.

28. Victor Margolin, *The Struggle for Utopia: Rodchenko, Lissitzky, Moholy-Nagy, 1917–1946* (Chicago: University of Chicago Press, 1997), 89.

29. Margolin, *The Struggle for Utopia,* 89.

30. Margolin, *The Struggle for Utopia,* 91.

31. Leah Dickerman sees Rodchenko's club as charting "a path between two rationalized poles—between the space of rational efficiency and hyperfunctionality. Much of the club's design in fact aimed at bodily control." Nonetheless, Dickerman imagines the exacerbated space of "media saturation" as producing an "active engagement with information," and she notes that "the games and activities within the club were to promote consciousness, putting ideology into practice." Leah Dickerman, "The Propagandizing of Things," in *Aleksandr Rodchenko* (New York: Harry N. Abrams, 1998), 75–76. My concern is not specifically with the desire to force certain effects on the beholder (although that raises important issues) but rather with the consequences of imagining nonbanal effects as transmitted by material properties.

32. Aleksandr Rodchenko, *Experiments for the Future: Diaries, Essays, Letters, and Other Writings,* ed. Alexander N. Lavrentiev, trans. Jamey Gambrell (New York: Museum of Modern Art, 2005), 128.

33. I address Rodchenko's photographic project in *Red Aesthetics: Rodchenko, Brecht, Eisenstein* (Lanham, Md.: Rowman & Littlefield, 2021), 37–80.

34. Isenstadt, "Richard Neutra," 98.

35. Barbara Lamprecht, *Richard Neutra, 1892–1970: Survival through Design* (Cologne: Taschen, 2004), 43.

36. Leet, *Richard Neutra's Miller House,* 172.

37. Gropius, *Apollo in the Democracy,* 148.

38. Gropius, *Apollo in the Democracy,* 79–80. For a brilliant analysis of this aspect of Bauhaus thought, see Éric Michaud, *Théâtre au Bauhaus (1919–1929)* (Lausanne: Éditions L'Age d'Homme-La Cité, 1978).

39. When Neutra arrived at the Bauhaus in the fall of 1930, he had his students produce competition designs for the Ukrainian state theater at Kharkov; Gropius also submitted a design for the theater. Aryeh Sharon reproduces Neutra's design in *Kibbutz + Bauhaus: An Architect's Way in a New Land* (Stuttgart: Kramer, 1976), 42.

40. Walter Gropius, "Modern Theatre Construction: Regarding the Rebuilding of the Piscator Theater in Berlin," *Drama* 18 (February 1928): 136.

41. Gropius, *Apollo in the Democracy,* 155.

42. Gropius, *Apollo in the Democracy,* 161.

43. Gropius, "Modern Theatre Construction," 136.

44. Gropius, "Modern Theatre Construction," 136.

45. Gropius, *Apollo in the Democracy,* 159.

46. Gropius, *Apollo in the Democracy*, 161.

47. Gropius, *Apollo in the Democracy*, 162.

48. Neutra, quoted in Lavin, *Form Follows Libido*, 56.

49. In *Architecture and Utopia*, Manfredo Tafuri describes the participatory turn in design thinking as masking coercion. Tafuri suggests that with the rise of "'open' space" architecture, wherein the user is "summoned to complete . . . the process," the subjective capacity to choose is reduced to a play of limited and preformed decisions. The new "open" forms offer a perfunctory image of freedom drained of alternatives beyond the delimited ones that are granted to the user to move a wall or shift furniture between two or three functions. "Architecture," Tafuri writes, "summoned the public to participate in its [completed] work of design." Design under the Bauhaus, he maintains, functioned as a means to control user response through participation. On this account, plastic spaces open to participatory exchange were formal equivalents of a form of subjectivity unable to conceive a difference between predigested choices and autonomous decisions. And yet Tafuri is as skeptical as Neutra in his attitude toward architectural agency. Neither of them can conceive a mode of practice that thinks through the unity of architect, material, and inhabitant in a way that imagines the work as expressive of architectural intention, but also one that understands the limits of control. Manfredo Tafuri, *Architecture and Utopia: Design and Capitalist Development*, trans. Barbara Luigia La Penta (Cambridge: MIT Press, 1976), 101. Despite his critical remarks on open planning, Tafuri goes on to offer a positive evaluation of Le Corbusier's ideal of "total involvement" by the public in the Obus plan for Algiers. For Tafuri, "maximum flexibility, interchangeableness, and accommodation to rapid consumption" take on a completely different cast in Le Corbusier's hands than they do within the Bauhaus (131).

50. Neutra, *Richard Neutra: Promise and Fulfillment*, 189. Neutra also reflected on his Bauhaus experience in "The Profession as Cooperation" (*NN*, 176–80).

51. Neutra, quoted in Hines, *Richard Neutra*, 95.

52. Neutra, *Richard Neutra: Promise and Fulfillment*, 190.

5. Functionalism with a Vengeance

1. For a useful survey of Soriano's career, see Wolfgang Wagener, *Raphael Soriano* (London: Phaidon, 2002).

2. Sarnoff Mednick, quoted in Serraino, *The Creative Architect*, 199.

3. Raphael Soriano, interview in Heyer, *Architects on Architecture*, 132, 131.

4. Here I am taking up my argument about Loosian normativity from chapter 1.

5. I have yet to describe Neutra's attitude toward historical associations, a complex topic that I address in what follows.

6. Soriano, interview in *Architects on Architecture*, 131.

7. Raymond Neutra has confirmed Soriano's account, although he suggests that he spoke with Soriano during a personal visit, not at a lecture. "What I meant was that after a time my father stopped experimenting with new industrial structures, while Raphael continued with steel and aluminum frames and their esthetic possibilities. My father settled into conventional timber frames and became more interested in calming conscious experiences, and unconscious impacts of his works." Raymond Neutra, email correspondence with author, March 8, 2017.

8. Soriano describes their different approaches to the module. For Neutra, the module is largely a matter of the wall, whereas for Soriano, the whole space is designed according to the module. Soriano explains that Neutra's plans are not modular in the "way I considered the modules, you see. Because I plan a precise strict module like a fugue of Bach. . . . But if you look at

the plans of Neutra. . . . They are totally different than mine. In that respect, I said I did my own innovations" (*SF*, 107).

9. G. H. Beale to Jan Lapp, July 17, 1981, quoted in Jan Lapp, *Beyond the Gene: Cytoplasmic Inheritance and the Struggle for Authority in Genetics* (Oxford: Oxford University Press, 1987), 105.

10. Lapp, *Beyond the Gene*, 157.

11. Lapp, *Beyond the Gene*, xiii. Neutra could not comment in *Survival through Design* on the discovery of DNA by James Watson and Francis Crick, as they did not publish their findings until 1953, but he does address the matter at length in later writings.

12. Tracy Sonneborn, quoted in Lapp, *Beyond the Gene*, 93.

13. Sonnborn, quoted in Lapp, *Beyond the Gene*, 92.

14. Lapp, *Beyond the Gene*, 174.

15. Sonneborn, quoted in Lapp, *Beyond the Gene*, 174.

16. Emil du Bois-Reymond, quoted in John Theodore Merz, *European Scientific Thought in the Nineteenth Century*, vol. 2 (1912; repr., New York: Dover, 1965), 478.

17. Neutra found evidence for his account of prenatal influence in Davenport Hooker's 1953 study *The Prenatal Origin of Behavior* (Lawrence: University of Kansas Press, 1953), an early attempt at genetic neurology. Neutra's copy of the book remains in the library of the VDL Research House.

18. Neutra, *Life and Human Habitat*, 20.

19. Neutra, "The Senses and the Setting," 8.

20. Cara Greenberg, *Mid-century Modern: Furniture of the 1950s* (London: Thames and Hudson, 1984).

21. Drexler and Hines, *The Architecture of Richard Neutra*, 48.

22. Drexler and Hines, *The Architecture of Richard Neutra*, 56.

23. Drexler and Hines, *The Architecture of Richard Neutra*, 21.

24. Drexler mentions one school, Palos Verdes High School of 1961, but only to flag the structure's "overtly regional and 'historical'" character, one that "anticipated the renewal of interest in historical allusion." Drexler and Hines, *The Architecture of Richard Neutra*, 112. Drexler relates it to the California missions and to farm buildings.

25. Drexler and Hines, *The Architecture of Richard Neutra*, 21.

26. See Sibyl Moholy-Nagy, review of *Survival through Design*, by Richard Neutra, *College Art Journal* 13, no. 4 (Summer 1954): 329–31.

27. With further research, Neutra believed, knowledge would emerge about how "design affects ever-greater portions of the innermost human being," which would inevitably show how "responsibilities begin to loom before us" (*SD*, 318).

28. Richard Neutra, "Architecture Conditioned by Engineering and Industry," *Architectural Record* 66, no. 3 (September 1929): 272.

29. Gregory Ain, interview by Thomas S. Hines, 1977, Thomas S. Hines Interviews Regarding Richard J. Neutra, 1972–1980, Series II, Box 2, Getty Research Institute.

30. Neutra, "Mural Conceptualism," 94.

31. Fuller, *Nine Chains to the Moon*, 41, 42, 348, 359. Along these lines Fuller writes of the architect doing the "best he could with the materials . . . for he did the most with the least out of the available materials and tool" (60).

32. This is not to say that the Eameses were strict in their attachment to structural expression; they were not. In CSH 9, the neighboring Entenza House, a collaboration between Saarinen

and the Eameses, the "structure is not expressed; walls are plastered, ceilings are covered with wood" (*EMR*, 172).

33. Richard Neutra, "Aesthetics and the Open Air," *The Studio* 99, no. 443 (1930): 80.

34. Richard Neutra, quoted in Hines, *Richard Neutra*, 101.

35. Jehane Burns Kuhn, "Eames Office Oral Histories: 'The Solution Is a Diagram of the Problem,'" interviews by Eames Demetrious, 1988–90, YouTube, https://www.youtube.com; Eames, Norton Lecture no. 5.

36. Kevin Roche, interview in Heyer, *Architects on Architecture*, 352.

37. Louis H. Sullivan, *Kindergarten Chats, and Other Writings* (New York: Wittenborn, 1976), 164.

38. Richard Neutra, remarks in Wurster et al., "Converging Forces on Design, Part 1," 15.

39. Neutra, remarks in Wurster et al., "Converging Forces on Design, Part 1," 15.

40. Charles raised the issue of the conflation of science and technology also in his criticism of Banham, a topic I address in my Conclusion.

41. See Roger J. Williams, *Biochemical Individuality: The Basis for the Genetotrophic Concept* (New York: John Wiley, 1963); *Free and Unequal: The Biological Basis of Individual Liberty* (New York: John Wiley, 1964); and *You Are Extraordinary* (New York: Random House, 1967). Neutra first referred to Williams's work in 1955.

42. Charles Eames, remarks in Wurster et al., "Converging Forces on Design, Part 1," 11.

43. Charles Eames, quoted in Dorothy Townsend, "Designer, Choreographer Discuss Creativity in Arts," *Los Angeles Times*, April 8, 1963, V1.

6. Burn after Use

1. *A Communications Primer*, directed by Ray and Charles Eames (1953), 2:10–2:20.

2. *A Communications Primer*, 3:10–3:31.

3. *A Communications Primer*, 4:16–4:36.

4. As Norbert Wiener remarked in 1954, "clichés" are "inherent in the nature of information." Literature and art "must say something substantially different from the community's previous common stock of information." Picasso is celebrated for his "destructive influence" on his contemporaries and successors. Norbert Wiener, *The Human Use of Human Beings: Cybernetics and Society*, rev. ed. (New York: Avon, 1967), 163. It is hard to overestimate the impact of Wiener's book on the Eameses' practice. I address the issue in a forthcoming essay on the Eameses and Wiener.

5. Justus Nieland, "Postindustrial Studio Lifestyle: The Eameses in the Environment of 901," in *In the Studio: Visual Creation and Its Material Environments*, ed. Brian R. Jacobson (Berkeley: University of California Press, 2020), 176. No doubt it is true that the members of the Eames Office were involved in a postindustrial (better, deindustrial) fantasy of production, their works inserted into and abetting the new world of "flexible networks of distribution and their traffic flows," as Nieland puts it (180), but it is also the case that the increasing flow of information rarely made its way into mass production, and, more significantly, this flow of information was *designed* to delay or forestall any such potential application. Nieland's analysis of the distribution and movement of information at the Eames Office and in the wider postwar U.S. culture in *Happiness by Design: Modernism and Media in the Eames Era* (Minneapolis: University of Minnesota Press, 2020) provides an important background to my argument. In a sense, Nieland's emphasis on the wide-ranging entanglements of the Eameses in a culture devoted to the production and consumption of "happiness" is the necessary reverse of my contention that the "fail-

ures" to realize that ideal are written into the project from the beginning. Nieland grasps that the Eameses are "anxious about human production in the unhappy shadow of catastrophe," but that anxiety is also the source of their commitment to the model and to a sustaining, if fraught, approach to (non)production. Nieland, *Happiness by Design,* 123.

6. *A Communications Primer,* 20:42–21:30.

7. Eames, quoted in Townsend, "Designer, Choreographer Discuss Creativity," V1.

8. Eames, remarks in Wurster et al., "Converging Forces on Design, Part 1," 11.

9. Ralph Caplan points to this quality when he describes the Eameses' "active involvement all the way: initiating design and taking responsibility for it in all the messy situations of distribution and use that can never be recorded in the visual presentations." Ralph Caplan, *By Design,* 2nd ed. (New York: Fairchild, 2005), 200.

10. The thematics of the intertwinement of production and consumption is brilliantly explored in the early work of Walter Benn Michaels. See Michaels, "Introduction: The Writer's Mark," in *The Gold Standard and the Logic of Naturalism: American Literature at the Turn of the Century* (Berkeley: University of California Press, 1987), 1–28.

11. Eames, oral history interview, July 28–August 20, 1980.

12. George Nelson picks up this thought when he describes how "an architect has a relatively limited time to solve a very complex set of problems, and when he has done so his design is picked up by a motley crew of masons, plumbers, carpenters and others who then proceed to execute it in a thoroughly unpredictable fashion" (*PD,* 147). The Eameses and Nelson could find support in an unlikely place: Geoffrey Scott's *The Architecture of Humanism: A Study in the History of Taste* (New York: Houghton Mifflin, 1914). Scott offers a similar picture of the noise that haunts architectural realization: "Architecture is the art of organizing a mob of craftsmen. This, the original meaning of the word, expresses an essential fact. You can pass, in poetry, at a leap from Pope to Blake, for the sleepiest printer can set up the most original remarks. But the conceptions of an architect must be worked out by other hands and other minds than his own. Consequently, the changes of style in architecture must keep pace with the technical progress of the crafts. And if, at the bidding of a romantic fashion, an abrupt change of style be attempted, then the technique and organization required by the new ideal must not be more exacting than those employed by the existent art. For neither technique nor organization can be called into being suddenly and at will" (42).

13. Henry van de Velde, "Chapter on the Design and Construction of Modern Furniture" (1897), in Benton et al., *Form and Function,* 18. Richard Rogers, inspired in part by the Eameses' example, had a different response to the "impossibility" of the "client–contractor relationship." Looking back on the first Team 4 houses, Rogers took a skeptical view of the desire for control: "The fact that by the time we completed the house either the wife had taken another husband, who didn't like us or the house, or they had another child, or the guy was single by then, and whatever happened it was always changing. And whatever happened the one thing that was clear was that we couldn't start an addition to our building [because] no one would pay for it, because we couldn't keep up with the changes of the program." Richard Rogers, lecture, Los Angeles, January 1, 1977, SCI-Arc Channel, https://channel.sciarc.edu/browse/richard-rogers-1977. Rogers's solution to keeping up with the changes—divorce for Rogers functions like noise for the Eameses—was to make everything an expression of change, to build flexibility into the very fiber of the structure. Of course, this was not to give up on control any more than the Eameses or Neutra did, but instead to ride the tides of change. As Deyan Sudjic rightly observes, Team 4's Reliance Controls Factory (1967) is "closer to Charles Eames or Craig Ellwood in its spirit than

to Mies van der Rohe." Sudjic adds that on a visit to Los Angeles in the early 1960s (inspired by James Stirling's previous visit), Norman Foster of Team 4 "discovered . . . Craig Ellwood and Charles Eames[,] who were to inform two key Team 4 projects: the house in Cornwall and the Reliance Controls factory." Deyan Sudjic, *The Architecture of Richard Rogers* (New York: Harry N. Abrams, 1995), 21, 40.

14. The Eameses' stated aim in *The India Report* was to set up a school that would "resist the rapid deterioration of consumer goods" within contemporary Indian culture (*EA*, 176). It is unclear how significant the setting was, given that they made the same claim about American consumer goods. The Eameses insisted on the autonomy of the newly proposed design school in order to "protect the objective from dilution and the method from deterioration" (*EA*, 182). The charged language of purity and dilution reiterates their basic concern with the survival of the idea in contexts of potential misuse by audiences.

15. John Entenza, "Case Study House for 1949 Designed by Charles Eames," *Arts and Architecture*, December 1949, 27.

16. Esther McCoy, "An Affection for Objects," *Progressive Architecture*, August 1973, 65.

17. *A Report by the Office of Charles and Ray Eames on the IBM Exhibition Center*, directed by Charles and Ray Eames, 1979.

18. Charles bluntly asserts that "the values are to be questioned, particularly those things having to do with physical stuff" (*EA*, 271). This is not exactly a "bad picture" of intent, as discussed in the Introduction. Charles does not separate intent and realization; rather, there is the work and there is "physical stuff." Once that "physical stuff" gets taken up into the work, it is no longer mere stuff.

19. This is the kind of experience the Eameses hoped to provide to anyone who visited their house or office. The role of the host is to "anticipate the needs of his guests," and following that logic, with the house they designed for themselves, they could play host to themselves (*EA*, 314).

20. Jean-Paul Sartre, *Existentialism Is a Humanism*, in *Existentialism from Dostoevsky to Sartre*, ed. Walter Kaufmann (New York: Meridian, 1956), 289.

21. Abraham Kaplan, "Lecture Three: Existentialism," in *The New World of Philosophy* (New York: Vintage Books, 1963), 107–8, 109. A professor of philosophy at UCLA (and one of Stanley Cavell's teachers), Kaplan collaborated with the Eameses on several projects.

22. William Whyte, in his popular study *The Organization Man*, laments the "bewildering multiplicity of choices [one has] to make. In making them, furthermore, [we] have less and less tradition to lean on." William H. Whyte Jr., *The Organization Man* (New York: Simon & Schuster, 1956), 314.

23. See Claudia Goldin and Robert A. Margo, "The Great Compression: The Wage Structure in the United States at Mid-century," *Quarterly Journal of Economics* 107, no. 1 (February 1992): 1–34.

24. Eames, interview by Terkel.

25. Eames, Norton Lecture no. 5; and Charles Eames, "I Care," overview of Norton Lectures, 1970, n.p., Work of Charles and Ray Eames, Manuscript Division, Library of Congress.

26. R. Buckminster Fuller, *Untitled Epic Poem on the History of Industrialization* (New York: Simon & Schuster, 1962), 208–9.

27. R. Buckminster Fuller, *Operating Manual for Spaceship Earth* (New York: Dutton, 1971), 56.

28. Fuller, *Utopia or Oblivion*, 109.

29. *An Eames Celebration*.

30. Office of Charles and Ray Eames, *The World of Franklin and Jefferson* (New York: Metropolitan Museum of Art, 1975), 31.

31. Elmer Bernstein described working with the Eameses as a "sort of unending agenda." Quoted in Eames Demetrios, *An Eames Primer*, updated ed. (New York: Universe, 2013), 213.

32. Ray Eames, quoted in Nieland, *Happiness by Design*, 61.

33. Charles Eames, letter to CBS executive, n.d., Part II, Box 173, Folder: "Omnibus," Work of Charles and Ray Eames, Manuscript Division, Library of Congress.

34. Charles developed an interest in Leonardo early, after reading Dmitry Sergeyevich Merezhkovsky's novel *The Romance of Leonardo da Vinci* (1900). He viewed Leonardo as emblematic of someone who was "completely involved in any subject he attacked" (*EA*, 206): "When we think of great imagination and farreaching perspective combined with infinite patience and attention to detail, we think of Leonardo Da Vinci." Charles notably describes Leonardo's achievement as "always beginning new projects, leaving others unfinished" (*EA*, 144).

35. Charles Eames, notes for *Omnibus* appearance, May 1956, 2, Part II, Box 173, Folder: "Omnibus," Work of Charles and Ray Eames, Manuscript Division, Library of Congress.

36. Eames, remarks in Wurster et al., "Converging Forces on Design, Part 1," 15.

37. Charles's notes indicate that a short film called *Toys, Other Designs* was to be played as he spoke (this has been lost, but the film included aspects of *Parade, or Here They Come Down Our Street* of 1952).

38. In a talk delivered at the National Film Theater for the British Film Institute in November 1975, Eames categorized *Blacktop* and *Toy Trains* as "Celebration" films.

39. Charles Eames, Norton Lecture no. 3, January 14, 1971, audio recording, Work of Charles and Ray Eames, Manuscript Division, Library of Congress.

40. Charles Eames, notes for an international design conference, 1978, Folder: "International Design Conference Notes," Work of Charles and Ray Eames, Manuscript Division, Library of Congress.

41. In a very different context, but, I argue, with a similar set of aims is the work of Aleksandr Rodchenko. See my *Red Aesthetics*, 37–80. On the identity of production and consumption, see also Michael Szalay, *New Deal Modernism: American Literature and the Invention of the Welfare State* (Durham, N.C.: Duke University Press, 2000), 67–69.

42. Deborah Sussman to Claes Oldenburg, April 27, 1966. It appears the Eameses made a slide show of Oldenburg works, but the show no longer exists. Charles photographed the set of Oldenburg's *Autobodys* in 1963. My thanks to Kelsey Williams at the Eames Office, who discovered this letter.

43. Eames, quoted in Townsend, "Designer, Choreographer Discuss Creativity," V8.

44. Eames, oral history interview, July 28–August 20, 1980.

45. *Something about Photography*, directed by Charles and Ray Eames, 1976.

46. This term recurs frequently in the Eameses' work (see, for example, *EA*, 106, 121, 163, 165, 349, 361).

47. Charles Eames, untitled note, n.d., but written after 1972, Work of Charles and Ray Eames, Manuscript Division, Library of Congress. The serious deciders in question are Claes Oldenburg, Pablo Picasso, Pliny, and Trajan.

48. Burns Kuhn, "Eames Office Oral Histories."

49. Eames, "Film as a Modeling Device," 1.

50. The title of this work is likely drawn from E. E. Cummings's "Listen my children and you," from *Is 5*, which tells of the "true story of Mr Do-nothing." Charles's provisional title

"I Care" for the Norton Lectures was likely drawn from Cummings's "Voices to voices, lip to lip" from this same collection. Cummings declares "who cares"—a point he is making about the relation between art and science. The Eameses, of course, cared very much about this relation. See E. E. Cummings, *A Selection of Poems* (New York: Harcourt, 1963), 64.

51. Eames, notes for *Omnibus* appearance, 3. This is what Charles frequently calls "this-is-how-it-should-be-ness," the material expression of the ideal of "unselfconsciousness" (*EA*, 317).

52. Charles Eames, talk for the American Association of Museums, Los Angeles, June 1975, 2, Box 217, Work of Charles and Ray Eames, Manuscript Division, Library of Congress.

53. Etsu Farfias, quoted in Demetrios, *An Eames Primer*, 228. Again, this is not a literal claim, as the "as though" signals.

54. Charles Eames, Norton Lecture no. 6, April 26, 1971, audio recording, Work of Charles and Ray Eames, Manuscript Division, Library of Congress.

55. Fuller, introduction to Youngblood, *Expanded Cinema*, 24.

56. In his 1949 Yale lectures, Eliot Noyes emphasized the necessity of working "without decided intent," a theme he elaborated on in his 1949 *Modern Design* exhibition at the Yale University Art Gallery, where a wall label read, "Inappropriate form is often deliberate." Quoted in Gordon Bruce, *Eliot Noyes: A Pioneer of Design and Architecture in the Age of American Modernism* (London: Phaidon, 2006), 94, 92. Noyes, it seems, did not fear production in the way the Eameses did. So-called good design was Noyes's ideal from beginning to end.

57. Mike Sullivan of IBM described how Charles could "sense . . . immediately" if someone was "role-playing." Quoted in Demetrios, *An Eames Primer*, 125.

58. Eames, Norton Lecture no. 6.

59. John Dewey, *Art as Experience* (1934; repr., New York: Penguin, 2005), 71.

60. Parke Meek, quoted in Demetrios, *An Eames Primer*, 152.

61. For a detailed account of Cage's German performances, see Amy C. Beal, "The Army, the Airwaves, and the Avant-Garde: American Classical Music in Postwar West Germany," *American Music* 21, no. 4 (Winter 2003): 474–513.

62. Charles Eames, quoted in Demetrios, *An Eames Primer*, 129.

63. For an important against-the-grain account of Cage as an artist who took up precisely the kinds of intentional issues raised by the Eameses, see Dani Follett, "Error, Intention, Contingency, Cage," *nonsite.org*, no. 32 (September 10, 2020), https://nonsite.org.

64. Charles Eames, in *An Eames Celebration*.

65. Demetrios, *An Eames Primer*, 227.

66. Charles made the same point in his Norton Lectures. See Charles Eames, Norton Lecture no. 4, March 15, 1971, audio recording, Work of Charles and Ray Eames, Manuscript Division, Library of Congress.

67. From very early on the Eameses conceived of tools as the idealized results of unselfconscious production. "From tools [students] learn vital lessons in 'fitness to need,' balance, and relation of form to the human scale" (*EA*, 23).

68. Several of the Eameses' films feature tools as their subject. Their film montages for Billy Wilder's *The Spirit of St. Louis* (1957), their film *Before the Fair* (1962), and the tool sequences in *House of Science* (1962) and *Think*, not to mention the series of computer films that figure the computer as a kind of supertool, point to the centrality of tools in their aesthetic imagination.

69. Caplan, "Making Connections," 39.

70. "The familiarity with tools and the experience of designing tools for specific purposes play a great part in our attitude toward any problem we approach" (*EA*, 149).

71. Eames, Norton Lecture no. 4.

72. *The Information Machine,* directed by Charles and Ray Eames, 1957.

73. The narrator is Vic Perrin, best known for providing the "control voice" for the 1963–65 science fiction television series *The Outer Limits.*

74. This picture is entirely compatible with Neutra's vision of the artist-architect as a super-sensitive predictive instrument. Taking a dig at architects (like the Eameses) who are backed by corporate foundations, Neutra describes the architect as an empathetic "clinician," one who is able to "make a more accurate architectural prediction for a life" placed in his hands (*LS,* 65). Although Neutra typically rejects computers, he does fantasize about the possibility of "feeding equations into an electronic computer" with a "multitude of variable parameters in the field of endocrine biochemistry" (*LS,* 316). But far more often he sees computers as inhuman number-crunching devices inimical to survival. Thus, it is the "lonely individual in the mass of linked contributors" who is held down by the "mathematically composed computers" that breed dissatisfaction (*LS,* 366).

75. Hugh Kenner muses how the "computer simulates thought when thought has been defined in a computer's way." Kenner, *The Counterfeiters,* 26. He would have rightly construed *The Information Machine* as satire.

Conclusion

1. For a discussion of Banham's antimonumentalism, see George Baird, *The Space of Appearance* (Cambridge: MIT Press, 1995), 155.

2. By the early 1960s, Banham was embracing notions of "expendability" alongside the "throwaway." For a useful survey of the moment, one that encompasses the work of Deborah Allen and Jane Thompson at *Industrial Design* magazine, see Alice Twemlow, *Sifting the Trash: A History of Design Criticism* (Cambridge: MIT Press, 2017), 19–89.

3. Reyner Banham, "Propositions," *Architectural Review* 127, no. 760 (June 1960): 382.

4. Reyner Banham, quoted in Nigel Whiteley, *Reyner Banham: Historian of the Immediate Future* (Cambridge: MIT Press, 2002), 147, 148. Banham is responsible for bringing Scheerbart into mainstream architectural discourse with an article on him in 1959.

5. Banham, quoted in Whiteley, *Reyner Banham,* 154.

6. Reyner Banham, *Theory and Design in the First Machine Age,* 2nd ed. (Cambridge: MIT Press, 1980), 142; hereafter cited in text as *TD.*

7. Alongside Moholy-Nagy, Whiteley rightly sees *"Bauhausler* Hannes Meyer" as "tailor-made to fit with Banham's theory of a Machine Age *architecture autre,"* even if Banham does not cite his work. Whiteley, *Reyner Banham,* 161.

8. Reyner Banham, "The Dymaxicrat" (1963), in *A Critic Writes: Essays by Reyner Banham,* selected by Mary Banham, Paul Barker, Sutherland Lyall, and Cedric Price (Berkeley: University of California Press, 1996), 93.

9. H. de C. Hastings, "Propositions," *Architectural Review* 127, no. 760 (June 1960): 387.

10. Eames, remarks in Wurster et al., "Converging Forces on Design, Part 1," 15.

11. *The Black Ships,* directed by Charles and Ray Eames, 1970.

12. Cedric Price, "Activity and Change," *Archigram* 2 (1962): n.p. On the question of the throwaway and expendability there was widespread consensus among avant-garde circles in Europe. Team X, Yona Friedman, Constant Nieuwenhuys's New Babylon, and Jean Baudrillard's Utopie all demonstrated a commitment to the primacy of performance.

13. Banham's vision of expendable architecture was shared by his colleague at the *Architectural Review* John McHale, a devoted disciple of Fuller. For an important series of discussions on this topic, see John McHale, *The Expendable Reader: Articles on Art, Architecture, Design, and Media (1951–79)*, ed. Alex Kitnick (New York: Columbia University Press, 2011).

14. Reyner Banham, "Schindler's Architecture—Thick and Thin," 1979, audio recording, Friends of the Schindler House Lecture Series, Architecture and Design Collection, Art, Design & Architecture Museum, University of California, Santa Barbara.

15. For a detailed engagement with this book, see Todd Gannon, *Reyner Banham and the Paradoxes of High Tech* (Los Angeles: Getty Research Institute, 2017), 89–118. Gannon closely tracks the changes in Banham's approach between the earlier (and more well-known) writings and the later work. As in the case of the Bauhaus and related figures, I am less persuaded of the weight of those differences and more by the high level of consistency in the commitment to biology-driven performance.

16. Reyner Banham, *The Architecture of the Well-Tempered Environment*, 2nd ed. (Chicago: University of Chicago Press, 1984), 171–94.

17. Banham, *The Architecture of the Well-Tempered Environment*, 190.

18. Fuller, *Education Automation*, 45.

19. Alison and Peter Smithson, "The New Brutalism," *Architectural Design* 27 (April 1957): 113.

20. Banham, *The Architecture of the Well-Tempered Environment*, 194.

21. Whiteley, *Reyner Banham*, 25. Whiteley sees Banham's politics as in line with the sentiments Harold Wilson expressed in his famous "white heat" speech, when he declared that Britain was "going to be forged in the white heat of this [scientific] revolution" (25, 179). As Whiteley clarifies in the aptly titled chapter "The Anti-establishmentarian and Class," for Banham, class is a matter of identity, not economics.

22. Whiteley, *Reyner Banham*, 380.

23. Like Nelson, Banham sees Fuller as the most original thinker on the theme of "the shelter-needs of mankind" (*DC*, 52). But Banham laments that Fuller's structures are being used "as alibis for fancy formalisms," that Fuller interiors are fast becoming places for "free and untrammeled exercises in architectural sensibility." Banham cites Mies's theater project in an air hangar as demonstrating this aesthetic misuse of engineering (*DC*, 53).

24. Reyner Banham, "The Science Side: Weapons Systems, Computers, Human Sciences," *Architectural Review* 127, no. 757 (March 1960): 188. For an important discussion of these matters (entirely from Banham's perspective), see Anthony Vidler, "Toward a Theory of the Architectural Program," *October* 106 (Fall 2003): 59–74.

25. J. M. Richards, "Positions," *Architectural Review* 127, no. 760 (June 1960): 386.

26. Reyner Banham, "Reply," *Architectural Review* 127, no. 760 (June 1960): 386.

27. Banham, "Reply," 387.

28. Erwin Panofsky, "The History of Art as a Humanistic Discipline," in *The Meaning of the Humanities: Five Essays* (Princeton, N.J.: Princeton University Press, 1940), 104.

29. Reyner Banham, *Scenes in America Deserta* (Layton, Utah: Gibbs M. Smith, 1982), 211, 213; hereafter cited in text as *AD*.

30. Reyner Banham, "This Is Tomorrow: Synthesis of the Major Arts," *Architectural Review* 120, no. 716 (September 1956): 188. See also Ian Trowell, "Collision, Collusion and Coincidence: Pop Art's Fairground Parallel," *Visual Culture in Britain* 17, no. 3 (2016): 329–50.

31. *Reyner Banham Loves Los Angeles*, directed by Julian Cooper (BBC, 1972), 37:50–40:06.

32. Brad prefigures at once Uber and Airbnb, and if we imagine him offering piano lessons from the van, a charter school as well—in other words, a neoliberal gig economy in the making.

33. Reyner Banham, *Age of the Masters: A Personal View of Modern Architecture* (New York: Harper & Row, 1975), 77.

34. Theodor W. Adorno, *Minima Moralia: Reflections from Damaged Life,* trans. E. F. N. Jephcott (London: New Left Books, 1974), 28.

35. Ray Bradbury, "Dark They Were, and Golden-Eyed," in *The Stories of Ray Bradbury* (New York: Alfred A. Knopf, 1980), 472.

36. Bradbury, "Dark They Were," 473, 475.

37. Bradbury, "Dark They Were," 476.

38. Ray Bradbury, "February 1999: Ylla," in *The Martian Chronicles* (1950; repr., New York: Bantam Books, 1962), 2.

39. Banham, *Age of the Masters,* 77.

Index

Page numbers in italics refer to figures.

TODD CRONAN is professor of art history at Emory University. He is author of *Against Affective Formalism: Matisse, Bergson, Modernism* (Minnesota, 2013) and *Red Aesthetics: Rodchenko, Brecht, Eisenstein.*